Politics of Citizenship and Migration

The *Politics of Citizenship and Migration* series publishes exciting new research in all areas of migration and citizenship studies. Open to multiple approaches, the series considers interdisciplinary as well political, economic, legal, comparative, empirical, historical, methodological, and theoretical works. Broad in its coverage, the series promotes research on the politics and economics of migration, globalization and migration, citizenship and migration laws and policies, voluntary and forced migration, rights and obligations, demographic change, diasporas, political membership or behavior, public policy, minorities, border and security studies, statelessness, naturalization, integration and citizen-making, and subnational, supranational, global, corporate, or multilevel citizenship. Versatile, the series publishes single and multi-authored monographs, short-form Pivot books, and edited volumes.

For an informal discussion for a book in the series, please contact the series editor Leila Simona Talani (leila.talani@kcl.ac.uk), or Palgrave editor Isobel Cowper-Coles (isobel.cowpercoles@palgrave.com).

This series is indexed in Scopus.

Jatinder Mann
Editor

Citizenship in Transnational Perspective

Australia, Canada, and Aotearoa New Zealand

2nd ed. 2023

palgrave
macmillan

Editor
Jatinder Mann
Department of History
University of Reading
Reading, UK

ISSN 2520-8896 ISSN 2520-890X (electronic)
Politics of Citizenship and Migration
ISBN 978-3-031-34357-5 ISBN 978-3-031-34358-2 (eBook)
https://doi.org/10.1007/978-3-031-34358-2

Cover illustration: Yau Ming Low / Alamy Stock Photo

This Palgrave Macmillan imprint is published by the registered company Springer Nature Switzerland AG.
The registered company address is: Gewerbestrasse 11, 6330 Cham, Switzerland

Paper in this product is recyclable.

Acknowledgments

I would like to express my gratitude to the wonderful contributors to this edited collection: Yasmeen Abu-Laban, Chadwick Cowie, Harry Hobbs, Pavithra Jayawardena, Carwyn Jones, Sukhmani Khorana, Craig Linkhorn, Jatinder Mann, Kate McMillan, Nisha Nath, Sangeetha Pillai, Kim Rubenstein, Paul Spoonley, Daiva Stasiulis, and Māmari Stephens for their thought-provoking chapters, without which this book would not have been possible. In particular I would like to thank Chad, Harry, Pavithra, Sukhmani, Jatinder, Nisha, and Sangeetha for their excellent new chapters which built on the strengths of the first edition to make this new second, revised edition a reality. I am also extremely grateful to Yasmeen, Jatinder, Kate, Kim, and Paul for updating their chapters for this second, revised edition.

I would like to give my thanks to Palgrave Macmillan, New York, for inviting me to publish a second, revised edition of this collection. I would specifically like to thank the editor of the Politics of Citizenship and Migration Series: Leila Simona Talani for agreeing for the second, revised edition of this book to be a part of her excellent series once again. My gratitude also to Anne-Kathrin Birchley-Brun and Isobel Cowper Coles for commissioning the second, revised edition of the collection in the first place, and Leila Simona Talani for being such a wonderful person to work with through the process to production.

And lastly, but certainly not least, I would like to give my heartfelt thanks to my family for all their love and support throughout the journey of producing this book: my husband John and our adorable fur babies, Jasmine, Sebastian, Tobias, and Serena.

Dr. Jatinder Mann
Maidenhead, United Kingdom

Contents

Notes on Contributors

Yasmeen Abu-Laban Professor and Canada Research Chair in the Politics of Citizenship and Human Rights, Department of Political Science, University of Alberta.

Chadwick Cowie Assistant Professor, Department of Political Science, University of Toronto (Scarborough and St. George Campuses).

Harry Hobbs Associate Professor, Faculty of Law, University Technology Sydney.

Pavithra Jayawardena Senior Lecturer, Department of International Relations, University of Colombo.

Carwyn Jones Lead Academic, Ahunga Tikanga (Māori Laws and Philosophy) program, Te Wānanga o Raukawa; and Honorary Adjunct Professor, School of Māori Studies, Te Herenga Waka - Victoria University of Wellington.

Sukhmani Khorana Scientia Associate Professor, Faculty of Arts, Design, and Architecture, University of New South Wales, Sydney.

Craig Linkhorn Barrister, Clifton Chambers and Co-Editor, *Māori Law Review*.

Jatinder Mann Visiting Research Fellow, Department of History, University of Reading; and Creator and Manager of the Australian, Canadian, and New Zealand Studies Network.

Kate McMillan Associate Professor, School of History, Philosophy, Politics, and International Relations, Te Herenga Waka—Victoria University of Wellington.

Nisha Nath Associate Professor of Equity Studies, Centre for Interdisciplinary Studies, Athabasca University.

Sangeetha Pillai Senior Research Associate, School of Global and Public Law, University of New South Wales, Sydney.

Kim Rubenstein Professor and Director of the 50/50 by 2030 Foundation, Faculty of Business, Government and Law, University of Canberra.

Paul Spoonley Distinguished Professor Emeritus, Massey University.

Daiva Stasiulis Chancellor's Professor Emerita, Department of Sociology, Carleton University.

Māmari Stephens (Te Rarawa) Reader, Faculty of Law, Te Herenga Waka—Victoria University of Wellington.

CHAPTER 1

Introduction

Jatinder Mann

The first edition of this collection[1] was based on an international symposium on "Citizenship in a Transnational Perspective," co-convened by Professor Janine Brodie and Dr. Jatinder Mann, that was held at the University of Alberta in Edmonton, Alberta, Canada, on 6–7 July 2016. The international symposium on which the original edition was based brought together leading international scholars from Canada, Australia, and Aotearoa New Zealand to explore citizenship in a transnational perspective, focusing on the three countries through the two overarching themes of Indigeneity and ethnicity. Since then there have been some significant global developments when it comes to citizenship, namely Brexit in 2016, the election of Donald Trump as president of the United States of America (USA) also that same year, and the Covid-19 pandemic in 2020. The vote for the United Kingdom (UK) to leave the European Union (EU) in the referendum of 2016 was seen by some as the rejection of globalisation by certain sections of the British population, namely those

J. Mann (✉)
Department of History, University of Reading, Reading, Berkshire, UK

Australian, Canadian, and New Zealand Studies Network, London, UK
e-mail: j.mann@reading.ac.uk

J. Mann (ed.), *Citizenship in Transnational Perspective*, Politics of Citizenship and Migration,
https://doi.org/10.1007/978-3-031-34358-2_1

that felt left behind and believed the EU had not protected its citizens in the UK from the ravages of the free market.[2] Why they did not blame their national government in Westminster (which was still responsible for domestic economic policy) however was unclear. Over the course of the UK's long and painful exit from the EU, support for Brexit was also viewed as a rejection of the EU's supranational nature and the continued importance of national citizenship, epitomised by Prime Minister Theresa May's infamous criticism of people considering themselves "Global Citizens."[3] The election of Trump saw the introduction of a travel ban of people to the USA from several Muslim countries, a prohibition on the admittance of Syrian refugees completely, and a halving of the USA's overall refugee intake.[4] The Covid-19 pandemic witnessed an unprecedented closure of national borders by numerous countries in an effort to curb the spread of the disease.[5] Although all of these major events would appear to indicate the importance of national citizenships, in the case of the first, most British people now agree Brexit was a mistake,[6] Trump's travel ban was ultimately overturned, and the closure of national borders in the wake of Covid-19 was also reversed.

Furthermore, this second, revised edition demonstrates the continued salience of exploring citizenship in a transnational perspective, as the chapters which all look at citizenship in terms of Indigeneity and ethnicity show that these themes or ideas very much cross national borders, which is the essence of a transnational approach. Moreover, in order to highlight this, all of the chapters do not need to adopt a transnational approach specifically per se, the chapters collectively in this edited collection illustrate this perspective instead. This important point is something that is missed by some.

The contributors to this collection approach the subject from a range of disciplinary perspectives: historical, legal, political, and sociological. Therefore, this book makes an important and unique contribution to the existing literature through its transnational, interdisciplinary and multidisciplinary perspectives. This second, revised edition builds on the strength of the first edition (certain chapters have been revised and updated—Mann, McMillan, Spoonley, Rubenstein, and Abu-Laban), but it also includes several new chapters by predominantly early career or mid-career scholars who demonstrate the cutting-edge research in the field (Jayawardena, Mann, Pillai and Hobbs, Cowie, Khorana, and Nath). This second, revised edition of the collection is particularly proud of the fact that a majority of its chapters are written by female scholars and People of

Colour. I thought this was important as so much scholarship in the Humanities and Social Sciences is still dominated by white, male scholars. And so it is crucial in my opinion to have a diversity of scholarly voices.

The twenty-first century has witnessed multiple and ever more recalcitrant challenges to conventional citizenship models and policies that typically understand citizenship as a package of rights, which are universally bestowed upon individuals as members of a distinct national community residing within and defined by the boundaries of a modern territorial state. Whether such membership is the result of an accident of birth or achieved through some form of probationary residence and mandatory citizenship test, conventional citizenship models have advanced the idea that there is a definitive alignment between identities, citizenship rights, and territorial boundaries. Even in cases where a national state contains diverse ethnic or religious groups, citizenship conveys the idea of a shared identity rooted in universal rights and obligations.

Critics of this model rightly point out that this promise of universality was never fully achieved, especially in settler societies[7] where national citizenship regimes were premised, in the first instance, on the denial and suppression of Indigenous forms of nationhood and understandings of political membership and community obligation. In the contemporary moment, conventional models of citizenship are further challenged by transnationalism. The apparent waning in significance of economic, social, and national boundaries in a globalised world has accelerated the mobility and migration of diverse populations, the incidence of denizens and dual citizens, and the multiplication of identities and deep diversities.

The edited collection brings together leading scholars whose work on citizenship in settler societies moves beyond the idea of inclusion (fitting into extant citizenship regimes) to innovative models of inclusivity (refitting existing models) to reflect the multiple identities of an increasingly post-national era and to promote the recognition of Indigenous citizenships and rights that were suppressed as a formative condition of citizenship in these societies.

First, the edited collection seeks to explore the value of comparative and cross-disciplinary analyses of citizenship regimes in settler societies. Australia, Canada, and Aotearoa New Zealand are generally subsumed under the category of "Anglo-American democracies" and are understood as most similar systems because of their similar colonial origins and their Westminster style government. They are thus, in the language of comparative research design, "most similar systems." The contributors to this edited collection, however, understand their similarity differently as former British settler societies, which have shared common moments in the development of citizenship regimes. These include the suppression and current resurgence of Indigenous claims for distinct forms of recognition, citizenship, and governance; a transformation from a British imperial model of political community to nationally constituted models of civic citizenship that are sufficiently robust to incorporate successive waves of migration and their attendant diversities; and the contemporary challenges of transnationalism and what some term as "deep diversity."

Second, the edited collection seeks to enhance comparisons of settler–Indigenous relations that have followed, quite distinct trajectories in the three countries under review. In particular, the book tracks three different and largely unsuccessful models of citizenship as well as contemporary pressures to refit existing citizenship regimes to accommodate Indigenous demands for "rangatiratanga" or self-governance, especially in Aotearoa New Zealand and Canada.

Third, the edited collection explores the challenges of transnationalism on conventional and nationally constituted citizenship regimes. In particular, contributors to this edited collection explore the multiplication of identities of migrant communities and different forms of belonging in national communities (dual citizens, temporary, and permanent residents, refugees, etc.). Several chapters focus on the growing tension between the pressures of transnationalism and the increasing securitisation and conditionality placed on national citizenship.

The edited collection includes early career, mid-career, and established citizenship scholars from a broad range of cross-disciplinary and cross-sector perspectives to address these thematic goals. A particular highlight is Daiva Stasiulis, who has published extensively on citizenship in Canada and Australia. The edited collection is organised into sections around the aforementioned themes. So, Stasiulis and Pavithra Jayawardena's chapters offer a truly transnational perspective on the subject of citizenship. Jatinder Mann, Kate McMillan, and Carwyn Jones and Craig Linkhorn explore the evolution and trajectory of citizenship regimes in settler societies. Sangeetha Pillai and Harry Hobbs, Chadwick Cowie, Paul Spoonley, and Māmari Stephens study settler–Indigenous citizenships. And Sukhmani Khorana, Kim Rubenstein, Yasmeen Abu-Laban, and Nisha Nath focus on transnationalism, deep diversity, and securitisation.

Going into more detail, the focus of Daiva Stasiulis' contribution is on how dual nationals access safety and services in two domains—to negotiate their "security" in the context of the 2006 Lebanon war and to access health care, and thus construct "social citizenship" in two national spaces and in more localised settings in Lebanon and Canada/Australia. While as citizens of Canada and Australia, these dual nationals generally expressed gratitude for the extraordinary evacuation services provided by the country of their more robust citizenship, some citizens, caught in heavily bombed areas, felt that more should have been done to bring them to safety. Similarly, while most citizens predictably rated the health care in Australia and Canada more highly than in Lebanon, some negotiated the deterioration of services in these countries by seeking private but more accessible services in Lebanon.

According to Pavithra Jayawardena in her chapter, Sri Lanka became bankrupt in 2022 mainly due to the country's dollar scarcity. Sri Lankan migrants around the world were willing to transfer foreign money to help the situation, demonstrating strong transnational financial abilities. However, during the subsequent people's uprising, when Sri Lankans in the country demanded the government's resignation, many Sri Lankan migrants overseas offered their compatriots support, by refusing to send money unless the government listened to the people's demands. These transnational acts along with many others tell us that Sri Lankan migrants possess strong transnational identities, although we do not have a wide body of knowledge to understand them yet. This chapter intends to fill this gap by exclusively looking at the case of the transnational identities of Sri Lankan migrants in Australia and Aotearoa New Zealand. Findings are based on observations and 49 semi-structured interviews with a variety of Sri Lankan migrants in Melbourne, Sydney, Auckland, and Wellington in 2019 and a round of follow-up interviews in 2022 and 2023. The chapter presents three key themes of the participants' transnational identities: becoming a transnational citizen, transnational politics, and transnational social lives. The chapter details the home and host country factors shaping those views and their complexities. Looking at Sinhalese and Tamil migrants comparatively, the chapter reminds us of the importance of contextual understandings of smaller migrant communities to not only make sense of them but also influence effective migrant policy.

Jatinder Mann's first substantial chapter maintains that in the 1950s, Australia very much identified itself as a British country and an integral part of a wider British World which had the UK at its centre. However, by the 1970s, this British World had come to an end, as had Australia's self-identification as a British nation. During this period, citizenship in Australia was redefined in a significant way from being an ethnic (British)-based one to a more civic-founded one which was more inclusive of other ethnic groups and apparently Aborigines. This chapter argues that this redefinition of citizenship took place primarily in the context of this major shift in national identity. After having established the context of the end of the British World in Australia (with a focus on the UK's application for entry into the European Economic Community (EEC) and the British withdrawal from "East of Suez"), it explores the *Australian Citizenship Act* 1973 to illustrate the way in which citizenship became more inclusive of other ethnic groups in the country. It then studies the 1967 constitutional referendum to highlight how citizenship in Australia also appeared to incorporate Aborigines at this time.

In his second substantial contribution, Mann argues that in the 1950s, English-speaking Canada also very much identified itself as an integral part of a wider British World. Canada's bicultural nature, with the French-Canadians, complicated this self-identity in Canada. However, by the 1970s, this British World had come to an end. During this period, citizenship in Canada was redefined in a significant way from being an ethnic (British)-based one to a more civic-founded one which was more inclusive of other ethnic groups and Indigenous peoples. The chapter asserts that this redefinition of citizenship took place primarily in the context of this major shift in national identity, focusing on key external events that led to this process. It then explores pieces of citizenship legislation and other moves which illustrate the redefinition of citizenship during this period.

Kate McMillan in her chapter maintains that in the mid-1970s, Aotearoa New Zealand, Canada, and Australia all ceased using "British subject" as a criterion for national voting rights. In all three countries, this represented a decisive step away from the British imperial model of political community towards a nationally constituted one. Unlike Australia and Canada, however, Aotearoa New Zealand did not replace "British subject" with national citizenship criterion; it simply removed "British subject," leaving the existing residency requirement intact. Aotearoa New Zealand became and remains the only country in the world to allocate national voting rights to all permanent resident non-citizens after one-year residence. This was a radical decision with far-reaching implications for the incorporation of immigrants into the national political community.

According to Carwyn Jones and Craig Linkhorn in their contribution, Article 3 of the Treaty of Waitangi, signed by Māori leaders and the British Crown in 1840, stated that Māori would enjoy "all the rights and privileges of British subjects." This new citizenship of a British colony was laid over the top of Māori forms of social organisation and understandings of nationhood and citizenship. The Aotearoa New Zealand state has struggled to come to terms with Indigenous forms of citizenship and over time has changed its approach to Māori citizenship to try to address this. The chapter considers the nature of Māori citizenship today in the era of Treaty of Waitangi settlements, exploring how citizenship in this period of transitional justice is informed by political, social, and justice dimensions of conceptions of Māori citizenship over time.

Sangeetha Pillai and Harry Hobbs in their chapter argue that the place and status of First Nations peoples within Australia has long been contested. In the 2020 decision of *Love v Commonwealth*, the High Court of Australia declared that Aboriginal and Torres Strait Islander peoples who satisfied the tripartite definition from *Mabo v Queensland (No 2)* were not aliens, even if they were not Australian citizens. The decision recognised the unique connection First Nations peoples have with the lands and waters of Australia, but it left many unopened questions. The immediate political reaction also suggested many non-Indigenous Australians remain uncomfortable with accepting the unique position First Nations peoples hold in this country. In this chapter, they tease out the legal and political challenges to Indigeneity and membership raised by *Love*.

Chadwick Cowie maintains in his contribution that the current relationships between First Nations peoples, who make up one of three groups considered "Indigenous" under the *Constitution Act* 1982, and the Canadian state is the product of a narrow and one-sided view that has developed over centuries. In regard to citizenship, there is an opportunity for First Nations to utilise the Canadian political system to recalibrate Canada's mentality towards their relationships. Although there is potential to utilise both First Nations and Canadian legal and social structures, and representative bodies to create change, the issue of sovereignty, as well as its impact on citizenship and participation in the Canadian state must be explored. The importance of sovereignty has been a source of ongoing discussion when considering the issues that impact Canada's relationship with First Nations that it shares territory with. In addressing the issue of sovereignty, treaties, as well as First Nations citizenship, the potential for First Nations participation in the Canadian electoral process could further entrench the recognition of First Nations sovereignty and nationhood alongside that of the Canadian state.

In her chapter, Māmari Stephens argues that Māori have persistently sought autonomy in decision-making regarding Māori social outcomes and in identifying Māori conceptions of citizenship that may differ from universalist understandings of citizenship. Language-based evidence and social and legal history suggest a Māori understanding of citizenship that is not only protective but perhaps also positive, confirming relational ways of doing things, under a Māori authority. One of those "ways of doing things" has been using collective processes in order to assist Māori individuals and collectives to attain basic physical and material well-being or welfare. An examination of welfare law and development in Aotearoa New Zealand is able to reveal both Māori persistence in having Māori notions of citizenship fully heard, and the sheer difficulty in having such notions recognised more broadly.

According to Paul Spoonley in his contribution, Aotearoa New Zealand is a classic settler society that has experienced distinct phases of citizenship development in its modern history. Colonisation saw the erasure of the preceding sovereignty of the Indigenous Māori. However, by the 1970s, the country began to debate nationality and citizenship in ways that differed (in part) from other modern liberal (including settler) societies. It is this history and those departures which are the focus here. It has two key elements: a pre-eminent focus on a biculturalism which recognises the Indigeneity of the original settlers, Māori, and the shift in the ethnic diversity that resulted from changes to immigration policy in the 1980s so that a significantly enhanced diversity has altered debates about identity, nationalism, and citizenship.

In her chapter, Sukhmani Khorana maintains that migrants have long been seen as striving for socio-economic mobility in the countries they migrate to. While these aspirations receive scholarly attention, less is known about how their subsequent generations experience belonging, what they mean by it, and how they enact it by trying to be part of the polity. Her chapter begins with an overview of the concepts of "belonging" and "active citizenship" as they pertain to second-generation migrants before unpacking why this cohort of migrants merits examination to understand how the enactment of citizenship is evolving in immigrant settler colonial nations like Australia. Two case studies pertaining to civic initiatives in the media and politics in Australia are then presented to exemplify the manifestation of belonging and citizenship. Media Diversity Australia was founded by the children of migrants and has an explicit focus on advancing the media careers of this group. Pathways to Politics and Women for Election have a more generic emphasis on women in politics, but have also been influential in facilitating the political careers of second-generation migrant women.

Kim Rubenstein's contribution argues that Australian citizenship has travelled from an acceptance and foundation of a form of cosmopolitan or supranational citizenship, to one of vulnerability for dual citizens. In doing so, it changes the relationship between the individual and the state, reverting Australian citizens back to their "subject" like status in principle even if not in title.

According to Yasmeen Abu-Laban in her chapter, one of the most potent legal regimes governing the division of advantage and disadvantage between peoples at global and national levels is citizenship. Utilising government documents, print media accounts, and secondary sources, her chapter examines the evolution of Canada's immigration policy between 2006 and 2023. Overall, this period has been characterised by greater exclusion. This is because policy reforms in the past decade have included numerous changes introduced by the Conservative government of Prime Minister Stephen Harper (in power from 2006 to 2015) which combined to make Canadian citizenship harder to obtain (and easier to lose), reduce the number of refugee claimants and control the flows of refugees (in the face of growing numbers globally), and intensify the surveillance of borders and belonging in ways that are racialised and gendered.

In her contribution, Nisha Nath offers a (re)reading of citizenship by turning to Canada's *Anti-Terrorism Act (ATA)* and in particular its amendment in 2015 through Bill-51. The intention here is to think through how citizenship regulates political normativity through relational securitization, wherein the positioning and governance of white, racialized non-Indigenous people and Indigenous people is specifically relational *as a strategy of the state*. In turning to the *ATA*, the intention is to hold the *ATA* as a provisional locus of analysis at a given moment of time and to think through this legislation as one site through which we can trace how "policies that infringe on Indigenous peoples' self-determination, the securitization of Canadian state borders, and imperialism abroad" are working together as citizenship regulates through race, security, and dissent. In exploring the structured relationships between Indigenous and non-Indigenous racialized peoples, and between citizens and non-citizens, she illustrates how the state's legitimacy and authority to act is also being consolidated. In this, she wants to both illustrate how the state is invested in "particular kinds of connections *and* disconnections" amongst and within citizens and non-citizens, and that through the mechanism of citizenship, this kind of regulation and securitization is happening in "profoundly reliant and relational ways." This has key implications for how we conceptualise the investment in citizenship, how we narrate political progress and change, but also for how Black, Indigenous, and other racialized people might think about the locus of their solidarities.

Several edited collections have been published in the past surrounding citizenship, even one looking at the three countries of this book.[8] However, none of them explore citizenship in Australia, Canada and Aotearoa New Zealand through the twin prisms of Indigeneity and ethnicity,[9] and they certainly do not address the contemporary issues that this edited collection does, such as dual citizenship and security. Hence, this book makes a unique and important contribution to the field.

The vast majority, if not all, of the chapters in this edited collection situate themselves in the settler colonial context. This as outlined earlier essentially argues that the Australian, Canadian, and Aotearoa New Zealand settler societies were established through the dispossession of Indigenous nations, which were already present in those territories. Although the effect of this colonisation process was extremely devastating, many of these Indigenous nations still exist, and most importantly, their current situation has to be understood through the context of their experience of European colonialism, which has lasting effects to this day. The literature on settler colonialism in Australia, Canada, and Aotearoa New Zealand is extremely vast. However, some key works are by James Belich,[10] Glen Coulthard,[11] Marilyn Lake and Henry Reynolds,[12] Lorenzo Veracini,[13] and Andrew Woolford.[14] Several of the chapters in this collection draw on some of these. However, they also build on them, especially with their focus on citizenship. And those chapters that combine an exploration of Indigeneity and ethnicity are also extremely unique.

A significant broader societal development common to Australia, Canada, and Aotearoa New Zealand is future demographic changes in these states—namely a shrinking white settler population and growing proportions of Indigenous and migrant populations. What impact this will have on citizenship issues in the three countries remains to be seen. This is something that Spoonley discusses in much more detail in his chapter, which he terms "superdiversity."

The issue of treaties (between Indigenous peoples and the settler colonial state) and citizenship is also another important theme in this edited collection. Several of the chapters discuss this issue. Specifically, Canada and Aotearoa New Zealand have them, but Australia does not currently.[15] This has certainly had an impact on relations between the settler colonial state and Indigenous peoples in the three countries. Although the Canadian and Aotearoa New Zealand experiences are also quite different, the settler colonial state in Canada only concluded treaties with certain Indigenous nations, not all. The Indigenous nations in British Columbia historically are a prominent example. In contrast to Aotearoa New Zealand, the Treaty of Waitangi was regarded for the longest time as being an agreement between the settler colonial state there and Māori. But again the Treaty of Waitangi was not one with all Māori iwi, only some. So, perhaps there might be more commonality between the Canadian and Aotearoa New Zealand experiences here.

Thinking about linkages between some of the chapters in this collection, Mann and McMillan, although focusing on Australia and Canada, and Aotearoa New Zealand, respectively, share a common emphasis on the shift away from a British-centred identity in these three settler societies in the post-Second World War period, and how this change was reflected in citizenship legislation in the 1970s.

Pillai and Hobbs and Cowie in their chapters explore the very basis of citizenship for Indigenous peoples in Australia and Canada, respectively: the former focusing on the distinct recognition of Indigeneity in the High Court of Australia and the latter the prospect of dual citizenship for First Nations in Canada. This relates to Benedict Anderson's writings on imagined communities,[16] whereby individuals believe, or are made to believe, that they are part of a mythical and usually benign community or nation, which has defined boundaries. However, as the experience of Indigenous peoples in Australia, Canada, and Aotearoa New Zealand demonstrates for much of the history of these settler colonial societies, they were in fact excluded and State interactions with them were anything but benign. This is certainly something to keep in mind especially when reading these two chapters, but the book in general as well.

Cowie, Jones and Linkhorn, and Stephens also share a similar approach to Indigeneity in Canada and Aotearoa New Zealand through their emphasis on the crucial role that Indigenous nations in those settler societies must play themselves in the definition of their own citizenship. Unfortunately, this is something that they have been denied for centuries, much to the detriment of those settler societies in my opinion. Without this, they all argue that citizenship is not feasible for Indigenous nations in the settler societies of Canada and Aotearoa New Zealand.

Spoonley and Jones and Linkhorn also both survey the history of citizenship for Māori in Aotearoa New Zealand from the late nineteenth century to the present. And Spoonley and McMillan also explore the increasing diversity of the Aotearoa New Zealand population, especially due to large levels of Asian migration.

Abu-Laban and Nath have a commonality in their focus on the recent citizenship regime in Canada, most notably during the Harper Conservative government of 2006–2015. However, they both complement each other, as Abu-Laban takes a more policy-focused approach, whereas Nath adopts a more security-focused one.

And lastly in terms of methodology, Stasiulis and Jayawardena both utilise the rich resource of qualitative sources, specifically one-on-one interviews with individuals involved directly in the events/subjects that they both explore. This enables them to provide a very rich and unique perspective "from below," which would not be possible if they had only relied on quantitative sources. Several of the other chapters (Mann, McMillan, Stephens, Rubenstein, Abu-Laban, and Nath) look at citizenship more "from above," by focusing on analysing legislation, which considering the nature of the subject of their articles is very fitting, and moreover they effectively contextualise that legislation—situating it in a broader historical and political context (so the descriptive term citizenship "from above" is not completely accurate). The remaining chapters (Jones and Linkhorn, Pillai and Hobbs, Cowie, Spoonley, and Khorana) use a range of other methodologies including focusing on treaties, case law, and organisations, so exploring citizenship "from the middle" perhaps. All of the approaches adopted by the different chapters in this collection collectively illustrate the multifaceted approaches you can take to studying citizenship. What is more, they all have advantages and disadvantages, neither of them is superior over the others in my opinion. But what this collection provides from these diverse approaches is a holistic view of citizenship in a transnational perspective in Australia, Canada, and Aotearoa New Zealand.

Notes

1. Jatinder Mann (Ed.), *Citizenship in Transnational Perspective: Australia, Canada, and New Zealand* (New York: Palgrave Macmillan, 2017).

2. "Brexit is a rejection of globalisation," 26 June 2016, *The Guardian*. Available: https://www.theguardian.com/business/2016/jun/26/brexit-is-the-rejection-of-globalisation [Accessed 24 February 2023].
3. "Theresa May treads the Brexit path of empathy and righteousness," 5 October 2016, *The Guardian*. Available: https://www.theguardian.com/politics/2016/oct/05/theresa-may-treads-the-brexit-path-of-empathy-and-righteousness [Accessed 24 February 2023].
4. "Trump's travel bans caused heartache and suffering. For what?," 25 January 2021, *Washington Post*. Available: https://www.washingtonpost.com/world/2021/01/25/trump-muslim-ban-legacy-biden/ [Accessed 25 January 2023].
5. "Closed borders, travel bans and halted immigration: 5 ways COVID-19 changed how – and where – people move around the world," 28 March 2021, *The Conversation*. Available: https://theconversation.com/closed-borders-travel-bans-and-halted-immigration-5-ways-covid-19-changed-how-and-where-people-move-around-the-world-157040 [Accessed 25 January 2023].
6. "Most Britons now think Brexit was a bad idea – the government just hasn't caught up yet," 21 November 2022, *The Guardian*. Available: https://www.theguardian.com/commentisfree/2022/nov/21/most-britons-now-think-brexit-was-a-bad-idea-the-government-just-hasnt-caught-up-yet [Accessed 24 February 2023].
7. These are nations primarily in the Americas, Africa, Asia, and Australasia or Oceania, which were colonised by European Imperial powers, their settlers dispossessing the Indigenous nations already present in those territories. The effects of this extremely destructive process are still felt to this day. For the purposes of this edited collection, the settler societies that will be focused on are Australia, Canada, and Aotearoa New Zealand. All three of these countries subsequently received a diverse immigration intake over the course of the late nineteenth and twentieth centuries, which transformed their populations.
8. Pierre Boyer, Linda Cardinal, and David Headon (Eds.), *From Subjects to Citizens: A Hundred Years of Citizenship in Australia and Canada* (Ottawa: University of Ottawa Press, 2004); Alan C. Cairns, John C. Courtney, Peter MacKinnon, Hans J. Michelmann, and David E. Smith (Eds.), *Citizenship, Diversity, and Pluralism: Canadian and Comparative Perspectives* (Montreal & Kingston: McGill-Queen's University Press, 1999); Paul Havemann (Ed.), *Indigenous Peoples' Rights in Australia, Canada, & New Zealand* (Auckland: Oxford University Press, 1999).
9. Jatinder Mann, *Redefining Citizenship in Australia, Canada, and Aotearoa New Zealand* (New York: Peter Lang Publishing, 2019) published since the first edition of this collection does actually do this. And the monograph

also adopts an interdisciplinary approach (history and politics in regard to subject and politics and law in terms of analysis). But unlike this edited collection, it focuses on the period of the 1950s-1970s.

10. James Belich, *Paradise Reforged: A History of the New Zealanders from the 1880s to the Year 2000* (Honolulu: University of Hawaii Press, 2002).
11. Glen Coulthard, *Red Skin, White Masks: Rejecting the Colonial Politics of Recognition* (Minneapolis: University of Minnesota Press, 2014).
12. Marilyn Lake and Henry Reynolds, *Drawing the Global Colour Line: White Men's Countries and the International Challenge of Racial Equality* (Cambridge: Cambridge University Press, 2008).
13. Lorenzo Veracini, *The Settler Colonial Present* (Basingstoke, Hampshire: Palgrave Macmillan, 2015).
14. Andrew Woolford, *This Benevolent Experiment: Indigenous Boarding Schools, Genocide, and Redress in Canada and the United States* (Lincoln, NE: University of Nebraska Press, 2015).
15. The referendum campaign currently underway in Australia for an "Indigenous Voice to Parliament" (this was one of the major calls of the *Uluru Statement from the Heart*—a petition by a constitutional convention which brought together over 250 Aboriginal and Torres Strait Islander leaders) is considered by its supporters as the first step on the journey of the negotiation of an actual treaty between the settler colonial state in Australia and the First Nations of the territory that is now known as Australia. https://www.aph.gov.au/About_Parliament/Parliamentary_Departments/Parliamentary_Library/pubs/rp/rp1617/Quick_Guides/UluruStatement.
16. Benedict Anderson, *Imagined Communities: Reflections on the Origin and Spread of Nationalism* (London: Verso, 1991).

Bibliography

Anderson, Benedict. *Imagined Communities: Reflections on the Origin and Spread of Nationalism*. London: Verso, 1991.

Belich, James. *Paradise Reforged: A History of the New Zealanders from the 1880s to the Year 2000*. Honolulu: University of Hawaii Press, 2002.

Boyer, Pierre, Linda Cardinal, and David Headon, eds. *From Subjects to Citizens: A Hundred Years of Citizenship in Australia and Canada*. Ottawa: University of Ottawa Press, 2004.

Cairns, Alan C., John C. Courtney, Peter MacKinnon, Hans J. Michelmann, and David E. Smith, eds. *Citizenship, Diversity, and Pluralism: Canadian and Comparative Perspectives*. Montreal & Kingston: McGill-Queen's University Press, 1999.

Coulthard, Glen. *Red Skin, White Masks: Rejecting the Colonial Politics of Recognition*. Minneapolis: University of Minnesota Press, 2014.

Havemann, Paul. ed. *Indigenous Peoples' Rights in Australia, Canada, & New Zealand*. Auckland: Oxford University Press, 1999.

Lake, Marilyn and Henry Reynolds. *Drawing the Global Colour Line: White Men's Countries and the International Challenge of Racial Equality*. Cambridge: Cambridge University Press, 2008.

Mann, Jatinder. ed. *Citizenship in Transnational Perspective: Australia, Canada, and New Zealand*. New York: Palgrave Macmillan, 2017.

Mann, Jatinder. *Redefining Citizenship in Australia, Canada, and Aotearoa New Zealand*. New York: Peter Lang Publishing, 2019.

Veracini, Lorenzo. *The Settler Colonial Present*. Basingstoke, Hampshire: Palgrave Macmillan, 2015.

Woolford, Andrew. *This Benevolent Experiment: Indigenous Boarding Schools, Genocide, and Redress in Canada and the United States*. Lincoln, NE: University of Nebraska Press, 2015.

PART I

Transnationalism

CHAPTER 2

Respatializing Social Citizenship and Security Among Dual Citizens in the Lebanese Diaspora

Daiva Stasiulis

I am immensely grateful for the financial support provided to this research by the Social Sciences and Humanities Research Council of Canada (Standard Research Grant, No. 410-2005-1395) and for teaching release through the Marston LaFrance Research Fellowship from the Faculty of Arts and Social Sciences, Carleton University, 2016–2017. I owe a great debt of gratitude to wonderful research assistants: Christophe Allaire-Sevigny, Zainab Amery, Louisa Romanous, and Dania Fawaz. I am also extremely grateful to the editor of this collection, Jatinder Mann, for his detailed feedback and helpful suggestions on my chapter.

D. Stasiulis (✉)
Department of Sociology, Carleton University, Ottawa, ON, Canada
e-mail: daiva.stasiulis@carleton.ca

J. Mann (ed.), *Citizenship in Transnational Perspective*, Politics of Citizenship and Migration,
https://doi.org/10.1007/978-3-031-34358-2_2

Introduction

The phenomenon of transnational migration, where people create and sustain meaningful social, economic, and political relations in (at least) their countries of origin and their countries of "immigrant settlement," has fractured assumptions about the eternal, essentialist, and exclusive character of "national belonging."[1] The fact that international migration can no longer be seen as a one-time move from "sending" to "receiving" states has also unsettled conventional understandings of the spatiality and lived experience of citizenship, especially among those mobile subjects who hold dual or multiple citizenship.

Multiple nationality holds a particular attraction to those whose homeland has a history of violent conflict and political destabilization. Thus, the Lebanese have a lengthy pattern of emigration to escape war and have "long sought out second passports as 'safeguards' to be used when things get rough" while permitting them to return regularly or indeed habitually reside in their homeland.[2] This chapter aims to contribute to the scholarship on the "new geographies of citizenship"[3] by exploring how a particularly dramatic moment internationally—the summer 2006 war in Lebanon—brought into sharp relief the efforts of dual citizens and other foreign nationals to seek security, then ruptured by an intense and unexpected war. It is based on interviews conducted with eighty Lebanese–Canadian and Lebanese–Australian dual citizens, ten members of community organizations, and then Australian Ambassador to Lebanon, conducted in Australia, Canada, and Lebanon between April 2007 and December 2009, who had been in Lebanon during the outbreak of the summer 2006 war.[4]

The ten-year anniversary of the 2006 outbreak of the 33-day summer war between Israel and Hezbollah was a relatively subdued affair in both Lebanon and Israel.[5] The memory of these hostilities has faded in international headlines on the Middle East which is currently preoccupied with the multisided armed conflict in Syria that has displaced over half of its population, with three million having fled to Syria's immediate neighbors—Lebanon, Jordan, and Turkey—and 1.2 million as of 2016 residing in Lebanon. In 2006, among the million Lebanese displaced by the war, many (approximately 180,000), especially in the blockaded south, sought their way to safety in Syria, while another half a million fled to shelter in the mountains.[6] Those holding citizenship in Australia or Canada commented on the strangeness of being Canadian or Australian "refugees" from Lebanon in Syria.[7]

In addition to the rapid devastation of Lebanese infrastructure during the summer 2006 war, this event was also notable for the international attention given to the unprecedented numbers of foreign nationals seeking immediate escape. The "summer of return" saw many people of Lebanese descent visiting Beirut, the "Paris of the Middle East" in all its restored glory, following the 1975–1990 civil war. For the Canadian government, it was the largest historical evacuation of its nationals. The discursive framing of this evacuation among Canadian politicians and media pundits emphasized the high costs (about C$94 million) of Canadian assistance and the illegitimacy of Canadian tax dollars meted out to "citizens of convenience," especially non-resident Canadians who took advantage of Canadian taxpayers' generosity to visit relatives or do tourism in Canada.[8] In Canada, as in many countries that have been "tolerant" of dual citizenship, multiple citizenship has become increasingly politicized, racialized, and conditional.

Dual citizenship[9] involves holding full, legal membership, with the attendant rights and responsibilities—in two or more states. Acquisition of dual citizenship can come about at birth (e.g. through an interplay of jus soli and jus sanguinis laws) or through naturalization. The broad recognition of multiple citizenships has entailed "a dramatic transformation of the relationship between individuals and states, from a segmentary system of exclusive belonging to a matrix of multiple and overlapping affiliations."[10] Indeed, for some scholars, the proliferation of persons with multiple citizenship worldwide at birth or through marriage, migration, or political change has signified "one of the most important reconfigurations in the relationship between the [Westphalian] state and the individual which is so central to modernity."[11]

Some writers have interpreted the augmenting acceptance by states of multiple citizenship as a prefiguration of post-national forms of membership in political communities that "dilute the nationalist core of conventional citizenship."[12] Others have suggested that the advent of a "post-national world" is fanciful insofar as people continue to manage the uncertainties related to rapid economic transformations associated with neoliberal globalization, political and military instability, and climate change by negotiating their citizenship relative to their allegiances and connections to particular countries and still imagine "citizenship in the vernacular of an all-encompassing system of states."[13] While "the proliferation of dual and multiple citizenships around the world…subverts the conventional expectation of citizenship exclusivity," this trend illustrates "not so much the post-nationalization as the multi-nationalization of citizenship status."[14] Part of the confusion resides in the fact that among political and legal scholars studying migration, the focus on the perspective of the state and on normative concerns relating to the desirability and costs of dual citizenship has neglected the active construction of citizenship from below.[15]

This lacuna has since begun to be addressed by social scientists who have adopted a bottom-up, multi-sited ethnographic approach that "can bring out the perspective of [dual] citizens themselves and reveal the situated meanings that citizenship acquires on the ground."[16] Such qualitative ethnographic research discloses a broad array of orientations toward the acquisition and holding of citizenships and passports among dual citizens.[17] In this chapter, I examine the lived experience of dual citizenship among dual Lebanese–Australian and Lebanese–Canadian citizens who were in Lebanon when the summer 2006 war broke out. The focus of this chapter is on how these dual national subjects access safety and services in two domains—to negotiate their "security" in the context of the Lebanon war, and to access health care—and thus construct "social citizenship" in two national spaces and in more localized settings in Lebanon and Canada/Australia. My analysis sees citizenship as constructed through enactment and practice, rather than merely formal status and membership, as individuals and families navigate structural and cultural obstacles and respond to opportunities.[18]

Do dual nationals behave like uni-nationals by restricting their social citizenship entitlements within the boundaries of one state (presumably the state associated with more robust social citizenship or where they have habitual residence)? Or do they increase their and their families' "citizenship portfolios" by strategically seeking and combining benefits and avoiding deficits through mobility between two national contexts?[19]

The prevailing understanding of social citizenship relies chiefly on T. H. Marshall's foundational text on modern nation-state citizenship and influential account of a troika of sequentially emergent citizenship rights—civil, political, and social. Social citizenship rights offered the fullest efflorescence of citizenship in the twentieth century. Many analyses equate Marshall's understanding of social citizenship with the core ideas of a Keynesian national welfare state, decommodification, "social democratic" notion of redistribution, and universal access to public services.[20] Martin

Powell has pointed out, however, how writers have overextended Marshall's meaning of social citizenship, "mistakenly assuming a strong or maximalist version of a weak or minimalist concept."[21] In fact, in Marshall's original mid-twentieth-century formulation, one finds reference to a continuum from a minimalist to an admittedly vague maximalist version. Marshall defined social citizenship in terms of "the whole range from the [minimalist] right to a modicum of economic welfare and security to the [maximalist] right to share to the full in the social heritage and to live the life of a civilized being according to the standards prevailing in society."[22]

Marshall's definition of social rights of citizenship has been subjected to many reformulations both theoretically and in light of twenty-first-century conditions, subjecting it to critiques from the perspectives of national contexts other than the United Kingdom (UK), and of women, Indigenous peoples, migrants, and cultural groups. Since the 1980s, the focus has shifted to the decline in social citizenship linked to neoliberal forms of globalization and government. This has suggested a replacement of nation-state social citizenship, "based on rights and equality" with a "hollowed-out, civil society model based on duties and inclusion."[23] Despite the many reappraisals of "social citizenship" in the twentieth century, few have examined how social citizenship is becoming respatialized in light of the augmenting interconnectedness of people and localities around the globe, of which the increase in multiple citizenships is one manifestation and modality. The ideas of "post-nationalism," "transnational social rights," and "global" or "cosmopolitan citizenship" suggest social rights as advanced beyond national state borders. However, in the absence of universally enforceable social rights, and in confronting the formidable levels of global inequality, the idea of social rights at a transnational level remains "a normative utopian idea" rather than a realistic recasting of citizenship as attached to a global community.[24]

In exploring the global spatialization of social citizenship, Thomas Faist utilizes a familiar and (somewhat Eurocentric) framework from international political economy in order to differentiate between what he terms four "different partial worlds" on a hierarchical scale of social citizenship from the strongest to the non-existent. Thus: "World I is broadly congruent with the wealthiest OECD countries; World II matches the transition countries in Eastern Europe and the Newly Industrialized Countries (NICs) in Southeast Asia; World III embraces…developing countries; and World IV comprises the most impoverished countries, in which the status of statehood, and consequently citizenship is extremely precarious...[including] failed states."[25]

Faist observes that when mapping social citizenship globally, one confronts a "highly fragmented world" with respect to the vast range of opportunities that nationality provides in different countries.[26] Faist makes two observations about social citizenship in these partial worlds that are germane to the current study. First, in "classic" welfare states of World I, social policies have stagnated and have not survived the neoliberal challenge of the last four decades to the tenets of the post-war welfare state (public investment and collective responsibility).[27] Yet in comparison to the other three "partial worlds," social citizenship provisions retain a higher degree of "heft" for a larger proportion of 'World I" national populations.[28]

A second notable observation that Faist makes, not captured in hierarchical rankings of states' social security systems, is the structural heterogeneity in formal and informal security systems in each of the partial worlds. In Worlds III and IV, informal security systems prevail that primarily comprise non-state actors, which might include religious communities, kinship systems, and oppositional political parties. Thus, private health care in low- and middle-income countries is very extensive and heterogenous, ranging from itinerant medicine sellers, through independent practitioners—both unlicensed and licensed—to corporate hospital chains and private insurers.[29]

According to Faist, when "citizens combine memberships in and of several states...we are dealing neither with exclusive citizenship in tightly bounded political communities nor with denationalized citizenship, but rather with a sort of multi-nationalized citizenship."[30] This raises the question of what sort of "multi-nationalized citizenship" is enacted by specific groups of people—in this case Lebanese–Canadians and Lebanese–Australians who are multiple citizens of countries with such contrasting quality and heterogenous structures of social provision.

In his foundational essay on the genealogy of modern citizenship, Marshall draws a direct link between the equalizing of status through social citizenship and a reduction in risk and insecurity on the part of citizens. To Marshall, equality of status would provide "a general enrichment of the concrete substance of civilised life, a general reduction of risk and insecurity, and equalisation between the more or less fortunate at all levels."[31] Diplomatic protection and consular assistance[32] comprise the extension on an extraterritorial plane of the right to protection by one's state or indeed the right to be acknowledged by one's state as a political subject deserving of special, national protection.[33] The intensification of travel and migration, and the increase in time individuals spend outside their country of primary residence, renders diplomatic protection an important social citizenship right in a hypermobile world.[34]

The pivotal moment in the research examined here is the summer 2006 war between Israel and Hezbollah that saw dozens of countries scrambling to find safe exit for their holidaying and resident nationals from the devastation of this unexpected war. The numbers—hundreds of thousands of foreign nationals in Lebanon—were so staggering that few embassies could effectively assist departure at such a scale. For most foreign governments, this was their largest evacuation by sea of non-combatants. The United States of America (USA) government was exceptional in its capacity to evacuate approximately 15,000 of an estimated 25,000 Americans in Lebanon at the time, utilizing its military assets (navy and army helicopters) and large consular presence in the region.[35] Altogether, some 45 countries evacuated their nationals or asked other nations to help.[36] The relative action or inaction of the various embassies made it starkly evident that holding citizenship in a wealthy, well-resourced state was an asset, while citizenship in a poor nation provided no such benefit.[37]

According to the Canadian Standing Committee on Foreign Affairs, by the end of the crisis, Canada had evacuated approximately 14,370 nationals of the 40,000–50,000 Canadians visiting or residing in Lebanon.[38] Only about 35 percent of the approximately 39,000 Canadians registered with the embassy at the peak of the crisis accepted the invitation of the Canadian government's assisted departure. Out of an estimated 25,000 Australian citizens in Lebanon at the outbreak of the war,[39] Australia's "Operation Ramp" assisted the departure of 5300 Australians and 1250 other foreign nationals from the ports of Beirut and Tyre.[40]

Among the dual citizens, we interviewed who were in Lebanon at the outbreak of war, half (17 of 34 Australians and 22 of 45 Canadians) received assisted departure from their Australian or Canadian government. Ten of these who accepted evacuation (six Australians and four Canadians) were "external citizens," residents in Lebanon at the time of war. A second group (numbering 24 of 79) found their own independent route out of Lebanon. A third group (numbering 16 of 79) chose to remain in Lebanon and weather the storm.

Many of those who were evacuated expressed a passionate attachment to their Australian and/or Canadian citizenship because of its perceived capacity to shield them from death or bodily harm. Numerous stories were told by both Canadians and Australians about the exceptional evacuation efforts of these governments. Thus, one Australian 37-year-old resident related how:

> in the beginning we didn't think much of the Government. We had no communication from the embassy except a message saying don't call us, we'll call you. It was like we had no country that cared. The reality of it—it was the first time the Australian government had to evacuate a large number of people from such a threat…In the end they pulled through tremendously. The support was outstanding and overwhelming. Being fed, given a bed to sleep on, brought home to safety, having strangers hug you upon arrival, a smile, a hand to help—who does that?… I am proud to call myself Australian. I am proud to feel safe with my own government.[41]

For the vast majority of dual citizens, there was no expectation that their Lebanese citizenship would shield them from the war or provide assisted departure. The Lebanese government, with its Parliament in disarray during the war, played no direct role in securing safe passage from the violence and carnage of the war for foreign nationals, other than coordinating and facilitating the assistance of local and international NGOs and aid agencies.[42] Eight Australian–Lebanese and four Canadian–Lebanese, when asked about citizenship benefits, exclaimed that there were "none" attached to holding Lebanese citizenship, whereas no respondents claimed "no benefit" from holding Canadian or Australian citizenship. In contrast, the high regard for a "safe" citizenship had been cultivated through their experience of sustained and periodic violence in Lebanon, with many respondents having lost family members in the civil war or during past occupations. The relief and gratitude for holding a "peaceful and safe" citizenship was most passionately expressed by young people, especially those who had grown up in Australia or Canada and for whom (unlike their parents who experienced the fifteen-year civil war), July 2006 was their first experience of war. A 25-year-old Canadian-born man with Lebanese and Canadian citizenship, who visited Lebanon for the first time during the summer 2006, responded to the question about the benefits of Canadian citizenship by exclaiming: "Wow, what a question! So many benefits, we can just live in a peaceful and best country in the world. No war, no violence, just great. I don't know, it's like almost a utopia."[43]

The associations of Canadian/Australian citizenship with peace and security and effective consular services, however, were quite different and more negative among those who were in the South (south of the Litani River), a region heavily bombarded by the Israeli Defense Forces (IDF). Twenty-four of our respondents found their own treacherous way out of south Lebanon, through convoys of private vehicles or hiring taxis to Syria. The danger of being maimed or killed was realistically felt to be heightened in the South, Baalbek, or southern Beirut which were considered by the Israelis to be Hezbollah strongholds. Our interview with Ahmed el-Akhras, the Montreal resident who lost eleven members of his family in one bomb blast, most poignantly illustrated the sense of betrayal felt by this family and others at the perceived inaction and callous disregard by the Canadian government to their plight. The perceived unwillingness of the Canadian government to take actions to protect its citizens or to condemn the Israeli government for its killing of civilians in south Lebanon made him "so upset and hurt, because the Canadian government did not condemn this awful crime of killing Canadian civilians. It is a war crime."[44]

A strong sense of betrayal by the Australian government was similarly expressed by some respondents, such as a fifty-year-old man who was in the southern town of Bint Jbeil to attend his daughter's wedding. Forced to flee with his family following the full brunt of the IDF bombing in southern Lebanon, this man was highly critical of the Australian government's response to the war. His narrative also suggests a sense of entitlement to effective consular protection by virtue of holding citizenship in a safe country:

> I give it five out of ten, not good enough! At least,...Australia should pressure Israel, to say okay, we've got foreigners, we've got our...citizens here...what I'm saying is if they have a battle, we have nothing to do with it. We are Australian. We should have been taken care of. The Australian government didn't do much, at first. And after that, they said okay, we're going to send a boat to Tyre. And Tyre is getting shelled constantly. How can we go to Tyre?[45]

Dual citizens from both Canada and Australia expressed a mixture of gratitude, disappointment, and anger for the quality of their government's departure assistance from Lebanon in 2006. For both groups, witnessing that other countries had effectively evacuated their nationals earlier fueled a sense that Canada and Australia were sluggish in their efforts to assist their citizens to safety. In part, when viewed in the context of the Canadian Senate Standing Committee's assessment of Canada's capacities for undertaking large-scale evaluations, however, one can see that these two countries' capacities for undertaking such consular assistance were relatively weaker than the best provisioned nations—such as the USA and the UK which could mobilize their own helicopters and aircraft in their rescue operations. Thus, Canadian and Australian (dual) nationals experienced that their "secure" citizenships were attached to, in the Standing Committee's words (referencing Canada), "a medium-sized country with relatively small standing military capabilities."[46]

The harshest criticisms regarding the limits on capacity or willingness of Canada and Australia to safeguard their nationals came from those who felt abandoned by their governments to Israeli bombing, especially in areas under Hezbollah's control.[47] The perception here was that the Canadian Harper and Australian Howard governments merely replicated USA foreign policy in the region, rejecting an immediate ceasefire in the hopes that Hezbollah would be dealt a death blow by America's "sister nation" of Israel. The constant refrain from these governments that Hezbollah was a "terrorist" organization justified Israel's indiscriminate bombings in south Lebanon. The policies of their "safe citizenship" countries—for example, in not calling for an immediate ceasefire or effectively negotiating a safe corridor of escape for their nationals— not only endangered their uni-citizen Lebanese family members but indeed imperiled their entitlements to consular protection and thus, they felt, undermined their full citizenship status as Canadians and Australians. Dual citizens in the heavily bombed south expressed their frustration over the unwillingness of the governments of their safe citizenship to negotiate safe avenues (such as temporary ceasefires) for the escape of these citizens.

For dual nationals who chose to stay in Lebanon, many relied on their own memories and familial experiences of violence, as well as ongoing communication with residents, to identify where violence clusters in space (and also time) and also where best to avoid it. They applied their knowledge of the "microgeographies of security" in order to maximize the safety of themselves and their loved ones.[48] Thus, many negotiated their understanding of "safe spaces" by calculating likely targets for Israeli bombing—Shi'ite areas under the local control of Hezbollah, rather than Christian or Sunni neighborhoods. They sought safer suburbs in Beirut and/or rented housing in mountainous and northern areas, which for the most part escaped the bombing. In the absence of any expectation of security stemming from their Lebanese citizenship, and with only uneven and "middle-power" consular assistance from their Australian/Canadian citizenship, these dual nationals exercised embedded agency in designing their own security strategies to escape the violence and carnage of war. In so doing, they relied for their safety not only on any state citizenship membership but on a connective form of selfhood and communication with family and kin both in Lebanon and in border spanning and even transnational familial and communal networks.[49]

When asked about the benefits of holding Australian and Canadian citizenship, dual citizens referred to both general and specific social citizenship/social security rights. Health care is often seen to be one of the central pillars of social policy and social citizenship.[50] It is instructive to explore how dual nationals manage their health care over two very different policy architectures pertaining to their citizenship in Lebanon and in Australia/Canada.

In international rankings, the respective positions of Canadian, Australian, and Lebanese health-care systems suggest that there is a sharp distinction between the quality of health care received by nationals in Canada and Australia on the one hand and Lebanon on the other. Thus in 2000, the World Health Organization's (WHO) ranking of 191 countries placed Canada at 30 and Australia at 32 suggesting that the two countries were similar in overall level and distribution of health in their respective populations and responsiveness and financing of health-care services. In contrast, Lebanon ranked much lower at rank No. 91.[51]

Canada and Australia are said to have similar "universal health-care systems," although their systems differ in the role of private insurance. Canada has a universal public insurance plan, which (with the exception of Quebec) prohibits the use of private insurance to pay for services covered by the public plan.[52] In contrast, Australia has a mixed private–public system with many cost-sharing requirements. Australians have been encouraged to use private insurance to subsidize the escalating costs of public care and about half are privately insured. About two-thirds of Canadians have private insurance, which covers services outside the public plan, with (as of 2013), approximately ninety percent of private health premiums paid through group contracts with employers, unions, or other organizations.[53] Provinces and territories in Canada have primary responsibility for organizing and delivering health services, with the federal government, co-financing provincial/territorial programs, which must adhere to the underlying principles of the *Canadian Health Act*, which include "universality" and "accessibility."[54] The federal government's contribution to funding provincial/territorial health care has however dwindled from the initial 50/50 cost sharing to about 24 percent in 2015–2016 through the Canada Health Transfer.[55]

"Health care" has often been cited as one of the most fundamentally important values in Canadian society, with universal coverage and publicly funded aspects of the system cited as key sources of pride and inexorably linked to "being Canadian" since the 1960s.[56] Nonetheless, since the 1990s, Canadians have observed a marked deterioration in the quality of their health-care system, particularly in regard to wait times for specialists and elective surgeries (particularly hip and knee replacements), availability of high-quality technology, and adequate numbers of doctors.[57] In both Canada and Australia, there are huge disparities in the quality of health care received by urban versus widely dispersed rural communities, with Indigenous people especially said to receive grossly inadequate health care.[58] Those with lower incomes report higher dissatisfaction with almost all aspects of accessing health care attributable to cost.[59]

There are many debates about the sources for deterioration and rising dissatisfaction in health care in Canada and Australia—for example, the role of the aging population as a cost driver in health care, high and rising costs of drugs, the abandonment (in Canada) of federal leadership, and national standards in health care. Neoliberalism, informed by principles of individualism, privatization and deregulation, and decentralization, has frequently been identified as the political rationality driving health-care reform in Anglo-American democracies including Canada and Australia. As Janine Brodie observes, "[b]eginning in the late 1980s, one Canadian federal government after another has abandoned the concepts of universality and social security, reduced social program spending to levels not seen since right after the Second World War, and shifted emphasis from so-called passive to active welfare interventions, that is policies offering a 'hand-up rather than a hand-out.'"[60] Australia in the 1980s and 1990s also followed a neoliberal turn in social policy.[61] Welfare reforms in line with market-based policies included the introduction in 1996 of "a rebate on private health insurance that threatened the public health-care system."[62] While "neoliberal governments have not abandoned the terrain of social governance," current transformations can be said to "betray representations of social citizenship as an apex in the development of liberal rights."[63]

In Lebanon, the health-care system was never structured for the central government to play a central funding or coordinating role. The minimal direct state role in assuring social security has long historical roots. "During the Ottoman and colonial mandate periods, religious organizations such as churches, missionary groups and Muslim organizations were important providers of social assistance."[64] After Lebanon gained independence from the French in 1948, an integral part of the Lebanese political system became the formalization of institutional representation based on confessional or sectarian affiliation, which meant the deliberate construction of a weak state to privilege group identities and interests over national ones.[65] Little progress was made in constructing national state institutions of social protection. Under the presidency of Fuad Shihab (1958–1964), who brought in national-scale reforms in social development, national health financing was established, and public infrastructure was expanded. However, the fifteen-year civil war (1975–1990) led to the systematic destruction of what remained of public provision in the 1970s, thus again leaving this space open for confessional groups in all of Lebanon's religious communities to further develop their own social welfare programs. This consociational system has been historically anchored in post-Ottoman-era colonialism (the "French mandate" that privileged the Christian Maronite community, shared power with the Sunni community, and disadvantaged the proportionately larger but poorer Sh'ia community).

The Lebanese welfare regime is therefore characterized by a "low involvement of the state in social provision and peculiar dependence on a public-private mix."[66] A central state weakened by prolonged civil war, and highly susceptible to chronic foreign influence, both "Asian/Middle Eastern" (e.g. Iran and Saudi Arabia) and Western, Lebanon's economic and social development has been left open to the "free-wheeling financial interests of the Lebanese bourgeoisie," dominated by Christian and Sunni Muslim elites. In this context, the vacuum created by a wounded public sector has been filled by a proliferating private sector, NGOs, and international donors. The health system is "highly fragmented" with multiple actors, governmental bodies involved as "official regulators," but with "private providers as the true influential parties in the health sector."[67] Fifty percent of Lebanon's citizens are uninsured, but this does not mean that they lack all access to health care. The Ministry of Public Health "provides services as the last resort, either through public hospitals or contracted private hospitals, and covers 95 and 85% of hospital care costs consecutively and 100% of medication costs for chronic and high-risk diseases."[68]

A recurring observation made about Lebanon's health services and its social welfare systems more broadly is that there appears to be no conflict between neoliberal globalization and the politics of confessionalism dominated by ties of confessional group, family, and kin. Another is that the sectarian–capitalist orientation and the complex relationship between state, finance capital, and confessional politics in the context of health sector reform have reinforced gross inequalities in access to health care.[69]

These then were some of the features of the health-care landscapes of the countries which the Lebanese–Australian and Lebanese–Canadian dual citizens evaluated and negotiated their own "citizenship portfolios" in health care: the stark contrast in public health-care systems and overall international (WHO) ranking of Canadian (No. 30) and Australian (No. 32) versus Lebanese (No. 91) health-care systems; the perceived deterioration in the quality of these services in Canada/Australia in line with neoliberal reforms to social policy; the greater encouragement in Australia than in Canada for private insurance for basic health services; the stark contrast in the types of mixed public–private systems in Canada/Australia versus Lebanon with the latter more highly privatized and sectarian, but with private providers expanding in all contexts, facilitated by all three governments embracing neoliberal rationality.

"Universal health care" has long been identified as a cornerstone of Canadian national values.[70] Thus, it is not unexpected that among eighty respondents, more dual nationals with Canadian citizenship ($N = 9$) identified health care as a benefit of Canadian citizenship in comparison with those holding Australian citizenship ($N = 2$), while none saw this is a benefit of Lebanese citizenship.

In general, dual nationals' country of habitual residence—whether Canadian, Australian, or Lebanese—predictably shaped their choice of their two countries of citizenship to access their health-care services. As one middle-aged woman who resided in Montreal stated, she sought health care in Canada "because we live here, it's more normal, okay?" Many Lebanese–Canadians and Lebanese–Australians stated that they accessed health care only in Canada or Australia, respectively, and never in Lebanon. In some cases, they stated that the quality of health services and the accessibility regardless of wealth in Canada/Australia were better than in Lebanon, although more Canadians than Australians cited "universal health care" as a benefit of holding citizenship in these countries. Both groups of dual nationals also spoke about their entitlements to good quality care in Canada and Australia, regardless of wealth. One Lebanese–Australian female, who already was in her mid-60s, said that she would likely retire in Australia, because of its superior health-care system.

Many respondents—both Canadian and Australian—commented that they did not have health coverage in Lebanon and that it is therefore expensive to access Lebanese health services. One 32-year-old woman, born in Australia where she lived for twenty years until she moved to Lebanon with her family and then became one of the 2006 evacuees to Australia, contrasted the two country's medical services:

> If you don't have enough money or health insurance you won't be able to take your child to the dentist or to the hospital, it's an expensive way of living. But there is no government that reaches out to you. We do have a Medicare card in Australia, but in Lebanon the government does not provide social welfare so we were on private insurance overseas. If you don't get private health insurance, it's very, very difficult financially to stay for a few days in the hospital. It's very difficult whereas here [Australia] we don't have private health insurance at the moment. But even the public system here is much better then overseas.[71]

Several of the respondents regarded the health-care system in Lebanon to be both expensive and difficult to access. Thus, one middle-aged man in Sydney opined: "In Australia, they give me a far better medical service, whereas in Lebanon, you need money and you also need to know someone and you need to kiss people's hands to get decent health care." A 25-year-old woman from south Lebanon who lived in Lebanon for nineteen years before immigrating to Australia stated bluntly: "I access health care services in Australia. In Lebanon, there isn't any social welfare." As to be expected, some nonresident dual citizens accessed urgent care when they were in Lebanon, whereas others stated that their visits to Lebanon were sufficiently short that they did not have to seek medical attention.

While the majority of dual nationals' views about and experiences with the health-care systems in Australia/Canada versus Lebanon generally conformed to the gap in the quality of their respective countries' health-care systems, reflected in the WHO study, a minority regarded Lebanese health care as better. For a minority of respondents (five out of eighty), Lebanese health care was perceived to be much better than Canadian in particular. It has "world-class services if you can afford them. Whatever you want, if you can afford it, you can have it. The rich people don't feel the backwardness of many of the services" (thirty-year-old male). Canadian health services, with their long wait times, were seen as poor. Lebanese health services were "much better, way better, yeah way better, because there is a possibility where you can pay and get good service. Here [in Canada] you cannot pay" (32-year-old male). In other words, the public nature of Canadian health-care services, which imposes wait times and is subject to various restrictions, is perceived to be poorer than in Lebanon where money and connections can access excellent services.

One Lebanese–Canadian woman who had stomach ailments felt that she received quicker access to diagnosis in Lebanon where she had traveled to attend her brother's wedding. "There is no waiting like in Canada." "Health care in Lebanon for major operations, they'll do it right away." Another recounted how her "son had a back problem in Canada. To see a specialist, he had to wait six months, just to see him. People die waiting in Canada for a specialist. But if you don't have money in Lebanon, they still do it right away. You apply to the government and they pay 85 percent of the cost. The health care in Canada is in shambles. You go to Emergency, you can wait for hours in pain."

A minority of respondents indicated that they did utilize both health-care systems, often taking into account relative waiting times and costs in the two contexts. Thus, one respondent "fixed her teeth" in Lebanon, where it was cheaper than in Australia, but her other health-care services were accessed in Australia where they were cheaper or publicly covered. Another respondent expressed his frustration that the deterioration of health care in Canada had driven him to get his health care in Lebanon. "In Canada, it used to be much better than in Lebanon. But in Canada, now it's not good. I've been looking for a doctor for more than three years in Ottawa…I came here [Canada] and I am getting my health care in Lebanon…."

There were a few interesting cases of a more coordinated approach of accessing health services in both countries of citizenship. Some of these cases involved chronic health issues. Thus, a woman in her 50s interviewed in Mount Lebanon who had lived in both countries had chronic back problems. She had surgery in Australia where she "knew and trusted all the doctors…but the main one that she trusted advised her to see doctors in Lebanon; they told her that there are very good doctors in Lebanon," and in Lebanon, she subsequently had three back surgeries to date, within the space of one year.

In sum, habitual residence and the assessment that affordable health care is better in Canada/Australia than in Lebanon accounted for the majority of dual citizens accessing their health care in the countries of their more robust citizenship, where the quality was seen as superior and where health care was regarded as a right and part of being a Canadian or Australian. Dual citizens who habitually lived in Lebanon also did not tend to seek out health services in Canada or Australia and, depending on income, would either access "free" services along confessional lines or buy the services privately. However, the deterioration in Canada and Australia's health care since the 1990s, which led to diminished access to family doctors and specialists, and long wait times for surgery compelled some dual nationals to seek health care periodically in Lebanon despite the knowledge of their private character and cost. The health-related behavior of these transnational dual citizens also reflected the complexity of changes wrought by neoliberalism, where the continued hold of the public system in Canada hindered access to services that they could more readily buy in the Lebanese context where private health care had long been regarded as the norm. Finally, while they form the clear exception, it is instructive to see that physicians in one country of more robust citizenship (Australia) encourage their dual citizen patients to seek what they consider to be good quality care in the country (Lebanon) that ranks considerably lower in health care.

Conclusion

While dual citizens identified affective attachments, family, and quality of life as overall more intense in Lebanon, they deeply appreciated the benefits of holding Canadian/Australian citizenship in terms of "security" and access to public services (particularly health and education). For some dual citizens, the fact that they felt "cared for" by having Australian/Canadian citizenship evokes an understanding similar to Foucault's understanding of "pastoral power" as a modern form of governmentality, fostering a strong sense of their belonging in their adopted country or country of birth.[72]

Given the actual or perceived threat to their lives stemming from military actions, "security" and "peace and safety" ranked understandably highly in the list of benefits of holding Canadian and Australian citizenship cited by dual citizens, who declare the constant threats of war and political violence and general instability to be the leading drawbacks of holding Lebanese citizenship. The growing significance of protecting their citizens abroad was acknowledged in a May 2007 Canadian Senate Standing Committee Report that examined the 2006 evacuation and made recommendations meant to improve Canada's large-scale crises operations overseas. The then–Foreign Minister Peter McKay stated to the Committee that "there is no higher priority" than the "safety and security of Canadians."[73]

Interestingly, the Report reflects a sense of Canada's responsibility toward its external citizens, recommending "more frequent assessments of its missions abroad, particularly those situated in areas with large Canadian resident populations and areas where the potential for destabilization is high."[74] During the evacuation, critics from across party lines and mass media chatter derided the use of assisted departure of Canadian passport holders who had not resided or paid taxes in Canada for some time. These critics heavily disparaged the perceived abuse of the generosity of the Canadian government by these "citizens of convenience," although the perception of such abuse rested purely on anecdotal evidence given that Canada's border services do not conduct exit controls. A Department of Foreign Affairs and International Trade (DFAIT) official responsible for consular affairs also confirmed the principle of equality among Canadian citizens, internal or external: "Until further notice, within the framework of the consular service, a Canadian is a Canadian; the rule is very clear."[75]

While the Senate Standing Report clearly affirms the recognition of the augmenting significance of consular services as a right among Canadian citizens which requires modernization and expansion of such services in light of increased patterns of travel, work, and residence abroad, it also places responsibility upon Canadians for their own safety. It suggests that many of the Canadians caught in Lebanon's summer 2006 war were irresponsible in failing to register with the Canadian embassy in Beirut. Moreover, the expectations of Canadians overseas are perceived as high and "cannot always be satisfied" as there exist "constraints on resources and on diplomatic and logistical access."[76] A form of neoliberal subjectivity and model of self-responsibilization are thus reflected in the Standing Committee's recommendations such as ensuring that Canadians residing and traveling abroad register with the Registration of Canadians Abroad program.[77]

An exploration of the dual citizens' patterns of accessing health services generally undermines the notion of a double advantage through access to two social security or health-care systems. For the most part, dual citizens behave similarly to their uni-citizen cousins in accessing health care in the country/province where they habitually reside. The contrasting quality of public funding and also perceived higher quality of health care in Canada/Australia versus Lebanon was noted by many dual citizens as the primary reason to access only Canadian/Australian services. This contrast in health-care systems, however, was not universally agreed upon among respondents, some of whose experiences with health care in Canada and Australia reflect deterioration in services, increase in wait times, and so on. Some of these dual citizens thus pursued dual national strategies in accessing health services, seeking to skirt long waiting times in Australia and Canada by paying for more readily available services in Lebanon. Given the assumed contrast in quality of health services in Canada/Australia versus Lebanon, this finding is notable. It is possible that familiarity with accessing private and confessional social services in a country with a weak state serves as an important habitus, rendering these dual citizens adept and proactive in seeking private services in Lebanon to skirt the sluggishness and drawbacks of public services in Canada or Australia. Such patterns of negotiating dual health systems reflect how the embedded agency of dual nationals in multiple locales is utilized to build their own border-spanning social safety nets.

Notes

1. Linda Basch, Nina Glick Schiller, and Cristina Szanton-Blanc, *Nations unbound: Transnational projects and the deterritorialized nation-state* (New York: Gordon and Breach, 1994); Doreen Massey, "Geographies of Responsibility," *Geografiska Annaler*, Series B, *Human Geography* 86, 1 (2004): 6.
2. Jennifer Skulte-Ouaiss, "Home is where the heart is: citizenship is where it is safe: dual citizenship and Europe," *Identities: Global Studies in Culture and Power* 20, 2 (2013): 133.
3. Luke Desforges, Rhys Jones, and Mike Woods, "New Geographies of Citizenship," *Citizenship Studies* 9, 5 (November 2005): 439–451.
4. The analysis is also based on government documents and secondary analyses.
5. James Haines-Young, "The 2006 Lebanon War: Hezbollah's expensive 'victory' ten years on," Al Arabiya English, 15 July 2016. Available:

http://www.perspective/features/2016/07/15/The-2006-Lebanon-War-Hezbollahs-expensive-victory-ten-years-on.html.

6. Ray Jureidini, "State and Non-State Actors in Evacuations During the Conflict in Lebanon, July–August 2006," In *The Migration-Displacement Nexus: Concepts, Cases and Responses*, ed. K. Koser and S. Martin (New York: Berghahn Books, 2011).
7. Several interviews were conducted by the author.
8. Lois Harder and Lyubov Zhyznomirska, "Claims of belonging: Recent tales of trouble in Canadian citizenship," *Ethnicities* 12, 3 (2012): 294.
9. Dual citizenship is also referred to in the literature and legislation as multiple or plural citizenship and dual or multiple nationality. These terms will be used interchangeably in this chapter.
10. Hossi Harpaz, "Rooted Cosmopolitans: Israelis with a European Passport – History, Property, Identity," *International Migration Review* 47, 1 (Spring 2013): 173; see also Skulte-Ouaiss, "Home is where the heart is," 173.
11. Harpaz, "Rooted Cosmopolitans," 174.
12. Aristide Zolberg, quoted in Dalia Abdelhady, *The Lebanese Diaspora: The Arab Immigrant Experience in Montreal, New York, and Paris* (New York: New York University Press, 2011), 190.
13. David Cook-Martin, *The Scramble for Citizens: Dual Nationality and State Competition for Immigrants* (Stanford: Stanford University Press, 2013), 13–14.
14. Linda Bosniak, *The Citizen and the Alien: Dilemmas of Contemporary Membership* (Princeton: Princeton University Press, 2006), 24–25.
15. Harpaz, "Rooted Cosmopolitans," 174.
16. Ibid.
17. See Daiva Stasiulis, "Contending Frames of 'Security' and 'Citizenship': Lebanese Dual Nationals during the 2006 Lebanon War," in *Mobilities, Knowledge, and Social Justice*, ed. S. Ilcan (Montreal: McGill-Queen's University Press, 2013), 25–58; Skulte-Ouaiss, "Home is where the heart is"; Abdelhady, *The Lebanese Diaspora*; Harpaz, "Rooted Cosmopolitans"; Valerie Preston, Myer Siermiatycki, and Audrey Kobayashi, In *Dual Citizenship in Global Perspectives: From Unitary to Multiple Citizenship*, eds. T. Faist and P. Kivisto (Houndmills: Palgrave Macmillan, 2007), 203–226.
18. In her case study of transnational Bulgarian Muslim migrant aging caregivers, Neda Deneva similarly embraces a definition of social citizenship as both rights and entitlements and as their enactment and lived experience. Neda Deneva, "Transnational Aging Carers: On Transformation of Kinship and Citizenship in the Context of Migration among Bulgarian Muslims in Spain," *Social Politics* 19, 1 (2012): 109.

19. My thanks to Janine Brodie for suggesting the concept of "citizenship portfolio."
20. G. Esping-Anderson, *The Three Worlds of Welfare Capitalism* (Cambridge: Polity Press, 1990). Martin Powell, "The Hidden History of Social Citizenship," *Citizenship Studies* 6, 3 (2002): 229–244.
21. Powell, "The Hidden History," 230.
22. T. H. Marshall, *Citizenship and Social Class* (Garden City: Doubleday & Co., 1964), 74.
23. Powell, "The Hidden History," 230.
24. Thomas Faist, "The Transnational Social Question: Social Rights and Citizenship in a Global Context," Working Paper No.14 (Center on Migration, Citizenship and Development, Universität Bielefeld, 2007), 10.
25. Ibid., 15.
26. Ibid., 21.
27. Ibid., 18; Ben Revi, "T. H. Marshall and his critics: reappraising 'social citizenship' in the twenty-first century," *Citizenship Studies* 18, 3–4 (June 2014): 452–464.
28. Audrey Macklin, "Who is the Citizen's Other? Considering the Heft of Citizenship," *Theoretical Inquiries in Law* 6, 2 (2007): 333–366.
29. Maureen Mackintosh et al., "What is the private sector? Understanding private provision in the health systems of low-income and middle-income countries," *Lancet* 388, 10044 (August 2016): 596.
30. Thomas Faist, "The Fixed and Porous Boundaries of Dual Citizenship." In Thomas Faist, ed., *Dual Citizenship in Europe: From Nationhood to Societal Integration* (Aldershot: Ashgate, 2007), 3.
31. Marshall, Citizenship and Social Class, 102.
32. Legal experts argue that there are fundamental differences between diplomatic protection and consular assistance but hold different views as to which government activities fall under diplomatic protection and which under consular assistance. Two Vienna Conventions of 1961 and 1963 have codified the rules with respect to diplomatic and consular relations, respectively. The Vienna Convention on Diplomatic Relations, UN Treaty Series, vol. 500, 95 (hereinafter: VCDR), and the Vienna Convention on Consular Relations, UN Treaty Series, vol. 596, 262 (hereinafter: VCCR). According to Künzli, the major distinction is that diplomatic protection involves judicial proceedings, whereas interventions outside the judicial process on behalf of nationals fall under consular assistance. Annemarieke Künzli, "Exercising Diplomatic Protection: The Fine Line Between Litigation, Demarches and Consular Assistance," Max-Planck-Institut für ausländisches öffentliches Recht und Völkerrech, ZaöRV 2006, 322. Available: http://www.zaoerv.de/66_2006/66_2006_2_a_321_350.pdf.

33. Daiva Stasiulis and Darryl Ross, "Security, Flexible Sovereignty, and the Perils of Multiple Citizenship," *Citizenship Studies* 10, 3 (2006): 329–348.
34. Craig Forcese, "Shelter from the Storm: Rethinking Diplomatic Protection of Dual Nationals in Modern International Law," *George Washington International Law Review* 37 (2005): 469–500.
35. Canada, Standing Senate Committee on Foreign Affairs and International Trade, "The Evacuation of Canadians from Lebanon in July 2006: Implications for the Government of Canada," May 2007, 11.
36. Guita G. Hourani, *The Impact of the Summer 2006 War on Migration in Lebanon: Emigration, Remigration, Evacuation and Return: A Preliminary Study* (Louaize, IN: Notre Dame University Press, 2006), 40–41.
37. Thus, countries of the Global South with large migrant populations in Lebanon (particularly female migrant domestic workers) such as Sri Lanka, the Philippines, and Ethiopia lacked the financial means and organizational capacity to arrange for the evacuations of their citizens. Poor Palestinians, including 400,000 Palestinians languishing in refugee camps around Lebanon, were forced to weather the crisis, with only a small number (about 1000) permitted to enter Syria. Jureidini, "State and Non-State Actors."
38. As Beirut's major international airport had been bombed and disabled by the Israeli Defense Forces (IDF), Canadians were evacuated through 34 departures by ship from the Port of Beirut and one from the Port of Tyre to holding centers in Cyprus and Turkey and from there by 61 chartered and four National Defence flights to Canada. The Department of Foreign Affairs and International Trade (DFAIT) oversaw the evacuation and coordinated the involvement of an array of other government departments and officials. Canada, the Standing Senate Committee on Foreign Affairs and International Trade, "The Evacuation," 16.
39. The Australian ambassador commented on the logistical nightmare for her staff, as various family members in Australia would register the same people, sometimes using different spellings of names (interview with Ambassador Lyndall Sachs, Beirut, August 2008).
40. Australia chartered seventeen ships, 22 Australian aircraft, and over 470 buses. Ray Jureidini, "State and Non-State Actors." Ambassador Lyndall Sachs noted civilians' unawareness of embassies' complex communications and logistical preparations for the operation and their competition for scarce resources such as ships (interview, Beirut, August 2008).
41. Interview, Sydney, 3 May 2008.
42. Jureidini, "State and Non-State Actors."
43. Interview, Ottawa, 12 May 2007.
44. Interview, Aytaroun, 14 August 2008.
45. Interview, Sydney, 4 May 2008.

46. Canada, Standing Senate Committee, "The Evacuation of Canadians," 18.
47. About twenty percent were in south Lebanon when war broke out.
48. Stasiulis, "Contending Frames," 40–41.
49. For further elaboration, see Stasiulis, "Contending Frames," 43.
50. Sue L. T. McGregor, "Neoliberalism and healthcare," *International Journal of Consumer Studies* 25, 2 (2001): 82–89.
51. World Health Organization, The World Health Report 2000. Available: http://www.who.int/whr/2000/en/whr00_en.pdf.
52. In 2005, the Supreme Court of Canada granted Quebecers access to private insurance when it ruled that excessive wait times infringed on patients' constitutional rights. That decision was argued under the Quebec Charter of Rights, rather than the Canadian Charter, and therefore its results constitutionally did not extend beyond Quebec.
53. Sara Allin and David Rudoler, "The Canadian Health Care System, 2015," In *2015 International Profiles of Health Care Systems*, eds. Elias Mossialos et al. (Commonwealth Fund), 21.
54. Ibid.
55. Ibid.
56. Benjamin Shingler, "What Unites Canada? Charter of Rights and universal health care, say poll respondents," iPolitics, 30 June 2014. Available: http://ipolitics.ca/2014/06/30/what-unites-canada-charter-of-rights-and-universal-health-care-say-poll-responde.
57. Matthew Mendelsohn, "Canadians' Thoughts on their Health Care System: Preserving the Canadian Model Through Innovation," Commission on the Future of Health Care in Canada, 2002. Available: http://www.queensu.ca/cora/ files/MendelsohnEnglish.pdf; Elizabeth A. Hardie and Christine R. Critchley, "Public perceptions of Australia's doctors, hospitals and health care systems," *Medical Journal of Australia* 189, 4 (2008): 210–214. "Public dissatisfaction with the health care system grew markedly in Canada between 1990 and 1998, likely reflecting the sharp curtailment in real national health spending and reduced hospital inpatient capacity during these years." Robert J. Blendon et al., "Inequities in Health Care: A Five-Country Study," *Health Affairs* 21, 3 (May/June 2002): 189.
58. Tarun Ghose, "The Real Crisis in Medicare: Canada needs (and can afford complete national health care," Canadian Centre for Policy Alternatives, 1 December 2012. Available: https://www.policyalternatives.ca/publications/monitor/real-crisis-medicare.
59. Hardie and Critchley, "Public perceptions of Australia's doctors, hospitals and health care systems," 210–214.
60. Janine Brodie, "The Social in Social Citizenship," in *Recasting the Social in Citizenship*, ed. E. Isin (Toronto: University of Toronto Press, 2008), 39.

61. "Economic rationalism" that sought "free market reforms" began under the Hawke Labor government (1983–1991) and was further refined under the Keating Labor government (1991–1996) and the Howard-led Liberal-National coalition government (1996–2007). Christopher Deeming, "Social democracy and social policy in neoliberal times," *Journal of Sociology* 50, 4 (2014): 577–600.
62. Deeming," Social democracy," 583.
63. Brodie, "The Social in Social Citizenship," 39.
64. Melani Claire Cammett, "Partisan Activism and Access to Welfare in Lebanon," *Studies in Comparative International Development* 46, 1 (March 2011): 70–97.
65. Laurie A. Brand, *Citizens Abroad: Emigration and the State in the Middle East and North Africa* (Cambridge: Cambridge University Press, 2006).
66. Rana Jawad, "Human Ethics and Welfare Particularism: An Exploration of the Social Welfare Regime in Lebanon," *Ethics and Social Welfare* 1, 2 (July 2007): 141.
67. Thus, there are "two employment-based social insurance schemes, four different schemes to cover the security forces, the Ministry of Health financing, which is the insurer of uninsured, the private insurance sector, in addition to out-of-pocket expenditures." Regional Health Systems Observatory—EMRO, World Health Organization, Health System Profile: Lebanon, 2006. Available: http://apps.who.int/medicinedocs/documents/s17301e/s17301e.pdf.
68. Karl Blanchet, Fouad Fouad, and Tejendra Pherali, "Syrian refugees in Lebanon: the search for universal health coverage," *Conflict and Health* 10, 2 (2016). Available: https://conflictandhealth.biomedcentral.com/articles/10.1186/s13031-016-0079-4.
69. Jawad, "Human Ethics and Welfare Particularism," 141.
70. As recently as June 2014, a national survey of Canadians by the Montreal-based Association of Canadian Studies found that universal health care was listed as a close second to the Canadian Charter of Rights and Freedoms in a ranking of eleven items in terms of the elements that were perceived to unite Canadians. Benjamin Shingler, "What unites Canada?"
71. Interview, Sydney, March 2007.
72. Foucault defines "pastoral power" as aiming to ensure well-being, health, security, and protection against accidents through comprehensive regulation of behavior. Michel Foucault. "The Subject and Power," in *Art After Modernism: Rethinking Representation*, ed. Brian Wallis (New York: The Museum of Contemporary Art, 1984).
73. Canada, Standing Senate Committee on Foreign Affairs and International Trade, "The Evacuation," 5.
74. Ibid., 16.
75. Ibid., 21.
76. Ibid., 8.
77. Ibid.,13.

Bibliography

Abdelhady, Dalia. *The Lebanese Diaspora: The Arab Immigrant Experience in Montreal, New York, and Paris.* New York: New York University Press, 2011.

Allin, Sara and David Rudoler. "The Canadian Health Care System, 2015." In *2015 International Profiles of Health Care Systems*, edited by Elias Mossialos et al.: 21–30. Commonwealth Fund, 2015. Available: http://www.commonwealthfund.org/~/media/files/publications/fund-report/2016/jan/1857_mossialos_intl_profiles_2015_v7.pdf.

Basch, Linda, Nina Glick Schiller, and Cristina Szanton-Blanc. *Nations unbound: Transnational projects and the deterritorialized nation-state.* New York: Gordon and Breach, 1994.

Blanchet, Karl, Fouad Fouad, and Tejendra Pherali. "Syrian refugees in Lebanon: the search for universal health coverage." *Conflict and Health.* 10, 2, 2016. Available: https://conflictandhealth.biomedcentral.com/articles/10.1186/s13031-016-0079-4.

Blendon, Robert J. et al. "Inequities in Health Care: A Five-Country Study." *Health Affairs.* 21, 3, May/June 2002: 182–204.

Bosniak, Linda. *The Citizen and the Alien: Dilemmas of Contemporary Membership.* Princeton: Princeton University Press, 2006.

Brand, Laurie A. Citizens Abroad*: Emigration and the State in the Middle East and North Africa.* Cambridge: Cambridge University Press, 2006.

Brodie, Janine. "The Social in Social Citizenship." In *Recasting the Social in Citizenship*, edited by E. Isin: 20–43. Toronto: University of Toronto Press, 2008.

Cammett, Melani Claire. "Partisan Activism and Access to Welfare in Lebanon." *Studies in Comparative International Development.* 46, 1, March 2011: 70–97. Canada, Standing Senate Committee on Foreign Affairs and International Trade. "The Evacuation of Canadians from Lebanon in July 2006: Implications for the Government of Canada," May 2007.

Cook-Martin, David. *The Scramble for Citizens: Dual Nationality and State Competition for Immigrants.* Stanford: Stanford University Press, 2013.

Deeming, Christopher. "Social democracy and social policy in neoliberal times." *Journal of Sociology.* 50, 4, 2014: 577–600.

Deneva, Neda. "Transnational Aging Carers: On Transformation of Kinship and Citizenship in the Context of Migration among Bulgarian Muslims in Spain." *Social Politics.* 19, 1, 2012: 105–128.

Desforges, Luke, Rhys Jones, and Mike Woods. "New Geographies of Citizenship." *Citizenship Studies.* 9, 5, November 2005: 439–451.

Esping-Anderson, Goran. *The Three Worlds of Welfare Capitalism.* Cambridge, Polity Press, 1990.

Faist, Thomas. "The Fixed and Porous Boundaries of Dual Citizenship." In *Dual Citizenship in Europe: From Nationhood to Societal Integration*, edited by Thomas Faist: 1–44. Aldershot: Ashgate, 2007a.

Faist, Thomas. "The Transnational Social Question: Social Rights and Citizenship in a Global Context." Working Paper No.14. Center on Migration, Citizenship and Development, Universität Bielefeld, 2007b.

Forcese, Craig. "Shelter from the Storm: Rethinking Diplomatic Protection of Dual Nationals in Modern International Law." *George Washington International Law Review*. 37, 2005: 469–500.

Foucault, Michel. "The Subject and Power." In *Art After Modernism: Rethinking Representation*, edited by Brian Wallis: 417–432. New York: The Museum of Contemporary Art, 1984.

Harder, Lois and Lyubov Zhyznomirska. "Claims of belonging: Recent tales of trouble in Canadian citizenship." *Ethnicities*. 12, 3, 2012: 293–316.

Hardie, Elizabeth A. and Christine R. Critchley. "Public perceptions of Australia's doctors, hospitals and health care systems." *Medical Journal of Australia*. 189, 4, 2008: 210–214.

Harpaz, Hossi. "Rooted Cosmopolitans: Israelis with a European Passport – History, Property, Identity." *International Migration Review*. 47, 1, Spring 2013: 166–206.

Hourani, Guita G. *The Impact of the Summer 2006 War on Migration in Lebanon: Emigration, Remigration, Evacuation and Return: A Preliminary Study*. Louaize, IN: Notre Dame University Press, 2006.

Jawad, Rana. "Human Ethics and Welfare Particularism: An Exploration of the Social Welfare Regime in Lebanon." *Ethics and Social Welfare*. 1, 2, July 2007: 123–146.

Jureidini, Ray. "State and Non-State Actors in Evacuations During the Conflict in Lebanon, July-August 2006." In *The Migration-Displacement Nexus: Concepts, Cases and Responses*, edited by K. Koser and S. Martin: Chapter 12. New York: Berghahn Books, 2011.

Mackintosh, Maureen et al. "What is the private sector? Understanding private provision in the health systems of low-income and middle-income countries." *Lancet*. 388, 10044, August 2016: 596–605.

Macklin, Audrey. "Who is the Citizen's Other? Considering the Heft of Citizenship." *Theoretical Inquiries in Law*. 6, 2, 2007: 333–366.

Marshall, T. H. *Citizenship and Social Class*. Garden City: Doubleday & Co., 1964.

Massey, Doreen. "Geographies of Responsibility." Geografiska Annaler, Series B, *Human Geography*. 86, 1, 2004: 5–18.

McGregor, Sue L. T. "Neoliberalism and health care." *International Journal of Consumer Studies*. 25, 2, 2001: 82–89.

Mendelsohn, Matthew. "Canadians' Thoughts on their Health Care System: Preserving the Canadian Model Through Innovation." Commission on the

Future of Health Care in Canada, 2002. Available: http://www.queensu.ca/cora/_files/MendelsohnEnglish.pdf.

Powell, Martin. "The Hidden History of Social Citizenship." *Citizenship Studies*. 6, 3, 2002: 229–244.

Preston, Valerie, Myer Siemiatycki, and Audrey Kobayashi. In *Dual Citizenship in Global Perspective: From Unitary to Multiple Citizenship*, edited by T. Faist and P. Kivisto: 203–226. Houndmills: Palgrave Macmillan, 2007.

Revi, Ben. "T. H. Marshall and his critics: reappraising 'social citizenship' in the twenty-first century." *Citizenship Studies*. 18, 3–4, June 2014: 452–464.

Skulte-Ouaiss, Jennifer. "Home is where the heart is: citizenship is where it is safe: dual citizenship and Europe." *Identities: Global Studies in Culture and Power*. 20, 2, 2013: 133–148.

Stasiulis, Daiva. "Contending Frames of 'Security' and 'Citizenship': Lebanese Dual Nationals during the 2006 Lebanon War." In *Mobilities, Knowledge, and Social Justice*, edited by S. Ilcan: 25–58. Montreal: McGill-Queen's University Press, 2013.

Stasiulis, Daiva and Darryl Ross. "Security, Flexible Sovereignty, and the Perils of Multiple Citizenship." *Citizenship Studies*. 10, 3, 2006: 329–348.

CHAPTER 3

The Transnational Identities of Sri Lankan Migrants in Australia and Aotearoa New Zealand

Pavithra Jayawardena

Introduction

Sri Lanka became bankrupt in 2022.[1] The country is in its worst financial crisis in decades and has failed to make an interest payment on its foreign debt for the first time in its history. This has led its citizenry to struggle to buy food, medicine, and fuel. The causes and effects of the economic crisis are not solely economic, however. It displays a serious crisis of governance of the country, on multiple fronts simultaneously, including politically, socially, in terms of security, and ideologically.

I am extremely thankful to the editor of this collection, Jatinder Mann, for his detailed feedback and helpful suggestions on my chapter.

P. Jayawardena (✉)
Department of International Relations, University of Colombo,
Colombo, Sri Lanka
e-mail: pavithraj@inr.cmb.ac.lk

J. Mann (ed.), *Citizenship in Transnational Perspective*, Politics of Citizenship and Migration,
https://doi.org/10.1007/978-3-031-34358-2_3

One of the important avenues through which the country has been receiving money is via foreign remittances sent to the country by migrants who are working and living outside Sri Lanka. As a way to get more dollars in this desperate situation, during the early days of the crisis, the government encouraged Sri Lankan migrants to send foreign remittances to the country only through official channels (so as to make it easier for the government to show international creditors the flow of money that was entering the country). The campaign asking migrants not to use any unofficial channels received wide coverage among Sri Lankan migrants.[2] Consequently, there was a positive response from Sri Lankan migrants and many of them used official channels to send money, although financially it would have been more beneficial to use methods such as undiyal money transfer. Many migrants expressed that their decision to use official channels was a result of their special feeling and belonging to their "mother country." This transnational financial act by Sri Lankan migrants was a way of showing their solidarity with the country to save it from economic collapse.

But Sri Lankan migrants used the same transnational financial capability in a different fashion to pressurise the government during late 2022. When thousands of Sri Lankan citizens were protesting in the streets demanding the government and specifically the then-President Gotabaya Rajapaksa resign, arguing that the government's mismanagement worsened the crisis, Sri Lankan migrants too demanded that the government listen to its people. Standing in solidarity with thousands of Sri Lankans who were protesting in every corner of the island, a large number of Sri Lankan migrants joined them in spirit as well as by organising several protests in the overseas countries that they lived in. These took place in major cities in countries including Australia, Canada, Aotearoa New Zealand, the United States (USA), and France. With these protests, Sri Lankan migrants became very concerned and vocal about the Sri Lankan economic situation and the grave situation faced by their compatriots in Sri Lanka. For example, several Sri Lankan migrant organisations sent essential goods such as medicine to Sri Lanka since there was a serious shortage. While engaging in such kinds of activities, as stated above, migrants also used their transnational financial capability to send foreign remittances to Sri Lanka as a way to put pressure on the government. They began to insist that they would only send foreign remittances to the country if the government and relevant individuals listened to the demands of the people of Sri Lanka.

Why would Sri Lankan migrants, especially those who are permanently settled overseas, conduct such transnational acts? What do such acts tell us about Sri Lankan migrants' transnational identities? And about their multiple belongings? The literature on transnationalism provides us some useful explanations to understand the behaviour and lives of migrant communities. It shows us the complexities of migrants' lives and the fact that they do not live either *here* or *there*, but they live in between. It reminds us that migrants often do not just possess national but transnational identities—identities that transcend national borders.

Although the research field in transnationalism and specifically on migrants' transnational identities is very wide and rich, it is not sufficient to understand the particular case of Sri Lankan migrants. This is because a majority of studies of transnational identities are based on larger migrant communities,[3] not so much on relatively smaller migrant communities. Therefore, the tendency is that the transnational identities of smaller migrant communities are often understood through the prism of knowledge produced on larger migrant communities. This will only result in a homogenous understanding of migrants' transnational identities, without paying enough attention to the complex and subjective identities of smaller migrant communities.

Although Sri Lankan migrants are a community that has been studied more compared to other smaller migrant communities, the elements and focus of those studies have been very limited, as explained further in the next section. Thus, this chapter pays close attention to Sri Lankan migrants' transnational identities and the home and host country factors that shape those identities.

I intend to explore in depth the nature of Sri Lankan migrants' transnational identities and how they have been shaped. The findings are based on a case study of Sri Lankan migrants who are living on a permanent basis in Australia and Aotearoa New Zealand. This involved observations, 49 interviews with Sri Lankan migrants who lived in Melbourne, Sydney, Auckland, and Wellington conducted in 2018 and 2019, and a round of follow-up interviews in 2022 and 2023. I interviewed both Sinhalese and Sri Lankan Tamil migrants. Sinhalese participants are from the majority ethnic community in Sri Lanka and Sri Lankan Tamils[4] represent the largest minority ethnic group in the country. All the participants were first-generation migrants who had spent two or three decades of their adult lives in Sri Lanka before moving to their respective host countries.

Participants represented a wide array of Sri Lankan migrants, ranging from skilled, student, family reunion, and refugee categories.

In this chapter, I first present a brief overview of the history of Sri Lankan migration and then survey the existing literature on Sri Lankan migrants' transnational identities, before discussing the findings of my case study—specifically, the transnational identities of Sri Lankans in Australia and Aotearoa New Zealand and what factors have affected those identities. I explore them through three key themes: becoming a transnational citizen, transnational political identities, and transnational social lives.

Sri Lankan Migration: A Brief History

The Sri Lankan origin permanent immigrant community is estimated to be approximately one million.[5] This population is largely distributed across countries in Europe, North America, and Australasia. This one million figure excludes the Sri Lankan temporary migrant population. Together with the temporary migrants, who live and work primarily in Middle Eastern countries, South Korea, and Japan, it has been recorded that there were 1.25 million Sri Lankan-born persons living outside the country in 2013—equivalent to 5.9% of the Sri Lankan population.[6] In terms of the one million permanently settled migrants: 500,000 are in North America, 400,000 in Europe, and the rest in Australasia.

Although one million may sound like a small number in comparison to other South Asian migrant populations, the number forms a unique in-house population to migrant population ratio. As Sri Lanka's total population stands at 21 million, the in-house population to Sri Lankan permanent migrant population ratio is 21:1. When the economic crisis worsened in 2022, the desire of Sri Lankans to leave the country only increased. So, in a few years' time the 21:1 ratio is likely to be much higher. Although Sri Lanka has always been a migrant-producing country, there has not been much scholarship about Sri Lankan migrants.

To provide a greater understanding of the Sri Lankan migrant community Dinuk Jayasuriya and Marie McAuliffe[7] have categorised them into five groups: temporary workers (skilled, semi-skilled, and unskilled), skilled migrants, students, asylum seekers, and tourists (including pilgrims to Nepal and India). As I have argued elsewhere, there have been five main waves of Sri Lankan out-migration since independence in 1948.[8] The first wave took place soon after Sri Lanka became independent from the United Kingdom (UK) in 1948. Burgher Ceylonese people—Sri Lankans of

European descent—started leaving the country in large numbers due to their fear and insecurity about the prospect of living under a different regime than British colonialism, during the latter of which they had held a privileged position.[9]

The second wave occurred after 1956. The Sri Lankan government brought about a very controversial language policy for the country, popularly called the Sinhala Only Act. The act made the majority ethnic language—Sinhala—the only national language.[10] Those who could not perform their professional and daily activities in Sinhala became increasingly concerned about their future in the country. As a result, many started leaving Sri Lanka for countries such as the UK, Canada, Aotearoa New Zealand, and Australia.[11] These migrants included Sinhalese and Sri Lankan Tamils, especially those from Westernised, upper-class, and English educational backgrounds. The remaining Burghers too continued to leave the country.

The third wave took place in the early 1970s as a result of the government's new nationalisation reforms.[12] These resulted in several hardships and generated anxiety among people about the future of the country. Sri Lankans from several professions such as doctors, engineers, accountants, and scientists left the country for Western countries, with the hope of earning higher salaries and providing better educational opportunities for their children.[13] The main destinations for these professionals at the time were Australia, Canada, the UK, Switzerland, and Germany,[14] as well as Nigeria and Papua New Guinea.[15] Meanwhile, Sri Lankan Tamil migrants' decisions to leave were motivated not only by economic factors but also by security concerns. They were frustrated due to facing discrimination based on their ethnicity, at both societal and governmental levels.[16] As Dhananjayan Sriskandarajah[17] notes, a high number of Sri Lankan Tamil students also left the country in the 1970s for education, because as a result of the government quota, they found it difficult to enter universities. However, apart from home country factors, such migratory acts were also influenced by pull factors from host countries. For example, from the 1970s onwards, Australia, Canada, Aotearoa New Zealand, and the USA relaxed their immigration laws.[18]

The fourth wave took place in the 1980s and represents the highest peak of Sri Lankan migration so far. Due to the separatist war in the northern and eastern parts of Sri Lanka, and the riots and insurrection in the southern part, many Sri Lankans left the country as refugees and sought asylum overseas.[19] The conflict in the north and east was a result of ethnic tensions in the country, namely discrimination against Sri Lankan Tamils by the state. Sri Lankan Tamil identity, among both those in the country and overseas, became much more strident due to these ethnic tensions.[20] With the 1983 riots across Sri Lanka, thousands of Sri Lankan Tamils left the country either as refugees or on other humanitarian grounds, fearing to continue to live in the country as a minority community.[21] This trend of Sri Lankan Tamils departing the country continued with the civil war. Reports show that 73,000 Sri Lankan Tamil refugees were living in 112 camps in Tamil Nadu, India, followed by another 34,000 in other camps in India.[22] The United Nations High Commission for Refugees (UNHCR) ranked Sri Lanka as one of the top ten asylum seeker sending countries.[23]

The fifth wave took place in the early 2000s. Young Sri Lankans started emigrating mainly due to their frustrations about domestic social, economic, and political conditions.[24] With the increased number of agencies that facilitate studying and settling abroad, countries such as Australia, the UK, Canada, Aotearoa New Zealand, and the USA became popular destinations. A trend also emerged of sailing to Australia through irregular maritime channels after the 2000s.[25] According to reports in 2012 and 2013, the number of Sri Lankans arriving on Australian shores increased to 6000.[26] Another new development was Sri Lanka's labour migration to South Korea: 28,000 Sri Lankans left for South Korea between 2014 and 2019.[27] Due to these complicated patterns, Sri Lanka is now known as one of the most prominent emigration nations in the contemporary world.[28]

Sri Lankan Migrants in Australia and Aotearoa New Zealand

As pointed out earlier both Australia and Aotearoa New Zealand are popular destinations among Sri Lankans. In the Australian census of 2016, it was reported that there are 109,853 Sri Lankan-born people living in Australia.[29] According to the census, 60.3% of them are Australian citizens, while 38.3% are not. Of those 109,853 people, 55,830 (50.8%) live in the state of Victoria,[30] while 28,732 people (26.2%) live in New South Wales. The first recorded Sri Lankan immigrant to Australia arrived in 1882.[31] In the late nineteenth and twentieth centuries, some Sri Lankans were brought to work in the sugar plantations of Queensland and pearl fisheries in the Torres Strait.[32] The next significant wave of Sri Lankans arriving in Australia took place after 1948 and then in the 1970s.[33] They included migrants from the professional, refugee, student, and family reunion categories. As mentioned above irregular maritime migration also led to an influx of 6000 Sri Lankans arriving on Australian shores in 2012 and 2013. Hence, the Sri Lankan immigrant community in Australia is extremely diverse.

In contrast, Sri Lankan immigration to Aotearoa New Zealand is relatively recent.[34] Peter Reeves and Rajesh Rai assert that it began in the 1970s, with around 150 Sri Lankan migrants living in Aotearoa New Zealand at the time.[35] According to the New Zealand Ministry of Foreign Affairs and Trade,[36] approximately 16,000 Sri Lankans now live in the country. Auckland (the largest city in Aotearoa New Zealand by some margin) is the most popular destination among Sri Lankans in Aotearoa New Zealand, with 61.3% of the total Sri Lankan population living there. Wellington is the second most popular city, hosting 16.8% of Aotearoa New Zealand's Sri Lankan population.[37]

Sri Lankan Migrants' Transnational Identities

The literature specifically on Sri Lankan migrants' transnational identities is not very large, although several areas of Sri Lankan migration have been studied. The most popular subjects have been the Sri Lankan Tamil diaspora, labour migration to the Middle East, and Sri Lankan migrants' integration in host societies. The limited work on the transnational identities of Sri Lankan migrants is confined to the Sri Lankan Tamil diaspora as a transnational group, with a few exceptions. The main academic scholarship on this subject includes work on the Sri Lankan Tamil diaspora as a model of transnational identity by R. Cheran[38] and Giuseppe Burgio[39] and the role of the Sri Lankan Tamil diaspora in Sri Lanka's civil war by Camilla Orjuela.[40]

Sarah Wayland's[41] work on the Sri Lankan Tamil diaspora's transnational activities in particular makes a significant contribution to this study. Placing transnationalism in the field of International Relations (IR), Wayland reminds us that IR has narrowly defined transnationalism to mean the international activities of non-governmental actors. Such a narrow definition has allowed IR to combine transnationalism with economic relations, for example, the role of transnational corporations in international affairs. Emphasising the importance of expanding the idea of transnational entities in the field of IR, Wayland focuses on the role of ethnic networks and diasporas in connecting domestic and transnational politics, specifically using the case of the Sri Lankan Tamil diaspora.

In this regard, Wayland situates the Sri Lankan Tamil diaspora as an important transnational community which shapes domestic and international politics from below. Wayland studies the operationalisation of the transnational ethnic networks of the Sri Lankan Tamil diaspora in combining the greater political freedom, community organising, and access to communication, and financial resources to fund the prolonged secessionist campaign in Sri Lanka. Defining a diaspora as a type of transnational community that permanently live in one or more host countries with a collective identity or myth of a homeland, Wayland identifies the Tamil diaspora as a product of ethnonationalist conflicts and persecution in the homeland. According to her, the large level of resources the Liberation Tigers of Tamil Eelam (LTTE—the militant Sri Lankan Tamil separatist group fighting against the government for an independent homeland) received were the result of a transnational mobilisation of the Sri Lankan Tamil diaspora. She indicates:

> In the diaspora, it became possible to explore and express Tamil cultural, linguistic, and religious identity as never before. Associations were formed, both with an eye toward facilitating integration in the host country as well as toward maintaining ties with the homeland, namely through supporting the quest for Tamil independence. Migration from Sri Lanka has resulted in Tamil identity-building from abroad as well as material support for the creation of a separate Eelam.[42]

Wayland reminds us that the Sri Lankan Tamil diaspora is linked by a common identity rooted not only in the ethnic persecution experienced in Sri Lanka but also in the shared trauma of migration, including the guilt of having left family, friends, and their country behind. It also indicates that the host country conditions, such as how much they could integrate in the host country or whether they perceived any economic or social marginalisation, have shaped Sri Lankan Tamil migrants' transnational identities. Wayland also highlights how such identities were then used and abused by politically motivated ethnic elites. She claims that ethnic elites could capitalise on this shared identity by promoting migrant networks to support their co-ethnic insurgents in the home country. Transnational networks engaged in activities in three broader ways: information exchange within the Sri Lankan Tamil community, outreach to the broader state and society about the Sri Lankan Tamil struggle, and fundraising. She concludes by saying that "the war is being fought within Sri Lanka, but Tamil efforts are supported by transnational ethnic networks."[43]

Some other scholars have also studied various elements that affect the transnational identities of the Sri Lankan Tamil diaspora. For example, Morton Beiser et al.[44] have worked on Sri Lankan Tamil migrants' integration in Canadian society. Sri Lankan Tamil refugees' psycho-social experiences in Canada were investigated by William Affleck et al.,[45] while Nirukshi Perera[46] studied the intergenerational perspectives of belonging of Sri Lanka Tamil migrants in Australia. Meanwhile, Diotima Chattoraj[47] explains how Sri Lankan Tamil migrants who were displaced due to the civil war construct their sense of home and belonging.

While the Sri Lankan Tamil diaspora has received some attention as a transnational community and has been somewhat explored, the transnational identities of Sinhalese and other ethnic diasporas have been hardly studied. The exceptions are W. S. Weerasooria's[48] work on Sri Lankan migrants in Australia's link between their home and host countries. Siri Gamage[49] has examined the composition of the Sri Lankan migrant community and their adaptation experiences in Australia. Meanwhile, Menusha De Silva[50] focuses on older adults in Sri Lankan-Australian transnational families. Hence, Sinhalese Sri Lankan migrants in Australia are a community that has received much more scholarly attention than other Sinhalese Sri Lankan communities in other parts of the world. Exceptionally, there are some studies that have looked into Sri Lankan migrants' transnational lives, such as R. Henayaka-Lochbihler's and M. Lambusta's[51] work where they study Sri Lankan migrants in Italy.

Another important related work is Shemana Cassim.[52] In her PhD thesis, she explores Sri Lankan migrants' transnational identities. Focusing on eight households of Sri Lankan migrants living in Aotearoa New Zealand ethnographically, Cassim studies how these migrants navigate distance (geographical, social, and imagined) and establish a sense of transnational continuity between the host and home. She argues that Sri Lankan migrants' transnational identities are shaped by historical and current contexts—at home and in the host country. She also emphasises that migrants' everyday lives are always negotiations of public, domestic, and mediated spaces, providing transnational links between here (host) and there (home). Moreover, she highlights the centrality of food-related material practices in establishing a transnational sense of normality, familiarity, and stability in Sri Lankan migrants' everyday lives.

Jagath Pathirage's[53] work also provides important insights to understand Sri Lankan migrants' transnational characters. He specifically studies the transnational features of religious practices of Sri Lankan migrants in

Darwin, Australia. He argues that the religious practices of transnational communities are connected to both global change and the precarious state of the national borders which are altered by both migrants and nation states. Pathirage finds that due to migrants' dislocation from their usual environment and long-term migration, migrants' religious beliefs and practices tend to change. Migration results in the boundaries of ritual practices and the meaning of inclusion and exclusion being renegotiated and the boundaries of participation being relaxed. Studying the religious practices of Sinhalese Buddhist migrants' lives in Darwin, Australia, Pathirage suggests that migrants' transnational meanings of what is sacred and profound are blurred and reinterpreted.

Apart from this limited work, there is a significant gap in the literature that needs attention to understand the complexities of Sri Lankan migrants' transnational identities. We do not understand adequately the factors that shape Sri Lankan migrants' transnational activities, their behaviours, and decision-making. We are also unaware of the effects that those identities have towards home and host societies. Although this is yet to be ascertained, I argue that those identities continue to have important implications on individual, community, and state levels.

Becoming a Transnational Citizen

The data of my study shows that participants' transnational identities are shaped by their imagination of who s/he is as a citizen, relative to home and host societies. As I have argued elsewhere, the ways through which migrants view citizenship (or becoming a citizen) are complex and different from native citizens.[54] While native citizens' thoughts about citizenship are often shaped by a singular relationship with their state, migrants, due to their migratory background, experience multiple affiliations, relations, and experiences with two or more countries simultaneously. Migrants are not able to view their home country citizenship exclusively from their host country citizenship and vice versa.

As I explain further, Sri Lankan migrants' acquisition of host citizenship was due to the situation in their home country. Once they acquired the host citizenship, it shaped their identity as *Sri Lankan-born Australian or New Zealand citizens*. Reviewing why they wanted to become host citizens, it was interesting to observe that there were significant differences between Sinhalese and Sri Lankan Tamil migrants. For Sinhalese, it was due to the fact that they are from a majority ethnic group. For Sri Lankan Tamils, it was related to their experiences of discrimination as a minority ethnic group.

In regard to Sinhalese participants, the main reason they wanted to become an Australian or New Zealand citizen was because they thought that they and their children would be able to enjoy better socio-economic conditions which are very poor in Sri Lanka. These socio-economic conditions included education for their children, other welfare facilities, a good standard of living, and a better income. They thought that obtaining the citizenship of their host country would enable them to enjoy the relevant rights and privileges. This means as *Sri Lankan-born Australian or New Zealand citizens,* they view themselves as people who are more privileged in comparison to their compatriots in Sri Lanka. This superior position that they considered themselves in also made them feel compelled to repay their home country in some way. Many participants commented that since they were now in a privileged situation as Australian or New Zealand citizens, they wanted to do something for their fellow Sri Lankan citizens, using that privilege. Therefore, participants' host country citizenship became a central reference point in redefining their identity as a Sri Lankan-born person, relocating them in a different position in their home society.

Sharing his views about the recent popular uprising in Sri Lanka, Rasika (44) said, "As a Sri Lankan, although I am an Australian citizen right now and I almost have no immediate family ties with Sri Lanka, I always feel I should do something for the Sri Lankans who are suffering at home." Rasika is a Sri Lankan-born Sinhalese Buddhist male Australian citizen, who lives in Melbourne with his family. He arrived in Australia in 2013 and works in a private company. Due to his feelings for Sri Lanka he has been very active in sending goods to Sri Lanka for those in need. He also joined two protests organised by some Sri Lankan community organisations in May and June 2022, during the *Aragalaya* period. (*Aragalaya* is the word that was widely used to describe the daily gathering of people protesting against the Sri Lankan president and the government during the period from April to August 2022. It was seen as a symbol of unity, creativity, and political enlightenment.) He said he felt proud about being a Sri Lankan and saw his people as brave, fighting against unjust rule and corruption.

Paying attention to himself as a host citizen, while appreciating the host citizenship for enabling him to feel privileged compared to an ordinary Sri Lankan citizen, interestingly however, Rasika did not show much interest in performing his duties as an active Australian citizen. He added that his duties as an Australian citizen are to pay taxes and live lawfully, but he did not think that voting or engaging in Australian politics as a citizen should be his priority. This view was shared by other Sinhalese participants too. In other words, although these participants' transnational identities as Sri Lankan migrants had significantly been affected by their host country citizenship, nonetheless, they performed that identity towards their home country in a much more active way.

Sri Lankan Tamil migrants' behaviour also had similarities with Sinhalese migrants, especially in their thoughts about their duty to help and assist fellow Sri Lankan Tamils. Nonetheless, Sri Lankan Tamil migrants also showed significant differences in their transnational identities and their performativity. Firstly, in comparison to Sinhalese, Sri Lankan Tamil migrants' expectations for becoming Australian or New Zealand citizens were different. Referring to their ethnic-based experiences at home, several Tamil migrants left Sri Lanka due to security and political reasons. Consequently, in becoming an Australian or New Zealand citizen, many of them viewed their host country citizenship as a symbol of safety and security (Stasiulis makes a similar point about dual Lebanese–Australian and Lebanese–Canadian citizens in her chapter in this collection as well). Therefore, differently from Sinhalese, Sri Lankan Tamil migrants felt more grateful to their host country.

Similarly to Sinhalese participants, once they become host country citizens, Sri Lankan Tamil participants too felt that they were in a superior position to their compatriots in Sri Lanka. With the ethnicised community experiences, participants' thoughts about the suffering of fellow Tamils living in Sri Lanka were central to not only their knowledge on common socio-economic poor conditions, but the discriminatory experiences that participants reflected on that they went through themselves on a daily basis when they were back in Sri Lanka also had an impact. Sri Lankan Tamil participants' memories about how things were in Sri Lanka had been frozen in time at the point they left the country. Thus, their views on how they should help Tamils in Sri Lanka as a Sri Lankan-born Tamil Australian or New Zealand citizen is based on that period. For example, Shiva (70), a Sri Lankan Tamil Hindu male Australian citizen, felt that it was his responsibility to help his fellow Sri Lankan Tamils. Although he had no immediate family or friends living in Sri Lanka anymore, he thought he should contribute to his community. As a result, he sent monetary donations on a monthly basis for a Hindu Temple in his village. He thought that the religious leaders of the temple would use his donation for community work.

Contrary to Sinhalese participants, Sri Lankan Tamil participants showed a higher engagement in their host country as host country citizens. As I have argued elsewhere, one reason for this difference is because Sri Lankan Tamil participants developed feelings of belonging and loyalty towards their host country faster than Sinhalese.[55] This is because Sri Lankan Tamil participants had a stronger feeling of detachment from their home country of Sri Lanka than Sinhalese, given their ethnic experiences, fear, and frustration, and as a result they tended to feel much more grateful to their host country faster. This also made their integration easier and swifter than Sinhalese. As a result, Sri Lankan Tamil participants' engagement in their host country, in terms of voting, being interested in political affairs, connecting with political groups, and so on, was higher than Sinhalese. This means, in contrast to Sinhalese, Sri Lankan Tamil participants' transnational identity as a Sri Lankan-born Tamil in Australia or Aotearoa New Zealand was displayed not only in their home country communities but also visibly in their host country.

Transnational Political Identities

My study is particularly focused on first-generation migrants who have spent the first two to three decades of their lives in their home country of Sri Lanka. The amount of time my participants had been in their host country ranged from 2 to 50 years. My findings show that the way in which they comprehend and engage in politics in both their home and host countries is transnational. Their home country political identities affected their host country interventions and vice versa. However, comparing the transnational political identities of Sinhalese and Sri Lankan Tamils shows some interesting differences. Sinhalese participants who represent the majority ethnic group in Sri Lanka displayed strong political affinities with their home country. Consequently, they showed a much greater interest to have an active involvement in political affairs in Sri Lanka. Many participants revealed that they were more aware of what was happening in their home country politically than what was actually taking place in their host country. This means, although physically they are living in Australia or Aotearoa New Zealand, psychologically they are political members of their home country in which they are no longer residents.

Describing how and why they are actively involved in Sri Lankan political affairs, Anusha (45) said, "Because [migrants] are the people who have been exposed to the governing systems of other countries [than those who are living in Sri Lanka], so we are in a better position to suggest Sri Lanka better policies and practices it wants." Hence, Anusha positioned herself in a superior position as a political member of Sri Lanka in comparison to her compatriots in the home country. Anusha is a Sinhalese Buddhist female who arrived in Aotearoa New Zealand in 2018 and is currently a Sri Lankan dual citizen. She believed that her political exposure in Aotearoa New Zealand had improved her knowledge to view Sri Lankan political society from a unique perspective.

Priyantha (57) who arrived in Sydney, Australia, in 1989 stated, "[However] when we suggest new ideas for Sri Lankan political issues and raise concerns through social media like Facebook, we are criticised by those who live in Sri Lanka. They say, you have no right to make comments or suggestions about Sri Lanka without living in there. They do not consider us as full Sri Lankans." Priyantha is a Sinhalese Buddhist male holding both Australian and Sri Lankan citizenship. When he was in Sri Lanka, he was a journalist and now he is an Australian government worker. According to him, the reason for acquiring Sri Lankan dual citizenship was as a symbol of becoming a full legal member of the Sri Lankan political community. This is because he thought Sri Lankans who are living in Sri Lanka cannot disregard his thoughts on the basis that he is not a bona fide Sri Lankan citizen. He added that he publicly announced acquiring Sri Lankan dual citizenship so that he can claim to be a legitimate member of the Sri Lankan political community. As I have argued elsewhere, this is a common response migrants face when they comment on Sri Lankan political affairs from another country.[56] Sri Lankans who live in the country hold serious doubts about the loyalty of their migrants and consequently consider themselves as the sole legitimate political community of the country.[57]

Reviewing how participants' transnational political identities affected host country politics, Sri Lankan Tamil participants' experiences were interesting. While Sinhalese migrants had a more active engagement towards home politics as explained earlier, Sri Lankan Tamil participants were more interested in becoming involved in host country political issues. While, at times, this involvement was directly related to their host country political concerns, in certain cases, it was actually aimed at getting their host country directly or indirectly involved in their home country politics.

Shiva (70), a Sri Lankan Tamil Hindu male, arrived in Aotearoa New Zealand in 1993 as a skilled migrant. Although his visa status was under the skilled category, he left Sri Lanka with his family due to the ethnic tensions in the country. Recalling some of the political issues that he became involved in his host country during the civil war period in Sri Lanka, Shiva said that he and some of his friends felt that they should lobby the Aotearoa New Zealand government to speak up for the Tamil people in Sri Lanka through diplomatic channels. Therefore, through a Sri Lankan Tamil diaspora group, they lobbied the Aotearoa New Zealand government to raise concerns at important international platforms, including the United Nations.

Eva Østergaard-Nielsen's[58] one type of transnational political practices, what she calls "diaspora politics," is useful here to understand Sri Lankan Tamil migrants' behaviours. Nielsen says that when a migrant community is barred from direct participation in home country politics or does not even have a homeland political regime, they tend to engage in politics in their host country in a way that they can have some impact at home. My Sri Lankan Tamil participants expressed their distrust about engaging politically with the government of Sri Lanka due to their ethnicised experiences of discriminatory behaviour and policies of the government. In contrast, they shared a higher level of trust towards their host country government. Therefore, Sri Lankan Tamil migrants' transnational political identities are shaped by their different relations and experiences about their home and host countries. This shows that two contrasting ethnic experiences in their home country of Sri Lanka for Sinhalese and Sri Lankan Tamils have affected their transnational political identities and behaviour in different ways.

Transnational Social Lives

My study shows that Sri Lankan migrants' transnational identities are shaped heavily by their social lives and practices. As in any other migrant community, Sri Lankan migrants too live in transnational social spaces—(re)negotiating the meanings of everything through home and host country experiences simultaneously. Participants repeatedly mentioned how their transnational social lives have been shaped—culturally, religiously, and through art and entertainment, among many other factors.

Culture

The Sri Lankan communities in all the four cities where I carried out my research—Melbourne, Sydney, Auckland, and Wellington—are very much interested in organising various kinds of cultural events to reproduce Sri Lankan memories, practices, and identities. For example, each year in April, there are Sri Lankan New Year celebration events organised in all these cities on various scales. On these occasions, Sri Lankan migrants often attempt to observe all the rituals and practices of their home country without exception. They manage to find the appropriate facilities, equipment, and cultural dress to ensure that the final event is authentic as New Year celebrations in Sri Lanka. Nilmini (55), a Sinhalese Buddhist female, noted that during her annual visit to Sri Lanka, "we buy clothes to the New Year celebration in here [Wellington] in the following year." Sri Lankans usually wear cultural dress for this event. She said, "It's kind of weird because we buy New Year dresses from Sri Lanka during the times that is nowhere closer to the actual event. We usually visit Sri Lanka every December."

This observing of Sri Lankan cultural practices is also aimed at gaining a special cultural identity for them in their host country. Although my participants, both Sinhalese and Sri Lankan Tamils, were very open about how the observation of their home country cultural practices in their host country shaped their cultural identities as migrants, the data did not specifically show whether it also happens in reverse. The exception though was the importance Nilmini placed on her son wearing a green stone pendant when he visits Sri Lanka (green stone pendants are recognised as the unofficial symbol of Aotearoa New Zealand and are worn as a symbol of national pride). Comparing herself with her son, Nilmini (55) noted:

> Although I have very clear feelings about Sri Lankan culture and New Zealand culture and can distinguish between them very clearly, [my son cannot do it]. My son was born and raised here in New Zealand. Although we speak in Sinhala at home and frequently attend the Sri Lankan cultural events taking place here, I know that my son could never view himself as a Sri Lankan. For me, it's not complicated like that. I am a Sri Lankan. No matter how long I live here, I know that I am a Sri Lankan and I can never be a New Zealander.

Nilmini's experience gives us a glimpse of the way that transnational cultural identities are constructed and potentially vary among first- and second-generation migrants. Further research is needed to confirm this assertion.

Religion

Sri Lankan migrants in Australia and Aotearoa New Zealand also showed a greater interest to continue celebrating several religious celebrations. For example, those who are Buddhist followers find various ways to continue their practices and rituals. All the cities where I conducted my interviews had Buddhist temples, on different scales. Some temples did not have the advanced infrastructure of a traditional temple in Sri Lanka. Adapting to the new conditions of their host country, migrants have helped monks to find alternative ways to construct temples. For example, in Sri Lanka, a Buddhist temple will often be built in a spacious location. But in a country like Aotearoa New Zealand, it is not easy to find or afford to buy such a spacious location to build a temple. Hence, they explore alternative options that they might not even think of in Sri Lanka, that is, renting a house. Not only Sinhalese but Sri Lankan Tamil migrants also are very concerned with continuing their religious rituals. For example, Shiva said how important it is for him and his wife to continue their Hindu pujas (worship) and other rituals. All of my participants who had children told me how much it mattered to them to send their children to religious schools in their host country, to continue Sri Lankan religious practices.

Arts and Entertainment

Arts and entertainment are also important factors that shape Sri Lankan migrants' transnational identity, especially in their host countries. Sinhalese participants highlighted how much they are engaged in Sri Lankan entertainment events in their host societies. Shehan (46) said, "I am glad that I chose my destination as Melbourne. I still feel like I am living in Sri Lanka. Every weekend there are concerts, dramas, Sri Lankan artists' tours. It is pretty cool." Shehan is a Sinhalese Buddhist male who arrived in Australia in 2007 as a student. He is currently a manager and owns his own cleaning service business. Shehan was of the opinion that there is no distance between Colombo and Melbourne. He said, "For example, we now even get film premiers of brand new Sri Lankan films showing here even before in Colombo." He also added, "Look at the popular Sri Lankan TV channel in Melbourne, it got senior professional hosts from Sri Lanka working here. I certainly do not feel like I am not in Sri Lanka."

Apart from these kinds of events, in all the cities where I conducted interviews, there are Sri Lankan dancing classes, music classes, and Sinhalese and Tamil language classes. Some of these classes are conducted by extremely experienced Sri Lankan teachers—experts in those areas. Some of them had already moved to the host cities with their families and then they started the classes. However, others moved to their respective host country because they were invited and sponsored by the Sri Lankan community in those countries. This shows how much Sri Lankan migrants in Australia and Aotearoa New Zealand are willing to invest to maintain their Sri Lankan identity. All the participants who were parents again showed their keen interest to have their children enrolled in these classes—to give them an opportunity to explore their Sri Lankan heritage in their opinion.

Pathum (45), a Sinhalese Christian male from Auckland, summarised this perspective with his own experience. He said, "I can't understand the logic of my own decision-making. Soon after we arrived here, I put my daughter into a Sri Lankan dancing class to learn traditional Sri Lankan dancing. But when we were in Sri Lanka, I never thought to put her to a Sri Lankan dancing class, but for ballet. When we came here, for some reason I don't want to put her to Ballet—unless she tells she wants it, but very keenly I thought my daughter should learn Sri Lankan dance." Pathum's dilemma in understanding his preferences about what kind of dancing style his daughter should learn illustrates the complexity and relativity of his transnational decision-making.

Neither *Here* nor *There*, but in Between

Sri Lankan migrants similar to other international migrants have always had good reasons to leave home. Generally, for Sinhalese it has been mainly for socio-economic reasons, while for Sri Lankan Tamils it has been for political and security reasons. Nonetheless, soon after reaching their host country, they tend to reconnect and re-engage in home country affairs in multiple ways. Sri Lankan migrants operate in transnational social spaces, (re)negotiating their home–host experiences, memories, and relations simultaneously.

This chapter therefore provides useful insight into understanding Sri Lankan migrants' transnational identities, as well as the factors that shape them. Participants' views about their transnational identities reflect three key themes as outlined earlier: becoming a transnational citizen, a political member, and leading a transnational social life. In the case of the Sri Lankan migrant community, their transnational identities have been further affected by their different ethnic experiences in Sri Lanka. Sinhalese and Sri Lankan Tamil migrants constitute their identity based on their different ethnic experiences in their home country of Sri Lanka as a majority or minority ethnic group respectively. Consequently, there are practical implications. For example, while Sinhalese participants showed more interest to be actively engaged in home country politics, Sri Lankan Tamil participants were more interested in engaging in host country politics. Undoubtedly, their different home country experiences have become decisive factors along their migratory journeys, forcing them to (re)negotiate their identities and positionalities as *Sri Lankan-born Australians or New Zealanders.*

Notes

1. Iqbal Athas, Chris Liakos, Rhea Mogul, and Daniela Gonzalez-Roman, "Sri Lanka is 'Bankrupt,' Prime Minister says," CNN, 6 July 2022. Available: https://edition.cnn.com/2022/07/05/asia/sri-lanka-bankrupt-fuel-crisis-intl-hnk/index.html.
2. "Bankrupt Sri Lanka Asks Citizens Abroad to Send Home Cash," France 24,2022.Available:https://www.france24.com/en/live-news/20220413-bankrupt-sri-lanka-asks-citizens-abroad-to-send-home-cash.
3. S. L. Sharma, "Perspectives on Indians Abroad," in *The Indian Diaspora: Dynamics of Migration*, ed. N. Jayaram (New Delhi: Sage, 2004), 44–65.
4. I refer to "Sri Lankan Tamils" in my chapter instead of "Tamils" so as to differentiate between Tamils in India. However, I refer to Sinhalese instead of Sri Lankan Sinhalese as this ethnic group is not found in large numbers outside of Sri Lanka in the South Asian region.
5. Pavithra Jayawardena, *Immigrants' Citizenship Perceptions: Sri Lankans in Australia and Aotearoa New Zealand* (New York: Peter Lang Publishing, 2023).
6. Graeme Hugo and Lakshman Dissanayake, "The Process of Sri Lankan Migration to Australia Focusing on Irregular Migrants Seeking Asylum," in *A Long Way to Go: Irregular Migration Patterns, Processes, Drivers and Decision-Making*, eds. Marie McAuliffe and Khalid Koser (Canberra: ANU Press, 2017), 197–226.
7. Dinuk Jayasuriya and Marie McAuliffe, "Placing Recent Sri Lankan Maritime Arrivals in a Broader Migration Context," *Irregular Migration Research Program Occasional Paper Series*, 2013.
8. Pavithra Jayawardena, "Sri Lankan Out-Migration: Five Key Waves since Independence," *University of Colombo Review (Series III)* 1, 1 (2020): 101–18.

9. Siri Gamage, "Curtains of Culture, Ethnicity and Class: The Changing Composition of the Sri Lankan Community in Australia," *Journal of Intercultural Studies* 19, 1 (1998): 37–56; Siri Gamage, "Adaptation Experiences of Sri Lankan Immigrants and Their Children in Australia in the Context of Multiculturalism and Anglo-Conformity," in *Exploring Cultural Perspectives: Integration and Globalization*, eds. A. Richardson, M. Wyness, and E. A. Halvorsen (Edmonton: International Cultural Research Network Press, 2002), 3–29; Sisira Kumara Pinnawala, "Sri Lankans in Melbourne: Factors Influencing Patterns of Ethnicity," PhD Thesis, Canberra, Australian National University, 1984.
10. Gamage, "Curtains of Culture, Ethnicity and Class"; Sarah Wayland, "Ethnonationalist Networks and Transnational Opportunities: The Sri Lankan Tamil Diaspora," *Review of International Studies* 30, 3 (2004): 405–26.
11. Jayawardena, "Sri Lankan Out-Migration."
12. Prema-chandra Athukorala and Sisira Jayasuriya, "Trade Policy Reforms and Industrial Adjustment in Sri Lanka," *The World Economy* 10, 2 (2000): 387–404.
13. Malsiri Dias and Ramani Jayasundere, "Sri Lanka: The Anxieties and Opportunities of out-Migration," in *Migrant Workers and Human Rights: Out-Migration from South Asia*, ed. Pong-Sul Ahn (International Labour Organization, 2004), 153–92; Gamage, "Curtains of Culture, Ethnicity and Class"; K. Ratnayake, "Female Migration from Sri Lanka to the Middle East: Is Remedy Worse than the Disease?," *Sri Lanka Journal of Population Studies* 2 (1999): 43–56; Swarna Ukwatta, "Sri Lanka, Migration 1960s to Present," in *The Encyclopedia of Global Human Migration*, ed. Swarna Ukwatta (Wiley, 2013).
14. R. Henayaka-Lochbihler and M. Lambusta, *The Sri Lankan Diaspora in Italy: An Explorative Mapping* (Berlin: Berghof Foundation, 2004).
15. Dhananjayan Sriskandarajah, "The Migration-Development Nexus: Sri Lanka Case Study," *International Migration* 40, 5 (2002): 283–307.
16. Ibid.
17. Ibid.
18. Brian Galligan and Winsome Roberts, "Australian Multiculturalism: Its Rise and Demise," in *Australasian Political Studies Association Conference Proceedings* (Hobart: University of Tasmania, 2003); Elsa Koleth, *Multiculturalism: A Review of Australian Policy Statements and Recent Debates in Australia and Overseas* (Canberra: Department of Parliamentary Services, 2010); Will Kymlicka, "Immigration, Citizenship, Multiculturalism: Exploring the Links," *The Political Quarterly* 74 (2003): 195–208; Mervin Singham, "Multiculturalism in New Zealand – the Need for a New Paradigm," *Aotearoa Ethnic Network Journal* 1, 1 (2006):

33–37; Jerzy Zubrzycki, "The Evolution of the Policy of Multiculturalism in Australia 1968–1995," in *Global Cultural Diversity Conference Proceedings* (1995).

19. Chesmal Siriwardhana and Kolitha Wickramage, "Conflict, Forced Displacement and Health in Sri Lanka: A Review of the Research Landscape," *Conflict and Health* 8, 22 (2014): 1–9; Sriskandarajah, "The Migration-Development Nexus."
20. Lavanya Sankaran, "'Homeland' & 'Hostland' Identifications in the Sri Lankan Tamil Diaspora," Working Papers in Urban Language and Literacies, 2019; Wayland, "Ethnonationalist Networks and Transnational Opportunities."
21. Sriskandarajah, "The Migration-Development Nexus."
22. Jennifer Pagonis, "Coming Home: Sri Lankan Refugee Return," 2010. Available: http://www.unhcr.org/4c657ec69.html.
23. Sriskandarajah, "The Migration-Development Nexus."
24. A. Pingama, "Reasons for Youth Migration in Sri Lanka with Emphasis on Regular and Irregular Youth Migrants," *2nd International Conference on the Humanities* (University of Kelaniya, Sri Lanka, 2016).
25. Hugo and Dissanayake, "The Process of Sri Lankan Migration to Australia Focusing on Irregular Migrants Seeking Asylum."
26. Emily Howie, "Sri Lankan Boat Migration to Australia: Motivations and Dilemmas," *Economic and Political Weekly* 48, 35 (2013): 97–104; Hugo and Dissanayake, "The Process of Sri Lankan Migration to Australia Focusing on Irregular Migrants Seeking Asylum."
27. Janaka Wijayasiri, "Helping Sri Lankan Workers in South Korea to Save Better," *Daily Mirror*, 26 November 2019. Available: http://www.dailymirror.lk/features/Helping-Sri-Lankan-workers-in-South-Korea-to-save-better/185-178488.
28. Hugo and Dissanayake, "The Process of Sri Lankan Migration to Australia Focusing on Irregular Migrants Seeking Asylum."
29. Australian Bureau of Statistics, "2016 Census Quickstats Country of Birth," Census 2016. Available: https://quickstats.censusdata.abs.gov.au/census_services/getproduct/census/2016/quickstat/7107_036.
30. Victoria State Government, "Sri Lanka-Born: Victorian Community Profiles: 2016 Census," 2018. Available: https://multicultural.vic.gov.au/images/2016_Census/CommunityProfiles2016/Sri-Lanka-Community-Profile-2016-Census.pdf
31. W. S. Weerasooria, *Links between Sri Lanka and Australia: A Book about Sri Lankans (Ceylonese) in Australia* (Colombo: Government Printer, 1988).
32. Ibid.
33. Jayawardena, "Sri Lankan Out-Migration"; Nirukshi Perera, "The Maintenance of Sri Lankan Languages in Australia – Comparing the

Experience of the Sinhalese and Tamils in the Homeland," *Journal of Multilingual and Multicultural Development* 36, 3 (2015): 297–312.
34. Peter Reeves and Rajesh Rai, eds. *The Encyclopedia of the Sri Lankan Diaspora* (Singapore: Editions Didier Millet, 2013).
35. Ibid.
36. New Zealand Foreign Affairs and Trade, "Consulate Services for New Zealanders," 2019. Available: https://www.mfat.govt.nz/en/countries-and-regions/united-nations/new-zealand-permanent-mission-geneva/consulate-services-for-new-zealanders/.
37. Statistics New Zealand, "2013 Census Quickstats about Culture and Identity," *2013 Census*, 2013. Available: http://archive.stats.govt.nz/Census/2013-census/profile-and-summary-reports/quickstats-culture-identity/birthplace.aspx?url=/Census/2013-census/profile-and-summary-reports/quickstats-culture-identity/birthplace.aspx.
38. R. Cheran, *Diaspora Circulation and Transnationalism as Agents for Change in the Post-Conflict Zones of Sri Lanka* (Berlin: Berghof Foundation, 2004).
39. Giuseppe Burgio, "When Interculturality Faces a Diaspora. The Transnational Tamil Identity," *Encyclopaideia* 44 (2016): 106–28.
40. Camilla Orjuela, "Distant Warriors, Distant Peace Workers?: Multiple Diaspora Roles in Sri Lanka's Violent Conflict," *Global Networks* 8, 4 (2008): 436–52.
41. Wayland, "Ethnonationalist Networks and Transnational Opportunities."
42. Ibid., 418.
43. Ibid., 424.
44. Morton Beiser, Alasdair M. Goodwill, Patrizia Albanese, and Kelly Mcshane, "Predictors of the Integration of Sri Lankan Tamil Refugees in Canada: Pre-Migration Adversity, Mental Health, Personal Attributes and Post-Migration Experience," *International Journal of Migration, Health and Social Care* 11, 1 (2015): 29–44.
45. William Affleck, Umaharan Thamotharampillai, Judy Jeyakumar, and Rob Whitley, "'If One Does Not Fulfil His Duties, He Must Not Be a Man': Masculinity, Mental Health and Resilience Amongst Sri Lankan Tamil Refugee Men in Canada," *Culture, Medicine, and Psychiatry* 42, 4 (2018): 840–61.
46. Nirukshi Perera, *A Sense of Viidu: The (Re)creation of Home by the Sri Lankan Tamil Diaspora in Australia* (Singapore: Palgrave Macmillan, 2020).
47. Diotima Chattoraj, *Displacement Among Sri Lankan Tamil Migrants: The Diasporic Search for Home in the Aftermath of War* (Cham: Springer, 2021).
48. Weerasooria, *Links between Sri Lanka and Australia*.
49. Gamage, "Curtains of Culture, Ethnicity and Class"; Gamage, "Adaptation Experiences of Sri Lankan Immigrants and Their Children in Australia in the Context of Multiculturalism and Anglo-Conformity."

50. Menusha De Silva, "The Care Pentagon: Older Adults within Sri Lankan - Australian Transnational Families and Their Landscapes of Care," *Population, Space and Place* 23, 8 (2017): e2061.
51. Henayaka-Lochbihler and Lambusta, *The Sri Lankan Diaspora in Italy.*
52. Shemana Cassim, "Oceans Away: Sri Lankan Migrants in New Zealand," PhD Thesis, Hamilton, University of Waikato, 2017.
53. Jagath Pathirage, "Liberalizing the Boundaries: Reconfiguration of Religious Beliefs and Practice amongst Sri Lankan Immigrants in Australia," in *Asian Migrants and Religious Experience from Missionary Journey to Labour Mobility*, eds. B. E Brown and Yeoh Brenda (Amsterdam: Amsterdam University Press, 2018), 101–26.
54. I use the term "native citizens" to refer to those who have become citizens by virtue of their birth, whose families have lived in a particular society for generations and/or who claim that they are the "owners" of a country—acknowledging the prejudices of the term. Jayawardena, *Immigrants' Citizenship Perceptions.*
55. Ibid.
56. Jayawardena, "Sri Lankan Out-Migration."
57. Ibid.
58. Eva Østergaard-Nielsen, "The Politics of Migrants' Transnational Political Practices," *International Migration Review* 37, 3 (2003): 760–786.

Bibliography

Affleck, William, Umaharan Thamotharampillai, Judy Jeyakumar, and Rob Whitley. "'If one does not fulfil his duties, he must not be a man': Masculinity, mental health and resilience amongst Sri Lankan Tamil refugee men in Canada." *Culture, Medicine, and Psychiatry.* 42, 4, 2018: 840–61. https://doi.org/10.1007/s11013-018-9592-9.

Athukorala, Prema-chandra and Sisira Jayasuriya. "Trade policy reforms and industrial adjustment in Sri Lanka." *The World Economy.* 10, 2, 2000: 387–404. https://doi.org/10.1111/1467-9701.00278.

Beiser, Morton, Alasdair M. Goodwill, Patrizia Albanese, and Kelly Mcshane. "Predictors of the integration of Sri Lankan Tamil refugees in Canada: Pre-migration adversity, mental health, personal attributes and post-migration experience." *International Journal of Migration, Health and Social Care.* 11, 1, 2015: 29–44. https://doi.org/10.1108/IJMHSC-02-2014-0008.

Burgio, Giuseppe. "When Interculturality faces a diaspora. The transnational Tamil identity." *Encyclopaideia.* 44, 2016: 106–28. https://doi.org/10.6092/issn.1825-8670/5992.

Cassim, Shemana. "Oceans away: Sri Lankan migrants in New Zealand." PhD Thesis. Hamilton: The University of Waikato, 2017.

Chattoraj, Diotima. *Displacement among Sri Lankan Tamil migrants: The diasporic search for home in the aftermath of war*. Cham: Springer, 2021.

Cheran, R. *Diaspora circulation and transnationalism as agents for change in the post-conflict zones of Sri Lanka*. Berlin: Berghof Foundation for Conflict Management, 2004.

Dias, Malsiri and Ramani Jayasundere. "Sri Lanka: The anxieties and opportunities of out-migration." In *Migrant workers and human rights: Out-migration from South Asia*, edited by Pong-Sul Ahn: 153–92. International Labour Organization, 2004.

Galligan, Brian and Winsome Roberts. "Australian multiculturalism: Its rise and demise." In *Australasian political studies association conference proceedings*. Hobart: University of Tasmania, 2003.

Gamage, Siri. "Curtains of culture, ethnicity and class: The changing composition of the Sri Lankan Community in Australia." *Journal of Intercultural Studies* 19, 1, 1998: 37–56. https://doi.org/10.1080/07256868.1998.9963454.

Gamage, Siri. "Adaptation experiences of Sri Lankan immigrants and their children in Australia in the context of multiculturalism and Anglo-conformity." In *Exploring cultural perspectives: Integration and globalization*, edited by A. Richardson, M. Wyness, and E. A. Halvorsen: 3–29. Edmonton: International Cultural Research Network Press, 2002.

Henayaka-Lochbihler, R. and M. Lambusta. *The Sri Lankan diaspora in Italy: An explorative mapping*. Berlin: Berghof Foundation, 2004.

Howie, Emily. "Sri Lankan boat migration to Australia: Motivations and dilemmas." *Economic and Political Weekly*. 48, 35, 2013: 97–104.

Hugo, Graeme and Lakshman Dissanayake. "The process of Sri Lankan migration to Australia focusing on irregular migrants seeking asylum." In *A long way to go: Irregular migration patterns, processes, drivers and decision-making*, edited by Marie McAuliffe and Khalid Koser: 197–226. Canberra: ANU Press, 2017.

Jayawardena, Pavithra. "Sri Lankan out-migration: Five key waves since Independence." *University of Colombo Review (Series III)*. 1, 1, 2020: 101–18.

Jayawardena, Pavithra. *Immigrants' citizenship perceptions: Sri Lankans in Australia and Aotearoa New Zealand*. New York: Peter Lang Publishing, 2023.

Kymlicka, Will. "Immigration, citizenship, multiculturalism: Exploring the links." *The Political Quarterly*. 74, 2003: 195–208.

Orjuela, Camilla. "Distant warriors, distant peace workers?: Multiple diaspora roles in Sri Lanka's violent conflict." *Global Networks*. 8, 4, 2008: 436–52. https://doi.org/10.1111/j.1471-0374.2008.00233.x.

Østergaard-Nielsen, Eva. "The politics of migrants' transnational political practices." *International Migration Review*. 37, 3, 2003: 760–86.

Pathirage, Jagath. "Liberalizing the boundaries: Reconfiguration of religious beliefs and practice amongst Sri Lankan immigrants in Australia." In *Asian migrants and religious experience from missionary journey to labour mobility*, edited by B. E Brown and Yeoh Brenda: 101–26. Amsterdam: Amsterdam University Press, 2018.

Perera, Nirukshi. "The maintenance of Sri Lankan languages in Australia – Comparing the experience of the Sinhalese and Tamils in the homeland." *Journal of Multilingual and Multicultural Development.* 36, 3, 2015: 297–312. https://doi.org/10.1080/01434632.2014.921185.

Perera, Nirukshi. *A sense of Viidu: The (re)creation of home by the Sri Lankan Tamil diaspora in Australia.* Singapore: Palgrave Macmillan, 2020.

Pingama, A. "Reasons for youth migration in Sri Lanka with emphasis on regular and irregular youth migrants." In *2nd international conference on the humanities proceedings.* University of Kelaniya, Sri Lanka, 2016.

Pinnawala, Sisira Kumara. "Sri Lankans in Melbourne: Factors influencing patterns of ethnicity." PhD Thesis. Canberra: Australian National University, 1984.

Reeves, Peter and Rajesh Rai, Eds. *The encyclopedia of the Sri Lankan diaspora.* Singapore: Editions Didier Millet, 2013.

Ratnayake, K. "Female migration from Sri Lanka to Middle East: Is remedy worse than the disease?" *Sri Lanka Journal of Population Studies.* 2, 1999: 43–56.

Sankaran, Lavanya. "'Homeland' & 'Hostland' identifications in the Sri Lankan Tamil diaspora." Working Papers in Urban Language and Literacies, 2019.

Sharma, S. L. "Perspectives on Indians abroad." In *The Indian diaspora: Dynamics of migration*, edited by N. Jayaram: 44–65. New Delhi: Sage, 2004.

Silva, Menusha De. "The care pentagon: Older adults within Sri Lankan - Australian transnational families and their landscapes of care." *Population, Space and Place.* 23, 8, 2017. https://doi.org/10.1002/psp.2061.

Singham, Mervin. "Multiculturalism in New Zealand – The need for a new paradigm," *Aotearoa Ethnic Network Journal.* 1, 1, 2006: 33–37.

Siriwardhana, Chesmal and Kolitha Wickramage. "Conflict, forced displacement and health in Sri Lanka: A review of the research landscape." *Conflict and Health* 8, 22, 2014: 1–9. https://doi.org/10.1186/1752-1505-8-22.

Sriskandarajah, Dhananjayan. "The migration-development nexus: Sri Lanka case study." *International Migration.* 40, 5, 2002: 283–307. https://doi.org/10.1111/1468-2435.00220.

Ukwatta, Swarna. "Sri Lanka, migration 1960s to present." In *The Encyclopaedia of global human migration*, edited by Swarna Ukwetta. Wiley, 2013.

Wayland, Sarah. "Ethnonationalist networks and transnational opportunities: The Sri Lankan Tamil diaspora." *Review of International Studies.* 30, 3, 2004: 405–26. https://doi.org/10.1017/S0260210504006138.

Weerasooria, W.S. *Links between Sri Lanka and Australia: A book about Sri Lankans (Ceylonese) in Australia.* Colombo: Government Printer, 1988.

Zubrzycki, Jerzy. "The Evolution of the Policy of Multiculturalism in Australia 1968–1995." In *Global Cultural Diversity Conference Proceedings.* 1995.

PART II

Evolution and Trajectory of Citizenship Regimes in Settler Societies

CHAPTER 4

The Redefinition of Citizenship in Australia, 1950s–1970s

Jatinder Mann

Introduction

In the 1950s, Australia very much identified itself as a British country and an integral part of a wider British World which had the United Kingdom (UK) at its centre. However, by the 1970s, this British World had come to an end, as had Australia's self-identification as a British nation. During this

This chapter draws on material from my monograph entitled *Redefining citizenship in Australia, Canada, and Aotearoa* New Zealand (New York: Peter Lang Publishing, 2019). I am grateful to Peter Lang Publishing for allowing me to use this material here.

I am extremely grateful to the editor of this collection, Jatinder Mann, for his detailed feedback and helpful suggestions on my chapter.

J. Mann (✉)
Department of History, University of Reading, Reading, Berkshire, UK

Australian, Canadian, and New Zealand Studies Network, London, UK
e-mail: j.mann@reading.ac.uk

J. Mann (ed.), *Citizenship in Transnational Perspective*, Politics of Citizenship and Migration,
https://doi.org/10.1007/978-3-031-34358-2_4

period, citizenship in Australia was redefined in a significant way from being an ethnic (British)-based one to a more civic-founded one which was more inclusive of other ethnic groups and apparently Aborigines. This chapter will argue that this redefinition of citizenship took place primarily in the context of this major shift in national identity. After having established the context of the end of the British World in Australia (with a focus on the UK's application for entry into the European Economic Community (EEC) and the British withdrawal from "East of Suez"), it will explore the *Australian Citizenship Act* 1973 to illustrate the way in which citizenship became more inclusive of other ethnic groups in the country. It will then study the 1967 constitutional referendum to highlight how citizenship in Australia also appeared to incorporate Aborigines at this time.

Theoretical Background

Before exploring these several themes, it will be useful to briefly discuss the theoretical background to citizenship in Australia during the 1950s and 1970s—namely the distinction between normative citizenship (citizenship as status) and substantive citizenship (citizenship as rights and obligations). T. H. Marshall formulated "citizenship" as a designation given to those who are full participants of a community. Through this he enlarged citizenship to incorporate civil rights, as well as political and social citizenship.[1] According to Wayne Hudson and John Kane, though, "What most Australians understand by citizenship is a mixture of legal and political citizenship...The history of legal and political citizenship in Australia, however, is problematic."[2] This relates to the fact that in the 1950s, citizenship in Australia was very much normative—it did not entail extensive rights and obligations. And to complicate things even more, British migrants could attain this status on much easier terms in comparison with non-British migrants. Aboriginal Australians, though possessing the "status" of Australian citizens, were deprived of rights which are usually associated with citizenship through a swathe of restrictive legislation—at both the federal and state levels. Helen Irving emphasises that "The political rights we most readily associate now with citizenship were...not what defined a citizen but what followed from being a citizen."[3]

David Dutton argues thus:

> The legal meaning of Australian citizenship has never been singularly defined, and must even now, be sought in the common law, and a multitude of Commonwealth and state statutes dealing with immigration, passports,

the franchise, jury service, employment in the public service, and social security.[4]

According to Sangeetha Pillai:

> The commencement of the *NCA 1948* signified the emergence of Australian statutory citizenship...However, this did not symbolize a radical shift in notions of formal membership of the Australian community, but rather a relatively gradual evolution from previous statutes which had shaped such notions without using the language of citizenship.[5]

Nevertheless, by the 1970s, citizenship in Australia was considerably more substantive compared with the 1950s, and all migrants were put on an equal basis in terms of attaining this citizenship. Ann-Mari Jordens neatly encapsulates this redefinition: "Over 30 years, the presence of large numbers of non-British migrants in Australia slowly eroded the conception of Australian citizenship from a status based on British ethnicity and culture to one based on equality of rights and responsibilities."[6] However, I will argue that a shift in national identity rather than increasing multi-ethnicity was the main reason for this redefinition. Jordens adds:

> A culturally normative conception of citizenship was clearly reflected in the definition of 'alien' embodied in the [1948] Act...A nation's understanding of itself is revealed by the categories of people it regards as foreign, alien and 'other'...From 1948 to 1987 Australia's citizenship legislation defined an alien as 'a person who does not have the status of British subject and is not an Irish citizen or a protected person.'[7]

Turning to Aborigines and citizenship, the most that one can really say about when Aboriginal groups became Australian citizens is that, primarily during the 1960s, Aboriginal groups gradually secured the substantive citizenship rights that up to that point had been withheld from them at the State and Commonwealth levels as State and Commonwealth statutes that limited their citizenship rights were slowly repealed.[8] Susan Dodds maintains that,

> In considering ways of thinking about Australian Aboriginal citizenship, the history of European engagement with indigenous Australians acts as a constant reminder of the gap between abstract idealisations of liberal democratic citizenship and the reality of colonial and post-colonial Australian

> social policy...Aboriginal and Torres Strait Islander peoples were not simply 'overlooked' in the process of nation building; their status as rights bearers was actively undermined.[9]

Ann Curthoys states:

> In Australia there have been for a long time two distinct yet connected public and intellectual debates concerning the significance of descent, belonging and culture...One revolves around the cleavage between indigenous and non-indigenous peoples, and especially the status of indigenous claims deriving from a history of colonization...The other debate centers on the immigrant, and his or her challenge to Australian society at large.[10]

This chapter contributes to both of these debates.

Context of the End of the British World

Having established this theoretical background, the chapter will now turn to exploring the context of the end of the British World as the major reason for the redefinition of citizenship in Australia between the 1950s and 1970s. In the post-Second-World-War period, Australia was very much a British society and an integral part of a wider British World. The *British Nationality and Australian Citizenship Act* 1948 is an excellent and very appropriate example of this. Although this Act established the concept of Australian citizenship for the very first time, it emphasised *British Nationality* over *Australian Citizenship*. Furthermore, the status of British subject was preserved, and white immigrants[11] from the British Commonwealth were given preferential treatment in terms of naturalisation.[12] The Suez Crisis of 1956[13] was a further demonstration of Australia's identification as an integral part of a wider British World. Throughout the episode, the Australian government fully supported the UK's position of overturning President Gamal Abdul Nasser's decision to nationalise the Suez Canal. Australia offered unequivocal support for the UK, as it considered itself a British country. The UK was still the centre of a wider British World, and, therefore, backing the UK was still regarded as supporting the "mother-country."[14]

However, in the early 1960s, the first signs that Australia's Britishness was beginning to wane started to emerge. The first application of the UK government for entry into the EEC in 1961 marked the beginning of the unravelling of the belief that Australia was part of a wider British World. It came as a psychological shock to the Australians, as they had previously received repeated assurances from the British that there was no question of them making a choice between Europe and the Commonwealth. However, the Australian government became increasingly concerned by the lack of communication from London during 1960 and 1961, when the UK was reconsidering its position towards the EEC. Despite repeated requests for information, the British refused to indicate which way they were thinking until a more solid agreement had been secured with the Six (this was the six original members of the EEC—France, Germany, Italy, Belgium, The Netherlands, and Luxembourg. The latter three were collectively known as Benelux).[15]

There were increasing rumours and speculation in early 1961 about a reversal of British policy. This led to the Australian government's sudden interest in European economic matters. Minister for Trade John McEwen announced to the Cabinet in February that although the entire picture was not clear, it appeared as if the UK was shifting closer and closer towards something along the lines of full membership of the EEC. The Australian Prime Minister Robert Menzies expressed the deep concerns of the Australian people about this eventuality. He specifically drew attention to the political and strategic effects that Britain's decision would have on the Commonwealth. If Britain were to join the EEC, how would it then consider Australia, Canada, and the rest of the Commonwealth?[16]

But unlike the UK, Australia did not have an alternative geographic grouping to redirect its interests to. Thus, the Australian government decided to use whatever means it could to ensure that British entry into the EEC would not lead to a fundamental shift in Australia's long-standing political and economic ties to the UK. Menzies' subsequent tough probing of the British government illustrated the level of Australia's concerns. The issue of Britain and Europe had initiated a re-evaluation of the very concept of "British interests," rather than being seen as just a temporary conflict of interest between Australia and Britain. Menzies increased the pressure by stating that the UK had a very hard choice between the Commonwealth and Europe. On 31 July 1961, British Prime Minister Harold Macmillan announced his government's decision to seek membership of the EEC.[17] Macmillan's EEC statement resulted in a diverse range of responses in Australia. The *Sydney Morning Herald* represented the general feeling, however, announcing that the British action was one of the most historic statements of the century.[18]

If the UK's application for membership of the EEC initiated the breakdown of Britishness in Australia, its resolve in 1967 to end its military role "East of Suez" was the culmination. This move was significant in itself as it illustrated the end of the UK's military world role. To commentators in both the UK and Australia, it appeared that the decline of one of the last symbols of the Anglo-Australian relationship would result in the demise of Australia's long-standing British self-identification. This was due to British race patriotism in Australia being founded on the idea that Britons in Australia and the UK had a community of interest, which the British decision to withdraw from "East of Suez" acted blatantly against. But some time before the UK announced its move, there had been increasing problems in the British-Australian strategic relationship, which had led to Australia progressively becoming a part of the United States of America sphere. Nevertheless, this had not affected Australia's Britannic identity in any significant way, as it had always (with a few noteworthy exceptions) preserved a differentiation between sentiment and interest, particularly when it came to foreign policy. Moreover, although the UK had not yet become a member of the EEC, its failed bid in 1961–63 had most definitely resulted in Australia questioning their future relationship and had led to initiatives to broaden Australian trade.[19]

As expected, there were Australian protests aimed at the British over their announcement. Alexander Downer Sr., Australian High Commissioner in London, tried to persuade the British government that it would be a travesty of history if the UK were to be simply a European power. But largely, Downer's emotive reaction was not typical of most Australians' views in 1967, or indeed of those of the new Holt government. Although Foreign Minister Paul Hasluck did suggest to Prime Minister Harold Holt that connections of familial ties and common wartime experiences should be emphasised in communications with the UK, this was only a small component of the overarching Australian plan. Even the most ardent disciples of the British heritage had been compelled to accept the existence of this new world.[20]

Holt attempted to articulate a unique Australian identity based on both a British heritage and the European migrant cultures. In an Australia Day speech in 1967, he acknowledged: "Ours is not a long story as the history of many other nations is counted but in that time we have evolved our distinctive national identity and character [...] We have been assisted to do so by our heritage of British democracy and the cultures of European civilization." But he did not elaborate on what this apparently special Australian character and identity of the country entailed.[21]

The end of Britishness and the question of whether an Australian nationalism could be located to replace it coalesced in the late 1960s under Prime Minister John Gorton. Although Holt asked important questions, Gorton's public addresses on this subject were an illustration of the confusion and problems faced by national leaders in the late 1960s. Acknowledging that they could now develop a homegrown national identity, but at the same time wanting to hold onto the British connection, they found themselves on the horns of a dilemma. Hence, Gorton attempted to push an idea of "Australianism." In his opinion, the development of a sense of national pride represented a central goal for his government.[22]

The Whitlam government has often been associated with an unexpected emergence of a more autonomous and confident Australian nationalism; however, Gorton can be regarded as a predecessor of this drive, particularly in his arts policy initiatives. By establishing the Australian Council for the Arts, facilitating the re-emergence of the Australian film industry, and laying the basis for the introduction of an Australia Film and Television School, Gorton was linking himself and his government with an emerging faith in Australia's cultural uniqueness. While Holt had laid the foundation for a federal arts programme, Gorton took it up and supported it, not so much because of a newly discovered love of the arts, but instead due to his political search for a "new nationalism." Therefore, he promoted homegrown dance, music, opera, and above all, television and film. He had limited success in the achievement of this goal, however.[23]

The Sunday Australian captured the substance of the "new nationalism" in early 1972: "A splendid opportunity exists to build a multi-national society, rich and diverse in its origins but cohesive in its identity [...] Australia must be a country in which our people are concerned with a common purpose and a sharing of common identity."[24] This talk of Australia as a multi-national society but with a particular focus on national cohesion, along with somehow also possessing a clear idea of community and identity, combined the key concepts and contradictions of the "new nationalism." The decline of the idea that Australia was a part of a wider British World was helped by the long-drawn-out way in which the UK entered the EEC, which occurred in 1973, a dozen years after the original application. It was also assisted by the realisation by Australian leaders that the nation's trading future was in Asia, which for the majority of its past had been its psychological enemy. A white British Australian identity was no longer wanted and no longer appropriate as the nation attempted to come to terms with its presence in a changed world. In the early 1960s, then, the concept of Australia as a "British" country started to lose credibility and relevance. Later in the decade the "new nationalism," which emphasised a domestic Australian identity, arose as a possible replacement for Britishness. But this entire period was one of questioning and uncertainty. Thus, apart from an emphasis on national cohesion and uniquely Australian creative effort, there was not much substance to the "new nationalism."[25] This was the context in which nationality and citizenship legislation was amended during the 1950s and 1970s.

The Australian Citizenship Act 1973

The *Australian Citizenship Act* 1973 was a major reform of Australian Citizenship and Nationality legislation. It built on the reforms of the *Citizenship Act* 1969. One of the major elements the Bill introduced was a suggested new Oath (or Affirmation) of Allegiance: firstly, it removed the renunciation of allegiance which had been a source of considerable emotional turmoil for some migrants, and secondly, allegiance was now to be sworn to the Constitution of Australia—specific mention of the Queen was not made. The Bill also provided for a transitional period of two years (after the new Act commenced) during which:

> Commonwealth citizens, Irish citizens, and South African and Pakistani citizens already resident in Australia, will be able to become Australian citizens after 1 year's residence; and...aliens who have lived in Commonwealth countries or served under those countries' Governments may have such residence or service accepted as part of the new qualifying period of 3 years' residence for the grant of Australian citizenship.[26]

The Bill did not adjust the context in which citizens of Commonwealth countries, whether they became Australian citizens or not, carried on having the status of British or Commonwealth of Nations subjects and hence had benefits including the vote and ability to be employed in the public service under Parliamentary legislation.[27] Nevertheless, it was emphasised that the Bill would remove (after a transitional period) the past previous discrimination between citizens of Commonwealth nations and others, particularly by requiring the same period of residence for all and providing everyone with the chance to attend citizenship ceremonies.[28]

In his second reading speech on the Bill, Minister for Immigration, Al Grassby, emphasised the main thrust of the legislation, which was to establish equality between all migrants:

> The guiding principles for the Government in the vitally important matter of the grant of Australian Citizenship is that there should not be discrimination between different groups of settlers seeking to join the family of the nation. Wherever they were born—whatever their nationality—whatever the colour of their complexion—they should all be able to become Australian citizens under just the same conditions....So it is that this Bill provides for all, regardless of origins, the same requirements as to residence, good character, knowledge of the language and of the rights and duties of citizenship, and intention to live here permanently.[29]

The Bill also stipulated that all those applying for citizenship, apart from children under 16, would need to take the Oath or Affirmation of Allegiance, with no regard to their previous nationality. This meant that migrants from all the 31 Commonwealth countries would now have the same chance as other migrants to participate in citizenship ceremonies appropriately marking the significant event of their becoming citizens.[30] Grassby also emphasised another notable change in the proposed legislation:

> It is important to end the confusion which has been permitted to continue since the Citizenship Act of 1949 and the use of terminology which has given many Australians the mistaken impression that they are not only Australian citizens but also citizens of the United Kingdom of Great Britain and Northern Ireland. This has not been the case for 24 years yet the past Government permitted Australians to remain confused on this point.[31]

The Opposition, however, opposed all main features of the Bill. Philip Lynch, former Minister for Immigration and Deputy Leader of the Opposition, fired the opening salvo:

> The Opposition rejects the major provisions of this Bill for a number of fundamental reasons. The legislation seeks to remove the position of preferment which British migrants have enjoyed since the inception of Australia's immigration program...our early arrivals with relatively limited exceptions,

came almost solely...from the British Isles...The Government seems intent on ending that special relationship...I have...indicated that the Opposition is opposed to the proposal to delete all references to the Queen from the oath of allegiance taken by migrants at citizenship ceremonies. It is equally opposed to the Government's proposal to omit the renunciation of allegiance to another country.[32]

But Grassby did also receive support from his side of the house. Maxwell Old-meadow, the member for Holt, rose to support the Bill and stated that he and his side of the house did not share the alarm expressed by Lynch. There were no disincentives to British migrants. He also drew attention to the fact that Grassby had stated that renunciation of former citizenship served no legal purpose, though his most salient comments were, "A nation which has come of age, which has confidence in its future and has successfully emerged from the shadows of colonialism neither requires nor will accept such a sacrifice...Australian citizenship must always be preserved and solidified by its highest common factors."[33] The Opposition, however, was not finished: Alexander Forbes, the member for Barker, chimed in with a reference to British migrants: "Just who does the Minister for Immigration think he is kidding? Since when did people who are placed in a privileged position object because there was discrimination in their favour?"[34] He scathingly added, with a reference to non-British migrants, that "Citizenship is an act of identification with the adopted country and with the values and mores of its inhabitants...Persons who cannot accept these things have not sufficiently identified as to be ready for citizenship."[35]

But the government was not to be cowed on the Bill. The ALP member for Bowman, Leonard Keogh, made a lively riposte to Forbes:

As the honourable member for Barker (Dr. Forbes) was making his speech this evening I expected him to break out at any time into a verse from "Rule Britannia." My colleague, the honourable member for Liley (Mr. Doyle) said to me when he walked into the chamber that he felt sure that he must have been in Rhodesia listening to Ian Smith...The Immigration policy of the Government seeks to rid the nation of the inconsistencies, inequalities and discrimination that we believe should no longer be allowed to exist when we are seeking to bring people from various countries and to welcome them as citizens in their own right in Australia.[36]

Therefore, Keogh criticised the Imperial hanging-on of the Opposition at the same time as stressing the positive moves the government was trying to make to remove the discrimination between different types of migrants. Grassby picked up on this theme in his reply to MPs' responses to his second reading speech:

> The Opposition has attempted tonight to turn back the tide of history. It has rejected the concept of Australian citizenship as the badge of a free, strong and independent people....How could any Minister responsible for immigration and citizenship go out to the million here and now and the tens of thousands still coming and draft them off like so many sheep and cattle, saying: "You go to the one year pen; you go to the 3-year pen; you to the 5-year pen....Italians, Dutch, Germans, Greeks and Lebanese to the right and wait for 3 years; Tongans, Zambians, Canadians, British and Indians to the left and wait for one year if you are light enough and 5 years if you are not."[37]

Grassby pleaded to all members of Parliament to look at the citizenship legislation in a non-partisan way instead of on the level of petty party politics. The Bill simply recommended that all discrimination be removed from the conditions for the granting of Australian citizenship to migrants.[38]

In another speech on the *Australian Citizenship Bill* of 1973, Grassby attempted to draw links between the current citizenship legislation and its predecessor in 1969:

> The present leader of the Opposition when Minister for Immigration introduced a Citizenship Bill in 1969 which showed a progressive outlook by recognising the growing importance of the status of Australian citizen. That Bill specifically provided that an Australian when asked to state his nationality had only to say "I am an Australian citizen"..."What this Government now puts to this House in the present Australian Citizenship Bill is that it is time we progressed still further towards reality by ending the artificial discriminations in the present Act, in the matter of requirements for Australian citizenship."[39]

However, his call fell on deaf ears. Though the Bill passed the House of Representatives relatively easily due to the government's majority in that house, it faced a much tougher time in the Senate, where the Opposition held the balance of power. Grassby was forced to accept some amendments to his legislation, in particular, migrants having the choice to swear allegiance to the Australian Constitution *or* to the Queen.

So, I have shown above how the end of the British World led to a redefinition of citizenship in Australia between the 1950s and 1970s in relation to other ethnic groups. The chapter will now turn to Aborigines and the redefinition of citizenship in Australia between the 1950s and 1970s.

The 1967 Referendum

There is some considerable historiographical debate surrounding the significance of the 1967 referendum. The referendum ultimately sought to repeal Section 127 of the constitution and repeal the words "other than the Aboriginal race in any State" from Section 51 (xxvi). According to Tim Rowse, "The common narration of the 1967 referendum is to exaggerate its benefits, declaring it to be the moment when Aborigines attained 'citizenship'...This is strictly speaking, a misconception."[40] Nevertheless, he does concede that the amendment of the Constitution in the 1967 referendum is regularly reflected upon by Aborigines of a younger generation as the point at which Aboriginal people were "granted citizenship."[41] Bain Attwood and Andrew Markus go even further and maintain that "The 1967 referendum to alter Australia's Constitution is now seen as an event that marked a major turning point in Aboriginal-European relations in Australia."[42]

Terry Widders and Greg Noble argue, though, that, "The supposed coming into political existence of indigenous people through the 1967 referendum, as it had been mythologised in white history, has by no means been a democratic panacea, and nor has it been seen as such by indigenous people."[43] Christine Flether contrarily asserts that "The 1967 constitutional referendum was the turning point in Aboriginal affairs—a watershed in their cultural and political freedoms."[44] And Michael Dodson states that "The 1967 referendum, at least in principle, lifted many of the formal and overt forms of discrimination...Citizenship provided a ticket of entry into the political system."[45] My own opinion is that though its practical effect is certainly debatable, its symbolic value was extremely important.

Government moves towards considering constitutional amendments regarding Aborigines began in early 1965 with a Cabinet Submission by the Attorney-General, Billy Snedden:

There would assuredly be international approbation of any move to repeal section 127, as it savours of racial discrimination. Its repeal could remove a possible source of misconstruction in the international field...I think also that the average elector would feel that either the Commonwealth should have the power in section 51 (xxvi) in relation to all races, including people of the aboriginal race or ought not to have the power at all; and I believe the failure to include a proposal to delete the underlined parts might well prejudice the success of a referendum that wants the repeal of section 127.[46]

However, the Cabinet only agreed to the abolition of Section 127 of the Constitution being put to referendum simultaneously as the question of the nexus.[47,48]

This led to pressure being applied on the government by New South Wales State Secretary of Federal Council for the Advancement of Aborigines and Torres Strait Islanders (FCAATSI), Faith Bandler, on 30 April 1965. FCAATSI was the leading organisation calling for constitutional amendments regarding Aborigines,[49] and Bandler was a particularly passionate and conscientious advocate of the organisation:

A Referendum to amend the Commonwealth Constitution will be held later this year and the Government has already agreed to include in this the repeal of Section 127 which discriminates against Aborigines by excluding them from the census. However there is another section of the Constitution which also discriminates against Aborigines and the Government is still hesitant as to whether or not to include repeal of Section 51 Clause xxvi in the forthcoming Referendum.[50]

Snedden attempted to secure Cabinet agreement to have the words "other than the aboriginal race in any State" removed from the Constitution again on 23 August 1965,[51] but the Cabinet once again refused to support this.[52] A few months later, the *Sydney Morning Herald* questioned whether the proposed referendum went far enough as "it will still leave the Commonwealth Government without any direct responsibility for Aboriginal advancement outside the Northern Territory, and it will still leave power of 'discrimination' in the hands of the various States."[53] Mrs. L. Lippmann, Convenor of the Legislative Reform Committee of FCAATSI, commented in a letter to Snedden early the following year that it appeared likely that proposals for the inclusion of the amendment of Section 51, Placitum xxvi of the Constitution would be put before Parliament. And she emphasised the importance of this initiative, which would enable FCAATSI and other organisations working for the advancement of Aborigines to vociferously campaign for the referendum proposals.[54] Her enthusiasm was most likely due to Menzies' successor as prime minister, Harold Holt, taking office just a few weeks earlier. He was considered more receptive to including the second proposal on Section 51 (xxvi), and consequently announced a few weeks later that the government had decided not to hold the proposed referendum (which included only the one proposal) that year.[55]

It was left to the new Attorney-General, Nigel Bowen, to raise the issue again at the beginning of 1967. He argued in a Cabinet Submission that

> The Government announce that it will hold a referendum to seek legislative power for the Commonwealth with respect to aborigines by omitting the words "other than the aboriginal race in any State" from section 51(xxvi.) and, if the referendum is successful, will hold discussion with the States to formulate a joint policy whereby the States will be responsible for administration, but the Commonwealth will have a role of policy participation.[56]

The Cabinet finally agreed to this course of action the following month.[57] Holt announced the government's intention to include two proposals concerning Aborigines in a constitutional referendum very soon after: "Our intention, Mr. Speaker, is to put through the necessary legislation relating to these proposals as soon as practicable...I expect it to be introduced in this House within the next week or two...We proposed to have the measures passed by the two Houses as expeditiously as possible."[58] The Leader of the Opposition, Gough Whitlam, expressed the Opposition's support for both measures.[59] The *Sydney Morning Herald* explained the government's shift in position as a reaction to the persuasive arguments made by William Wentworth, a government backbencher who had introduced a Private Members Bill along similar lines the previous year.[60]

FCAATSI immediately swung into action. It published several information pamphlets to promote a "Yes" vote for the two Aboriginal proposals in the upcoming referendum.[61] It is no exaggeration to say that FCAATSI's extensive campaigning was the reason for the success of the Aboriginal proposals in the referendum on 27 May 1967. An illustration of this is an expose on Bandler in *The Australian Women's Weekly* in May 1967. She maintained that, "A Yes vote will mean that the Aboriginal people can come under Commonwealth law...Aborigines are the only Australians who live under six separate laws, one for each State...The eyes of the world are on Australia and her handling of black Australians...Not only Asia is watching but Africa and the whole Western world."[62] The general press reaction to the Aboriginal referendum proposals was overwhelmingly positive.[63] A few days before the referendum, Bandler drew attention to the public confusion on the Aboriginal issue in the *Sydney Morning Herald*. She pointed out that many Australians thought a "Yes" victory on the Aboriginal question in the referendum would give Aborigines the vote—whereas in actual fact they already had this. Bandler laid the blame for this confusion firmly at the doorsteps of the federal government and political parties, as they had not played much of a role at all in the campaign. She suggested that perhaps the government thought the Aborigines question would assist it in also securing support on the nexus question. Bandler showed this through the fact that the fifteen-page pamphlet which the Commonwealth government handed out to all voters included only two and a half pages on the Aborigines question.[64]

In the actual event there was an overwhelming majority in support of the constitutional amendments in regard to Aborigines—over ninety per cent (the biggest Yes vote in the history of federal plebiscites)—whereas the nexus proposal failed dismally.[65] Nevertheless, The *Sydney Morning Herald* pointed out that it was depressing that the largest No vote was recorded in parts of Australia where the question had real impact—in other words, in places where there were Aborigines to resent and to be prejudiced about: "The No vote was worst in the three States—Western Australia, South Australia and Queensland—that have been most criticised for their treatment of the remaining Aboriginal population."[66]

After the 1967 referendum the federal government was reluctant to act on its new authority to legislate for Aborigines. The federal government set up an Office of Aboriginal Affairs after the 1967 referendum, but there was little substantive change until the new government in 1972.[67] Hence, Attwood and Markus conclude:

> that the government's belated decision to conduct the referendum was a rather uninterested, even cynical, one that had little if anything to do with any program of change in Aboriginal affairs, and much more to do with maintaining the status quo, shoring up the government's position at home, and bolstering Australia's image abroad.[68]

But as well as allowing the Whitlam government in 1972 to enter the policy field, the successful referendum also put pressure on the subsequent Fraser government to stand up to the Queensland and Western Australia state governments. In this sense, its practical impact was important in the longer term.

Conclusion

This chapter has shown how the end of the British World and its replacement with a "new nationalism" led to a redefinition of citizenship in Australia between the 1950s and 1970s. The UK's first application for entry into the EEC in 1961 and the announcement of its military withdrawal from "East of Suez" in 1967 were particular highlights which signalled the end of the British self-identification of Australia. Through focusing on the *Australian Citizenship Act* 1973, the chapter has demonstrated how non-British migrants were gradually put on a much more equal basis to their British counterparts in being able to attain Australian citizenship and exercise the benefits of Australian citizenship, such as employment in the Public Service. It has also illustrated how the 1967 referendum led to the removal of the constitutional discriminations against Aborigines and actually allowed them to exercise the rights of Australian citizenship which they had theoretically held since 1948.

Notes

1. Kim Rubenstein, *Australian Citizenship Law in Context* (Pyrmont, NSW: Lawbook, 2002), 10.
2. Wayne Hudson and John Kane, "Rethinking Australian Citizenship," in *Rethinking Australian Citizenship*, ed. Wayne Hudson and John Kane (Cambridge: Cambridge University Press, 2000), 2.
3. Helen Irving, *To Constitute a Nation: A Cultural History of Australia's Constitution* (Cambridge: Cambridge University Press, 1997), 158.
4. David Dutton, *Citizenship in Australia: A Guide to Commonwealth Government Records* (Canberra: National Archives of Australia, 1999), 17.
5. Sangeetha Pillai, "The Rights and Responsibilities of Australian Citizenship: A Legislative Analysis," *Melbourne University Law Review* 37, 3 (January 2014): 736–85.
6. Ann-Mari Jordens, *Alien to Citizen: Settling Migrants in Australia, 1945–75* (St. Leonards, NSW: Allen & Unwin, 1997), 189. However,

there was still protection for British subjects who were on the electoral roll as late as 1983 to remain on the roll, even if they were not citizens.

7. Ann-Mari Jordens, *Promoting Australian Citizenship, 1949–71* (Canberra: Administration, Compliance and Governability Program, 1991), 1.
8. John Chesterman and Brian Galligan, "Indigenous Rights and Australian Citizenship," in *Individual, Community, Nation: Fifty Years of Australian Citizenship*, ed. Kim Rubenstein (Melbourne: Australian Scholarly Publishing, 2000), 67.
9. Susan Dodds, "Citizenship, Justice and Indigenous Group-Specific Rights-Citizenship and Indigenous Australia," *Citizenship Studies* 2, 1 (1998): 106.
10. Ann Curthoys, "An Uneasy Conversation: The Multicultural and the Indigenous," in *Race, Colour and Identity in Australia and New Zealand*, eds. John Docker and Gerhard Fischer (Sydney: UNSW Press, 2000), 21.
11. The White Australia Policy which had been established in 1901 and was primarily aimed at preventing Asian immigration to Australia was very much alive and well at this time.
12. For more on the *British Nationality and Australian Citizenship Act* 1948 see Jatinder Mann, "The Evolution of Commonwealth Citizenship, 1945–48 in Canada, Britain and Australia," *Commonwealth & Comparative Politics* 50, 3 (July 2012): 293–313.
13. This was a crisis precipitated by the nationalisation of the Suez Canal by Egyptian President Gamal Abdul Nasser in July 1956, which in turn led to the UK and France, who had substantial commercial interests in the canal, entering into a clandestine agreement with Israel to invade Egypt in October 1956, thus giving the two powers the opportunity to in turn send troops into the canal zone on the pretext of "separating the warring parties."
14. For more on the prevalence of Britishness in Australia at this time, see Jatinder Mann, *The Search for a New National Identity: The Rise of Multiculturalism in Canada and Australia, 1890s-1970s* (New York: Peter Lang Publishing, 2016), Chapter 4. It should be emphasised, however, that Australia's Britishness was not a sign of inferiority, rather, Australian Britons saw themselves as superior to those in the "mother-country." It was argued that the extreme Australian climate, the exigencies of colonial life, and a better diet had produced a stronger and fitter British population in the Antipodes.
15. Stuart Ward, *Australia and the British Embrace: The Demise of the British Ideal* (Carlton South, Vic.: Melbourne University Press, 2001), 69, 70.
16. Ibid., 71, 79.
17. Ibid., 81, 85, 86, 88.
18. *Sydney Morning Herald (SMH)*, August 2, 1961, cited in Ward, *Australia and the British Embrace*, 89.

19. Jatinder Mann, "'Leavening British Traditions': Integration Policy in Australia, 1962–1972," *Australian Journal of Politics and History* 59, 1 (March 2013): 49.
20. Ibid., 49–50.
21. Ibid., 50.
22. Ibid., 53.
23. Ibid.
24. NLA, MS 6690/Series 12/Box 40/File 22: Immigration Advisory Council, Extract from *Sunday Australian*, 13 February 1972, "Pride and Prejudice," 8.
25. Mann, "'Leavening British Traditions'," 54, 55, 62.
26. NAA, A446/75532: Citizenship Circular 4/73 by G. E. Hitchins (for Secretary) on "Australian Citizenship Bill 1973," 12 April 1973, 2.
27. Ibid.
28. NLA, MS 7798/Series 3/Box 40: Papers of Al Grassby—Notes on "Discrimination in Citizenship Legislation and Policy of Previous Government."
29. NAA, A446/75532: Second Reading Speech on Citizenship Bill 1973 by the Hon. A. J. Grassby, Minister for Immigration, 1, 2.
30. Ibid., 4–5.
31. Ibid., 5–6.
32. Australian Parliamentary Debates, *House of Representatives (H of R)*, Vol. 83, 9 May 1973, Phillip Lynch, 1899, 1900, 1901.
33. Australian Parliamentary Debates, *H of R*, Vol. 83, 9 May 1973, Maxwell Oldmeadow, 1902, 1903.
34. Australian Parliamentary Debates, *H of R*, Vol. 83, 9 May 1973, Alexander Forbes, 1908.
35. Ibid.
36. Australian Parliamentary Debates, *H of R*, Vol. 83, 9 May 1973, Leonard Keogh, 1911, 1913.
37. Australian Parliamentary Debates, *H of R*, Vol. 83, 9 May 1973, Al Grassby, 1925, 1926.
38. Ibid., 1926.
39. NLA, MS 7798/Series 3/Box 40: Speech by Minister for Immigration, The Honourable A. J. Grassby on Australian Citizenship Bill 1973, 2.
40. Tim Rowse, "Diversity in Indigenous Citizenship," *Communal/Plural* 2 (1993): 49.
41. Tim Rowse, "Indigenous Citizenship," in *Rethinking Australian Citizenship*, eds. Wayne Hudson and John Kane (Cambridge: Cambridge University Press, 2000), 92.
42. Bain Attwood and Andrew Markus, "Representation Matters: The 1967 Referendum and Citizenship," in *Citizenship and Indigenous Australians:*

Changing Conceptions and Possibilities, eds. Nicolas Peterson and Will Sanders (Cambridge: Cambridge University Press, 1998), 118.

43. Terry Widders and Greg Noble, "On the Dreaming Track to the Republic: Indigenous People and the Ambivalence of Citizenship," *Communal/Plural* 2 (1993): 106.
44. Christine Fletcher, "Living Together but not Neighbours: Cultural Imperialism in Australia," in *Indigenous Peoples' Rights in Australia, Canada & New Zealand*, ed. Paul Havemann (Auckland: Oxford University Press, 1999), 336.
45. Michael Dodson, "First Fleets and Citizenship: The Citizenship Status of Indigenous Peoples in Post-Colonial Australia," in *Citizenship in Australia: Democracy, Law and Society*, ed. S. Rufus Davis (Carlton, Victoria: Constitutional Centenary Foundation, 1996), 215.
46. NAA, A5840 507: Submission No. 660—Constitutional Amendments: Sections 24 to 27, 51 (xxvi.), 127 by B. M. Snedden, Attorney-General, 22 February 1965, 12, 14.
47. The nexus referred to the constitutional arrangement in which there had to be roughly double the number of Senators in the House of Representatives in the Australian Parliament.
48. NAA, A5840 507: Cabinet Minute—Decision No. 841, 7 April 1965.
49. Murray Goot and Tim Rowse, explore the Impact of FCAATSI's Campaign Efforts on Australian Public Opinion in *Divided Nation: Indigenous Affairs and the Imagined Public* (Carlton, Victoria: Melbourne University Press, 2007), 55–59.
50. NLA, 2683 Series 10/Box 27/File 9: Letter from Mrs. Faith Bandler, N.S.W. State Secretary, The Federal Council for Advancement of Aborigines and Torres Strait Islanders (FCAATSI), 30 April 1965.
51. NAA, A5827 VOLUME 31: Cabinet Submission No. 1009—Constitutional Amendments: Sections 24–27, 127 and 51 (xxvi.) by B. M. Snedden, Attorney-General, 23 August 1965, 5.
52. NAA, A5827 VOLUME 31: Cabinet Minute—Decision No. 1175—Submission

    No. 1009—Constitutional Amendments: Sections 24–27, 127 and 51 (xxvi.), 30 August 1965, 2.
53. "Does Referendum Go Far Enough," *SMH*, 17 November 1965, 2.
54. NAA, A432 1967/3321 PART 1: Mrs. L. Lippmann, Convenor, Legislative Reform Committee, The Federal Council for Advancement of Aborigines' and Torres Strait Islanders (FCAATSI) to B. M. Snedden, Attorney-General, 2 February 1966.
55. NAA, A432 1967/3321 PART 1: Referendum—Statement by the Prime Minister, Mr. Harold Holt, 15 February 1966, 1.

56. NAA, A406 E1967/30: Cabinet Submission on "Constitutional Amendment: Aborigines" by Nigel Bowen, Attorney-General, January 1967, 8.
57. NAA, A5840 79: Cabinet Minute—Decision No. 79, 22 February 1967.
58. Australian Parliamentary Debates, *H of R*, Vol. 54, 23 February 1967, Harold Holt, 115.
59. Australian Parliamentary Debates, *H of R*, Vol. 54, 1 March 1967, Gough Whitlam, 264.
60. "Aborigines," *SMH*, 28 February 1967, 2.
61. NLA, MS 8256/Series II/Sub-Series II/Box 175: "YES" vote—Information (1)—Referendum—Federal Council for the Advancement of Aborigines and Torres Strait Islanders, 31 March 1967, 1, 2.

    NLA, MS 8256/Series II/Sub-Series II/Box 175: "YES" vote—Information (3)—Referendum—Federal Council for the Advancement of Aborigines and Torres Strait Islanders, 31 March 1967, 1, 2.

    NLA, MS 8256/Series II/Sub-Series II/Box 175: Vote "YES" on both questions— Referendum Day—Voting is Compulsory, 27 May 1967.
62. NLA, MS 8256/Series 11/Sub-Series II/Box 175: Says a friend of the Aborigines: "Let's tell the world there's only one Australia, and his color doesn't matter at all" by Kay Keavney, *Australian Women's Weekly*, 10 May 1967.
63. "Appeal For Yes Vote To Realise 'Dream,"' *SMH*, 13 May 1967, 9. "Holt Puts Yes Cases," *SMH*, 16 May 1967, 1.

    "The Yes Case," *Age*, 17 May 1967, 5.

    "A Good Look at the Aborigines," *SMH*, 17 May 1967, 6.

    "The Final Week," *SMH*, 22 May 1967, 2.

    "Holt, Whitlam end 'Yes' Case," *Canberra Times*, 25 May 1967, 12.

    "YES Vital to Help Aborigines," *Age*, 26 May 1967, 3.

    "No. 2: Aborigines," *SMH*, 26 May 1967, 4.

    "Shoulder to the Wheel," *Age*, 26 May 1967, 5.
64. "Public Confusion Evident on Aboriginal Issue," *SMH*, 24 May 1967, 4.
65. "Record Yes on Second Issue," *SMH*, 29 May 1967, 1.
66. "The referendum," *SMH*, 29 May 1967, 2.
67. John Chesterman and Brian Galligan, *Citizens Without Rights: Aborigines and Australian Citizenship* (Cambridge: Cambridge University Press, 1997), 186.
68. Attwood and Markus, "Representation Matters," 125.

Bibliography

Attwood, Bain and Andrew Markus, "Representation Matters: The 1967 Referendum and Citizenship." In *Citizenship and Indigenous Australians: Changing Conceptions and Possibilities*, edited by Nicolas Peterson and Will Sanders: 118-40. Cambridge: Cambridge University Press, 1998.

Chesterman, John and Brian Galligan, *Citizens Without Rights: Aborigines and Australian Citizenship*. Cambridge: Cambridge University Press, 1997.

Chesterman, John and Brian Galligan. "Indigenous Rights and Australian Citizenship." In *Individual, Community, Nation: Fifty Years of Australian Citizenship*, edited by Kim Rubenstein: 64-72. Melbourne: Australian Scholarly Publishing, 2000.

Curthoys, Ann. "An Uneasy Conversation: The Multicultural and the Indigenous." In *Race, Colour and Identity in Australia and New Zealand*, edited by John Docker and Gerhard Fischer: 21-36. Sydney: UNSW Press, 2000.

Dodds, Susan. "Citizenship, Justice and Indigenous Group-Specific Rights-Citizenship and Indigenous Australia." *Citizenship Studies* 2, 1, 1998: 105-19.

Dodson, Michael. "First Fleets and Citizenship: The Citizenship Status of Indigenous Peoples in Post-Colonial Australia." In *Citizenship in Australia: Democracy, Law and Society*, edited by S. Rufus Davis: 189-223. Carlton, Victoria: Constitutional Centenary Foundation, 1996.

Dutton, David. *Citizenship in Australia: A Guide to Commonwealth Government Records*. Canberra: National Archives of Australia, 1999.

Fletcher, Christine. "Living Together but not Neighbours: Cultural Imperialism in Australia." In *Indigenous Peoples' Rights in Australia, Canada & New Zealand*, edited by Paul Havemann: 335-50. Auckland: Oxford University Press, 1999.

Hudson, Wayne and John Kane. "Rethinking Australian Citizenship." In *Rethinking Australian Citizenship*, edited by Wayne Hudson and John Kane: 1-11. Cambridge: Cambridge University Press, 2000.

Irving, Helen. *To Constitute a Nation: A Cultural History of Australia's Constitution*. Cambridge: Cambridge University Press, 1997.

Jordens, Ann-Mari. *Promoting Australian Citizenship, 1949–71*. Canberra: Administration, Compliance and Governability Program, 1991.

Jordens, Ann-Mari. *Alien to Citizen: Settling Migrants in Australia, 1945–75*. St. Leonards, NSW: Allen & Unwin, 1997.

Mann, Jatinder. "The Evolution of Commonwealth Citizenship, 1945–48 in Canada, Britain and Australia." *Commonwealth & Comparative Politics* 50, 3, July 2012: 293–313. https://doi.org/10.1080/14662043.2012.692923

Mann, Jatinder. "'Leavening British Traditions': Integration Policy in Australia, 1962–1972." *Australian Journal of Politics and History* 59, 1, March 2013: 47–62. https://doi.org/10.1080/14662043.2012.692923

Mann, Jatinder. *The Search for a New National Identity: The Rise of Multiculturalism in Canada and Australia, 1890s-1970s.* New York: Peter Lang Publishing, 2016.
Pillai, Sangeetha. "The Rights and Responsibilities of Australian Citizenship: A Legislative Analysis." *Melbourne University Law Review* 37, 3, January 2014: 736–85.
Rowse, Tim. "Diversity in Indigenous Citizenship." *Communal/Plural* 2, 1993: 47–63.
Rowse, Tim. "Indigenous Citizenship." In *Rethinking Australian Citizenship*, edited by Wayne Hudson and John Kane, 86–98. Cambridge: Cambridge University Press, 2000.
Rubenstein, Kim. *Australian Citizenship Law in Context.* Pyrmont, NSW: Lawbook, 2002.
Ward, Stuart. *Australia and the British Embrace: The Demise of the British Ideal.* Carlton South, Vic.: Melbourne University Press, 2001.
Widders, Terry and Greg Noble, "On the Dreaming Track to the Republic: Indigenous People and the Ambivalence of Citizenship." *Communal/Plural* 2, 1993: 95–112.

CHAPTER 5

The Redefinition of Citizenship in Canada, 1950s–1970s

Jatinder Mann

Introduction

In the 1950s, English-speaking Canada very much identified itself as a British country and an integral part of a wider British World, which had the United Kingdom (UK) at its centre. Canada's bicultural nature, with the French-Canadians, complicated this self-identity in Canada. However, by the 1970s, this British World had come to an end, as had Canada's

I have also published a broader monograph on the subject entitled *Redefining citizenship in Australia, Canada, and Aotearoa* New Zealand (New York: Peter Lang Publishing, 2019).

I am extremely thankful to the editor of this collection, Jatinder Mann, for his detailed feedback and helpful suggestions on my chapter.

J. Mann (✉)
Department of History, University of Reading, Reading, Berkshire, UK

Australian, Canadian, and New Zealand Studies Network, London, UK
e-mail: j.mann@reading.ac.uk

J. Mann (ed.), *Citizenship in Transnational Perspective*, Politics of Citizenship and Migration,
https://doi.org/10.1007/978-3-031-34358-2_5

self-identification as a British nation. During this period, citizenship in Canada was redefined in a significant way from being an ethnic (British)-based one to a more civic-founded one—which was more inclusive of other ethnic groups and apparently Indigenous peoples. This chapter will argue that this redefinition of citizenship took place primarily in the context of this major shift in national identity. After having established the context of the end of the British World in Canada (with a focus on the Suez Crisis of 1956 and the UK's application for entry into the European Economic Community [EEC]), it will explore the *Canadian Citizenship Act* 1977 to illustrate the way in which citizenship became more inclusive of other ethnic groups in the country. It will then study the awarding of the right to vote for First Nations (I will use the contemporary term "First Nations" in this chapter to describe Indigenous groups who were historically referred to as "Indians." However, any quotes from historical sources will of course employ the term used at the time) in 1960 to highlight the way in which citizenship in Canada also appeared to incorporate Indigenous groups at this time.

Theoretical Background

Before studying these several key points, it will be prudent to spend some time on the theoretical context to citizenship in Canada during the 1950s and 1970s—primarily the difference between normative (citizenship as status) as opposed to substantive citizenship (citizenship as rights and obligations). According to Christina Gabriel, "Conceptualizations of citizenship are generally characterized by issues of inclusion and exclusion, rights and duties, and full participation....The nature of each of these issues, however...is historically specific, shifting, and the object of political debate."[1] Post-war ideas of citizenship have been heavily influenced by T. H. Marshall's theory of citizenship rights.[2] Marshall maintains that "Citizenship is a status bestowed on those who are full members of a community...All who possess the status are equal with respect to the rights and duties with which the status is bestowed,"[3] though not everyone who has citizenship shares equitably in the social, political, and economic benefits of their society. However, it does bestow specific crucial rights.[4] Will Kymlicka and Norman Wayne argue that "Citizenship is not just a certain status, defined by a set of rights and responsibilities…It is also an identity, an expression of one's membership in a political community."[5] Jane Jenson asserts:

> Citizenship involves much more than the recognition provided by a passport…It has come to mean the attribution to citizens of a range of rights, including civil rights that protect individuals and groups from state interference; political rights of democratic participation; and substantive social and economic rights which recognize society's responsibility for all its members.[6]

Due to shifting outlooks and the large numbers of non-British migrants in the 1950s and 1960s, the difference in the way that British subjects and aliens were treated started to be criticised by the latter. The idea that citizenship is a privilege and not a right was also questioned by increasing non-British migrants.[7] Canadian citizens however continued to be British subjects until 1977, when Canadian citizenship was acknowledged as a right in relation to a series of new initiatives incorporated in changes to the *Citizenship Act*. According to Linda Cardinal and Marie-Joie Brady:

> The new Citizenship Act constituted a framework that served to denounce the discriminatory practices that had defined the linkages between the British Crown and its many subjects such as Aboriginal peoples, British citizens, French Canadians, or immigrants…Until the first half of the twentieth century, Aboriginal peoples living in reserves had the status of minors.[8]

Darlene Johnston maintains that,

> Citizenship…The very word conjures up notions of freedom and autonomy, the right to participate, a sense of belonging…The Western political tradition regards the evolution of citizenship as its crowning achievement…However, for the First Nations over whom Canada asserts jurisdiction, the experience of Canadian citizenship has been somewhat less ennobling.[9]

Kenneth Carty and Peter Ward argue thus:

> In postwar Canada, newly ascendant liberal views on race and ethnic relations challenged traditional biases in electoral law, and, in response, governments dismantled these barriers one by one…But not until 1960 was universal suffrage, the proclaimed goal of popular democracy, truly achieved.[10]

Context of the End of the British World

Having laid this theoretical foundation, the chapter will now turn to studying the context of the end of the British World as the key cause for the redefinition of citizenship in Canada between the 1950s and 1970s. After the Second World War English-speaking Canada very much still saw itself as an integral part of a wider British World. As stated above, this Britannic identity was complicated by the presence of a competing founding European group: the French-Canadians.[11] The *Canadian Citizenship Act* 1947 is an excellent example of the bicultural nature of Canada at the time. The legislation enshrined the concept of Canadian citizenship for the very first time, but it also maintained the status of British subject and British subjects from other parts of the Commonwealth were given privileged positions compared to non-British subjects in terms of naturalisation.[12] However, English-speaking Canada's Britishness began to unravel with the Suez Crisis of 1956.[13] According to Jose Igartua:

> The Suez incident became a litmus test of Canada's sense of place on the international scene, of Canadian values, and of national unity...It provoked both defenders and opponents of the Canadian position at the United Nations into arguments based on varying conceptions of what Canada was as a country, and what it should be.[14]

The Liberal government did not support the Anglo-French action. Though Prime Minister Louis St. Laurent saw President Gamal Abdul Nasser as a dictator, he believed that to respond to aggression with aggression, except under the auspices of the United Nations (UN), would lead to an estrangement in relations with neutral nations such as India and would offer the Soviet Union an excuse to interfere even more in the Middle East.[15] The United States of America (USA) was also firmly opposed to the Anglo-French action, partly for the same reason. This consequently also influenced the Canadian government's position, as Canada was a core ally of the Americans in the context of the Cold War and the threat of communism.[16] In contrast, John Diefenbaker, the Progressive Conservative spokesman on external affairs (and future prime minister), expressed his party's position of being solidly behind the UK on the issue. He called on the St. Laurent government to support the UK in criticising Nasser's action as the abrogation of an international contract.[17]

After the British and French had invaded Egypt, the position of the Canadian government shifted from lack of support for the Anglo-French action to open criticism and condemnation of it. But the Progressive Conservative Shadow Minister for Foreign Affairs, Howard Green, scathingly maintained that:

> The United States would have far more admiration for Canada...if this government stopped being the United States chore boy...Now this government, by its action in the Suez Crisis, has made this month of November, 1956, the most disgraceful period for Canada in the history of this nation.[18]

The Progressive Conservatives hence argued that the Liberal government was taking such a firm line against the Anglo-French action in Suez because it was keen to be seen as following the USA position. They instead believed that Canada should support the UK 100 per cent. An Anti-American tone from the Progressive Conservatives is clearly obvious. This would later become exemplified through the personal animosity between Diefenbaker, when he became prime minister, and President John F. Kennedy.

The English language press, usually loyal to Britain, was now divided. A survey of the 26 English-language dailies displayed a 50–50 split between those who agreed with the government and those who supported the Anglo-French intervention.[19]

The positions of the two parties were polarised even further when Canada took a leading role in the UN Emergency Force (which the USA sponsored) into Egypt, which signalled an embarrassing retreat for the UK and France, and symbolised to the whole world that they were no longer global superpowers.[20] To the Progressive Conservatives, it appeared to be only yet another instance of the Liberal government's readiness to follow American policy, but once they themselves were in power, they came to realise that the ties with the "mother-country" were not as strong as they once were.[21]

In the context of concerns over USA dominance in Canada, the UK's decision to seek membership in the EEC in 1961 was a deathblow to British race patriotism in English-speaking Canada. British Prime Minister Harold Macmillan's European ambitions were in no way the first disagreement between the UK and Canadian governments in terms of their own interests. However, it represented a clash of interests in a completely different league from those that had affected the harmony of the

Commonwealth in the past. As Andrea Benvenuti and Stuart Ward make clear, "The prospect of British adoption of a European common tariff, and the long-term political implications of European unity, raised fundamental questions about the material and ideological foundations of a 'Greater Britain.'"[22] Before proclaiming any formal decision to seek membership, the Macmillan government believed that it was necessary to make some moves towards "consulting" Commonwealth governments. Unsurprisingly, Duncan Sandys, the Secretary of State for the Colonies and Commonwealth Relations, met with a cool reaction in Ottawa and evidently failed to persuade the Diefenbaker government. Regardless of his reassurances that the UK cabinet had not yet made a firm decision to seek membership in the EEC, the Canadian ministers got the general view that the UK had in fact already decided to open negotiations.[23]

Canadian irritation with British methods arose more clearly a few months later at the Commonwealth Economic Conference in Accra, when Canada's Finance Minister Donald Fleming and Trade Minister George Hees carried out a direct attack on the UK's promises to the Commonwealth, made openly over several years, which they argued were plainly set to be broken.[24]

The Liberal opposition, headed by Lester Pearson, accused the government of leading the criticism of the UK and announced their unqualified backing for the UK's EEC membership application. Fleming was made to openly refute the view that Canada had acted in an aggressive way against the UK.[25] He justified his government's reaction to the EEC question in an address at Winnipeg:

> Like all families, we have had our differences; like all human associations ours is not a perfect one, but by and large our aims have been common, and where they have diverged we have brought our differences to the conference table and discussed them as members of a family.[26]

The language used by Fleming illustrates how Britishness still had some resonance in English-speaking Canadian society.

Diefenbaker agreed to not officially attack the British government publicly; he did however take the chance to express his worries to Macmillan privately. One such opportunity arose when Macmillan visited Ottawa in April 1962. On his visit, Diefenbaker emphasised the impact of trade preferences "in maintaining the cohesion of the Commonwealth" in its entirety, and for Canada specifically "as a means of staving off United

States domination." The political economic shift in Canada to a continental economy had begun in a large way after 1945. Diefenbaker stressed that the Canadian government "was keenly concerned with the preservation of the Commonwealth and feared that its future would be endangered by the political implications of United Kingdom entry."[27] Benvenuti and Ward argue:

> These comments reveal the extent of Canadian anxieties concerning the less tangible aspects of British entry into Europe – the unravelling of the British world raised acute awareness of the "other quiet revolution," and posed difficult questions about Canada's sense of place and purpose in the post-imperial world.[28]

"It was our purpose to develop national symbols which would give us pride and confidence and belief in Canada."[29] Now Prime Minister Lester Pearson's comment on the adoption of the new Maple Leaf Flag in 1965 encapsulates the essence of the "new nationalism" during this period. It emerged as something to fill the supposed void left by the demise of Britishness in English-speaking Canada. The "new nationalism" involved the construction of local symbols of identity to replace those of British race patriotism. In this respect, an earlier antecedent was the establishment of the Canada Council for the Arts in 1957, which aimed at supporting uniquely Canadian cultural endeavour.

At the same time, as the "new nationalism" was developed under Pearson, the Quiet Revolution was progressing in Quebec (this was the mass modernisation of the province of Quebec economically, politically, and socially) and its consequences were becoming more apparent. René Lévesque, the Liberal Minister of Natural Resources in Quebec (and future premier), when asked by a journalist at *Le Devoir* whether people exaggerated when they discussed the Quiet Revolution in Quebec, replied:

> There is no exaggeration, and indeed we have not yet finished measuring the significance of the recent changes in Quebec…What is the result? A nation awake, in full swing, fed up with being seen as a museum, as 'the quaint old province of Quebec,' a nation bend on advancing, rising: no longer just content to endure.[30]

Pearson responded to this growing nationalism in Quebec by stressing a Canadian identity that incorporated French-Canadians. He stated in April 1965:

> We must become increasingly proud of the composition and character of our people – the French part, the English part, and the third force[31] (these were Canadians of neither British nor French origin)...I don't believe that the Anglo-Saxon element in our society need be subordinated or minimized, because Canada is now a multiracial society.[32]

This was a ground-breaking statement as it was the first time that any Canadian leader had described their country as a multiracial society. This was the background in which citizenship legislation was amended during the 1960s and 1970s.

The Canadian Citizenship Act 1977

The *Canadian Citizenship Act* was amended in 1951, 1957, 1962, 1967, and 1977. However, it was in 1967 and then in 1977 that major reforms were introduced. Due to the limitations of space, I will only explore the *Canadian Citizenship Act* 1977 in this chapter. This Act finally removed the remaining privileges that British subjects had over other migrants to Canada. Similar to its predecessor, the *Canadian Citizenship Act* 1977 had a very long legislative process. At the beginning of 1974, the Cabinet agreed that the draft Citizenship Bill, initially prepared for introduction in 1972, be forwarded to the Department for Justice for revision. J. Hugh Faulkner, the Secretary of State, would revise the oath included in the draft Bill, to incorporate references to both the Queen and to Canada, and would forward the finished product to caucus for its deliberation.[33] Faulkner would also confer with caucus regarding the issue of plural nationality. And, announcement of the introduction of the Bill should be incorporated in the Speech from the Throne for the next session of Parliament.[34] Some months later, the President of the Privy Council and the Government Leader in the House of Commons highlighted that the Bill would remove special treatment for British subjects. The Cabinet agreed to consider the draft Bill entitled "An Act Respecting Citizenship" dated 24 April 1974 at a subsequent date.[35]

The Bill finally reached Parliament at the end of 1975—the delay seems to imply that it was not a high priority for the government—although it would later claim that this was due to a detailed consultation process with various representative ethnic group organisations. Jake Epp, the Progressive Conservative member for Provencher, maintained that more emphasis should be placed in the current Citizenship Bill on the obligations of citizenship for new prospective citizens. He thought that this was particularly important as Canada was receiving considerable immigration from countries that did not have strong democratic traditions.[36]

However, the Progressive Conservative member for Perth-Wilmot, Bill Jarvis, was much more critical of the Bill, particularly the time it had taken to reach the house:

> I hope later in my remarks to be a little more charitable, but at the outset may I say it is my opinion that this bill has been gathering dust in the citizenship branch for years and all through the twenty-ninth parliament. It is absolutely ridiculous that we are sitting here in the closing days of 1975 debating whether an 18 year old can apply for citizenship...The bill received first reading in October, 1974. Seven months later we got around to having the second reading debate. Now, well along in 1975, we are just getting into the third day of debate on this very important piece of legislation.[37]

But Jarvis' more substantive comments related to the change in the status of British subjects. He asserted that this was a major change. Jarvis was not so much concerned with the change in status itself, rather he was extremely critical of the "rotten job" as he put it that the government had done in announcing the changes to British subjects. He said that he had never heard of a so-called advertising campaign by the government or any public pronouncements by the Secretary of State informing British subjects of their change in status or their change in voting rights.[38]

Walter Baker, the Progressive Conservative member for Granville-Carleton, also discussed the change in status of British subjects in the new bill, but unlike his colleague, he criticised the change itself:

> I think it is correct to say that, by virtue of this bill, we are to treat those who are not British, and not members of the Commonwealth of Nations, in the same way as we treat British subjects...the minister implied that we were wrong to treat the British subject differently. But I suggest there was good reason for treating him differently...We must bear in mind that many people who come to this country have enjoyed the British parliamentary system, British justice, and other protections of the law as a matter of traditions. An

> advantage is enjoyed by the citizen from Great Britain, a Commonwealth country...in terms of the necessity of absorbing new traditions.[39]

This illustrates that even though English-speaking Canada's self-identification as a British nation had declined in the 1950s and 1960s, it was a gradual process and remnants still remained, even as late as the 1970s.

Len Marchand, the Liberal member for Kamloops-Cariboo, offered a contrary view to Baker on the change in status of British subjects:

> A bone of contention over the years regarding citizenship has been the term 'British subject'...I always felt uneasy about the term because in no way did I feel like I was a British subject. I can understand how people coming from many other lands must feel. To me the term 'British subject' connotes that a person comes from Britain...There will no longer be a privileged status for anyone. People wishing to become Canadian citizens will be treated the same regardless of where they came from...This is a very progressive change and I welcome it.[40]

This had been a long-standing view held by many French-Canadian parliamentarians since the inception of the *Canadian Citizenship Act* in 1947. The difference now though was that quite a large number of English-speaking Canadian parliamentarians shared that position.

Faulkner in a message in July 1976 announced the passage of the *Canadian Citizenship Act* the previous week. He acknowledged that the act had a long process of discussion and development. But Faulkner did mention that his office had consulted numerous ethno-cultural organisations, both during the drafting of the Bill and through its passage through parliament.[41] More detail was given in a news release the following month:

> The Secretary of State, J. Hugh Faulkner, stated that 'This new Act will make the acquisition of citizenship a more logical, equitable and consistent process and I envisage that it will encourage many resident across the country to become official members of our great Canadian family.' Under the new Act, applicants for naturalization are treated alike, regardless of...country of origin and citizenship now becomes a right, provided certain conditions are met.[42]

The *Canadian Citizenship Act* 1977 was a ground-breaking piece of legislation as it finally removed all inequalities, especially in terms of ethnicity that had existed in previous citizenship legislation for such a long time. So, I have shown above, through the use of one prominent example, how the context of the end of the British World in Canada led to the redefinition of citizenship in relation to other ethnic groups. I will now turn to exploring how this context led to apparent shifts in the way in which Indigenous peoples in Canada were regarded when it came to citizenship.

Awarding of the Right to Vote for First Nations in 1960

Pressure from the UN and decolonisation movements contributed towards the federal government addressing the issue of the federal franchise and First Nations in the early 1960s. There was considerable internal discussion within the Department of Citizenship and Immigration about the awarding of the right to vote for First Nations in late 1959. Reports from agencies on the ground indicated that there was a high level of interest in voting amongst some First Nations and relative indifference in others. In general, the consensus was that First Nations regarded the right to vote initially with suspicion. But largely, they had become politically more conscious after they were awarded the franchise in provincial elections, and this had resulted in their having a larger feeling of affinity with their fellow residents in the areas in which they resided.[43] H. M. Jones, Director, Department of Citizenship and Immigration in a memorandum to the Deputy Minister, agreed completely with the idea that First Nations should be awarded an unrestricted right to vote. Those living on reserves had certainly not come forward in large numbers to receive the right to the franchise under the terms imposed by the existing legislation (Under the revisions to the *Indian Act* [which from its first inception in 1876 regulated the lives of First Nations living on reserves in the country] in 1950, First Nations living on reserves could be awarded the right to vote only if they become "enfranchised"—which was essentially giving up their status as First Nations living on reserves. This was achieved through them executing a waiver of exemption from taxation on money earned on reserves). Jones then outlined the steps that would be required to achieve this end, which were primarily amendments to the *Indian Act* and the *Canada Elections Act*.[44] A few days later, Ellen Fairclough, Minister for Citizenship and Immigration, in a letter to her colleague, E. D. Fulton, Minister of Justice, announced her intention to introduce legislation to award the federal franchise to First Nations along the lines that Jones had suggested.[45]

Fairclough in a memorandum to cabinet on the subject in November 1959 made a persuasive case for the change:

> The present legislation has created an anomalous situation: some of the most primitive Indians in Canada in the James Bay area of Quebec and Ontario and also in the Yukon and Northwest Territories have the right to vote because they do not live on reserves and, in fact, voted in the last federal election. On the other hand, the most educated Indians in the southern parts of the provinces because they live on reserves and have never felt they should execute a waiver of exemption from taxation, are not eligible to vote. It is considered that the present restrictions should be removed and the Indians given the same privileges with respect to voting as other Canadian citizens.[46]

Thus, the changes to the *Indian Act* in 1950 had not led to a large number of First Nations living on reserves deciding to become "enfranchised" and thereby being awarded the federal vote. The Cabinet approved the recommendations of the minister the following month.[47]

There was also popular pressure for the government to act. In a brief submitted by the Primate of all Canada on behalf of the Anglican Church of Canada to the Joint Committee of the Senate and House of Commons on Indian Affairs[48] in January 1960, it was "urged that the federal vote be granted to all Indians residing on reserves without prejudice to their status."[49] However, the Aboriginal Native Rights Regional Committee of the Interior Tribes of British Columbia in its brief argued that "If we are to have the Federal vote at the expense of losing our aboriginal rights, we flatly refuse." They further added that "we would appreciate a system of voting similar to the Maoris of New Zealand, where all the Indians of Canada would vote for an Indian or Indian representatives in Parliament."[50] Concerns by First Nations that they would lose rights guaranteed to them by the *Indian Act* and the long-standing treaties that some of them had with the Crown[51] (which predated the *Indian Act*) if they were awarded the federal franchise were a recurring one.

The Senate finally approved the awarding of the federal franchise to First Nations in April 1960. The *Saskatoon Star-Phoenix* drew attention however to critical remarks by Liberal Senator Thomas A. Crerar of Manitoba who said that passage of the legislation would lead to inequality and anomalies: "If the Indian is to become a full citizen he must accept all the responsibilities and not receive these favors[52]...We are setting up a discrimination between citizens and that is not what we want to do."[53] Hence, there was not unanimous agreement that the proposed changes were a positive thing.

There was so much concern amongst certain First Nations that the changes proposed would lead to a loss of rights they had under the *Indian Act* and their own treaties with the Crown that some bands sought legal advice on their impact. There was particularly worry over military conscription during wartime.[54] However, the Department of Citizenship and Immigration emphasised that "There is no compulsory feature in the legislation...It merely extends to the Indians the right to vote if they wish to do so." In the past, other legislation such as making the Family Allowances and Old Age Pensions payable to First Nations had engendered similar fears but they had proven to be groundless.[55]

The *Globe and Mail* offered a First Nation perspective on the changes proposed through a First Nation person (unfortunately their name was not given in the article) writing an editorial in the newspaper in which he asserted that "Many Indians in Canada look towards the granting of the Federal vote with suspicion, scepticism, distrust, and fear." The main cause of this according to the author was the continued existence of Section 112 of the *Indian Act*, which allowed the Minister of Indian Affairs to force a First Nation person, even an entire band or tribe to be ejected from a First Nation Reserve.[56] The *Regina Leader-Post* also maintained that there would be extreme reluctance by First Nations to vote, as they were worried that by so doing they would lose rights guaranteed to them by the *Indian Act*. The newspaper argued that a written assurance by Prime Minister Diefenbaker detailing that this would not be the case would go a long way towards allaying their fears.[57]

Fairclough wrote to those First Nation individuals who had executed a waiver of exemption from taxation in order to be able to exercise the federal franchise in May 1960 informing them that under the new legislation, they were no longer bound by the waiver. They were exempt again from taxation on income earned on reserves as well as being able to vote in federal elections.[58] Nevertheless, there was still some considerable anxiety expressed by various First Nation group representatives that their people would lose rights guaranteed by the *Indian Act* if they exercised the federal franchise and that voting would be compulsory.[59] Fairclough did her best to assuage these concerns in individual replies.[60] But she realised that a general statement on the subject would be more effective and so, she released a press release the following month:

> Dominion Day 1960 marks another step forward in the progress of Canada's Indians. On July 1 all Indians aged 21 and over will gain the right to vote in federal elections...Parliament approved amendments to the Indian Act and the Canada Elections Act to permit the inclusion of Indian people on federal voters' lists...Indians will lose none of their rights or privileges by voting in federal elections. Repeated reassurances to this effect have been given in the House of Commons by the Prime Minister and by the Superintendent General of Indian Affairs, Mrs. Fairclough.[61]

This statement seemed to put concerns by First Nation representatives finally to rest, although the anxiousness of First Nations was completely understandable as in the previous reform of the *Indian Act* in 1950 First Nations people had had to become "enfranchised" in order to vote in federal elections.

Conclusion

This chapter has illustrated how the end of the British World led to a redefinition of citizenship in Canada between the 1950s and 1970s. The key highlights of the unravelling of Britishness in Canada were the Suez Crisis of 1956 and the UK's decision to apply for membership in the EEC in 1961. This resulted in a shift away from a British-centred citizenship to one that was more inclusive of ethnic groups and Indigenous peoples. The *Canadian Citizenship Act* 1977 demonstrated the greater inclusivity towards ethnic groups, as the last distinctions between British subjects and other migrants were removed from Canadian citizenship legislation. And on the Indigenous side, the awarding of the right to vote for First Nations in federal elections in 1960 was a major milestone in their being able to exercise one of the major privileges of citizenship.

Notes

1. Christina Gabriel, "Citizens and Citizenship," in *Critical Concepts: An introduction to politics*, eds. Janine Brodie and Sandra Rein (Toronto: Pearson, 2009), 166.
2. Ibid.

3. T. H. Marshall, *Citizenship and Social Development: Essays by T. H. Marshall* (Westport, Connecticut: Greenwood Press, 1964), 84.
4. William Kaplan, "Who Belongs? Changing Concepts of Citizenship and Nationality," in *Belonging: The Meaning and Future of Canadian Citizenship*, ed. William Kaplan (Montreal & Kingston: McGill-Queen's University Press, 1993), 252.
5. Will Kymlicka and Wayne Norman, "Return of the Citizen: A Survey of Recent Work on Citizenship Theory," *Ethics* 104 (1994): 369.
6. Jane Jenson, "Citizenship Claims: Routes to Representation in a Federal System," in *Rethinking Federalism: Citizens, Markets and Governments in a Changing World*, eds. Karen Knop, Sylvia Ostry, Richard Simeon, and Katherine Swinton (Vancouver: UBC Press, 1995), 99.
7. Valerie Knowles, *Forging our Legacy: Canadian Citizenship and Immigration, 1900–1977* (Ottawa: Citizenship and Immigration Canada, 1997), 88.
8. Linda Cardinal and Marie-Joie Brady, "Citizenship and Federalism in Canada: A Difficult Relationship," in *Contemporary Canadian Federalism: Foundations, Traditions, Institutions*, ed. Alain-G. Gagnon (Toronto: University of Toronto Press, 2009), 384.
9. Darlene Johnston, "First Nations and Canadian Citizenship," in *Belonging: The Meaning and Future of Canadian Citizenship*, ed. William Kaplan (Montreal & Kingston: McGill-Queen's University Press, 1993), 349.
10. R. Kenneth Carty and W. Peter Ward, "The Making of a Canadian Political Citizenship," in *National Politics and Community in Canada*, eds. R. Kenneth Carty and W. Peter Ward (Vancouver: UBC Press, 1986), 74.
11. For more on the prevalence of Britishness in English-speaking Canada at this time and the French-Canadian reaction to it see Jatinder Mann, *The Search for a New National Identity: The Rise of Multiculturalism in Canada and Australia, 1890s–1970s* (New York: Peter Lang Publishing, 2016), 15–48. It should be pointed out though that English-speaking Canada's Britishness was not a sign of inferiority, rather English-speaking Canadian Britons saw themselves as superior to those in the "mother-country". It was maintained that the harsh Canadian climate, the realities of colonial life, and a healthier diet had resulted in a fitter and stronger British population in Canada.
12. For more on the *Canadian Citizenship Act* 1947 see Jatinder Mann, "The evolution of Commonwealth citizenship, 1945–48 in Canada, Britain and Australia," *Commonwealth and Comparative Politics* 50, 3 (2012): 293–313.
13. This was a crisis precipitated by the nationalisation of the Suez Canal by Egyptian President Gamal Abdul Nasser in July 1956, which in turn led to the UK and France, who had substantial commercial interests in the canal,

entering into a clandestine agreement with Israel to invade Egypt in October 1956, thus giving the two powers the opportunity to in turn send troops into the canal zone on the pretext of "separating the warring parties".

14. Jose Igartua, "'Ready, Aye, Ready' No More?," in *Rediscovering the British World*, ed. Phil Buckner (Calgary: University of Calgary Press, 2005), 48.
15. Dale C. Thomson, *Louis St. Laurent: Canadian* (New York: St. Martin's Press, 1968), 459.
16. Robert Bothwell, *The Penguin History of Canada* (Toronto: Penguin Canada, 2006), 381–383.
17. Thomson, *Louis St. Laurent*, 459.
18. Debates, *House of Commons (H of C)*, 1956–57, 27 November 1956, Howard Green cited in Igartua, "'Ready, Aye, Ready' No More?," 47.
19. Ibid., 61–62.
20. Ibid., 58.
21. Jack L. Granatstein, *Canada 1957–1967: The Years of Uncertainty and Innovation* (Toronto: McClelland and Stewart, 1986), 43.
22. Andrea Benvenuti and Stuart Ward, "Britain, Europe, and the 'Other Quiet Revolution' in Canada," in *Canada and the End of Empire*, ed. Phil Buckner (Vancouver: UBC Press, 2006), 168.
23. Ibid., 169, 170.
24. Ibid., 171.
25. Ibid., 172–173.
26. National Archives of the UK, DO 159/52, Fleming, speech at Winnipeg, 19 January 1962 cited in Benvenuti and Ward, "Britain, Europe, and the 'Other Quiet Revolution' in Canada," 173.
27. Library and Archives Canada (LAC), RG25, vol. 5519, file 12447–40 (pt. 51), record of meeting between Prime Minister Macmillan and Prime Minister Diefenbaker, Ottawa, 20 April 1962 cited in Benvenuti and Ward, "Britain, Europe, and the 'Other Quiet Revolution' in Canada," 176–7.
28. Benvenuti and Ward, "Britain, Europe, and the 'Other Quiet Revolution' in Canada," 177.
29. Lester Pearson, "Symbols and realities," in *Mike: The Memoirs of the Right Honourable Lester B. Pearson: Volume 3, 1957–1968*, eds. J. A. Munro and A. I. Inglis (London: Victor Gollancz, 1975), 270.
30. "The Quiet Revolution in Quebec," *Citizen*, vol. 10, no. 5, December 1964, 10, 11.
31. The first major reference to a "third force" was by Senator Paul Yuzyk, who was of Ukrainian descent in his maiden speech to the Senate in 1964. He subsequently emerged as one of the strongest proponents of multiculturalism.

32. LAC, MG32-C67/Vol. 91/File 1, Prime Minister Lester Pearson, in the Weekend Magazine, no. 14, 3 April 1965, has seen fit to make the following significant statement to all Canadians.
33. LAC, RG2/Series A-5-a/Vol. 6436, Citizenship Legislation, 10 January 1974, 11.
34. LAC, RG2-B-2/Vol. 26589/Cab. Doc. 1235–73, Record of Cabinet Decision by R. B. Charron, Supervisor of Cabinet Documents – Citizenship Legislation, 11 January 1974, 2.
35. LAC, RG2/Series A-5-a/Vol. 6436, An Act Respecting Citizenship, 8, 9.
36. Debates, *H of C*, vol. IX, 1975, Jake Epp, 9802, 9803.
37. Debates, *H of C*, vol. IX, 1975, Bill Jarvis, 9809.
38. Debates, *H of C*, vol. IX, 1975, Bill Jarvis, 9810.
39. Debates, *H of C*, vol. X, 1975–76, Walter Baker, 9899.
40. Debates, *H of C*, vol. X, 1975–76, Len Marchand, 9904.
41. LAC, R11236/Vol. 135/File 148–4-8, A Message from the Secretary of State (including short press release), 23 July 1976.
42. LAC, R11236/Vol. 135/File 148–4-8, J. Hugh Faulkner, The Secretary of State for Canada to Bud Cullen, Minister of National Revenue (including copies of a press release to the ethnic press and women's groups and the bill itself), 6 August 1976, 1.
43. LAC, MG32-B1/Vol. 94/File IA-166/File 18, Memorandum by H. M. Jones, Acting Director, Department of Citizenship and Immigration to the Deputy Minister, 20 November 1959, 1–2.
44. LAC, MG32-B1/Vol. 94/File IA-166/File 18, Memorandum by H. M. Jones, Director, Department of Citizenship and Immigration to the Deputy Minister, 25 November 1959, 1.
45. LAC, MG32-B1/Vol. 94/File IA-166/File 18, Ellen L. Fairclough, Minister for Citizenship and Immigration to E. D. Fulton, Minister of Justice, 27 November 1959.
46. LAC, RG2-B-2/Vol.2745/Cab.Doc. 383–59, Memorandum by Fairclough to the Cabinet Re: Proposed amendment to the Indian Act and Canada Elections Act concerning voting by Indians, 27 November 1959.
47. LAC, RG2/Series A-5-a/Vol. 2745, Legislation—Amendment to the Indian Act and Canada Elections Act concerning voting by Indians, 15 December 1959, 5.
48. This was a major committee set up by the Diefenbaker government to look into relations between First Nations and the Canadian state, with the ultimate goal of revising the *Indian Act*, which had not been reformed in any significant way since 1950. The awarding of the right to vote on the federal level to First Nations was one of the issues it discussed.
49. LAC, MG32-B1/Vol. 88/File IA-12 J, A brief submitted by the Primate of all Canada on behalf of the Anglican Church of Canada to the Joint

Committee of the Senate and the House of Commons on Indian Affairs, January 1960, 5.

50. LAC, MG32-B1/Vol. 88/File IA-12 J, Brief Prepared by the Aboriginal Native Rights Regional Committee of the Interior Tribes of British Columbia, 20.
51. Generally speaking, the Crown concluded treaties with First Nations in parts of Atlantic Canada, Ontario, Quebec, Manitoba, Saskatchewan, and Alberta when British settlers first arrived in what became Canada by which the First Nations agreed to surrender large tracts of their land and live on reservations for compensation of some sort, usually financial. However, there were no treaties for the longest time with First Nations in British Columbia, the Métis (Indigenous people of mixed First Nation and European descent), and Indigenous peoples in the territories (Inuit). The treaties that did exist between the Crown and the First Nations were often not honoured though, which was a rightful cause of complaint by those First Nations that had signed the treaties in good faith.
52. This was a reference to the continued right of First Nations living on reserves not to have to pay tax on any income they earned there.
53. LAC, MG32-B1/Vol. 95/File IA-166/File 1, Extract from the *Saskatoon Star-Phoenix* – 'Senate Group Approves Federal Vote for Indians,' 1 April 1960.
54. LAC, MG32-B1/Vol. 95/File IA-166/File 1, Fred. R. & David Conroy Barristers et al. to Department of Citizenship and Immigration, 2 April 1960.
55. LAC, MG32-B1/Vol. 95/File IA-166/File 1, H. B. M. Best, Private Secretary, Minister to Fred R. & David Conroy Barristers et al., 11 April 1960, 2–3.
56. LAC, MG32-B1/Vol. 95/File IA-166/File 1, Extract from the *Globe and Mail* 'The Indian and the Vote,' 4 April 1960.
57. LAC, MG32-B1/Vol. 95/File IA-166/File 1, Extract from the *Regina Leader-Post* – 'Guarantee Indian's rights,' 14 April 1960.
58. LAC, MG32-B1/Vol. 95/File IA-166/File 1, Letter by Fairclough, 20 May 1960.
59. LAC, MG32-B1/Vol. 95/File IA-166/File 1, Translation of letter from Chief Alphonse T. Picard to Fairclough, 6 June 1960.
60. LAC, MG32-B1/Vol. 95/File IA-166/File 1, Fairclough to Chief Alphonse T. Picard, 20 June 1960; Fairclough to Chief Councillor Alex Oakes, 13 June 1960, 2.
61. LAC, MG32-B1/Vol. 95/File 1A-166/File 1, Press Release, 28 June 1960.

Bibliography

Benvenuti, Andrea and Stuart Ward. "Britain, Europe, and the 'Other Quiet Revolution' in Canada." In *Canada and the End of Empire*, edited by Phil Buckner: 165–82. Vancouver: UBC Press, 2006.

Bothwell, Robert. *The Penguin History of Canada*. Toronto: Penguin Canada, 2006. Cardinal, Linda, and Marie-Joie Brady. "Citizenship and Federalism in Canada: A Difficult Relationship." In *Contemporary Canadian Federalism: Foundations, Traditions, Institutions*, edited by Alain-G. Gagnon: Chapter 15. Toronto: University of Toronto Press, 2009.

Carty, R. Kenneth and W. Peter Ward. "The Making of a Canadian Political Citizenship." In *National Politics and Community in Canada*, edited by R. Kenneth Carty and W. Peter Ward: 65–79. Vancouver: UBC Press, 1986.

Gabriel, Christina. "Citizens and Citizenship." In *Critical Concepts: An introduction to politics*, edited by Janine Brodie and Sandra Rein: Chapter 12. Toronto: Pearson, 2009.

Granatstein, Jack L. *Canada 1957–1967: The Years of Uncertainty and Innovation*. Toronto: McClelland and Stewart, 1986.

Igartua, Jose. "'Ready, Aye, Ready' No More?." In *Rediscovering the British World*, edited by Phil Buckner: 47–65. Calgary: University of Calgary Press, 2005.

Jenson, Jane. "Citizenship Claims: Routes to Representation in a Federal System." In *Rethinking Federalism: Citizens, Markets and Governments in a Changing World*, edited by Karen Knop, Sylvia Ostry, Richard Simeon, and Katherine Swinton: 99–118. Vancouver: UBC Press, 1995.

Johnston, Darlene. "First Nations and Canadian Citizenship." In *Belonging: The Meaning and Future of Canadian Citizenship*, edited by William Kaplan: 349–67. Montreal & Kingston: McGill-Queen's University Press, 1993.

Kaplan, William. "Who Belongs? Changing Concepts of Citizenship and Nationality." In *Belonging: The Meaning and Future of Canadian Citizenship*, edited by William Kaplan: 245–64. Montreal & Kingston: McGill-Queen's University Press, 1993.

Knowles, Valerie. *Forging our Legacy: Canadian Citizenship and Immigration, 1900–1977*. Ottawa: Citizenship and Immigration Canada, 1997.

Kymlicka, Will and Wayne Norman. "Return of the Citizen: A Survey of Recent Work on Citizenship Theory." *Ethics* 104, 1994: 352–81.

Mann, Jatinder. "The evolution of Commonwealth citizenship, 1945–48 in Canada, Britain and Australia." *Commonwealth and Comparative Politics* 50, 3, July 2012: 293–313. https://doi.org/10.1080/14662043.2012.692923

Mann, Jatinder. *The Search for a New National Identity: The Rise of Multiculturalism in Canada and Australia, 1890s-1970s*. New York: Peter Lang Publishing, 2016.

Marshall, T. H. Citizenship and Social Development: Essays by T. *H. Marshall*. Westport, Connecticut: Greenwood Press, 1964.

Pearson, Lester. "Symbols and realities." In *Mike: The Memoirs of the Right Honourable Lester B. Pearson: Volume 3, 1957–1968*, edited by J. A. Munro and A. I. Inglis. London: Victor Gollancz, 1975.

Thomson, Dale C. Louis St. *Laurent: Canadian*. New York: St. Martin's Press, 1968.

CHAPTER 6

The Bridge Between Imperial and Multicultural Belonging: Non-citizen Voting Rights and Aotearoa New Zealand's Citizenship Regime

Kate McMillan

Introduction

In 2016, New Zealanders voted on whether to change their national flag. Central to public debates in the lead-up to the referendum was the question of whether the existing flag, which combines the Union Jack and four stars representing the Southern Cross, remained an appropriate national emblem in the twenty-first century. Winston Peters, leader of Aotearoa

I am extremely grateful to the editor of this collection, Jatinder Mann, for his detailed feedback and helpful suggestions on my chapter.

K. McMillan (✉)
School of History, Philosophy, Politics, and International Relations, Te Herenga Waka / Victoria University of Wellington, Wellington, New Zealand
e-mail: kate.mcmillan@vuw.ac.nz

J. Mann (ed.), *Citizenship in Transnational Perspective*, Politics of Citizenship and Migration,
https://doi.org/10.1007/978-3-031-34358-2_6

New Zealand's populist and nationalistic New Zealand First Party, argued that because the flag debate was about Aotearoa New Zealand's national identity, only citizens and not what he called "outsiders"[1] should be able to participate. "Why", he asked, "should thousands of immigrants who have come here in recent years be involved in making a decision that goes, in the words of the flag committee, 'to the very heart of who we are and what we are as a nation'?"[2]

Peters' comments refer to the fact that non-citizen immigrants have been able to vote in national elections and referenda in Aotearoa New Zealand since 1975. Aotearoa New Zealand is one of only five countries (the others are Malawi, Chile, Ecuador, and Uruguay) to extend this right to all permanent residents, but of those five is by far the most lenient, requiring only that immigrants are continuously and legally resident in the country for at least one year before they get to vote. It is this feature of Aotearoa New Zealand's citizenship regime that distinguishes it most clearly from those of Canada and Australia; two countries where, as in Aotearoa New Zealand, a "national" model of citizenship and political community evolved gradually and in some respects incompletely over the nineteenth and twentieth centuries out of the British imperial model of belonging. In Aotearoa New Zealand's case, the granting of national voting rights to non-citizens has given its post-imperial model of political community a highly flexible and permeable character. It has also, I argue, led the Aotearoa New Zealand government to promote an unusually inclusive definition of national citizenship.

This chapter explores the nature of Aotearoa New Zealand's citizenship "regime",[3] with a particular focus on the role that non-citizen voting rights have played in Aotearoa New Zealand's evolution from the Commonwealth's "most dutiful daughter"[4] to what Foreign Minister Murray McCully described in 2012 as a "young multicultural country".[5] I place Aotearoa New Zealand's franchise law in the context of other aspects of its citizenship regime: its membership rules and categories; the gradated set of rights associated with different membership categories; and attempts by the state to communicate the nature of national citizenship.

The chapter begins by identifying the membership classes available to those associated with the Aotearoa New Zealand polity and the rules governing their allocation. A second section examines the public welfare and political goods available to those in each membership class. The third section traces the process by which Aotearoa New Zealand parliamentarians came to adopt the most liberal franchise rules in the world for non-citizens in 1975. Here I argue that non-citizen national voting rights were less the product of an innovative desire to enfranchise new immigrants from diverse national backgrounds than the result of a lingering reluctance to distinguish non-citizen "Britons" from their imperial kin, white "New Zealanders". As such, non-citizen voting rights functioned as a hyphen connecting the older British model of imperial political community to the national model evolving in its place. In the contemporary period, however, this same hyphen now serves to connect immigrants from a diverse range of national backgrounds with Aotearoa New Zealand citizens, creating in the process a political community whose borders are highly permeable to international migrants.

Such permeability has implications for official narratives about the nature and advantages of citizenship, and about the link between formal membership, rights, and identity. In most countries, the borders around the community of citizens and the political community are co-terminus, providing states with a core membership over which to exercise processes of identity building for purposes of both state legitimacy and social solidarity. In Aotearoa New Zealand, however, non-citizen voting rights mean that the community of citizens is a *subset* of the political community, necessitating a more broadly inclusive explanation of the membership–rights nexus.

The next section, then, examines the 2014 official publication, *Choice Whiriwhiria: The New Zealand Citizenship Story Te Kōrero Raraunga o Aotearoa*, through which the centre-right National Government then in power sought to promote a national citizenship model. It is a model that is accessible to, and inclusive of, new members, whilst also appealing to what might be called "legacy" members—that is, New Zealanders whose membership is inherited and may, in some cases, extend back many generations. Ten years after its publication *Choice Whiriwhiria* is still promoted by the Department of Internal Affairs, the government department responsible for issuing citizenship to new migrants.

Membership Categories and Rules Governing Their Allocation in Aotearoa New Zealand

Nationally constituted communities draw boundaries around themselves through establishing a range of membership categories or classes. These specify who belongs and who does not, the criteria for membership, and the processes by which an individual can move from one membership category to another. They can include full, inalienable membership (citizenship), more partial and temporary categories (such as permanent or temporary residency), and non-membership. Such categories are the referent categories used in legislation and policy specifying the distribution of legal, welfare, and political goods at the state's disposal among those in each of the various classes.

In Aotearoa New Zealand, four broad categories of membership exist: New Zealand citizen, New Zealand Permanent Resident, New Zealand Resident, and temporary visitor. Several contemporary features of this categorisation system and the processes by which it operates are notable. First, Aotearoa New Zealand's immigration legislation and policy continues to play a major role in determining the criteria for entry into different residency and visitor categories, in allocating new members into particular categories, and in determining the proportion of the population who fall into each of the various available categories. In many respects, citizenship policy in Aotearoa New Zealand is immigration policy's shadow.

Second, as a result of high levels of immigration from diverse source countries prior to the COVID-19 pandemic, and the creation of multiple membership classes over the past couple of decades, a much larger proportion of the local population fall into partial and temporary forms of membership than has been the case in the past.

Third, high levels of immigration prior to the pandemic, combined with the multinational nature of the Aotearoa New Zealand Realm,[6] and Aotearoa New Zealand's liberal approach to dual citizenship mean a large proportion of those who hold a membership status within the Aotearoa New Zealand political community concurrently hold memberships in other political communities.

Lastly, due to Aotearoa New Zealand's geographical isolation, inhospitable sea barriers, and effective airport security, few of those on the Aotearoa New Zealand territory at any one time will not have some form of legal Aotearoa New Zealand membership status.

Citizenship, the premier class of membership in Aotearoa New Zealand, can be obtained in three ways: *jus soli, jus sanguinis*, and by grant. *Jus soli* in Aotearoa New Zealand was inherited from the British imperial model of subjecthood under which all those born in territories claimed as British were British subjects and, as Caroline Sawyer and Helena Wray point out, was based on concepts of allegiance that pre-date the concept of nationality.[7] Aotearoa New Zealand was slow to change from this model, maintaining full *jus soli* for a decade after the UK itself withdrew it from those without a British citizen or permanent resident parent. Prior to 2005, *jus soli* was available to all children born on Aotearoa New Zealand soil but the *Citizenship Amendment Act* 2005 restricted it to those born in Aotearoa New Zealand to an Aotearoa New Zealand citizen or resident parent.[8]

Jus sanguinis is available to those born overseas to an Aotearoa New Zealand citizen or resident parent but cannot be passed on to subsequent generations, something that has caused some controversy, particularly in relation to Māori born overseas.[9] A grant of citizenship is available to those who can meet character, English language, residency, intention to reside, and knowledge of the rights and privileges of Aotearoa New Zealand citizenship requirements. In 2005, the residency requirements for citizenship were increased from three to five years.[10]

Non-citizen Voting Rights in Aotearoa New Zealand

In practice, there is little to distinguish *jus soli, jus sanguinis*, or citizenship by grant, except that citizenship by grant may be revoked if it is found to have been obtained via fraud, false representation, or wilful concealment of relevant information.[11] Most significantly, all three prioritise residency over other principles of belonging, such as ancestry or commitment to and knowledge of particular cultural characteristics.

Jus soli and *jus sanguinis* citizenship have also been extended to Cook Island, Tokelauan, and Niuean nationals since the *British Nationality and New Zealand Citizenship Act* 1948 bestowed the status of Aotearoa New Zealand citizenship onto all British subjects who had been born in Aotearoa New Zealand, naturalised in Aotearoa New Zealand, resident in Aotearoa New Zealand for twelve months, or born to a father who had been born in Aotearoa New Zealand or naturalised in Aotearoa New Zealand.[12] As the Cook Islands, Tokelau, and Niue were Aotearoa New Zealand territories at the time of the Act, and thus British subjects, they too became Aotearoa New Zealand citizens when the Act came into force on 1 January 1949. Cook Islanders and Niueans retained their status as Aotearoa New Zealand citizens even after their countries assumed the status of self-government in free association with Aotearoa New Zealand in 1965 and 1974, respectively. Tokelau remains a part of the territory of Aotearoa New Zealand and its nationals are Aotearoa New Zealand citizens.

If Aotearoa New Zealand citizenship might be considered the premier status membership in Aotearoa New Zealand, "Silver" status would be that of Permanent Resident, a visa status granted by the New Zealand Immigration Service. Successful applicants for permanent residency status must have already lived in Aotearoa New Zealand on an Aotearoa New Zealand Resident visa for at least two years, including for the three months immediately prior to their application, and have met the terms of their resident visa, be able to prove their identity, meet character requirements, and be committed to living in Aotearoa New Zealand permanently. Additional requirements exist for those who seek to transfer from an Investor Residence category to Permanent Resident status.[13]

Another form of permanent residency exists within the Aotearoa New Zealand Realm: Cook Islanders and Niueans hold permanent residency in their home islands, a status only available for those who qualify by birth or ancestry rules set out in the constitutions of the Cook Islands and Niue. Cook Islanders and Niueans thus hold a kind of dual status as Aotearoa New Zealand citizens and permanent residents or nationals of their home islands.

A third-tier membership class is that of Aotearoa New Zealand Resident, available via a range of Residency visas developed by Immigration New Zealand in line with the government's wider economic, social, and security policy goals. In 2023, these included a variety of business, family, skilled migrant, and work-to-residence visas, along with special visas available to those from the Pacific, and for those entering Aotearoa New Zealand under its Refugee and Humanitarian categories. In order to be granted one of these residence visas, applicants must meet the immigration criteria specific to each visa type: criteria designed in most cases to ensure that those who are granted residency in Aotearoa New Zealand help "grow a stronger economy" and create jobs.[14]

Alongside the three residence membership classes are a range of temporary visas allowing holders to be present in Aotearoa New Zealand for time-limited periods: student visas, temporary work visas, visitor visas, and transit visas. Each of the membership categories discussed above brings with it access to a set of welfare and political public goods. These are laid out in the next section.

Membership Classes and Access to Public Goods in Aotearoa New Zealand

Access to the residence categories outlined in the previous section is competitive and can usually only be gained by those with considerable labour, educational, or financial resources to invest in the country. Once obtained, however, residence status gives almost immediate access to a wide range of publicly created goods. Permanent Residents can access most of the welfare benefits available to citizens, although some are only available after two years' residence.[15] After five years' residence in Aotearoa New Zealand, Permanent Resident visa holders are eligible to apply for New Zealand citizenship.

Those on a New Zealand Resident visa are also eligible for many of the benefits of citizenship and permanent residency. They are, for example, able to reside indefinitely in Aotearoa New Zealand and are eligible for publicly funded health and disability care, early childhood, primary and secondary education services, and domestic fees for tertiary education. The main difference between the public welfare goods available to New Zealand Residents and New Zealand Permanent Residents is that Residents are not eligible for a range of income support benefits such as the jobseeker support (unemployment) benefit; accommodation support; child support (including disability); and superannuation.[16] Many will be eligible to apply for Permanent Resident status after two years' residence in Aotearoa New Zealand and three years after that for New Zealand citizenship.

In addition, under Aotearoa New Zealand law, both Australian citizens and those with an Australian Permanent Resident visa who travel to Aotearoa New Zealand under the Trans-Tasman Travel Arrangement (a free travel arrangement agreed to by the Aotearoa New Zealand and Australian prime ministers in 1973) are treated as having New Zealand Permanent Residency status and are entitled to the same public welfare goods as New Zealand Permanent Residents.

For those on temporary visas, such as work and student visas, eligibility for publicly funded welfare benefits depends on the terms of the visa, particularly its length. The children of those on some work permits and student visas may be eligible for free early childhood, primary and secondary education, and free vaccinations, accident compensation payments to cover the cost of treatment for accidents, and some forms of emergency and compulsory healthcare services.[17] Many of those on temporary visas will seek to transfer on to a permanent visa after a period of time.

What really distinguishes the Aotearoa New Zealand citizenship regime—and not only from Australia and Canada's but also from almost all other democracies—however, is the right of those on Permanent Resident and Resident visas, including Aotearoa New Zealand-resident Australian citizens and Permanent Residents, to vote in national and local body elections after one year's legal residence. A consequence of non-citizen voting rights is that the "political community", as constituted by those who have national decision-making power, is inclusive of a large number of migrants who have been resident in Aotearoa New Zealand only for a short period of time, and who may or may not plan on living permanently in Aotearoa New Zealand.

This is consistent with Aotearoa New Zealand's emphasis on residency rather than ancestry or formalised loyalty through naturalisation as a method of allocating membership and the goods associated with it. It also does more to protect the political rights of internationally mobile individuals than do more traditional national models of political community which make much greater loyalty and identity demands on such individuals at the expense of their political agency. As is explored in the next section, however, this multicultural, immigrant-friendly form of political community was, perhaps ironically, the product of Aotearoa New Zealand's reluctance to let go of an imperially constituted model of national community.

Non-citizen Voting Rights and Multicultural Political Integration in Aotearoa New Zealand

The ability to participate in self-government is a defining feature of contemporary citizenship. It follows that franchise laws, which define the "self" to be governed, are also a central element of any citizenship regime. In almost all countries, the ability to participate in national elections is restricted to citizens,[18] although exceptions exist in some countries for citizens of former colonies. The extension of voting rights to non-citizens in local and regional elections, on the other hand, is common enough for David Earnest to query whether it is emerging as an international "democratic norm".[19] Such norms have, however, been established relatively recently, particularly where national citizenship emerged out of a slow and sometimes reluctant process of decolonisation.

In Aotearoa New Zealand, as in Canada and Australia, the decision to cease using British subjecthood as a qualification for voting did not emerge until quarter of a century after each country passed national citizenship laws. The new franchise arrangements, which limited voting rights to citizens in the case of Canada and Australia[20] but not Aotearoa New Zealand, were precipitated by Britain's own gradual replacement of an imperial conception of political community with a nationally constituted one.[21]

Until 1975, Aotearoa New Zealand's electoral laws required that voters be a "British subject ordinarily resident in NZ [who] had resided in NZ continuously for at least 1 year". With the passing of the *Electoral Amendment Act* 1975, the "British subject" part of this requirement was dropped, leaving the residency requirement that remains in force today. Only citizens, however, were allowed to stand for Parliament.

Aotearoa New Zealand law makers in 1975 were aware that an emerging international norm tied franchise rights to citizenship. The Select Committee considering the law change had been given extracts from Michael Ameller's 1966 study of parliaments, which clearly identified nationality as the "primary condition" for voting rights in electoral laws around the world.[22] They also had access to detailed reports about Canada's decision to replace British subjecthood with Canadian citizenship as a qualification for voting in 1975, and Australian debates about doing the same.

Other parts of the proposed electoral amendment, however, garnered much more attention and debate than those relating to the franchise: those relating to Māori electoral representation, reduction of the voting age from twenty-one to eighteen, prisoners' voting rights, and mechanisms for establishing electoral boundaries. Only three out of thirty-four submissions to the Select Committee focused on the proposed deletion of British subjecthood as a requirement for voting rights. All three of these were in favour of removing subjecthood, but only the Republican Movement suggested replacing it with Aotearoa New Zealand citizenship, saying:

> The Electoral Act is one of the ugliest colonial fossils embedded in New Zealand's legislative record. Many of its provisions are simply carry-overs from the British Parliamentary Representation Act. It gives foreigners from England a vote in a country which is not theirs.[23]

The other two submissions were concerned that the introduction of a citizenship requirement would "discriminate" against permanent residents who, in the words of the Auckland Labour Club, "have as much concern about this country as citizens".[24] This view appeared to be shared by the Select Committee and the Government of the day. In the second reading of the *Electoral Amendment Bill* 1975, Labour Member the Hon. Michael Bassett said:

> Some people born in other countries have liked to go through the naturalization ceremomy and become New Zealand citizens, but some have not wanted to do that. It has often been a matter of like or dislike of the ceremony, and I do not see why the right to vote should be attached to those people who are prepared to go through the ceremony and denied to the others.[25]

Analyses of the 1975 decision have focused on both Aotearoa New Zealand's liberality and pragmatism in relation to franchise rights. Christina Rodríguez, for example, has argued that "New Zealand's identity as a nation-state is intimately tied to its status as a historical, global leader in the expansion of the franchise".[26] Fiona Barker and Kate McMillan also identify liberal egalitarianism as an influential factor in the 1975 decision but suggest that "this inclusiveness was intended less for ethnic minority non-citizens than it was for the 'kin migrants'[27] from the UK who dominated migrant flows at that time".[28]

Over 97% of the Aotearoa New Zealand population in 1975 were categorised as either European or Māori, and the vast majority would have been British subjects.[29] Dropping the "British subject" franchise requirement in 1975, then, really only enfranchised the few "alien" migrants who were neither British subjects nor naturalised New Zealanders, most of whom were Dutch, American, or Yugoslavian, and the non-naturalised proportion of the 2.6% of the population comprising non-European migrants, primarily from Fiji, Tonga, India, and China,[30] some of whom would have been British subjects in any case. The imposition of an Aotearoa New Zealand citizenship requirement, on the other hand, would have disenfranchised many non-naturalised British subjects who had previously enjoyed the right to vote. A reluctance to do the latter is apparent in the Select Committee's concern that a number of British and Irish migrants had not naturalised and would, therefore, be unable to vote if citizenship became necessary for voting rights.[31]

It would be overstating the case, however, to say that citizenship was seen by lawmakers in 1975 as irrelevant to the constitution of the political community. In relation to passive voting rights, that is, the right to stand for Parliament, Aotearoa New Zealand followed the international norm of limiting eligibility to citizens: clearly, citizenship was thought to carry some heft in relation to distinguishing members from non-members of the political community. Further, it must be noted that the Electoral Select Committee did not actually rule out citizenship as a basis for voting rights. Rather, prevaricating, they recommended that the introduction of such a requirement be considered more fully the following year by a Committee which they expected would be established to "consolidate" the new electoral legislation.[32] In the event, no such Committee was established, and the residency requirement remained in place.

The historical record thus provides little if any evidence for the view that the parliamentarians who decided in 1975 to create non-citizen voting rights in national elections envisaged a future in which tens of thousands of new migrants from all around the world would annually become eligible for national voting rights in Aotearoa New Zealand after twelve months' residency. Nor does it seem likely they imagined that the new law would create a unique and innovative, "multicultural" model of political integration, unmatched elsewhere in the world. Indeed, as Barker and McMillan argue, it seems more probable that "the granting of voting rights to non-citizens looks less like an example of New Zealand politicians exercising a national trait of franchise inclusivity and more like another example of a 'quick fix' measure that endured past its intended use-by date".[33]

Nonetheless, the law has remained almost wholly uncontroversial since its introduction. Winston Peters' comment, cited above, provides an exception to the general rule that non-citizen voting rights remain a feature of Aotearoa New Zealand's electoral system that is more remarked upon outside of the country than within. Yet, the context in which non-citizen voting rights now operate is quite different to that in which the policy was developed. What was originally conceived of as a policy to smooth the transition from imperial franchise qualifications to national ones now operates in an "age of migration",[34] characterised in the Aotearoa New Zealand case by high levels of inward and outward migration, from and to a highly diverse range of countries. In 1975, the vast majority of non-citizens were not only co-members of a fading British Empire but also co-ethnics; by 2016, those non-citizens are just as likely to be Chinese,

Filipino, Indian, or Korean. Moreover, where in 1975 those unnaturalised British immigrants who were the target of the law were, in most cases, permanently settled in Aotearoa New Zealand, a good proportion of those who are enfranchised by the law in 2016 were not settled and may never settle permanently in Aotearoa New Zealand. And, of those who do, many will retain an active interest and, frequently, citizenship in their country of origin.

Citizenship as "Choice": Explaining the Citizenship–Rights Nexus in Aotearoa New Zealand

Any process of defining membership categories, such as citizenship, requires a certain logic of belonging: some criteria to justify the inclusion of some and exclusion of others, as well as the distribution of goods to some but not others. In the Aotearoa New Zealand context, in which the borders around different membership categories do not neatly coincide with the welfare and political or even cultural communities (see Spoonley in this collection), the logic of belonging, and of the rights–membership nexus, needs to be a particularly inclusive one.

It is in this context that the New Zealand Department of Internal Affairs, responsible for administering Aotearoa New Zealand citizenship policy and practice, produced a document in 2014 entitled *Choice Whiriwhiria: The New Zealand Citizenship Story*. The document, intended primarily to "welcome new citizens", asserts a vision of national citizenship that responds to the demands of inclusivity and diversity described above. Its name is illustrative:

> 'Choice' is a word that has two meanings in New Zealand. One meaning is to decide on an action or option. The other, more informal, meaning is 'good, great, excellent'. 'It's choice!' Choice here is expressed as Whiriwhiria. 'Whiri' is the word which means 'choice' in Māori. It also means 'plait', and the two meanings are thought to originate from the constant choices made as weavers selected each thread to plait together. It's a great image of the way different people and cultures draw together to create New Zealand society.[35]

Presenting the stories of eleven citizens who have migrated from Malaysia, Somalia, Zimbabwe, Syria, Austria, China, Samoa, Colombia, India, Canada, and Ireland, the document details what each citizen immigrant likes about Aotearoa New Zealand and their pride in becoming New Zealanders. While the instrumental benefits of Aotearoa New Zealand citizenship are identified by some in relation to the ease of travel on an Aotearoa New Zealand passport, the overwhelming emphasis is on things such as how safe, friendly, and beautiful Aotearoa New Zealand is, the quality of life it offers, and how lucky the immigrants feel to live there.

Several things are notable about *Choice Whiriwhiria* and the vision of citizenship it presents. First, most interestingly, it tells the story of citizenship through immigrants' stories, rather than telling immigrants a story of Aotearoa New Zealand citizenship with the explicit or implicit assumption that they fit themselves appropriately into that story. It imposes no expectations on immigrants that they conform to particular "Aotearoa New Zealand" cultural norms or values, although it does lay out the legal basis of constitutional government in Aotearoa New Zealand and identifies the rights and duties of Aotearoa New Zealand citizenship, along with a legal history of Aotearoa New Zealand citizenship.

Aesthetically, the document references the beauty of Aotearoa New Zealand's natural environment. The cover design maps Aotearoa New Zealand as a starry constellation in the night sky; below, early dawn lights a path across calm sea towards a distant bay. Notes explain that the cover design concept is derived from the Māori New Year celebration of Matariki (a particular constellation that appears in southern skies in mid-winter) and, as such, references "new life, new beginnings".[36]

Centrally, citizenship is portrayed as something that can be *chosen*, not something that is necessary in order to enjoy the benefits associated with formal membership. Through the eyes of the immigrants whose stories the document tells, citizenship is an emotional attachment and commitment to Aotearoa New Zealand, itself portrayed as a natural environment, an outdoor lifestyle, a friendly people, and a long-standing democracy. These are all, notably, features of Aotearoa New Zealand's international branding, used extensively in tourist and immigrant attraction materials abroad, suggesting considerable alignment between constructions of national identity and citizenship for political and commercial purposes.[37]

Choice Whiriwhiria thus plays little attention to historical narratives of national identity or character and, in so doing, enacts a welcoming of individuals from diverse national, ethnic, religious, and cultural backgrounds, demanding little from them in the way of conformity to the contours of a pre-existing nationally constituted political community. It is, in other words, a highly inclusive vision of citizenship that asserts citizenship as a way to bind together the multicultural population of a country with high levels of inward and outward migration.

Conclusion

As was the case in Australia and Canada, Aotearoa New Zealand's citizenship regime has developed rather gradually and incompletely out of the British imperial model of belonging and loyalty. Aotearoa New Zealand took many of the steps involved in this transition only reluctantly. In 1947, for example, when Canada announced it was to create the status of Canadian citizenship, the Aotearoa New Zealand Under-Secretary of Justice said, "It is very doubtful whether there is any general desire in New Zealand for the creation of a New Zealand nationality or citizenship as distinct from British nationality. I believe that if any Bill of this type were introduced in New Zealand it would have a mixed, and probably hostile reception."[38] He was right: when Aotearoa New Zealand's hand was forced by the passing of the *British Nationality Act* 1948, which required Commonwealth countries to pass national citizenship legislation,[39] the Aotearoa New Zealand Minister of Internal Affairs, W. E. Parry, said: "Speaking for New Zealand, I am bound to say that this action would not have been initiated by our Government at the present time. We did not seek this freedom for ourselves."[40]

Such loyalty to Empire and Commonwealth was still apparent in 1975 when Aotearoa New Zealand politicians demonstrated a greater reluctance than Australia and Canada to replace an imperially derived understanding of political community with a "national" one. That reluctance, however, has had what appear to be unintended consequences. With more than 25% of Aotearoa New Zealand's population now born overseas,[41] and with Asia the region in which more immigrants were born than any other region,[42] non-citizen voting rights now perform a function quite different from that they were designed to perform in 1975. Originally intended to minimise distinctions between naturalised and non-naturalised kin migrants, non-citizen voting rights went on to facilitate the political incorporation of highly diverse immigrants.

Official attempts to explain what Aotearoa New Zealand citizenship means have, as a result, relied heavily on civic rather than ethnic understandings of "nation" or identity, illustrated particularly through references to Aotearoa New Zealand's physical rather than cultural or political landscape.

As the flag debate illustrated, however, persuading the public of the logic of the membership–rights–identity nexus portrayed through the *Choice Whiriwhiria* document remains an incomplete project. The Union Jack still flutters in the corner of the national flag, but the referenda "ignit[ed] unexpectedly intense passions encompassing wildly conflicting notions of nationhood, identity, culture and identity".[43] Older imperial notions of belonging and identity jostled both with exclusive nationalistic ones and with more recent conceptions of Aotearoa New Zealand as a multicultural, lifestyle-oriented destination for internationally mobile residents.

These competing conceptions are visible in the Word Cloud (Fig. 6.1) developed out of more than 20,000 submissions in response to the Flag Consideration Project's requests for statements about what they, as New Zealanders, stood for and what the Aotearoa New Zealand flag should stand for. Here, font size reflects the frequency with which each word appeared in the submissions. We see older conceptions of belonging, membership, and identity—such as "commonwealth", "heritage", and "British"—appearing in middle-sized fonts, as do newer forms of identity—such as "kiwi", "pacific", and "Māori"—along with a range of other terms referencing landscape, culture, history, and civic values. In the largest fonts, however, are the words "equality", "history", and "freedom". As this chapter has argued, "equality" and "freedom" as understood by politicians clinging on to imperial concepts of belonging led, in one historical context, to the granting of national voting rights for non-citizens. These voting rights, and the values that underpin them, are now enacted in a quite different post-imperial, multicultural context characterised by high levels of migration from diverse source countries.

Fig. 6.1 "What we stand for." Source: http://www.standfor.co.nz/

The future contours of Aotearoa New Zealand's citizenship regime will continue to be shaped by dynamic interaction between the ideals of equality and freedom, as well as other logics of membership, belonging, rights, and identity. In the Aotearoa New Zealand case, unlike most other democracies, residents as well as citizens will have a say in how those logics are translated into policies, and how those policies, in turn, are narrated as logic.

Notes

1. Sam Sachdeva, "Winston Peters: only NZ citizens should be able to vote in flag referendum," Stuff.co.nz, 28 February 2016. Available: http://www.stuff.co.nz/national/politics/77355528/Winston-Peters-only-NZ-citizens-should-be-able-to-vote-in-flag-referendum [Accessed 4 June 2016].
2. Ibid.
3. Jane Jenson, "The European Union's Citizenship Regime. Creating Norms and Building Practices," *Comparative European Politics* 5 (2007): 53–65; Maarten Peter Vink and Rainer Bauböck, "Citizenship configurations: Analysing the multiple purposes of citizenship regimes in Europe," *Comparative European Politics* 11, 5 (2013): 621–648.
4. William K. Hancock, *Survey of British Commonwealth Affairs* (London: Oxford University Press, 1940).
5. Murray McCully, "Speech to China Foreign Affairs University Beijing," Beehive. govt.nz, 6 April 2012. Available: https://www.beehive.govt.nz/speech/speech-china-foreign-affairs-university-beijing. [Accessed 8 June 2016].
6. The Realm of Aotearoa New Zealand includes all those territories over which the King of Aotearoa New Zealand is sovereign and includes Aotearoa New Zealand, the Cook Islands, Niue, Tokelau, and the Ross Dependency.
7. Caroline Sawyer and Helena Wray, *EUDO Citizenship Observatory Country Report: United Kingdom* (Florence: European Union Institute, 2013). Available: http://cadmus.eui.eu/bitstream/handle/1814/33839/EUDO-CIT_2014_01_UK.pdf?sequence=1; Kate Macmillan and Anna Hood, *Country Report: New Zealand Citizenship* (Italy: European University Institute and European Democracy Observatory, 2016). Available: http://cadmus.eui.eu/handle/1814/42648
8. Provisions for citizenship by birth are also available to children born outside Aotearoa New Zealand to an Aotearoa New Zealand citizen parent who is the head of an Aotearoa New Zealand mission; an employee of the

State Services; a person working overseas for the public service of Niue, Tokelau, or the Cook Islands; an office or employee of New Zealand Trade and Enterprise; or an officer or employee of the New Zealand Tourism Board. *Jus soli* provisions also exist for people who would have been born in Tokelau and have been Aotearoa New Zealand citizens by birth but who out of medical necessity were born in Samoa. Macmillan and Hood, *Country Report: New Zealand Citizenship.*

9. Simon Collins, "18 percent of Māori now live overseas," *New Zealand Herald*, 29 November 2011. Available: http://www.nzherald.co.nz/nz/news/article.cfm?c_id=1&objectid=10769488
10. Specifically, applicants are required to have been present in Aotearoa New Zealand for 1350 days in the five years preceding their application, including at least 240 days in each of those years.
11. New Zealand Government, "Being stripped of New Zealand Citizenship." Available: https://www.govt.nz/browse/nz-passports-and-citizenship/changing-your-nz-citizenship/being-stripped-of-nz-citizenship/
12. *The British Nationality and New Zealand Citizenship Act* 1948 also bestowed Aotearoa New Zealand citizenship on British subjects born in Western Samoa immediately prior to the commencement of the Act, or who was married to someone eligible for Aotearoa New Zealand citizenship. Macmillan and Hood, *Country Report: New Zealand Citizenship.*
13. Immigration New Zealand, "Operational Manual," Immigration New Zealand, Wellington, 2016. Available: http://onlineservices.immigration.govt.nz/opsmanual/
14. Ministry of Business, Innovation, and Employment (MBIE), "Vote Immigration: Briefing to the Incoming Minister," MBIE, Wellington. Available: http://www.mbie.govt.nz/publications-research/publications/mbie-corporate/Immigration.pdf
15. Superannuation (universal old age benefit) requires a ten-year residency in Aotearoa New Zealand, five of which must be after the age of fifty but is available to those who meet the residency requirements. Ministry of Social Development, "Residency requirements for New Zealand benefits and pensions," Work and Income, Wellington, 2016. Available: http://www.workandincome.govt.nz/pensions/travelling-or-moving/moving-to-nz/residency-requirements-for-new-zealand-benefits-and-pensions.html#null
16. Ministry of Social Development, "A-Z benefits and payments," Work and Income, Wellington, 2016. Available: http://www.workandincome.govt.nz/products/a-z-benefits/index.html
17. Immigration New Zealand, "Paying for Healthcare services, 2016." Available: https://www.newzealandnow.govt.nz/living-in-nz/healthcare/paying-for-healthcare-services

18. André Blais, Louis Massicotte, and Antoine Yoshinaka, "Deciding who has the right to vote: a comparative analysis of election laws," *Electoral Studies* 20, 1 (2001): 41–62; European Union Democracy Observatory on Citizenship, "Conditions for Electoral Rights," 2015. Available: http://eudo-citizenship.eu/electoral-rights/conditions-for-electoral-rights-2015 [Accessed 8 June 2016].
19. David Earnest, "Noncitizen Voting Rights: A Survey of an Emerging Democratic Norm" (Paper prepared for delivery at the American Political Science Association meeting, 2003). Available: http://ww2.odu.edu/~dearnest/pdfs/Earnest_APSA_2003.pdf
20. With some exceptions for British subjects previously entitled or enrolled to vote.
21. Kate McMillan, "National Voting Rights for Permanent Residents: New Zealand's Experience," in *Global Migration: Old Assumptions, New Dynamics*, eds. Diego Acosta Arcarazo and Anja Wiesbrock (Santa Barbara: Praeger, 2015).
22. Michael Ameller, *Parliaments: A Comparative Study on the Structure and Functioning of Representative Institutions in Fifty Five Countries*, A new and completely revised edition (London: Cassell, and Interparliamentary Union, 1966). (Archives New Zealand reference number ABCL W4035 Box 8, Record Number E 1/2, Part 2, 1974–1975).
23. Republican Movement of New Zealand, "Submission to the Electoral Select Committee," (Archives New Zealand reference number ABCL W4035 Box 8, Record Number E 1/2, Part 2, 1974–1975).
24. Auckland University Labour Club, "Submission to the Electoral Select Committee," (Archives New Zealand reference number ABCL W4035 Box 8, Record Number E 1/2, Part 2, 1974–1975), cited in McMillan, "National Voting Rights for Permanent Residents."
25. Michael Bassett, "Second Reading of the Electoral Amendment Bill," New Zealand Parliamentary Debates 398 (12 June 1975), 2095.
26. Christina M. Rodríguez, "Noncitizen voting and the extra constitutional construction of the polity," *I • CON* 8, 40 (2010): 30–49.
27. Malcolm McKinnon, *Immigrants and Citizens: New Zealanders and Asian Immigration in Historical Context* (Wellington: Institute of Policy Studies, 1996).
28. Fiona Barker and Kate McMillan, "Constituting the Democratic Public: New Zealand's extension of national voting rights to non-citizens," *New Zealand Journal of Public and International Law* 12, 1 (2014): 61–80.
29. New Zealand Department of Statistics, *The Population of New Zealand 1974, United Nations Committee for International Coordination of National Research in Demography Series* (Wellington: Department of Statistics, 1974). Available: http://www.cicred.org/Eng/Publications/pdf/c-c37.pdf [Accessed 9 June 2016].

30. New Zealand Department of Statistics, *The Population of New Zealand 1974.*
31. Electoral Select Committee, "Report of the Electoral Act Committee 1975," *Appendices to the Journals of the House of Representatives*, I.15, Vol. IV (Wellington: Government Printer, 1975).
32. Electoral Select Committee, "Report of the Electoral Act Committee 1975."
33. Fiona Barker and Kate McMillan, *Access to Electoral Rights: New Zealand* (European University Institute and European Union Democracy Observatory, 2016). Available: http://cadmus.eui.eu/handle/1814/42884
34. Stephen Castles and Mark Miller, *The Age of Migration*, 4th ed. (London: Palgrave Macmillan, 2009).
35. Department of Internal Affairs, *Choice Whiriwhiria: The New Zealand Citizenship Story. Te Kōrero Raraunga o Aotearoa* (2014). Available: https://www.dia.govt.nz/Services-Citizenship-Choice-The-New-Zealand-citizenship-story
36. Ibid.
37. John Urry, *Global Complexity* (Cambridge: Polity Press, 2003).
38. Cited in Kate McMillan, "Developing Citizens. Subject, aliens and citizens in New Zealand since 1840," in *Tangata Tangata The Changing Ethnic Contours of New Zealand*, eds. Paul Spoonley, Cluny Macpherson, and David Pearson (Victoria: Thomson Dunmore Press, 2004).
39. For more on this see Jatinder Mann, "The evolution of Commonwealth citizenship, 1945–48 in Canada, Britain and Australia," *Commonwealth and Comparative Politics* 50, 3 (2012): 293–313.
40. Parry, cited in McMillan, "Developing Citizens."
41. Statistics New Zealand, "2013 Census Quick Stats about culture and identity," 2014. Available: http://www.stats.govt.nz/Census/2013-census/profile-and-summary-reports/quickstats-culture-identity/birthplace.aspx
42. Statistics New Zealand, "2013 Census Quick Stats about culture and identity."
43. Karl du Fresne, "Two flags, 4.5 million differing views of them," Stuff.co.nz, 18 March 2016. Available: http://www.stuff.co.nz/dominion-post/comment/columnists/77973239/two-flags-45-million-differing-views-of-them [Accessed 5 June 2016].

Bibliography

Barker, Fiona and Kate McMillan. *Access to Electoral Rights: New Zealand*. European University Institute and European Union Democracy Observatory, 2016. Available: http://cadmus.eui.eu/handle/1814/42884.

Barker, Fiona and Kate McMillan. "Constituting the democratic public: New Zealand's extension of national voting rights to non-citizens." *New Zealand Journal of Public and International Law*. 12, 1, 2014: 61–80.

Blais, André, Louis Massicotte, and Antoine Yoshinaka. "Deciding Who has the Right to Vote: a Comparative Analysis of Election Laws." *Electoral Studies*. 20, 1, 2001, 41–62. https://doi.org/10.1016/S0261-3794(99)00062-1

Castles, Stephen and Mark Miller. *The Age of Migration*. 4th ed. London: Palgrave Macmillan, 2009.

Hancock, William K. *Survey of British Commonwealth Affairs*. London: Oxford University Press, 1940.

Jenson, Jane. "The European Union's Citizenship Regime. Creating Norms and Building Practices." *Comparative European Politics*. 5, 2007: 53–65.

Mann, Jatinder. "The evolution of Commonwealth citizenship, 1945–48 in Canada, Britain and Australia." *Commonwealth and Comparative Politics*. 50, 3, 2012: 293–313. https://doi.org/10.1080/14662043.2012.692923

McKinnon, Malcolm. *Immigrants and Citizens: New Zealanders and Asian Immigration in Historical Context*. Wellington: Institute of Policy Studies, 1996.

McMillan, Kate and Anna Hood. *Country Report: New Zealand Citizenship*. Italy: European University Institute and European Democracy Observatory, 2016. Available: http://cadmus.eui.eu/handle/1814/42648.

McMillan, Kate. "National Voting Rights for Permanent Residents: New Zealand's Experience." In *Global Migration: Old Assumptions, New Dynamics*, edited by Diego Acosta Arcarazo and Anja Wiesbrock: 101–128. Santa Barbara: Praeger, 2015.

McMillan, Kate. "Developing Citizens. Subject, aliens and citizens in New Zealand since 1840." In *Tangata Tangata The Changing Ethnic Contours of New Zealand*, edited by Paul Spoonley, Cluny Macpherson, and David Pearson: 267–290. Victoria: Thomson Dunmore Press, 2004.

Rodríguez, Christina M. "Noncitizen Voting and the Extra Constitutional Construction of the Polity." *I • CON*. 8, 40, 2010: 30–49.

Sawyer, Caroline and Wray, Helena. *EUDO Citizenship Observatory Country Report: United Kingdom*. Florence: European Union Institute, 2013. Available: http://cadmus.eui.eu/bitstream/handle/1814/33839/EUDO-CIT_2014_01_UK.pdf?sequence=1.

Urry, John. *Global Complexity*. Cambridge: Polity Press, 2003.

Vink, Maarten Peter and Rainer Bauböck. "Citizenship configurations: Analysing the Multiple Purposes of Citizenship Regimes in Europe." *Comparative European Politics*. 11, 5, 2013: 621–648. https://doi.org/10.1057/cep.2013.14.

CHAPTER 7

"All the Rights and Privileges of British Subjects": Māori and Citizenship in Aotearoa New Zealand

Carwyn Jones and Craig Linkhorn

Introduction

Article 3 of the Treaty of Waitangi, signed by Māori leaders and the British Crown in 1840, confirmed that Māori would enjoy "all the rights and privileges of British subjects." This Article of the Treaty is often described as the equality or citizenship clause. However, this new subjecthood within

We are extremely thankful to the editor of this collection, Jatinder Mann, for his detailed feedback and helpful suggestions on our chapter.

C. Jones (✉)
Ahunga Tikanga (Māori Laws and Philosophy) Programme, Te Wānanga o Raukawa, Ōtaki, New Zealand
e-mail: carwyn.jones@twor-otaki.ac.nz

C. Linkhorn
Māori Law Review, Aotearoa, New Zealand
e-mail: craig.linkhorn@cliftonchambers.co.nz

J. Mann (ed.), *Citizenship in Transnational Perspective*, Politics of Citizenship and Migration,
https://doi.org/10.1007/978-3-031-34358-2_7

a British colony and an empire in turn was laid over the top of Māori forms of social organisation and understandings of nationhood and citizenship. For most of the time since 1840, the Aotearoa New Zealand state has struggled to come to terms with the pre-existing, Indigenous forms of citizenship. Over time, the state has changed its approach to Māori citizenship. The state has recognised Māori as citizens of the national political, social, and justice systems by virtue of being landowners, as individuals in their own right, and as members of kin-based groups of Indigenous peoples. This chapter considers the plural and evolving nature of Māori citizenship today in the era of negotiated settlements for historical grievances. We explore how this is informed by the history of Māori citizenship both before and after 1840.

Citizenship in the Māori World

Before the Treaty of Waitangi in 1840 declared that Māori would have the rights and privileges of British subjects, Māori society was operating in accordance with some clear ideas about the nature of citizenship and the rights and obligations entailed in being a citizen. For most of the time since 1840, the Aotearoa New Zealand state has struggled to come to terms with those pre-existing understandings of citizenship or to effectively recognise that Māori participate in public life as citizens of kinship groups (known as iwi, hapū, and whānau) and, simultaneously, as citizens of the nation-state and before that the Dominion and Crown colony of New Zealand.

Māori forms of social organisation and citizenship are important not only at the beginning of the relationship established by the Treaty of Waitangi. These citizenships remain highly relevant to Māori collective activity as Māori groups move through a phase of transitional justice. The landscape of Māori citizenship in the context of transitional justice is examined later in this chapter.

This first part of the chapter sets out the basic framework of citizenship in Māori society. A basic understanding of Māori forms of social organisation is helpful in order to comprehend the development of Māori citizenship in the context of the Treaty of Waitangi and the establishment of the nation-state of Aotearoa New Zealand. Māori identity revolves around the central concept of whakapapa (genealogy). Whakapapa provides a framework of kinship connections that link an individual to his or her family and the wider world. All relationships in the Māori world are framed as kin relationships of one sort or another. That is to say that relationships, which are not literal kin relationships, are nonetheless conceptualised through a kinship framework. The concept of whakapapa provides an infinite network of connections within which an individual can situate one's self. Key markers of identity for Māori are relationships with landscape features such as mountains and rivers as well as the social groupings iwi, hapū, and whānau. These are all forms of kin-based groups. The whānau can be understood as the extended family. Iwi and hapū have been described as follows:[1]

> Māori iwi and hapū are two of the categories of descent groups—groups of kin linked primarily by their direct descent from a common ancestor—through which Māori organised and organise their lives. … Iwi and hapū are often referred to in a bilingual mix as 'tribes' and 'sub-tribes'. 'Peoples' (persons composing a community, tribe, race or nation) and 'clans' (a group with a common ancestor) would be better classes than 'tribes' and 'sub-tribes' because they avoid the structural connotations of the latter terms.

Pākehā historian, Angela Ballara, produced one of the most carefully considered studies to date of Māori social structures. Her book, *Iwi: The Dynamics of Māori Tribal Organisation from c. 1769 to c. 1945*, describes, within the period of her study, how the primary corporate group within Māori society shifted from the hapū to the iwi. Nevertheless, Ballara suggests in *Iwi* that the hapū might be re-emerging as a more relevant social unit. We would argue that the hapū has experienced significant resurgence as a social grouping in the nearly twenty years since the publication of *Iwi*.

It is useful to identify a number of the key themes addressed by Ballara as she points to persistent ideas in Māori society about identity and kinship obligations and also illustrates the fluidity and flexibility that is characteristic of Māori forms of social organisation. These features of belonging and citizenship in the Māori world perhaps also help to explain the Aotearoa New Zealand state's pragmatic and evolutionary approach to conceptualising Māori as both state citizens and members of distinct polities of Indigenous peoples.

As we noted above, whakapapa (genealogy) plays a central role in Māori identity. Both iwi and hapū are kin groups, usually based primarily upon descent from a common ancestor. However, central to Ballara's thesis is recognising the flexibility of Māori social organisation and further recognising that this flexibility derives from using descent as a defining feature of group identity. This apparent paradox—flexibility arising from something as fixed as one's lineage—can be explained simply by the fact that even though an individual's whakapapa or genealogical connections are fixed, which branches of the family tree that an individual chooses to prioritise is not.

Through detailed case studies, Ballara demonstrates that in the eighteenth century, Māori social groupings were highly dynamic. At that time, hapū were unquestionably the primary political and corporate unit and these hapū grew in size or shrank, joined together or split apart, depending on a range of circumstances. A key factor in this fluidity was the ability to identify a common ancestor for a community that would bind the group together and maintain the kin-based nature of the social unit. This flexibility remains an important factor in Māori identity and citizenship in the Māori world today.

But, as Ballara points out, there have also been important changes in Māori social organisation since the eighteenth century. One of the most significant has been the changing balance between iwi and hapū. Some of those changes have undoubtedly been influenced by the processes of colonisation and the activities of settlers and government from the mid-nineteenth century onwards in particular.[2]

Throughout the twentieth century, governments tended to prefer to try to engage with larger rather than smaller Māori groupings as distinctive political entities, whether through statutorily defined collective or representative bodies, iwi organisations, or the "large, natural groups" of the policy settings for the present Treaty of Waitangi settlement process.

The following section provides a brief outline of important political and social aspects of state approaches to Māori citizenship from the signing of the Treaty of Waitangi in 1840 through into the period of transitional justice of the late twentieth and early twenty-first centuries.

State Approaches to Māori Citizenship

Political Citizenship

The English text of the Treaty of Waitangi stated that Māori would have "all the rights and privileges of British subjects." Through the second half of the nineteenth century and up until at least the 1920s, these rights were predominantly given effect as rights of political citizenship and within the justice system.

Expression of political rights can be seen in state instruments such as the 1852 *Constitution Act*. This Act established Aotearoa New Zealand as a self-governing colony and provided for political participation of Māori as well as the settler population. However, this was by no means a universal franchise. The 1852 Act contained both gender and property restrictions. The latter disproportionately limited Māori voting because the communal nature of Māori land tenure made it difficult for Māori men to meet the requirements of property ownership. The gender restriction limited the franchise amongst both the Māori and the non-Māori communities in this period. Although never used, Section 71 of the 1852 Act also provided for the possibility of establishing "aboriginal districts" which would be self-governing Māori districts.

The *Constitution Act* 1852 can be seen as "an early demonstration of the tension created when Aotearoa New Zealand governments attempted to encourage Māori into the folds of a citizenship conflating nation and state."[3]

Political citizenship provided by the state jostled in this period with political dimensions of the exercise of self-determination by Indigenous peoples including, famously, prominent movements like the Kingitanga and Kotahitanga movements.

Although Section 71 of the 1852 Act was never used before it was finally repealed over a century later, the Aotearoa New Zealand state continued to adopt measures that both directly and indirectly affected Māori citizenship.

The 1860s saw several pieces of legislation, which would have profound effects on Māori citizenship and Māori society in general. In 1862 and 1865, the first *Native Land Acts* were passed into law. These Acts established the Native Land Court (a body that continues today as the Māori Land Court). The function of the Native Land Court was to ascertain who held customary title to Māori land. It could then approve processes to convert the title to a Crown-derived title. In very large measure, this led to the creation of individual ownership interests at the expense of prior customary collective interests. This greatly facilitated the alienation of Māori land. It has also created long-term issues in relation to the management of Māori land and the control by communities of land as a collective resource rather than a set of individuated interests in land. This had a significant impact on the Māori economy and Māori social structures. It also paved the way for the state to recognise Māori as citizens by virtue of being landholders in two important ways. First, it created a situation whereby the state could substitute recognition of the traditions of Māori as Indigenous peoples with recognition instead of landholding bodies as political entities. We return to this point briefly below. Second, it began to create a group of Māori individuals who could meet the property requirements necessary to vote in general elections. Yet, it was also clear that it would take some time for the individualisation of Māori title through Native Land Court hearings to have any significant effect on the franchise. This is the context in which the *Māori Representation Act* 1867 was enacted. This legislation would have major implications for Māori political participation and citizenship of the colony.

The *Māori Representation Act* 1867 provided for the establishment of four Māori seats in the General Assembly. It seems as though the motivation for introducing this legislation may have had more to do with balancing the influence of disparate groups within the settler population rather than being entirely aimed at providing effective representation for Māori at the national level. Whatever the motivation, given that the Māori voting population (men of voting age) at the time was approximately 50,000, and the settler voting population of approximately 250,000 was represented by 72 seats in Parliament, the establishment of 4 Māori seats could hardly be seen as proportionate or providing fair levels of political representation. The Act divided the North Island into three Māori electorates and the fourth Māori electorate would cover the whole of the South Island. The Act was initially intended to be a temporary measure but was renewed for a further five years in 1872 and eventually renewed indefinitely. The four Māori seats continued in that form until Aotearoa New Zealand shifted to a system of proportional representation in 1996.

Since the creation of a regular Māori electoral option, Māori today have the choice of voting on the Māori electoral roll for the Māori seats or the general roll. The separate Māori electoral roll remains but now the number of Māori seats is calculated every five years on the basis of the number of Māori who choose to vote on the Māori roll. In the 2020–2023 parliament, there were 7 Māori seats in a 120-seat Parliament. Two of these seats were held by members of a political party expressly established to represent a Māori voice in Parliament—the Māori Party. There were also Māori MPs from various parties across the Parliament who held the remaining Māori seats and a number of general seats. There were twenty-five Members of Parliament in 2023 who self-identified as being of Māori descent, or 21% of the total Parliament.

The Māori seats provide a fascinating example of the way in which Māori citizenship draws on both citizenship of the state and the idea of Māori communities as being distinct polities. The Report of the Royal Commission on the Electoral System (1986), which eventually led to the introduction of the mixed member proportional electoral system, gave particular attention to Māori representation.[4]

Māori political representation and participation in state processes are complicated by individuals' additional and simultaneous identification as citizens of iwi and hapū as distinct political units. At both the central and local government level and at other sites where Māori are engaged in state processes, Māori and the state will often need to grapple with the tensions that are inherent in political participation premised on citizenship of the iwi and hapū as well as of the state. As the section further on illustrates, similar types of issues arise when we consider the social dimensions of citizenship.

Justice Citizenship

The new colony's justice system had early impact but limited practical reach from 1840. The first murder trial was in April 1840 and contained a cross-cultural encounter as a war party of 300 interrupted the trial threatening summary justice until reassured.[5] The extension and application of the coloniser's justice system was in many respects a negotiated affair as it extended slowly beyond the colony's beachhead towns and penetrated into districts remaining under Māori control.[6]

Part of this negotiated movement involved making room for Māori communities to continue to dispense justice within their own legal traditions and through increasing application of law created for the whole colony. The Native Exemption Ordinance of 1844 anticipated gradualism in the application and enforcement of colonial laws. Resident Magistrates sitting with Native Assessors provided a further mode to attempt the gradual application of parts of the justice system to Māori citizens of the colony.

A native district system saw districts created for law councils (known as Rūnanga) to operate with a civil and criminal jurisdiction. These state-created Rūnanga did not endure but found a mirror-like reflection in the form of tribes creating their own Rūnanga. Time has shown that it has been the self-determined tribal variant providing an enduring example of citizens' access to legal traditions within their tribes.

Through into the twentieth century, the citizenship confirmed by the 1840 Waitangi Treaty has been the great means of using access to the justice system to attempt to hold the state to account in civil proceedings and, latterly, rights-based litigation. Faith in the rule of law is seen in statements such as that attributed to Te Kooti Arikirangi Te Turuki, "The canoe for you to paddle after me is the Law. Only the Law can be set against the Law."[7] Belief in the justice system and the independence of the courts saw many causes pursued, across generations, culminating in the last generation's pursuit of transitional justice both to address the impacts of colonisation on Indigenous peoples and to establish a constitutional foundation in the Treaty of Waitangi.

Social Citizenship

Māori citizenship also leads to distinct forms of engagement with the social and welfare state in Aotearoa New Zealand. We do not examine issues relating to social service delivery to Māori in any great detail in this chapter (Stephens focuses on this in her chapter in this book). The objective of this part of the chapter is instead to consider the role of Māori citizenship in shaping the approach of the state and Māori to implementing Māori use of Aotearoa New Zealand's welfare state, which emerged from the end of the nineteenth century.

The rise of the modern welfare state through the twentieth century had serious implications for Māori social organisation and Māori citizenship. As one commentator has suggested, the basic philosophy underpinning systematic social welfare has "subordinated Māori cultural differences to a 'universal' citizenship based on equality, even when the rights of citizenship were rarely applied to Māori in an 'equal' or 'universal' manner."[8]

As with the political dimensions of Māori citizenship, the approach to the social aspects of Māori citizenship has been significantly influenced by the fundamental changes imposed on Māori land tenure. As noted above, this had a major impact on Māori social structures. Ultimately radical land loss from tribal communities after individuated rights were created became tied with a significant migration to urban areas after the Second World War. The resulting loosening of bonds to home districts with their traditional social supports saw changes in how Māori groups connected with their urbanised kin-folk and the springing up of urban institutions and other forms of social support to replicate Māori forms of social organisation.

It is fair to say that the state's role in supporting both urban Māori[9] and supra-tribal institutions has been mixed and has brought its fair share of frustrations.[10] The implications of state activity in this area have been significant for the recognition of Māori polities and collective authority as Māori. These issues of identity, authority, and citizenship are likely less understood than matters relating to property rights held by Māori where a narrative of dispossession has been the major theme behind the transitional justice programme of negotiated settlements of historical claims with large natural groups in Aotearoa New Zealand. Those settlements are now reasonably well accepted in Aotearoa New Zealand society but with only a limited understanding of what is being settled and what history this represents. The regeneration for Indigenous peoples that these settlements offer means that the issue of Māori polities also regenerating is only going to come more to the fore once a measure of economic restoration (of an asset base) has occurred.

The loss of community control about decisions over land and other natural resources from the nineteenth century onwards focused engagement with Māori on an individual basis. After the Second World War, the focus on human rights instruments emphasised universalism and less emphasis on group rights until more recent work to secure support for a United Nations Declaration of the Rights of Indigenous Peoples (UNDRIP). State recognition of Māori citizenship as focused predominantly on individuals meant, for example, no distinct space was held for local communities to exercise control over human and natural resources or over their own tribal people's use of those resources.

As we mentioned above, mass internal migration (urbanisation) of Māori took place in the post-war years of the twentieth century. Here too, people were viewed increasingly as individuals and less and less as citizens of distinct subnational communities.

Māmari Stephens has noted that Māori polities have long extended beyond the Māori ethnos to the Māori demos (a civic collectivism beyond immediate kin groups).[11] Many of these bodies have been in the vanguard of responses to these immense changes in Māori societies and the loss of control wrought by these changes. For instance, the Kotahitanga movement; the Māori Women's Welfare League; and Urban Māori Authorities, more recently.

The major enterprise of the transitional justice programme in the second half of the twentieth century has been negotiating settlements that include compensation aimed at helping Indigenous peoples to re-establish a tribal economic base. The policy has been to encourage settlement where possible with the largest possible groups—iwi. Given the compensatory, rather than restorative, elements to the settlement redress, there is a modern pragmatism to this.

Questions of governance over settlement assets have raised afresh issues about citizenship of the tribal societies, including social citizenship. It seems like very early days in working out how this will unfold. We suggest that it is an area that is under-examined in legal scholarship. Most focus appears to instead be on the particular vehicles chosen to administer the various settlements and the status of tribal members, typically, as beneficiaries of these post-settlement governance entities (PSGEs) or mandated iwi organisations.

Te Whānau o Waipareira Report

As indicated above, this chapter does not interrogate the social service delivery mechanisms of the Aotearoa New Zealand state and their responsiveness (or not) to Māori. Yet, there are useful insights about Māori citizenship that can be gleaned from examining forms of Māori social organisation that are designed to operate within the modern welfare state. Te Whānau o Waipareira Trust provides a helpful case study. The next part of the chapter discusses a 1998 Waitangi Tribunal report relating to the Waipareira Trust, which deals with the question of whether or not the Trust ought to be considered as an iwi for the purposes of its interactions with the state.

The community that describes itself as Te Whānau o Waipareira has its origins in the migration of Māori from rural areas to West Auckland that occurred in the post-war years. Welfare work has long been undertaken by Māori leaders associated with this community, particularly in relation to supporting others who had lost their connection with traditional tribal support structures through the process of urbanisation. The central issue in the claim that the Trust brought before the Waitangi Tribunal was related to the then Department of Social Welfare's approach to funding community organisations like the Trust. At a more fundamental level, the Trust asserted that it ought to be recognised as a Treaty of Waitangi partner and consulted as such alongside iwi and hapū in order to reflect the way in which this community of urban Māori had chosen to come together. It is notable that this assertion draws on the flexibility of Māori forms of social organisation discussed above.

The Waitangi Tribunal addressed the question of what constitutes an iwi, noting the way in which the parties generally approached the issue. The Tribunal noted that both the Crown and the claimants in that inquiry used the term "'iwi' to refer to 'traditional' tribal bodies, groupings of hapū whose members are linked by descent."[12] However, Te Whānau o Waipareira did not claim to be a traditional tribal group in this way. Membership of the group was not based on genealogy or literal kin connections. Likewise, Te Whānau o Waipareira Trust did not exercise customary rights to land over a traditional territory in the way that an iwi would. Instead, the Trust described its intentions as being to "recreate an 'iwi' environment for urban people who cannot trace their links to their traditional iwi, or who seek the comfort and solace of that environment in the urban context where they live."[13]

In addressing the Trust's claims, the Waitangi Tribunal noted that the recognition of the autonomy/self-determination (or "rangatiratanga") of the Trust is not in conflict with the recognition of traditional hapū in the same area.[14] It was not necessary for the Trust to demonstrate that it represented "every individual Māori in West Auckland" for the members of Te Whānau o Waipareira to be recognised as a community that may collectively exercise the autonomy protected by the Treaty of Waitangi.[15] This recognition need not impact upon the autonomy of traditional, tribal groups in West Auckland. Those groups are also entitled to have their collective self-determination recognised under the Treaty.[16]

Furthermore, it appears that the Tribunal focused on the way in which community members understood their relationship with the community of Te Whānau o Waipareira.[17] The central question was: how do the members of Te Whānau o Waipareira understand their relationships with each other and the nature of their rights and obligations to the collective? For the Tribunal, it was the "structure, organisation and values of Te Whānau o Waipareira" that were critical in terms of understanding the dynamics of group membership in this instance.[18] In other words, it was the internal relationships and the relational rights and duties that inhered within the community that spoke to Māori forms of citizenship and social organisation.

The Tribunal also makes some important observations about the flexibility of Māori forms of social organisation:[19]

> We observe that this approach may be seen as consistent with custom. It is clear that far from being static, Māori communities have changed over time. No doubt they will continue to do so. They have changed throughout history with hapu growing, disappearing and emerging, their political alliances reshaping continuously, and sometimes with major migrations occurring, the migrants regularly gathering adherents from communities far and wide. It is thus apparent that, in 1840, Māori were not organised into the same communities as they were only 20 years before. There were major and pan-tribal movements in the interim, as the migrations to Wellington in the 1820s and 1830s well show. And those that exist today did not all exist in 1840. The concept of iwi authorities has grown, exercising corporate functions previously unheard of, and so too national bodies, each valid if they serve the needs of Māori in a new age. In addition new urban communities have grown as well, and these for many may now represent the communities of their choice.

The Waitangi Tribunal's comments in Te Whānau o Waipareira Report provide a useful analysis of the nature of Māori citizenship and the distinctive rights and obligations it entails in the context of the Treaty of Waitangi. The following section turns to consider the settlement of historical Treaty of Waitangi claims and issues relating to post-settlement governance and Māori citizenship.

Opportunities in Revitalizing Māori Legal Traditions of Citizenship Through Transitional Justice

Aotearoa New Zealand now has many settlements as a result of a deliberate programme of transitional justice. It is founded on a reasonably strong consensus that some compensation should be made for dispossession of Māori from natural resources, especially land and fisheries, but increasingly also relationships with waterways. More recent settlements have included regimes for natural resource management often labelled co-governance or co-management. This innovation is premised on the idea that there is a Treaty partner, a tribal group, to co-govern with.

Both regular settlements and co-governance settlements have dealt piecemeal with questions of post-settlement governance on behalf of the iwi or hapū kin groups whose claims are settled. The focus has mostly been on governance of settlement assets to be fair (and the entitlement to membership of a class of beneficiaries by individuals with the correct whakapapa [lineage]).

By and large, post-settlement governance entities are just that—governance for that particular settlement. They do not of themselves recognise or constitute a tribal government. There has been much less focus through settlements, and in the law more generally, on the tribes' internal constitutional existence and relationships between these Indigenous peoples and their members.

The Ngāi Tahu people of Te Waipounamu (the South Island) obtained private legislation from the Parliament of Aotearoa New Zealand. The resulting Act constituted Te Runanga o Ngāi Tahu for Ngāi Tahu members to exercise internal self-governance. Other tribes have worked in their own customary spheres or under existing models supported by general legislation with mixed results.

There was a move to provide a legislated template vehicle for both tribal and supra-tribal governance. Much of the analysis by the Law Commission for the reasons behind the proposed Waka Umanga law remains very useful.[20] But the idea of a generic vehicle failed to gather sufficient support and was seen as cutting across tribal autonomy.

This is one area where the state has preserved the benefits of flexibility and avoided a one-size-fits-all prescription. Time will tell therefore how this unfolds as the tribes chart their own pathways. It seems to us that this flexibility for tribes minimises the risks of juridification distorting the tribe's own law. In this respect, we suspect that we are now more optimistic than Kirsty Gover's 2010 analysis of tribal membership in Aotearoa New Zealand appears to be (and it seems to us that the work was more about membership of beneficiary classes under particular settlements in Aotearoa New Zealand by that stage than the final word on tribal constitutionalism).[21]

We tend to see no necessary inconsistency between formality in constitutional settings for tribes (within tribal law or national law) and Indigenous legal traditions. As John Borrows[22] has described, there are a number of sources of Indigenous law. Custom is one. Indigenous legal systems can contain formalised laws and institutions. We agree with Gover that looking for Māori agency is crucial in determining whether modern tribal constitutions are acts of cultural production or reproduction or unacceptable distortions of the particular Indigenous peoples' legal traditions.

We also note that an area to watch is whether, increasingly, decisions by tribal governments affecting their citizens are treated as questions of public law (and the exercise of public power) rather than completely private questions.

For instance, membership of a tribe by virtue of descent may be part only of an assessment of one's entitlement to the rights and privileges of establishing and maintaining citizenship of the tribe. There is a longstanding current of thought that acts (of ascription) are also important to demonstrate participation in Māori community life. In a post-urbanised Aotearoa New Zealand, let alone with global mobility, this can be demanding when the homelands are distant. Maintenance of connection with the tribe remains a very important strain of traditional Māori philosophy in an environment where the strands of whakapapa, today, offer people a number of choices.

By way of further example, tribes increasingly expect to develop beyond a restored economic base assisted by settlements of historical claims about natural resources to take a significant role in strategic partnerships with the state in the social sector to deliver education, health, and welfare services, while at the same time accepting that their citizens have the option of either a mainstream or tribally channelled service. Even if much of that provision continues to come within the ambit of a contractual model for now as between a service delivery entity acting on behalf of the tribe and central government,[23] tribal members will be experiencing the exercise of power that may well be more public than private in nature.[24] These are markers in a journey of self-determination for Indigenous peoples in Aotearoa New Zealand.

Conclusion

Despite this era of settlements and those groups who have settled exercising a greater degree of self-determination as Indigenous peoples with citizens of their iwi or hapū, Māori also continue to be citizens of the state of Aotearoa New Zealand. Consistent with the compromise in UNDRIP about the territorial integrity of states with Indigenous peoples, the overlay of state citizenship that is formally assured by the Treaty of Waitangi remains. However, the relationship between these two forms of citizenship held by Māori has never been fixed and is not definitively settled now.

The Treaty settlement process and the increased autonomy of tribes after settlement illustrate the way in which the relationship between iwi/hapū citizenship and state citizenship continues to be negotiated and to evolve. This flexible and pragmatic approach to Māori citizenship is consistent with the way in which the Aotearoa New Zealand state has historically engaged with the subject. It also resonates with the nature of Māori identity and iwi and hapū citizenship. Although the Treaty of Waitangi settlement process is formalising and recording agreements about a range of rights and obligations between settling groups and the state, Māori continue to engage with the state across a range of different sites, sometimes as citizens of iwi or hapū, sometimes as registered members of PSGEs, and sometimes as citizens of the state. The location of these sites and the nature of the engagement will no doubt continue to be negotiated as the settlements of historical Treaty claims are concluded. For its part, the state is demonstrating itself willing to test constructively the waters of increasing pluralism (even if this is in what theorists might describe as a weak form) in relation to Indigenous peoples. The nature of Māori constitutionalism and citizenship within those Indigenous peoples itself looks set to continue to develop in a flexible and pragmatic manner as the relationship between citizenship of iwi and hapū and citizenship of the state is debated and contested in the context of the Treaty of Waitangi partnership.

Notes

1. Angela Ballara, *Iwi: The Dynamics of Māori Tribal Organisation from c. 1769 to c. 1945* (Wellington: Victoria University Press, 1998), 17.
2. *Ibid.*, 279.
3. Louise Humpage, "Revision Required: Reconciling New Zealand Citizenship with Māori Nationalisms," *National Identities* 10 (2008): 251.
4. John Wallace, John Darwin, Kenneth Keith, Richard Mulgan, and Whetumarama Wereta, *Report—Royal Commission on the Electoral System: Towards a Better Democracy* (December 1986).
5. Vincent O'Malley, "English Law and the Māori Response: a case study from the Runanga system in Northland, 1861–65," *Journal of the Polynesian Society* 116 (2007): 7.
6. Alan Ward, "Law and law-enforcement on the New Zealand frontier, 1840–1893," *New Zealand Journal of History* 5, 2 (1971): 128.
7. Judith Binney, "Te Kooti Arikirangi Te Turuki" in the Dictionary of New Zealand Biography, Te Ara—the Encyclopedia of New Zealand. Available: http://www.TeAra.govt.nz/en/biographies/1t45/te-kooti-arikirangi-te-turuki.
8. Humpage, "Revision Required," 252.

9. Waitangi Tribunal, *Te Whānau o Waipareira Report* (Wellington: GP Publications, 1998).
10. Waitangi Tribunal, *Whaia te Mana Motuhake—In Pursuit of Mana Motuhake: Report on the Māori Community Development Act* (Wellington: Waitangi Tribunal, 2014).
11. Māmari Stephens, "A Loving Excavation: Uncovering the Constitutional Culture of the Māori Demos," *New Zealand Universities Law Review* 25, 4 (2013): 820–843.
12. Waitangi Tribunal, *Te Whanau o Waipareira Report* (Wellington: GP publications, 1998), 6.
13. *Ibid.*, 6.
14. *Ibid.*, 14.
15. *Ibid.*
16. *Ibid.*
17. *Ibid.*
18. *Ibid.*
19. *Ibid.*, 218.
20. New Zealand Law Commission, *Māori Custom and Values in New Zealand Law* (Wellington, 2001).
21. Kirsty Gover, *Tribal Constitutionalism: States, Tribes and the Governance of Membership* (Oxford: Oxford University Press, 2010).
22. John Borrows, *Canada's Indigenous Constitution* (Toronto: University of Toronto Press, 2010), 23–58.
23. For further discussion of the issues confronted by Indigenous peoples in terms of the institutional supremacy of the nation-state, see Bruce Duthu, *Shadow Nations: Tribal Sovereignty and the Limits of Legal Pluralism* (Oxford: Oxford University Press, 2013).
24. Hon. Justice Joseph Williams, "Property or interests, private or public?," Administrative Law Intensive (Wellington: New Zealand Law Society, 2011).

Bibliography

Adds, P., B. Bonisch-Brednich, R. Hill, and G. Whimp, eds. *Reconciliation, Representation and Indigeneity: 'Biculturalism' in Aotearoa New Zealand.* Heidelberg: Universitatsverlag Winter, 2016.

Ballara, Angela. *Iwi: The Dynamics of Māori Tribal Organisation from c. 1769 to c. 1945.* Wellington: Victoria University Press, 1998.

Binney, Judith. "Te Kooti Arikirangi Te Turuki" in the Dictionary of New Zealand Biography, Te Ara—the Encyclopedia of New Zealand. Available: http://www.TeAra.govt.nz/en/biographies/1t45/te-kooti-arikirangi-te-turuki

Borrows, John. *Canada's Indigenous Constitution*. Toronto, University of Toronto Press, 2010.

Durie, Mason. *Te Mana, Te Kawanatanga: The Politics of Māori Self-Determination*. Oxford: Oxford University Press, 1998.

Duthu, Bruce. *Shadow Nations: Tribal Sovereignty and the Limits of Legal Pluralism*. Oxford: Oxford University Press, 2013.

Gover, Kirsty. *Tribal Constitutionalism: states, tribes and the governance of membership*. Oxford: Oxford University Press, 2010.

Hickford, Mark. *Lords of the Land: Indigenous Property Rights and the Jurisprudence of Empire*. Oxford: Oxford University Press, 2011.

Hill, Richard. *Māori and the State: Crown-Māori Relations in New Zealand/ Aotearoa, 1950–2000*. Wellington: Victoria University Press, 2009.

Humpage, Louise. "Revision required: Reconciling New Zealand citizenship with Māori nationalisms." *National Identities*. 10, 2008: 247–261. https://doi.org/10.1080/14608940802249858

New Zealand Law Commission. *Māori Custom and Values in New Zealand Law*. Wellington, 2001.

O'Malley, Vincent. "English Law and the Māori Response: a case study from the Runanga system in Northland, 1861–65." *Journal of the Polynesian Society*. 116, 2007: 7–34.

Stephens, Māmari. "A Loving Excavation: Uncovering the Constitutional Culture of the Māori Demos." *New Zealand Universities Law Review*. 25, 4, 2013: 820–843.

Tully, James. *Public Philosophy in a New Key*. Cambridge: Cambridge University Press, 2008.

Waitangi Tribunal. *Te Whānau o Waipareira Report*. Wellington: GP Publications, 1998.

Waitangi Tribunal. *Whaia Te Mana Motuhake – In Pursuit of Mana Motuhake: Report on the Māori Community Development Act*. Wellington: Waitangi Tribunal, 2014.

Wallace, J., J. Darwin, K. Keith, R. Mulgan, and Whetumarama Wereta. *Report – Royal Commission on the Electoral System: Towards a Better Democracy*. December 1986.

Ward, Alan. "Law and law-enforcement on the New Zealand frontier, 1840–1893." New Zealand Journal of History. 5, 2, 1971: 128–149.

Williams, Hon. Justice Joseph. "Property or interests, private or public?," Administrative Law Intensive. Wellington: New Zealand Law Society, 2011.

Wilson, M. and A. Yeatman, eds. *Justice & Identity: Antipodean Practices*. Wellington: Bridget Williams Books, 1995.

PART III

Settler-Indigenous Citizenships

CHAPTER 8

Indigeneity and Membership in Australia After *Love*

Sangeetha Pillai and Harry Hobbs

Introduction

Aboriginal and Torres Strait Islander peoples have occupied, possessed, and cared for the Australian continent for at least 60,000 years.[1] Despite their enduring spiritual connection to the lands and waters that comprise the territorial community of Australia, however, the place and status of First Nations peoples within the Australian political community have long been contested. For many years following invasion and colonisation,

We are extremely grateful to the editor of this collection, Jatinder Mann, for his detailed feedback and helpful suggestions on our chapter.

S. Pillai
School of Global and Public Law, University of New South Wales, Sydney, NSW, Australia
e-mail: sangeetha.pillai@unsw.edu.au

H. Hobbs (✉)
Faculty of Law, University Technology Sydney, Sydney, NSW, Australia
e-mail: hobbs.harry@uts.edu.au

J. Mann (ed.), *Citizenship in Transnational Perspective*, Politics of Citizenship and Migration,
https://doi.org/10.1007/978-3-031-34358-2_8

discriminatory law and practice sought to distance and exclude Aboriginal and Torres Strait Islander peoples from the broader non-Indigenous community. This approach continued into the early decades of the Australian Commonwealth. First Nations peoples did not participate and played no role in the drafting of the Australian Constitution. In 1902, they were expressly denied the right to vote for the Australian Parliament.

Over the course of the twentieth century exclusion and restrictions were progressively removed. This has been underpinned by significant shifts in constitutional and common law. In 1967, Australians voted overwhelmingly in a referendum to alter the Constitution and amend two discriminatory references to Aboriginal and Torres Strait Islander peoples (see Mann's first substantial chapter in this collection).[2] In 1992, in the case of *Mabo v Queensland (No 2)*,[3] the High Court held that the idea that Australia was "terra nullius," or empty land, at the time of British occupation was a legal fiction and that native title rights existed and were held by all Indigenous persons. Limited native title rights have since been incorporated into statute. Notwithstanding these significant changes, however, legal recognition of First Nations peoples' distinct rights possessed by virtue of their status as prior self-governing communities remains incomplete.

The Australian Constitution offers little guidance in considering the relationship between Indigeneity and membership of the Australian community. In fact, it offers little guidance on membership at all. The constitutional framework that governs membership of the Australian community is infamously focused on maximising parliamentary powers of exclusion. There is no express or clearly implied constitutional concept of citizenship or membership. In 1947 a statutory concept was first introduced and has remained in place ever since, but it is thin and formal, doing little other than conferring the status of citizenship upon people deemed eligible. Substantive rights in Australia are primarily conferred through a range of other statutes, and for the most part do not hinge upon possession of citizenship. Non-citizens—even if they hold permanent residency and have lived in Australia for their entire lives—remain vulnerable to visa cancellation and removal from Australia in a wide range of circumstances.

Australia's citizenship frameworks, thus, do little to nothing to make space for the unique rights of First Nations peoples. Moreover, while the majority of First Nations peoples hold Australian statutory citizenship, some do not. This may happen, for instance, where a First Nations person is born outside Australia, and they or their parents have not gone through the administrative task of applying for citizenship by descent.

These factors collectively create a number of hanging questions about the place of First Nations peoples within the Australian constitutional community. For example, does the unique position First Nations people hold as the original custodians of Australian land exempt them from being excluded from Australia under migration legislation passed under the aliens power, irrespective of whether or not they hold statutory citizenship? Along similar lines, does it immunise them against having their citizenship revoked?

The first of these questions was explored by the High Court in 2020 in the case of *Love ; Thoms v Commonwealth*[4] ("*Love*"). By the narrowest of majorities, the Court held that, for at least some First Nations people, exclusion from Australia under the banner of the aliens power was constitutionally impossible. The *Love* decision has been regarded as a controversial one, and, due to the lack of a clear thread in the majority's reasoning, has been seen as a vulnerable precedent. A mere two years later, the Commonwealth sought to overturn *Love* in the case of *Montgomery v Minister for Immigration, Citizenship, Migrant Services and Multicultural Affairs*[5] ("*Montgomery*"), though this challenge was ultimately withdrawn following a change in government.

While *Love* remains good law, the lack of a clear majority voice throws open several questions about what exactly the decision means for the relationship between Indigeneity and membership in Australia. In our chapter, we explore some of these questions. Our chapter is divided into four substantive sections. In the first section, we set out the legal frameworks that govern citizenship and community membership in Australia. As we explain, questions about the boundaries of membership in the Australian community are largely expressed through the language of alienage rather than citizen—terms that are not necessarily synonymous. In the second section, we trace how Australian law has moved from excluding to including First Nations peoples. We note, however, that this journey is incomplete. Many Australians continue to raise anxieties over recognising Indigenous difference and Indigenous-specific rights. In the third section, we turn to the *Love* case. Concerning the capacity of the Australian government to exclude First Nations peoples who do not possess statutory citizenship, *Love* is situated in the middle of disputes over Indigeneity and membership in the Australian community. In the final section we offer some reflections on the judgement and tease out ongoing complications that are yet to be resolved.

Citizenship and Community Membership in Australia

The word "citizen" only features once in the Australian Constitution—in s 44(i), which provides that a citizen of a foreign power is ineligible to serve as a member of the federal Parliament. On Australian citizenship, the Constitution is completely silent. This silence eventuated because the Constitution's framers could not agree on fundamental aspects of citizenship. Some saw it as a status that served as a gateway to particular rights or immunities,[6] while others saw it as something that derived from the possession of those rights and immunities.[7] Others still believed that citizenship was connected to particular rights and duties, but that it was not necessary to reflect this legally, because the idea that a democratically elected Parliament would infringe upon the fundamental rights of citizens was inconceivable.[8]

There was also disagreement about who ought to be entitled to citizenship. At Federation, the fullest form of formal community membership throughout the British Empire was British subject status.[9] While the framers wanted to grant full rights to settle in Australia to those born in the UK,[10] they also had a unanimous desire to exclude people who were British subjects, but were not regarded as being of "British type." This meant that a national citizenship that was coexistent with British subject status was undesirable. The idea of granting the Commonwealth Parliament the power to legislate with respect to citizenship was discussed, but was not proceeded with. There was some concern expressed that granting such a power to the Parliament might open up the possibility of citizenship deprivation via legislation.[11]

Instead, Parliament was granted broad powers over "naturalisation and aliens" and "immigration and emigration," which worked hand in hand to facilitate racially based statutory exclusion on the broadest possible basis. At Federation, and for several decades thereafter, British subjects were regarded as outside of the scope of the aliens power, but within the scope of the immigration power. This enabled Parliament to legislate in a way that shaped the Australian community via whatever migration mix it chose. In the early years of Australian federation, it did so via the statutes that gave effect to the White Australia Policy, which remained in place for a number of decades.[12] The naturalisation limb of the naturalisation and aliens power enables it to recognise desirable migrants as formal members of the Australian community via naturalisation, while the aliens limb, in conjunction with the immigration limb of the immigration and emigration power, allows it to partially or completely exclude migrants who are considered less desirable.

Despite the lack of an express legislative power with respect to citizenship, it is well-settled today that the Commonwealth Parliament has the constitutional power to define the concept of Australian citizenship through legislation. Since 1949 such legislation has existed. The legislative concept of Australian citizenship is relatively thin and formal. It prescribes the various ways in which a person can acquire citizenship (automatically at birth, by descent upon application, and by conferral, upon application following a period of permanent residency). It also prescribes the circumstances in which citizenship may be lost by voluntary renunciation or by Ministerial revocation on the basis of fraud or prescribed conduct.

The constitutional basis for Parliament's power to pass citizenship legislation has never been conclusively ruled on by the High Court. It is accepted that the naturalisation and aliens power provide support, at least to the extent that citizenship is being conferred on people who were previously aliens, via a process of naturalisation.[13] But this legislation also confers statutory citizenship on people who it is not clear were ever aliens. For example, when citizenship is conferred automatically at birth on a child born in Australia to Australian parents, it would be strange to describe this as the naturalisation of an alien; it is more a recognition that the citizen has, since birth, been a core member of the Australian community and a non-alien.

There is no practical need to comprehensively chart who is and is not a constitutional alien. When Parliament grants a person statutory citizenship, it is generally unimportant to determine the basis on which this is constitutionally possible. But when a person with a claim to constitutional non-alienage is *denied* citizenship, or the rights of citizenship, questions about the boundaries of Parliament's power become more important, and constitutional ambiguities about what rights go hand in hand with citizenship have practical consequences.

Citizenship is not the main gateway to rights in Australia. The *Australian Citizenship Act* 2007 says nothing about the rights that attach to citizenship. A plethora of other statutes confer substantive rights on members of the Australian community, but overwhelmingly these do not hinge upon possession of citizenship. There are two significant legal benefits that are strongly associated with citizenship. The first is the right to vote held by adult citizens (a statutory right with a degree of constitutional protection). The second is simply the right to be in Australia, or an immunity against being removed.[14]

The overwhelming power to make exclusionary legislation under the umbrella of the aliens power has been employed by Parliament to its fullest, particularly in the last decade. The *Migration Act* 1968 provides that where a non-citizen fails a "character test," they are vulnerable to visa cancellation, detention, and deportation (ss 501, 189, 198). Visa cancellation is *mandatory* (though reversible by ministerial discretion on application) where a non-citizen is convicted of an offence and sentenced to at least twelve months imprisonment (ss 501(3A)(i)). These laws purport to apply to *all* non-citizens, regardless of how long they have spent in Australia or the strength of their ties to the country. But because the laws rely on the aliens power for constitutional support, there are deep questions about their validity or applicability in circumstances where a person is a non-citizen, but also has a viable claim of non-alienage.

This was the legal and practical question at the heart of the *Love* case. Could the *Migration Act* be used to deport a First Nations person who does not hold Australian statutory citizenship from Australia, or are First Nations peoples, regardless of their citizenship status, constitutional non-aliens who are immune from removal? This question brings into play deeper questions about the relationship between First Nations people and Australian law. As we outline below, this issue is itself unsettled.

First Nations Peoples and Membership in Australia

A historical sweep examining how Australian law has engaged with First Nations peoples reveals a gradual shift from exclusion to inclusion. As we outline in this short background, however, what inclusion means remains contested. First Nations peoples understand inclusion to mean both legal recognition of equal rights as equal citizens *and* legal protection of their unique rights and interests as Indigenous peoples. In contrast, many within the Australian community struggle with the notion of providing legal recognition of Indigenous difference.

Exclusion began early. Colonisation in Australia proceeded on the basis that the Indigenous inhabitants had no law or rights worthy of protection. The British and later colonial governments did not attempt to negotiate their presence on the continent, nor did they seek to understand the intricate and complex normative systems that had secured the survival of First Nations peoples for thousands of generations. Despite the evidence before them, British politicians considered that Aboriginal people were "entirely destitute … of the rudest forms of civil polity,"[15] while the Supreme Court of New South Wales declared that Aboriginal people had only "the wildest most indiscriminatory notions of revenge."[16] Colonial authorities became convinced that First Nations peoples "would be exterminated by the progress of civilisation."[17] This attitude "contributed significantly to the pervasive ideologies that formed the racist, protectionist policies framed by" colonial governments.[18]

It also helps us understand how the Australian Constitution does or does not engage with First Nations peoples. The Constitution was drafted at a series of constitutional conventions in the 1890s by leading colonial politicians. Reflecting the attitudes of the day, First Nations peoples were not invited and did not contribute to the drafting. The new Constitution ignored the hundreds of First Nations communities and the multiple intricate bodies of social ordering they had developed.[19] It also discriminated against First Nations people in at least three sections. Section 25 anticipated that a State Parliament could exclude people from voting in elections on the basis of their race, section 51(xxvi) empowered the Federal Parliament to make special laws for the people of any race, other than the Aboriginal race, and section 127 excluded First Nations people from being counted for constitutional purposes. While these provisions did not necessarily indicate ill-intent,[20] they symbolically excluded First Nations peoples from membership of the new polity. Exclusion was confirmed the following year with the passage of the *Commonwealth Franchise Act* 1902, which disqualified Indigenous Australians from voting. Even though there was no concept of Australian citizenship at this stage, First Nations peoples were clearly not considered part of the Australian community.[21]

Aboriginal and Torres Strait Islander peoples contested the place that had been set for them in the new nation. In the first half of the twentieth century, focus centred on dismantling racist law and policy and recognising their rights as equal members of the community.[22] In 1928, for instance, Noongar elder William Harris led a deputation to Philip Collier, the Premier of Western Australia, arguing for changes to the discriminatory *Aborigines Protection Act* 1905. The following decade, Yorta Yorta man, William Cooper, collected almost 2000 signatures from Aboriginal people in a petition to send to the King. Denied the right to vote, Cooper and his petitioners desired a voice in national affairs, calling for someone "who can speak for us in Parliament, influencing legislation on our behalf and safeguarding us from administrational officers."[23] Cooper's demand for dedicated representation in Parliament was dismissed by Cabinet, but First Nations peoples continued to call for political and legal reform.

First Nations peoples' activism may have encouraged a shift in government policy in the 1930s from protectionism (which favoured exclusion) towards assimilation. Assimilation recognised Aboriginal and Torres Strait Islander peoples were unjustly excluded from the Australian polity and sought to include them. However, inclusion would be on the terms of non-Indigenous Australians; Aboriginal people would be expected to "attain the same manner of living as other Australians and live as members of a single Australian community enjoying the same rights and privileges, accepting the same responsibilities, observing the same customs and influenced by the same beliefs, hopes and loyalties as other Australians."[24] In 1962, the Commonwealth belatedly extended the franchise to all First Nations peoples (*Commonwealth Franchise Act* 1962). Paul Hasluck, the Minister for the Territories, praised the Act as "one step further towards the ideal of one people in one continent."[25]

That ideal appeared another step closer in 1967. That year, Australians voted overwhelmingly in a referendum to alter the Constitution and amend two discriminatory references to Aboriginal and Torres Strait Islander peoples. The referendum amended s 51(xxvi) and excised s 127. As we have seen, section 127 did not legally exclude Aboriginal and Torres Strait Islanders from being counted as citizens, but it excluded them from "membership of the constitutional community."[26] Similarly, while the states could make laws for Aboriginal and Torres Strait Islanders, alteration of s 51(xxvi) empowered the Commonwealth to do so on the same basis as all other "races." The referendum symbolically and practically expanded the idea of Australian identity by making room for First Nations peoples as equal members of a "single-status community."[27] Indigenous and non-Indigenous Australians alike could enjoy political equality.

The referendum was a momentous change, but it fell short of meeting First Nations peoples' aspirations. As Guugu Yimithirr lawyer and activist Noel Pearson later remarked, the absence of any explicit recognition of Aboriginal and Torres Strait Islander normative distinctiveness recorded their citizenship in neutral terms.[28] Indeed, following the referendum, Aboriginal and Torres Strait Islander peoples have increasingly articulated demands for recognition of their unique rights *as* First Nations peoples. These aspirations are embedded in and drawn from long histories as self-governing communities operating under their own source of laws prior to colonisation. When citizenship is understood as membership of a single-status community, these claims cannot be heard.

One of the more prominent early calls for the legal recognition of First Nations peoples' distinct rights occurred in August 1966. That month, Vincent Lingiari led 200 Gurindji stockmen, house servants, and their families off the Wave Hill Cattle Station in the Northern Territory following years of exploitation. While media and politicians initially saw the strike as a fight for fair wages and conditions, the Gurindji's motivations were clear: they wanted their land back.[29] Their resolve—alongside the determination of the Yolngu and Larrakia peoples who were advocating at the same time—led directly to enactment of the first land rights legislation in the country (*Aboriginal Land Rights (Northern Territory) Act* 1976). Similar legislation is now in place in all States.

The strength of the Gurindji and other First Nations communities has pushed Australia to recognise Indigenous peoples' differentiated status. Legal recognition comes in several major forms, including the establishment of distinct entitlements to land through native title and land rights regimes, and the protection of cultural heritage. An Indigenous sector that delivers services and represents First Nations peoples is also increasingly significant. Yet, these advances are precarious. As many First Nations peoples have remarked, understandings of Australianness continue to marginalise Aboriginal and Torres Strait Islander peoples' unique rights. The "psychological terra nullius" continues to exclude First Nations peoples as First Nations peoples.[30]

Concerns along these lines featured prominently in political and legal debate following the High Court's decision in *Mabo v Queensland (No 2)*, which held that the Australian common law could recognise Indigenous peoples' pre-colonial interests in land. A few weeks after the decision was handed down, President of the Western Australia Liberal Party, Bill Hassell, noted succinctly: "Mabo creates privilege—legal privilege based on race."[31] A Queensland legal scholar was particularly incensed, labelling the decision akin to "apartheid."[32]

Although expressed more subtly, the same anxiety is present in contemporary debate on constitutional recognition of Aboriginal and Torres Strait Islander peoples. In 2016, former Prime Minister Tony Abbott rejected growing calls for a treaty between First Nations peoples and the Australian state, noting: "A treaty is something that two nations make with each other, and obviously Aboriginal people are the first Australians, but in the end we're all Australians together, so I don't support a treaty."[33]

Likewise, the Institute for Public Affairs has persistently rejected the need for a First Nations Voice to be put in the Constitution, on the basis that "Indigenous Australians already have a voice to Parliament"—they can vote in the federal Parliament like every other citizen.[34] At the core of these statements is an understanding of Australian citizenship that denies space for First Nations peoples' distinct rights. For this line of thinking, constitutional reform unfairly positions Aboriginal and Torres Strait Islander people "as a favoured class of Australians entitled to pursue advantageous claims not available to others."[35] Sitting at the intersection of non-Indigenous anxieties over identity, membership, and belonging was the *Love* case.

The *Love* Litigation

Daniel Love and Brendan Thoms are both Aboriginal men who were born outside Australia. Love was born in Papua New Guinea (PNG) in 1979 to an Australian citizen father and PNG citizen mother. At birth, he became a citizen of PNG. He identifies as and is recognised by at least one elder as a Kamilaroi man. Thoms was born in Aotearoa New Zealand in 1988 to an Australian citizen mother and an Aotearoa New Zealand citizen father, and automatically became a citizen of Aotearoa New Zealand at birth. He identifies and is recognised by other members as a member of the Gunggari people. The Federal Court has recognised Gunggari native title and Thoms himself is a native title holder.[36] Both Love and Thoms came to Australia as children and have lived in the country into adulthood. Both were eligible for Australian citizenship by descent, but never took out this citizenship.

As adults, both Love and Thoms were convicted of separate offences and sentenced to a period of imprisonment of twelve months or more. As a result, both men had their visas cancelled by a delegate of the Minister for Home Affairs in accordance with s 501(3A) of the *Migration Act*. This provision relies on the aliens power for constitutional support and imposes mandatory (but reversible) visa cancellation on any non-citizen who is convicted of an offence and sentenced to more than twelve months imprisonment.

Love and Thoms challenged the cancellation of their visas on the grounds that, due to their Indigeneity, they were not constitutional aliens and therefore could not be deported under a statutory provision that relied on the aliens power for support. By contrast, the Commonwealth's argument was that Love and Thoms were aliens because they did not possess statutory citizenship, and in fact had not endeavoured to acquire it despite being eligible for citizenship by descent.

At the heart of the case was a question about the scope of the constitutional aliens power. The Constitution merely states that Parliament has a power to legislate with respect to "naturalization and aliens." It does not define or qualify what an "alien" is. Alien is originally a common law term used to denote people who were not British subjects. At common law, at least from 1608 when *Calvin's Case*[37] was decided, British subjects were regarded as those born in Crown territory. They owed "permanent allegiance" to the Crown (who owed them a corresponding duty of protection), while aliens did not. By the time Australia federated in 1901, these concepts had shifted, as a result of legislative developments in the UK. A changing set of statutory criteria defined who was entitled to British subject status, and British subjects could, in certain circumstances, renounce their subjecthood and divest themselves of their allegiance. In short, the law on alienage at Federation was fluid and actively shaped by legislative developments.[38]

A number of High Court judges over the years have concluded that this means that the Commonwealth Parliament has the power to affect who qualifies as a constitutional alien via its legislative development of Australian citizenship. Some have gone so far as to say that the terms "alien" and "non-citizen" are synonymous.[39] It is accepted that there are boundaries to this equivalence. Alien is a term inserted into the Constitution to place limits on Parliament's legislative capacity. If Parliament were able to define an alien to be anything it wanted, this limit would be illusory, and the *Constitution's* purpose would be frustrated.[40]

It is therefore more accurate to say that Parliament can, through citizenship legislation, define who is a citizen and who is an alien, but only within the bounds that the *Constitution* allows. A person who is capable of being regarded as a constitutional alien will be a non-alien if Parliament elects to grant them citizenship, and an alien if Parliament elects not to do so. But a person who is not capable of being regarded as a constitutional alien will always be a non-alien, whether or not Parliament grants them citizenship. Prior to 2020, non-citizens in a number of categories had argued that they were constitutional non-aliens. These included children born in Australia to non-citizen parents,[41] permanent residents who have lived in Australia since they were babies,[42] people who were British subjects—and therefore non-aliens prior to Australia acquiring legal independence from the UK[43]—and people born in PNG who had held Australian citizenship prior to PNG's independence.[44] The High Court held that people in all of these categories were capable of being regarded as aliens.

Love and Thoms were the first people to argue that First Nations people are constitutional belongers, incapable of being regarded as aliens. With precedent in other aliens power cases heavily underlining the breadth of Parliament's discretion, their claim required careful argument. While First Nations peoples are distinct from other classes of people who might assert non-alienage, by virtue of their deep and enduring connection to country and their legal systems predating Australian Federation, this is not reflected in the Australian Constitution. The constitutional text devotes significant attention to ensuring Parliament has flexibility over who can be excluded from Australia, while being silent on the question of who is definitively included. It does not state, in terms, that Aboriginal and Torres Strait Islander peoples are belongers, or expressly exclude them from the scope of the aliens power. Rather, since the changes made in the 1967 referendum, it does not mention them at all. At the time of Federation, Australia was regarded—erroneously—as terra nullius. It took until *Mabo (No 2)* in 1992 for this error to be legally recognised, and that case was a common law, rather than a constitutional decision. As we noted above, although the legal position of First Nations peoples has changed radically since Federation, this has largely fallen short of amounting to secure, substantive recognition of their differentiated status.

All seven members of the High Court acknowledged that Aboriginal and Torres Strait Islander peoples have a unique and significant connection to country. The point of difference between the majority and minority judges was whether that connection had constitutional force.

The three minority judges (Kiefel CJ and Gageler and Keane JJ) said that it did not. In their view, the breadth of the discretion afforded to Parliament under the aliens power and the lack of reference in the constitutional text to First Nations peoples being included amongst the body politic or excluded from the reach of the aliens power made it impossible to conclude, using accepted methods of constitutional interpretation, that Parliament could not treat Love and Thoms as aliens.[45] Both Gageler J and Keane J acknowledged that Love and Thoms' argument had moral force,[46] but found that, in the absence of constitutional recognition of First Nations people—which would require a referendum—it did not have legal force.[47] Both referred to the fact that the conversation about whether to amend the *Constitution* to include such recognition was currently underway.[48]

By contrast, the four majority judges (Bell, Nettle, Gordon, and Edelman JJ) found that Aboriginal Australians, understood according to the three-part test in *Mabo (No 2)*, are not within the reach of the aliens power.[49] They said that due to Aboriginal and Torres Strait Islander peoples' long-standing and deep connection to country, they cannot be said to be aliens, or outsiders to the Australian community, even if they do not hold statutory citizenship.[50]

There were some variances in how the majority judges reached this conclusion. Justices Gordon and Edelman drew attention to the inseparability of ties between First Nations peoples and the land that makes up Australia. Justice Edelman described First Nations peoples as "belongers to the Australian political community,"[51] and noted that their "metaphysical bonds" to country were "far stronger than those forged by the happenstance of birth on Australian land or the nationality of parentage."[52] Justice Gordon said:

> The constitutional term 'aliens' conveys otherness, being an 'outsider,' foreignness. The constitutional term 'aliens' does not apply to Aboriginal Australians, the original inhabitants of the country. An Aboriginal Australian is not an 'outsider' to Australia. ... Failure to recognise that Aboriginal Australians retain their connection with land and waters would distort the concept of alienage by ignoring the content, nature and depth of that connection. It would fail to recognise the first peoples of this country. It would fly in the face of decisions of this Court that recognise that connection and give it legal consequences befitting its significance.[53]

Justices Bell and Nettle found that it would be incongruous to recognise—as the High Court had in *Mabo (No 2)*—that First Nations peoples have a unique, spiritual connection with country, while also finding that they are capable of being described as constitutional aliens.[54] Justice Nettle went on to say that the common law recognition of Aboriginal societies "as the source and sanctuary of traditional laws and customs" means that the Crown owes an obligation to protect those societies and that they in turn owe a permanent allegiance to the Crown in right of Australia.[55]

The majority judges in *Love* did not necessarily conceive of the constitutional protection afforded to First Nations peoples in the same way. For example, Nettle J observed that since the protection of First Nations societies is a product of the common law, it is "conceivable that it could be abrogated by statute" and that this would bring First Nations peoples who were non-citizens within the reach of the aliens power.[56] By contrast, Gordon and Edelman JJ's draw on, but place less weight on, the common law position, and it seems implicit in their judgements that the constitutional position that First Nations peoples occupy cannot be dismantled through legislation.

Reflections on *Love* and First Nations Peoples' Membership in Australia

At one level, the decision in *Love* is limited. The judgment prevented the government's intended deportation of Daniel Love and Brendan Thoms. It also precludes the government from deporting other Aboriginal non-citizens under the *Migration Act*. This is not many people. The Department of Home Affairs informed the Parliament that at least twenty-three people in immigration detention may be Aboriginal non-citizens.[57] At a broader level, however, *Love* speaks to the contested nature of the place and status of First Nations peoples within the Australian community. In this final section we conclude with several reflections on *Love*.

The first point to note is that *Love* offers little concrete on the legal relationship of First Nations peoples to Australia. Justice Edelman describes Aboriginal peoples as "belongers" to the Australian political community. But for First Nations peoples who do not hold citizenship, all that *Love* really guarantees is immunity against expulsion under laws made pursuant to the aliens power. It is not clear that this status carries with it any of the other rights hinged upon statutory citizenship (e.g., voting rights), and it certainly does not amount to the kind of substantive belonging that First Nations peoples have been asking for, as described in the third section of this chapter. Can this really be described as belonging, in any meaningful sense?

One of the judges in the minority is alive to this problem. Justice Gageler draws attention to these challenges, noting that the majority's decision admits the existence of a category of non-citizen non-aliens who are "consigned to inhabit a constitutional netherworld."[58] His Honour also noted that at the *Love* hearing, a "notable absence" from the viewpoints expressed was "the viewpoint of any Aboriginal or Torres Strait Islander body representing any of the more than 700,000 citizens of

Australia who identify as Aboriginal or Torres Strait Islander."[59] While at least one Aboriginal person participated in the case, they did so intervening on behalf of the State of Victoria, rather than as a representative of First Nations peoples. Justice Gageler goes on to say:

> On the basis of the case as presented, I cannot presume that the political and societal ramifications of translating a communal, spiritual connection with the land and waters within the territorial limits of the Commonwealth of Australia into a legislatively ineradicable individual connection with the polity of the Commonwealth of Australia are able to be judicially appreciated.[60]

There are also complications in the way members of the majority reach their conclusion. Perhaps most curious is Nettle J's imputation that the common law recognition of First Nations peoples' connection with country amounts to a duty of protection on the Crown's part that carries with it an obligation that Aboriginal societies "owe permanent allegiance" to the Crown.[61] While his Honour recognises there might be instances of renunciation, this reasoning does not seem particularly in line with the kind of recognition that First Nations peoples have been advocating for as described in the third section. As Keane J recognised, it also smacks of paternalism:

> To accept the argument would be to accept limitations on the freedom of persons of Aboriginal descent to pursue their destiny as individuals. The autonomy of such persons would be constrained in a way that does not affect people who are not of Aboriginal descent.[62]

The political reaction to *Love* suggests further challenges going forward. Reflecting the decision's challenge to the government's policy of deporting non-citizens convicted of serious offences, members of the government were furious with the result. Many also focused on the notion that the decision violated the principle of equality by privileging Indigenous people over non-Indigenous people. Almost immediately, calls were made to reopen the decision. In 2021, in the *Montgomery* case, the government asked the High Court to overturn its decision. Following a change of government at the 2022 federal election, however, the case was withdrawn.

Conservative legal commentators have derided *Love* as "fundamentally challenging the idea that all Australians are equal," and nothing more than "ethno-nationalism frocked up as progress." Others, including prominent federal politicians, have claimed the decision enshrined "racism" in Australian law, by dividing "those who reside in Australia along racial lines."[63] At root in this criticism is the view that Aboriginal and Torres Strait Islander peoples' status as prior self-governing communities should have no legal significance in modern Australia. First Nations peoples' membership in the Australian community should be on the same terms as all Australians.

Australians will soon be asked whether they agree with this position. In the 2017 Uluru Statement from the Heart, Aboriginal and Torres Strait Islander peoples called for structural reform to "empower our people and take a rightful place in our own country."[64] The Statement called for a First Nations Voice to be put in the *Constitution*, and a Makarrata Commission to supervise agreement-making and truth-telling. In late 2023, Australians are expected to vote in a referendum on the Voice. An Indigenous representative body, the First Nations Voice, would empower Aboriginal and Torres Strait Islander peoples with the capacity to have their voices heard and interests considered in the processes of government. While debate is ongoing at this time, it is likely that the Voice will be authorised to make representations to Parliament and the Executive Government on law and policy that affect Indigenous Australians.

Referendums are difficult to win in Australia. Only eight referendums have succeeded from forty-four attempts since 1901. The political reaction to *Love* suggests inserting a Voice in the *Constitution* will be challenging. Indeed, conservative politicians and legal commentators have argued that the *Love* case weakens the prospect of a successful Yes vote. Senator James Paterson has warned that the judgement "perfectly illustrates the warnings constitutional conservatives" have "about the legal risks" of constitutional recognition.[65] Similarly, Morgan Begg has argued that "[t]o approve constitutional recognition would be an endorsement of the High Court's dangerous decision and empower future courts to make similar decisions."[66]

The legal consequences of *Love* are uncertain and, at this stage, limited. Nevertheless, the political reaction suggests that something as fundamental as the place of First Nations peoples within Australia remains unsettled. The Uluru Statement from the Heart seeks to resolve these tensions. As the Statement explains, constitutional reform will allow Aboriginal and Torres Strait Islander peoples "ancient sovereignty to shine through as a fuller expression of Australia's nationhood."[67]

Notes

1. Peter Veth and Sue O'Connor, "The Past 50,000 Years: An Archaeological View," in *The Cambridge History of Australia: Volume 1: Indigenous and Colonial Australia*, eds. Alison Bashford and Stuart Macintyre (Cambridge: Cambridge University Press 2013), 19.
2. Bain Attwood and Andrew Markus, *The 1967 Referendum: Race, Power and the Australian Constitution* (Canberra: Aboriginal Studies Press, 2007).

   For a more recent treatment of this and an analysis of other notable changes in terms of Indigeneity and citizenship in Australia between the 1950s and 1970s, see Jatinder Mann, *Redefining Citizenship in Australia, Canada and Aotearoa New Zealand* (New York: Peter Lang Publishing, 2019).
3. *Mabo v Queensland (No 2)* (1992) 175 CLR 1.
4. *Love; Thoms v Commonwealth* (2020) 270 CLR 152.
5. *Montgomery v Minister for Immigration, Citizenship, Migrant Services and Multicultural Affairs*, High Court of Australia, Case No S192/2021.
6. See John Williams, "Andrew Inglis Clark: Our Constitution and His Influence," *Papers on Parliament* 61 (2014): 89–91.
7. *Official Record of the Debates of the Australasian Federal Convention* Melbourne 1898, vol. 5, 1782, Josiah Symon.
8. *Official Record of the Debates of the Australasian Federal Convention* Melbourne 1898, vol. 4, 688, John Cockburn.
9. *Singh v Commonwealth* (2004) 222 CLR 322, 367.
10. *Official Record of the Debates of the Australasian Federal Convention* Melbourne 1898, vol. 1, 1760.
11. *Official Record of the Debates of the Australasian Federal Convention* Melbourne 1898, vol. 5, 1764, Josiah Symon.
12. See further Jatinder Mann, *The Search for a New National Identity: The Rise of Multiculturalism in Canada and Australia, 1890s–1970s* (New York: Peter Lang Publishing, 2016).
13. *Hwang v Commonwealth* (2005) 87 ALD 256, 259–60 [10].
14. See further Sangeetha Pillai, "The Rights and Responsibilities of Australian Citizenship: A Legislative Analysis." *Melbourne University Law Review* 37, 3 (2014): 736–785.
15. Great Britain House of Commons, 1837, 125–6.
16. Bruce Kercher, "Recognition of Indigenous Legal Autonomy in Nineteenth Century New South Wales," *Indigenous Law Bulletin* 4, 13 (1998): 7–9.
17. Russell McGregor, *Imagined Destines: Aboriginal Australians and the Doomed Race Theory, 1880–1939* (Melbourne: Melbourne University Press, 1997), 14–22.

18. Robin Holland, "The Impact of 'Doomed Race' Assumptions in the Administration of Queensland's Indigenous Population by the Chief Protectors of Aboriginals from 1897 to 1942," (MA Thesis) (Queensland University of Technology, 2013).
19. Harry Hobbs, *Indigenous Aspirations and Structural Reform in Australia* (Oxford: Hart Publishing, 2021), 18.
20. Anne Twomey, "An Obituary for Section 25 of the Constitution," *Public Law Review* 23, 2 (2012): 125–141.

    Greg Taylor, "A History of Section 127 of the *Commonwealth Constitution*," *Monash University Law Review* 42, 1 (2016): 206–237.
21. Elisa Arcioni, "Tracing the Ethno-Cultural or Racial Identity of the Australian Constitutional People," *Oxford University Commonwealth Law Journal* 15 (2015): 175.
22. John Chesterman, *Civil Rights: How Indigenous Australians Won Formal Equality* (Brisbane: University of Queensland Press, 2005).
23. Andrew Markus, "William Cooper and the 1937 Petition to the King," *Aboriginal History* 7 (1983): 57.
24. Paul Hasluck, *Shades of Darkness: Aboriginal Affairs 1925–1965* (Melbourne: Melbourne University Press, 1988), 93.
25. Commonwealth Parliament of Australia [Hansard], *House of Representatives Parliamentary Debates*, House of Representatives, 1 May 1962, 1771.
26. Elisa Arcioni, "Excluding Indigenous Australians From 'The People': A Reconsideration of s 25 and 127 of the Constitution," *Federal Law Review* 40 (2014): 17–18.
27. Geneviève Nootens, *Popular Sovereignty in the West: Polities, Contention, and Ideas* (Abingdon: Routledge, 2013), 58.
28. Noel Pearson, "Aboriginal Referendum a Test of Nation's Maturity." *The Australian*, 26 January 2011, https://capeyorkpartnership.org.au/news/aboriginal-referendum-a-test-of-national-maturity/.
29. Gurindji Petition to Lord Casey, Governor-General of Australia, 19 April 1967.
30. Larissa Behrendt, "White Picket Fences: Recognising Aboriginal Property Rights in Australia's Psychological *Terra Nullius*," *Constitutional Forum* 10, 2 (1999): 50.
31. Bill Hassell, "Mabo and Federalism: The Prospect of an Indigenous Peoples' Treaty," *Upholding the Australian Constitution: Proceedings of the Second Conference of The Samuel Griffith Society* 2 (1993): 36.
32. L. J. M. Cooray, "The High Court in Mabo: Legalist or L'égotiste," in *Make a Better Offer: The Politics of Mabo*, eds. Murray Goot and Tim Rowse (Sydney: Pluto Press, 1994), 95.
33. George Williams and Harry Hobbs, *Treaty*, 2nd ed. (Sydney: Federation Press, 2020), 138.

34. Institute of Public Affairs, *Four Reasons to Reject the Referendum Council Recommendations*, Parliamentary Research Brief, 28 July 2017.
35. Barry Maley, "Abandon Changes to the Constitution," *The Australian*, 5 August 2014, http://www.theaustralian.com.au/opinion/abandon-change-to-constitution/news-story/05889b172417cd71d09d226bafd52f8a.
36. *Kearns v Queensland* [2013] FCA 651; *Foster v Queensland* [2014] FCA 1318.
37. *Calvin's Case* (1608) 77 Eng Rep 377.
38. *Chetcuti v Commonwealth* [2021] HCA 25 [41] (Gordon J), [69] (Edelman J). See also Sangeetha Pillai, *The Legal Parameters of Australian Citizenship*. Doctoral dissertation, UNSW, 2015. UNSWorks: https://unsworks.unsw.edu.au/entities/publication/b0862db3-a924-42e2-9ac1-865dcae8480d, ch. 4.
39. See, for example, *Chu Kheng Lim v Minister for Immigration* (1992) 176 CLR 1, 25 (Brennan, Deane and Dawson JJ).
40. See, for example, *Pochi v Macphee* (1982) 151 CLR 101, 109 (Gibbs CJ).
41. *Singh v Commonwealth* (2004) 222 CLR 322; *Koroitamana v Commonwealth* (2006) 227 CLR 31.
42. *Minister for Immigration and Multicultural and Indigenous Affairs v Nystrom* (2006) 228 CLR 566.
43. *Shaw v Minister for Immigration and Multicultural Affairs* (2003) 218 CLR 28.
44. *Re Minister for Immigration and Multicultural and Indigenous Affairs; Ex parte Ame* (2005) 222 CLR 439.
45. *Love* 2020, Kiefel CJ [8] and [31], Gageler J [126]–[131], Keane J [177]–[181].
46. *Ibid.*, Gageler J [128], Keane J [178].
47. *Ibid.*, Gageler J [135], Keane J [178].
48. *Ibid.*, Gageler J [134], Keane J [178].
49. *Ibid.*, Bell J [81].
50. *Ibid.*, Bell J [74], Gordon J [296], Nettle J [276]–[278], Edelman J [398].
51. *Ibid.*, Edelman J [396].
52. *Ibid.*, Edelman J [396], Nettle J [276]–[278].
53. *Ibid.*, Gordon J [296]–[297].
54. *Ibid.*, Bell J [71], Nettle J [268]–[272].
55. *Ibid.*, Nettle J [272], [279].
56. *Ibid.*, Nettle J [283].
57. Evidence to Senate Legal and Constitutional Affairs Committee, 2020, 109.
58. *Love* 2020, Gageler J [131].
59. *Ibid.*, Gageler J [134].
60. *Ibid.*
61. *Ibid.*, Nettle J [279].

62. *Ibid.*, Keane J [217].
63. See Harry Hobbs, "The New Right and Aboriginal Rights in the High Court of Australia," *Federal Law Review* 51, 1 (2023): forthcoming.
64. Uluru Statement, 2017.
65. James Paterson, "The High Court *Love* Decision," Samuel Griffith Society, Online Speaker Series, 2020, 4.
66. Morgan Begg, "Courting Calamity," *IPA Review*, 2020.
67. Uluru Statement, 2017.

Bibliography

Arcioni, Elisa. "Excluding Indigenous Australians From 'The People': A Reconsideration of s 25 and 127 of the Constitution." *Federal Law Review*. 40, 2014: 1–29.

Arcioni, Elisa. "Tracing the Ethno-Cultural or Racial Identity of the Australian Constitutional People." *Oxford University Commonwealth Law Journal*. 15, 2015: 173–195. https://doi.org/10.1080/14729342.2016.1173350

Attwood, Bain and Andrew Markus. *The 1967 Referendum: Race, Power and the Australian Constitution*. Canberra: Aboriginal Studies Press, 2007.

Begg, Morgan. "Courting Calamity." *IPA Review*, 2020.

Behrendt, Larissa. "White Picket Fences: Recognising Aboriginal Property Rights in Australia's Psychological *Terra Nullius*." *Constitutional Forum*. 10, 2, 1999: 50–58.

Chesterman, John. *Civil Rights: How Indigenous Australians Won Formal Equality*. Brisbane: University of Queensland Press, 2005.

Cooray, L. J. M. "The High Court in Mabo: Legalist or L'égotiste." In *Make a Better Offer: The Politics of Mabo*, edited by Murray Goot and Tim Rowse: 82–96. Sydney: Pluto Press, 1994.

Hasluck, Paul. *Shades of Darkness: Aboriginal Affairs 1925–1965*. Melbourne: Melbourne University Press, 1988.

Hassell, Bill. "Mabo and Federalism: The Prospect of an Indigenous Peoples' Treaty." *Upholding the Australian Constitution: Proceedings of the Second Conference of The Samuel Griffith Society* 2, 1993: 34–46.

Hobbs, Harry. *Indigenous Aspirations and Structural Reform in Australia*. Oxford: Hart Publishing, 2021.

Hobbs, Harry. "The New Right and Aboriginal Rights in the High Court of Australia." *Federal Law Review*. 51, 1, 2023: forthcoming.

Kercher, Bruce. "Recognition of Indigenous Legal Autonomy in Nineteenth Century New South Wales." *Indigenous Law Bulletin*. 4, 13, 1998: 7.

Mann, Jatinder. *The Search for a New National Identity: The Rise of Multiculturalism in Canada and Australia, 1890s–1970s*. New York: Peter Lang Publishing, 2016.

Mann, Jatinder. *Redefining Citizenship in Australia, Canada and Aotearoa New Zealand*. New York: Peter Lang Publishing, 2019.

Markus, Andrew. "William Cooper and the 1937 Petition to the King." *Aboriginal History*. 7, 1983: 46–60.

McGregor, Russell. *Imagined Destines: Aboriginal Australians and the Doomed Race Theory, 1880–1939*. Melbourne: Melbourne University Press, 1997.

Nootens, Geneviève. *Popular Sovereignty in the West: Polities, Contention, and Ideas*. Abingdon: Routledge, 2013.

Pillai, Sangeetha. "The Rights and Responsibilities of Australian Citizenship: A Legislative Analysis." *Melbourne University Law Review*. 37, 3, 2014: 736–785.

Twomey, Anne. "An Obituary for Section 25 of the Constitution." *Public Law Review*. 23, 2, 2012: 125–141.

Taylor, Greg. "A History of Section 127 of the *Commonwealth Constitution*." *Monash University Law Review*. 42, 1, 2016: 206–237.

Veth, Peter and Sue O'Connor. "The Past 50,000 Years: An Archaeological View." In *The Cambridge History of Australia: Volume 1: Indigenous and Colonial Australia*, edited by Alison Bashford and Stuart Macintyre: 17–42. Cambridge: Cambridge University Press, 2013.

Williams, George and Harry Hobbs. *Treaty*, 2nd ed. Sydney: Federation Press, 2020.

Williams, John. "Andrew Inglis Clark: Our Constitution and His Influence." *Papers on Parliament*. 61, 2014.

CHAPTER 9

Questioning Canadian/First Nations Relations: An Argument for Dual-Citizenship

Chadwick Cowie

Introduction

The current relationship between First Nations[1] peoples, who make up one of three groups considered "Indigenous" under the *Constitution Act* 1982, and the Canadian state is the product of a narrow and one-sided view that has developed over centuries.[2] In regard to citizenship, there is an opportunity for First Nations to utilize the Canadian political system to recalibrate Canada's mentality towards their relationships. Although there is potential to utilize both First Nations and Canadian legal and social structures and representative bodies to create change, the issue of sovereignty, as well as its impact on citizenship and participation, in the

I am extremely thankful to the editor of this collection, Jatinder Mann, for his detailed feedback and helpful suggestions on my chapter.

C. Cowie (✉)
Department of Political Science, University of Toronto (Scarborough & St. George Campuses), Toronto, ON, Canada
e-mail: chadwick.cowie@utoronto.ca

J. Mann (ed.), *Citizenship in Transnational Perspective*, Politics of Citizenship and Migration,
https://doi.org/10.1007/978-3-031-34358-2_9

Canadian state must be explored. The importance of sovereignty has been a source of ongoing discussion when considering the issues that impact Canada's relationship with First Nations that it shares territory with. In addressing the issue of sovereignty, treaties, as well as First Nations citizenship, the potential for First Nations participation in the Canadian electoral process could further entrench the recognition of First Nations sovereignty and nationhood alongside that of the Canadian state.

This chapter will argue that the Westphalian idea of sovereignty should be replaced with a more contemporary version that acknowledges the ability of multiple nations[3] existing together within a shared territory. With the understanding of this new interpretation of sovereignty, Canada and First Nations could move forward and embrace a form of treaty federalism. The potential of treaty federalism to enhance First Nations recognition in, and alongside, the Canadian state could also be achieved if First Nations embraced the concept of dual-citizenship. By embracing dual-citizenship, First Nations could participate in the Canadian state while seeking changes internally for proper recognition of their rights and existence as distinct nations from the Canadian state. With dual-citizenship in practice, the issue of infringement on First Nations becomes non-assimilationist, a concern for opponents to such participation.

By arguing for a new understanding of sovereignty, Canada as a treaty federal state, and the idea of First Nations as dual-citizens, their participation in Canadian politics could become less threatening to First Nations and their recognition. In fact, as this chapter will argue, First Nations participation, as dual-citizens, in Canada's federal electoral process could be positive for First Nations because it allows them to directly influence who is being sent to the Canadian House of Commons. Traditionally, voter turnout for First Nations is low and, although debated, may be linked to numerous causations, such as a lack of concern and understanding from many Canadian politicians on the true Canadian/First Nations relationships. Today, change to the current First Nations/Canadian relationship is slow, if not stalemated at times. Therefore, whether First Nations could influence the Canadian political process should be an option to investigate. To consider the option of political participation, concerns over sovereignty must be assessed first.

Blended Recognition: The Importance of a New Concept of Sovereignty

The issue of sovereignty is problematic for the relationship between Canada and First Nations because of how it has been conceptualized since the *Peace of Westphalia* in 1648.[4] According to Frederico Lenzerini, the formation of Westphalian sovereignty "resulted in a concept of sovereignty that may be defined as supreme authority within a territory ... [with] authority, which has been defined as the right to command and correlatively the right to be obeyed."[5] Additionally, as Lenzerini points out, the ability to have the right to control territory is central to the definition of Westphalian sovereignty because it forms legitimacy for internal matters to be controlled by the sovereign.[6] In other words, the treaty outlined a new concept of sovereignty that defined how nation-states had control in their own territory to the exclusion of all outside forces.[7] The only ways for Westphalian sovereignty to be challenged or usurped by outside forces are if a territory claimed independence, a war occurred, or treaties that ceded territory to another sovereign state. It is this concept of sovereignty that has been consistently used by academics like Tom Flanagan and Alan Cairns to bolster their arguments against First Nations claims of sovereignty.

Lenzerini asserts that due to western dominance around the world for centuries, the idea of Westphalian sovereignty became adopted in situations of colonization for international law.[8] Thus, when individuals in various oppressed or colonial populations, like the American colonies, began pressing for their independence, their first step was to assert their sovereignty within the territory they claimed. The control of a territory was key for international recognition and Westphalian sovereignty. If a group of people were able to obtain control of a territory, such as the American colonists, their legitimacy under the concept of Westphalian sovereignty became harder to ignore.[9]

For instance, important requirements that coincide with the idea of Westphalian sovereignty are a permanent population, a defined territory, a government, and a capacity to enter relations with other states and polities.[10] If these items are key to sovereignty, then First Nations should have had sovereignty recognized in the Westphalian context as well, albeit with a view of protecting land rather than owning it. Additionally, the fact that the European states, especially Great Britain, entered treaties with First Nations would mean that they were indeed recognized sovereign entities. To add more credit to First Nations falling into the category of having had Westphalian sovereignty, the ruling made by the United States of America (USA) Chief Justice of the Supreme Court, John Marshall, in the case *Johnson v M'Intosh*, highlights recognition of First Nations sovereignty. The ruling stated that:

> North America … was held, occupied, and possessed, in full sovereignty, by various independent tribes or nations of Indians, who were sovereigns of their respective portions of the territory … and who neither acknowledged nor owed allegiance or obedience to any European sovereign or state.[11]

Furthermore, Chief Justice Marshall did identify cases where jurisdiction was shared and/or where First Nations had surrendered some forms of sovereignty, but as domestic and dependent nations to that of the USA through treaties.

Treaties were also a key part of non-Indigenous settlement in parts of present-day Canada. However, many Canadian court cases have asserted the possibility of rights for First Nations to pursue self-determination.[12] Moreover, the Canadian courts have ruled that Indigenous title had not necessarily been extinguished through the treaty process. By the courts acknowledging that title may not have been extinguished, the need to consult, negotiate, and meet with Indigenous peoples when relating to said land should be required.[13] However, these rulings have been used in a very narrow view that often favours Canadian dominance instead of recognizing both as sharing sovereignty through the original relationship. For example, in *Delgamuukw v British Columbia*, the court was cautious in its decision and elaborated that proof must be presented rather than claiming in favour of First Nations sovereignties.[14] Additionally, in *R v van der Peet*, the courts outlined a more constrictive "cultural" test to assess how, and when, Indigenous rights can be limited in order to protect the economic benefits of all those now residing in the Canadian state.[15] *Delgamuukw v the Queen* and *R v van der Peet* are only two examples where the Canadian state has chosen to ignore Indigenous sovereignties as well as an opportunity to comprehend the First Nations viewpoints on what sovereignty means to them. The importance of including First Nations understandings of sovereignty is important as it highlights the differences in understanding between western and First Nations philosophies regarding the subject.

Both Patricia Monture-Angus and David Wilkins assist in highlighting the differences between Westphalian sovereignty and First Nations concepts of sovereignty at the time Europe formulated, and agreed to, the *Peace of Westphalia*. Wilkins points out that for many First Nations, their structures and understandings of land pre-date Westphalian sovereignty and European contact. Hence, First Nations views on land hold far more credibility to First Nations and must be given due credit by Canada if First Nations are to embrace working with the state.[16] Furthermore, the concept of having control over territory goes against First Nations philosophies that exist about the earth being a fellow citizen and thus something one cannot own.[17] Instead, the idea of "sovereignty," or self-determination as Monture-Angus calls it, is "not about ownership of territory in the way that [Western] politicians and lawyers would define those words ... [but as referring to] *tewatatha:wi*, [which translates to] we carry ourselves."[18] Monture-Angus continues that tewatatha:wi means that "sovereignty to [her] is a responsibility. It is a responsibility to carry ourselves: collectively as nations, as clans, as families, as well as individually in a good way ... in order to take care of the Earth."[19] In Monture-Angus' context of "sovereignty," it becomes clear that for First Nations sovereignty is about more than just a land base but is about autonomy and control over their own sustainability.

Therefore, the western and First Nations understandings of sovereignty are quite different, and this has added to the misunderstandings that exist between both Canada and First Nations. The differences between Westphalian sovereignty and the idea of "sovereignty" outlined by Monture-Angus, thus, highlight the need for a more contemporary view that recognizes First Nations and the Canadian state for a better partnership and coexistence for all those involved. Fortunately, as the world shifted to a more globalized perspective, so have the theories on sovereignty.

With the establishment of the United Nations (UN) in the 1940s and the horrors witnessed and learned from World War II, the idea of sovereignty and European domination in the world faced questions of validity. With the decline of European control and dominance over colonies around the world, western thought continued to influence international relations and rules. However, a noticeable trend occurring through international structures such as the UN and the International Criminal Court, according to Lenzerini and Wilkins, is beginning to challenge western theory of sovereignty.

For instance, Lenzerini highlights how concessions made by states vis-à-vis other governments with the purpose of satisfying shared individual interests, such as the North American Free Trade Agreement or the

European Union, have blurred the lines of state jurisdiction and parts of Westphalian sovereignty.[20] With international law and agreements bringing various sovereign states together in times of mutually shared needs, a question of whether or not treaties between First Nations, the British Crown, and Canada could also be viewed this way needs to be considered.

Lenzerini points to the International Court of Justice's (I.C.J.) 1975 Advisory Opinion, in relation to the Spanish colonization of the Western Sahara, as an example of the international community rejecting key practices used for colonizing. To bolster the I.C.J. example, he explains that the Advisory Opinion on Spanish colonization of the Western Sahara was the first time the international community recognized that *terra nullius* was invalid and not a sufficient reason for the forceful colonization of territories that had been inhabited by others.[21] The opinion further expressed that whether the population was nomadic or not, they were socially and politically organized in tribes and under chiefs that had been competent to represent them at the time of contact.[22] The I.C.J. ruling and the fact the majority of the international community agreed with it had an impact on many modern states when working with Indigenous nations they shared territory with. Furthermore, the recognition that colonization did not remove Indigenous jurisdictions and nationhood bolsters the idea that Canada must recognize Indigenous nations it shares territory with as equal partners with their own jurisdictions and citizenship codes.

Despite this ruling and the opportunities presented with it, many states, including Canada, fear visiting the issue of First Nations sovereignty because of the reliance on a Westphalian mentality. In other words, for many states the dominant interpretation of self-determination is linked to independence and complete control over their own territory.[23] But Canada should be less fearful to visit the idea of a contemporary form of sovereignty as the treaties allow for the existence of both treaty partners in the territory they share. In fact, the recognition of both sides of the relationships would give more credibility to Canada's existence as the treaty process would then be followed rather than ignored, the relationship of mutual respect and working together re-established, and First Nations citizenship to their respective nations recognized. A concern that may arise, despite treaty recognition solidifying Canada's existence, is whether First Nations would then seek status as autonomous states.

Roderic Pitty and Shannara Smith address this concern when discussing First Nations recognition. As Pitty and Smith point out, many First

Nations "do not wish to be states ... and while they claim autonomy, they do not claim a blanket principle of non-interference."[24] In other words, for First Nations who are in a relationship with the Canadian state, a modern understanding of sovereignty, where both sides can exist together and maintain separate forms of sovereignty, could be achieved without fear of dismantling Canada. The ability for joint recognition and sovereignty is even more probable because of Canada's *Constitution Act* 1982, which protects existing treaty rights.[25] A problem, however, with the reliance on the *Constitution Act* 1982, is that it has been used to bolster Canadian sovereignty, authority, and control over territory and First Nations rather than recognize an equal and shared existence.

Another example that could help with the development of a new understanding of sovereignty between First Nations and Canada is through the United Nations Declaration on the Rights of Indigenous Peoples (UNDRIP). The UNDRIP, as Pitty and Smith express, is one of the most important documents that not only represent Indigenous rights but also an opportunity to challenge and replace the notion of Westphalian sovereignty and its use to limit Indigenous claims of recognition and rights.[26] With the use of UNDRIP, the potential to move forward with a form of joint recognition of sovereignty because of the rights it seeks to protect, such as self-determination, jurisdiction, as well as citizenship.

If UNDRIP is about rights, then past international examples showing "support for rights treaties [as having] unanticipated consequences in civil society and within the government, so that what were thought to be empty pledges might actually change domestic authority structures."[27] The example Pitty and Smith use to highlight how a rights treaty, that was originally thought to be empty pledges, has actually influenced various states is that of the United Nations Declaration of Human Rights (UNDHR). Although not every state follows the UNDHR, the majority that have agreed to it have been forced or shamed into implementing better human rights standards. In Canada, the UNDHR had helped in advancing Indigenous claims of inequality, such as the treatment of Indigenous women. Nevertheless, it is UNDRIP that could be the most promising for Indigenous/Canadian relations and cooperation.

Although UNDRIP was adopted by the UN General Assembly in 2007, Australia, Aotearoa New Zealand, the USA, and Canada voted against it due to concerns such as the integrity of their own sovereignty.[28] The specific article that was of concern for Canada and other states was Article 3, which outlined the right of Indigenous people to self-determination.[29] As stated earlier in this chapter, the right to self-determination in a Westphalian sense is one of independence. However, many of those involved in the UN Indigenous committee had continuously tried to express that UNDRIP was a declaration that could allow Indigenous nations and modern states to co-exist. To this end, Cree representative Ted Moses expressed that "the Cree have no interest in secession from Canada. We want self-determination to be recognized so that we can finally become part of Canada."[30]

With the development of the UN, Human Rights Agreements that complement treaty relationships, and a more globalized world and view of sovereignty, the potential for Canada to re-establish a mutual relationship and an understanding of shared territory could be recovered. The development of international organizations and the signing of international agreements have helped demonstrate this possibility for Canada and the Indigenous nations. A similar understanding could come into existence, which would see the Indigenous nations working alongside and within Canada rather than as separate entities in the Westphalian sense—this will be elaborated on in more detail when considering dual-citizenship. The recognition of Indigenous sovereignties does not infringe on Canadian existence, especially when looked at from a more contemporary view of sovereignty. Rather, Indigenous sovereignty should be viewed as being parallel to the Canadian state. Doing so could alleviate the Canadian concern of sovereignty and witness the birth of Canada into a contemporary federalist state that would, thus, recognize First Nations as partners.

Treaty Federalism: Working Together to Rebuild the Relationship

The concept of treaty federalism is something that has been given little consideration at the present time. Treaty federalism, although primarily a view that is brought forth by First Nations academics, is one that recognizes First Nations as being partners to the state of Canada. The entrenchment of section 35 in the *Constitution Act* 1982 enhances the idea of treaty federalism, according to Sakej Youngblood Henderson, as it highlights the importance of treaty rights that were outlined in the treaties formulated between the British Crown and First Nations.[31] By doing so, the place of First Nations and the treaties they signed are important to the existence of Canada. As Henderson has argued, the treaties signed allow the Canadian federation to exist as they grant the ability for non-Indigenous people to settle on the land peacefully, alongside Indigenous nations.

A consideration of similar examples to such an understanding of equal recognition in Canada is needed to see if Henderson's idea on treaty federalism may work. The province of Quebec and its unique recognition in the Canadian state could highlight the potential for dual recognition and treaty federalism because of the agreements brokered for its decision to federate. John Borrows, in his book *Canada's Indigenous Constitution*, highlights the example of Quebec because of its recognition as a nation within the Canadian state. Borrows furthers Quebec as an example, specifically to bolster the potential of recognition for First Nations, because:

> Canada's founders rejected the idea of forced cultural coercion, at least as it related to the most critical challenges they encountered: French and English, juridical, cultural, religious, and linguistic differences. Although this framework was not [originally] extended to Indigenous peoples, it is not too late to do so.[32]

Since Canada recognized the place of Quebec and the social differences that Quebec brought to federation, according to Borrows, Canada can properly include and recognize First Nations territories, jurisdictions, and differences of First Nations. Canada's actions in recognizing First Nations as such would bring forth treaty federalism and could then allow a stronger and entrenched recognition of the duality of the relationship between Canada and First Nations. Quebec is not the only example that could bolster the concept of treaty federalism for First Nations.

Kiera Ladner illustrates how similar agreements recognized First Nations as equal partners and thus gives credibility to the potential of treaty federalism to exist. Ladner expresses that although it is mainly a First Nation concept today, it was one that the original settler governments recognized and validated. One such example was in 1705 when a Royal Commission concluded and recognized the Mohegan nation to be a sovereign entity and was not subservient to the British colonies that it was now sharing territory with.[33] In other words, the Mohegan nation was not controlled by the British Colonies but instead was an equal and possibly, a partner in the territory on which both were residing. With consideration of First Nations as equal partners in the relationship, the potential for a renewed understanding and First Nations to embrace recognition as dual entities inside both Canada and their respective nations is possible. Since First Nations had not relinquished key components of their sovereignty, the constitutional orders that encompass their political and legal ways must be recognized and allowed to flourish for distrust towards Canadian citizenship and the state to dwindle.[34]

The concept of recognizing First Nations legal and political orders also has credit in the British common-law system due to the practice of *lex loci*. As Russell Lawrence Barsh has concluded, the idea of *lex loci* is to "hold that local laws and governing institutions of a territory are respected and become incorporated under the common law."[35] Barsh further points out that there were many examples in the British Empire where, regardless of how a territory became part of the Crown's area of influence, the local laws remained. But even if the local laws were inconsistent with British law, they remained in place unless expressly changed or modified by both sides.[36] Kiera Ladner and Michael McCrossan add to Barsh's *lex loci* argument by showing how it was forgotten as a more colonial mindset replaced the idea of peace and friendship. Despite the change in mindset, First Nations never forgot their laws or British tradition of *lex loci*. Thus, the potential for treaty federalism to exist has further opportunity due to past agreements that Britain, and to some extent Canada, had signed and supposedly agreed to honour. Further credit and potential for treaty federalism may also exist with the constitutional amendments of 1982, specifically section 35.

According to Ladner, McCrossan, and Henderson, section 35 of the *Constitution Act* established a post-colonial roadmap for Canada by complementing the idea of *lex loci* and bringing Indigenous legal orders, laws, and jurisdictions into constitutionally recognized and guaranteed rights.[37] By recognizing and practicing *lex loci*, alongside section 35, the possibilities of the Canadian/Indigenous relationships gaining momentum for proper re-establishment become a greater possibility for coexistence and inter-development. A Royal Commission that was established by the Mulroney Government would come to a similar conclusion.

The Royal Commission on Aboriginal Peoples (RCAP) (1996) also highlighted the importance of a *lex loci* concept being law in British North America, even after Canada's federation. For instance, the report expressed that:

> Over time and by a variety of methods, Aboriginal people became part of the emerging federation of Canada while retaining their rights to their laws,

> lands, political structures and internal autonomy as a matter of Canadian common law … the treaties form a fundamental part of the constitution and for many Aboriginal peoples, plays a role similar to that played by the *Constitution Act*, 1867 in relation to the Provinces.[38]

The significance of the above excerpt from the RCAP is important as it offers additional validity to the concept of not only *lex loci* and nation-to-nation relationships but also what the idea of treaty federalism could stand for if implemented. Additionally, RCAP is an example of the Canadian state being notified of where it belongs in the First Nations/Canadian relationship—as an equal partner in living on the land and the federation of the Canadian state. Unfortunately, the Chretien government and the opposition parties did little to address what RCAP had framed as suggestions that Canada could implement to foster a better and more mutually beneficial relationship with First Nations. Furthermore, it would be interesting to delve further into whether a lack of First Nations influences on Canadian politicians inside and outside of the House of Commons may have contributed to Canada's laissez-faire attitude towards *RCAP's* findings and the potential of treaty federalism.

If Canada began to implement and recognize the option of treaty federalism, the issue of oppression and domination can be ended and the process of decolonizing the Canadian/First Nations relationships begun. In doing so, according to Ladner, the institutional conditions that are needed for a colonial state to move forward can be achieved and recognition that First Nations have rights and differences would be met.[39] Ladner highlights this point by assessing the clause of Peace, Order, and Good Governance (POGG) that have been included in some of the numbered treaties that Canada has signed, such as Treaty Six and Treaty Seven.

In Ladner's interpretation of Treaty Six and Treaty Seven, the potential for the POGG clause to, in some ways, illustrate treaty federalism is considerable. Moreover, the POGG clause may also be a guarantee for the Treaty Six and Treaty Seven signatories to have a right to delegated representation in the Canadian political system. Ladner elaborates on POGG when she shows that:

> Constructing a system [such as with a peace, order and good governance clause] which recognizes the existence of nations and whereby the leaders of the Cree, Blackfoot, Blood, and Peigan [the First Nations that signed treaties six and seven] could share, in the responsibility of maintaining peace

and order, particularistic representation would be a reflection of, and thus not a detraction from Treaties Six and Seven.[40]

In other words, the potential wording of the clause for POGG could allow for First Nations who signed Treaties Six and Seven to send delegates to the Canadian Parliament. Additionally, the statements that coincide with POGG could be viewed as suggesting that Canada expected First Nations to also keep peace and order in their territories, with the other First Nations, as well as with non-Indigenous peoples.[41] Meanwhile, the Canadian government would also be responsible for keeping peace and order throughout the entire territory, and in doing so would mean that POGG would allow them political representation through delegates in the Canadian House of Commons.[42] According to Ladner, this interpretation recognizes the change in the relationship that has occurred while also continuing to recognize First Nations as having their own jurisdictions and sovereignties alongside Canada.

Unfortunately, the concept of POGG and treaty federalism being thought of to recognize and affirm sovereignty of the First Nations alongside that of the Canadian state has gained little acknowledgement or attention from the courts and/or the Canadian government. Henderson believes that a shift to treaty federalism has yet to occur because of the lack of will from Canadian politicians to embrace it. For instance, Henderson believes that "Canadian politics lacks creative capacity to construct political relations with others."[43] If Ladner and Henderson are correct in their views that there is little interest and political will from inside the Canadian political system, First Nations must consider other options to convince them otherwise—such as influence through the ballot box.

Voting as Canadian citizens, using dual-citizenship, may be needed since section 35 of the *Constitution Act* 1982 and the suggestions from RCAP have been of little use to bringing Canada to accept the concept of treaty federalism. Although there is a debate amongst First Nations in relation to electoral participation, with fears of it undermining their sovereignties and accepting Canadian imposition, whether voting is a possible solution needs to be assessed. In fact, the potential of a contemporary version of sovereignty, and the view of treaty federalism, could give greater support to the idea of First Nations as dual-citizens. The concept of dual-citizenship may offer additional support in moving Canada forward to a more open and revitalized view of Canadian/First Nations relationships.

Dual-Citizenship: The Myth of Participation Equaling Assimilation

The Canadian government in the past has used citizenship rights to assimilate First Nations and degrade their identities as belonging to sovereign and separate nations and confederacies. These tactics assisted in tarnishing the relationship and trust that First Nations had towards the Canadian state, government, and citizenship. However, in the cases of First Nations, the ability to participate in Canadian citizenship, and hence also with the electoral process, did not hinder the status of their nationhood as had been thought.

In some cases, as Ladner has argued, parts of the numbered treaties could be used to claim that First Nations involved may have a right to delegated representation. Borrows expands this idea for all treatied areas because "treaties between Indigenous peoples and the Crown promote peace and order across cultures and are the basis of the country's formation and continued reformation."[44] In other words, Borrows believes that because of the treaties signed, respect and inclusion of treatied First Nations were recognized. Respect and inclusion of First Nations also extends into the Canadian political process because both societies were to share the territory that was treatied. Borrows highlights that this is even more probable because not all First Nations people reside within their own communities or territories.

Borrows elaborates further on First Nations stating that even though some may live in their traditional territories or in designated communities, many also live in Canadian towns and cities. Furthermore, influences from national and international forces, such as education, culture, and spirituality, will continue to impact First Nations, their way of life, and viewpoints no matter how remote or traditional they may be.[45] Hence, even if First Nations became completely autonomous, they would encounter a geography, history, economic system, and political landscape that would require a working relationship alongside Canada to reach any objectives they may seek in the globalized world of today.[46] With treaty federalism and dual-citizenship, First Nations could still have their autonomy while also working within and alongside Canada. By working with Canada through an interdependent nation-to-nation view, First Nations would have more opportunity to garner what is needed in a globalizing world rather than trying to do so on their own.

The idea of jointly working with Canada from within the Canadian system may lead some First Nations to believe Borrows is promoting the same ideas that Cairns and Kymlicka have suggested when looking at the place that First Nations have in Canada. Borrows rebuts such accusations, stating that:

> Assimilation implies a loss of political control, culture and difference. Aboriginal control of Canadian affairs has the potential to facilitate the acquisition of political control, culture, and difference because it could change contemporary notions of Canadian citizenship.[47]

With Borrows explaining that his view is not promoting assimilation but another method to expand and re-establish First Nations authority, the possibility for influencing the Canadian political system, by voting as dual-citizens, could also be considered another option.

To further his own point of using the Canadian system, Borrows assesses the *Gus Wen Tah*, two-row wampum treaty. The two-row wampum treaty is a part of the "peace and friendship" treaties that spoke to two boats going down the river side-by-side without interfering with one another. Although this has been the common reflection of the Gus Wen Tah, Borrows explains that there is another interpretation to consider. Borrows details how there are more than two purple rows and that the three rows of white beads represent a counter-balancing message.[48] Borrows highlights that the white rows of the Gus Wen Tah are the bed of the agreement and stand for peace, friendship, and respect.[49] When the principles of peace, friendship, and respect are combined, according to Borrows, it can be thought to include "that ideas of cooperation have also been rooted in notions of mutuality and interconnectedness."[50] Through mutuality and interconnectedness, Borrows argues, First Nations should feel they have the right and ability to be involved in the Canadian state and not fear degrading their citizenship to their respective nations as they seek to practise the use of shared territory and recognition.[51]

Moreover, another belt that came after the Gus Wen Tah was exchanged at Niagara in 1764 and may add more credit to Borrows' point. This other belt emphasized the interdependence between First Nations and British subjects in North America. Borrows describes it as:

> A ship woven into one end of the belt with its bow facing towards Quebec. At the other end of the belt is an image of Michilimackinac, a place in the

centre of the Great Lakes regarded as the heart of the Chippewa-Anishinaabe homelands. Between the two objects were woven twenty-four Indians holding one another's hands, with the person furthest to the right holding the cable of the ship, while the one on the extreme left has his foot resting on the land at Quebec. Representatives of the twenty-two First Nations assembled at Niagara in 1764 touched this 'Belt of Peace' as a symbol of friendship and as a pledge to become 'united.'[52]

In other words, by considering Borrows' view of the Gus Wen Tah and the additional belt from 1764, the idea of cooperation and interdependence is a plausible option that not only responds to the Royal Proclamation of 1763 but also highlights the idea of treaty federalism and the potential of dual-citizenship. But Borrows' point only highlights for those who were involved with the 1764 treaty process and does not take into consideration any future treaties that the Crown and the Canadian state may have made with First Nations later. Therefore, it is important to find broader proof that highlights how First Nations may not be vulnerable to further degradation by practising dual-citizenship and participation in the Canadian state.

One such example comes from David Wilkins, who believes that such recognition could help influence Canada in recognizing First Nations once again. Wilkins believes First Nations, by participating in the state they share territory with, are not infringing on the sovereignty of First Nations because:

Tribal nations continued to exist as separate sovereign entities since citizenship only applied to individual Indians, not Indian nations. Second, established voting eligibility criteria, and being well aware of the ongoing vitality of tribal sovereignty as evidenced by a) treaty rights which exempt Indian lands and their members from most regulations and taxation; and b) clauses that detail that state governments cannot extend their jurisdiction or taxing authority over Indian lands held in trust status.[53]

Although Wilkins' argument on First Nations sovereignties is more focused on the USA/First Nations relationship, there is potential for a similar understanding to be developed in Canada. By reviewing Canada's own laws that granted voting to First Nations (1960) (see Mann's second substantial chapter in this collection), there is no hint that the legislation removed their jurisdiction in their territories and that Canadian citizenship erased their rights as citizens to their nations. Although previous policies relating to citizenship did force First Nations to surrender their Indigeneity, the legislation used to grant citizenship in 1870, 1954, and 1960 had not.

Wilkins would point out that this is like how in the USA citizenship was transferred to each Indigenous person as an individual rather than imposed on the actual nation itself. In other words, the sovereignty of each Indigenous nation was not impacted as it was granted to the individual and did not restrict their Indigeneity.[54] Instead, Indigenous people have been granted a form of dual-citizenship.

The idea of dual-citizenship, in the Canadian context, was also suggested in RCAP's conclusions in 1996.[55] Yet, the potential of First Nations recognizing themselves as dual-citizens has not yet been achieved because it is yet to be a concept discussed, debated, or considered in the Canadian context. In other words, although the discussion and concept have been considered and partially recognized in the USA, a similar understanding has yet to be fully broached in relation to Canadian/First Nations relationships. If the idea of dual-citizenship was to be considered, the potential for further recognition by influencing the Canadian political process is a viable option that does not threaten First Nations sovereignties.

Despite this potential it has been avoided, other than in RCAP's findings, in the Canadian context. The possible reasons could range from not knowing that such possibility exists to the fact many may not realize the potential political power such recognition could have. However, if First Nations viewed themselves as dual-citizens of their nations and the Canadian state, as Borrows argues, the use of Canada's legal and political institutions would be less threatening.[56] Influence on the legal and political institutions of Canada could allow for First Nations to protect, maintain, and affirm their political, economic, and sociological systems.[57]

Taiaiake Alfred would disagree. He maintains that the only way to rebuild and recognize the sovereignties of First Nations is to remove western influences from their lives and return to their traditional ways. Alfred, in *Wasase*, gives examples of other nations who he believes have been able to achieve recognition through their own ways. To bolster his view, he examines the Philippines, India, and Myanmar. Regarding the Philippines, Alfred addresses the Filipino concept of identity that is based on *kapwa*, a Tagalog word meaning "shared being." The shared being highlights that there is no concept of a separate existence from others and everything shared.[58] Alfred points out that Filipinos, no matter where they may live, now have held on to this concept. Additionally, Alfred cites India as being another example, for decolonizing itself after removing British control over its territory some six decades ago through the Gandhian movement, and Myanmar due to Aung San Suu Kyi's resistance to the totalitarian military rule that continues to control her home territory.[59]

Although Alfred's points are poignant, there are problems with his conclusion regarding the examples above. In fact, the three examples could be used more appropriately for why dual-citizenship and mutual recognition can exist. For instance, in the case of Filipinos, it is an example of a key concept of an Indigenous culture surviving the colonization and establishment of the Philippines over territory held by dozens of Indigenous peoples, while still utilizing western forms of government and economics. Regarding India, there are also problems with Alfred's points as modern India is also the result of British influences and comprises more than a dozen different Indigenous states that were forcibly unified. India also still reflects the differences of the groups who reside there yet makes use of a western form of government, economic structures, as well as British-like boarding schools. Lastly, Myanmar's Aung San Suu Kyi has used the political process, which was established by its colonial British past, to push for democracy and changes to the state. Thus, the examples Alfred uses are not ones that bolster his point exclusively but rather show what can be achieved, albeit not yet perfected, when people make use of the tools that they have around them. The use of Canada's political systems and dual-citizenship to entrench and push for recognition of the original Canadian/First Nations relationship may have just as much potential to do so because of Alfred's own examples that contradict his argument.

Borrows furthers this argument by highlighting the need for First Nations to work not only as individuals and groups within their nations but also in the Canadian state. By participating in the Canadian state at large, the potential to increase First Nations influence over matters of importance will gain more traction within Canada.[60] The point of increasing their influence would also mean welcoming people into their nations who may not be related by blood.[61] The idea of welcoming individuals who are not blood related into an Indigenous nation follows many traditional forms of societal structures amongst First Nations. Hence, recognition of non-First Nations peoples as possible citizens of an Indigenous nation would increase better understanding, respect of First Nations ways of life but also cohesion between Canada and each respective nation. Pam Palmater adds to this concept of extending citizenship to non-Indigenous people to think beyond blood as being how one becomes a citizen of an Indigenous nation. In fact, welcoming those who come from around the world and who follow the key principles that an Indigenous nation outlines in their citizenship codes, matches the natural system that many used prior to colonization. The difference is that including Canadians and those who immigrate to Canada would allow many individuals to not only participate but also see what First Nations legal, political, social, and citizenship standards truly are.[62] Therefore, granting dual-citizenship to non-Indigenous peoples could allow for First Nations philosophies to be adopted and pushed by non-First Nations on to the Canadian state.

One such view that is an important cornerstone to many First Nations is the recognition of the earth as an equal and fellow citizen within their nation. Various Indigenous nations have long recognized the importance of the earth, and all it offers, because without its sustenance they would cease to exist. Borrows describes the importance of the earth being a fellow citizen and that First Nations need to look past just control over their own affairs since the land is now shared with other societies and peoples.[63] According to Borrows:

> Our births, lives, and deaths on [the land] have brought us into citizenship with the land. We participate in its renewal, have the responsibility for its continuation, and grieve for its losses. As citizens of this land, we also feel the presence of our ancestors, and strive with them to have the relationship of our polity respected.[64]

In other words, the view of the land as a fellow citizen is a key component to many First Nations societies. Moreover, many continue to push for recognition of the land as a fellow citizen due to the historical and sustainable connections that are important to their nationhood and citizenship codes, as outlined by Monture-Angus and Borrows.

Using voting as dual-citizens, Borrows further explains the potential for First Nations input on how the earth is regarded would be more likely listened to. In turn, the activity of First Nations having their views regarded could lead to the earth being recognized as an entity in the Canadian state that all citizens must be mindful towards.[65] But both Borrows and Wilkins acknowledge that if First Nations are to participate in the Canadian state in order to make these type of changes occur, a great deal of influence within Canada's political institutions must be made to see such items implemented in party policy and legislation. By First Nations directly impacting who may sit in Canada's House of Commons, there may be a greater likelihood that what First Nations seek in recognition regarding Canadian/First Nations relations could be implemented. Thus, the option for First Nations to view themselves as dual-citizens could ease fear of further degradation towards their nations as they seek recognition of the original relationship and their sovereignty by casting a ballot in Canada's electoral process.

Conclusion

Without consideration of contemporary forms of sovereignty and recognition of potential change using the Canadian political process within both the Canadian and First Nations psyches, the idea of dual-citizenship will continue to be unused. In addition, the potential of treaty federalism and jointly recognized sovereignty will be even less achievable if dual-citizenship is unpractised. Furthermore, how dual-citizenship can be practised and recognized may further rely on individual studies of the treaties that the various First Nations have entered. Despite the need for additional research on individual treaties in relation to dual-citizenship, this chapter has pointed to important concepts of sovereignty, treaty federalism, and dual-citizenship. These concepts relate directly to First Nations sovereignties and how many First Nations opt for non-involvement in the Canadian political process due to fears that doing so will degrade their nation, identity, and citizenship codes.

In assessing Westphalian sovereignty, it becomes clear that the definition of sovereignty has been one to benefit the European states that existed and dominated the world at the time of its inception. With it also comes a Eurocentric understanding of citizenship. But new viewpoints arose due to more interconnected nations and peoples around the world and a recognition of some states of the need to work alongside each other through treaties and organizations that tie them together. Although it was a non-binding document, the best and most recent example of this is UNDRIP.

The potential for treaty federalism coming into play, with the adoption of a more contemporary view of sovereignty, allows for both First Nations and the Canadian state to move forward together in a retrenched and mutually respectful relationship, as highlighted by RCAP. In fact, recognition of treaty federalism in Canada could allow for mutual respect, with many First Nations opting to take a similar level of recognition as the Canadian provinces and therefore not impacting the ability of the Canadian state to govern in the territory shared. Lastly, citizenship rights that were enacted in 1960 were not like previous experiences of enfranchisement that the Canadian government had imposed (see Mann's second substantial chapter in this collection).[66] Instead, by using Wilkins' argument in the Canadian context, it could have brought forth a form of dual-citizenship. In other words, since citizenship can only be granted to an individual, it must stipulate whether they must rescind other forms of recognition of citizenship to other nations. By First Nations no longer having Canadian citizenship imposed and replacing their Identity, but rather co-existing alongside of it, using their dual-citizenship can bring forth change to the Canadian state mentality. First Nations jurisdictions, treaty federalism, as well as joint sovereignty could be recognized by First Nations having their philosophies integrated into the state as well as the mindsets of Canada's citizens and politicians.

The ability for such recognition may not rest with just the concept of dual-citizenship but also from the potential First Nations peoples may wield in Canada's electoral process. First Nations sway on Canada's electoral process is also important to consider when discussing the utilization of the Canadian state to cause change from within because without direct impact on elected officials, the potential for such change is drastically limited.

Notes

1. For this chapter, First Nations refers to those considered to be "Status" First Nations and Non-Status First Nations (in relation to section 27 of the *Indian Act*). First Nations also represents over fifty different and distinct nations and confederacies that share territory with the Canadian state—most of which is agreed upon through treaty agreements and arrangements.
2. See Chadwick Cowie's "A Vote for Canada or Indigenous Nationhood? The Complexities of First Nations, Métis, and Inuit Participation in Canadian Politics," *The Conversation Canada*, 1 November 2021. Available: https://theconversation.com/a-vote-for-canada-or-indigenous-nationhood-the-complexities-of-first-nations-metis-and-inuit-participation-in-canadian-politics-169312 [Accessed 20 December 2022].
3. The term "nation" relates to the concept that specifies nations as groups of people who have a shared culture, ethnicity, history, and land base for centuries, if not millennia, like that of First Nations. This understanding of "nation" is different from a "state" such as Canada, as a state traditionally relates to borders and governance structures that govern over various territories that do not represent ethnic lines specifically but rather a citizenship to a larger political structure in a larger land mass.

4. Federico Lenzerini, "Sovereignty Revisited: International Law and Parallel Sovereignty of Indigenous Peoples," *Texas International Law Journal* 42 (2006–2007): 157.
5. *Ibid.*
6. *Ibid.*
7. *Ibid.*
8. *Ibid.*, 163.
9. *Ibid.*, 158.
10. *Ibid.*, 163.
11. *Ibid.*, 165.
12. Patricia Monture-Angus, *Journeying Forward: Dreaming First Nations Independence* (Halifax: Fernwood Publishing, 1999), 36; Kiera Ladner and Michael McCrossan, "The Road Not Taken," in *Contested Constitutionalism: Reflection on the Canadian Charter of Rights and Freedoms,* eds. James Kelly and Christopher Manfredi (Vancouver: University of British Columbia Press, 2009), 266.
13. Monture-Angus, *Journeying Forward,* 36; Ladner and McCrossan, "The Road Not Taken," 266.
14. Supreme Court of Canada, "Delgamuukw v British Columbia," *Supreme Court of Canada*, 11 December 1997. Available: http://scc.lexum.org/en/1997/1997scr3-1010/1997scr3-1010.html [Accessed 2 December 2022].
15. Supreme Court of Canada, "R. v Van der Peet," *Supreme Court of Canada*, 21 August 1996. Available: https://scc-csc.lexum.com/scc-csc/scc-csc/en/item/1407/index.do [Accessed 2 December 2022].
16. Monture-Angus, *Journeying Forward*, 36.
17. *Ibid.*
18. *Ibid.*
19. *Ibid.*
20. Lenzerini, "Sovereignty Revisited," 159.
21. *Ibid.*
22. *Ibid.*, 167.
23. Roderic Pitty and Shannara Smith, "The Indigenous Challenge to Westphalian Sovereignty," *Australian Journal of Political Science* 46, 1 (2011): 127.
24. *Ibid.*
25. Lenzerini, "Sovereignty Revisited," 170.
26. Pitty and Smith, "The Indigenous Challenge to Westphalian Sovereignty," 125.
27. *Ibid.*, 126.
28. *Ibid*, 121; United Nations, "United Nations Declaration on the Rights of Indigenous Peoples," 2007. Available: http://www.un.org/esa/socdev/unpfii/en/drip.html [Accessed 2 December 2022].
29. *Ibid.*

30. Pitty and Smith, "The Indigenous Challenge to Westphalian Sovereignty," 126.
31. James Youngblood Henderson, "Empowering Treaty Federalism," *Saskatchewan Law Review* 58, (1994): 241–300.
32. John Borrows, *Canada's Indigenous Constitution* (Toronto: University of Toronto Press, 2010), 124.
33. Kiera Ladner, "Treaty Federalism: An Indigenous Vision of Canadian Federalisms," in *New Trends in Canadian Federalism*, eds. Francois Rocher and Mariam Smith (Peterborough: Broadview Press, 2003), 187–188.
34. Ladner and McCrossan, "The Road not Taken," 265.
35. Russell Lawrence Barsh, "Indigenous Rights and the *Lex Loci* in British Imperial Law," in *Advancing Aboriginal Claims: Visions, Strategies, Directions*, ed. Kerry Wilkins (Saskatoon: Purich Publishing, 2012), 97–98.
36. *Ibid.*; Ladner and McCrossan, "The Road Not Taken," 276.
37. Ladner and McCrossan, "The Road Not Taken," 276.
38. Royal Commission on Aboriginal Peoples (RCAP), *Report of the Royal Commission on Aboriginal Peoples*, Volume 2 (Ottawa: Canada Communications Group, 1996).
39. Kiera Ladner, *Peace and Good Order: A Treaty Right to Parliamentary Representation?*, A dissertation presented to the Department of Political Science at Carleton University (Ottawa: Carleton University, 1996), 97.
40. *Ibid.*, 90.
41. *Ibid.*, 56.
42. *Ibid.*
43. Henderson, "Empowering Treaty Federalism," 316–317.
44. Borrows, *Canada's Indigenous Constitution*, 124.
45. John Borrows, "Landed Citizenship: Narratives of Aboriginal Political Participation," in *Citizenship in Diverse Societies*, eds. Will Kymlicka and Wayne Norman (Oxford: Oxford University Press, 2012), 332.
46. *Ibid.*
47. *Ibid.*, 333.
48. *Ibid.*, 335.
49. *Ibid.*
50. *Ibid.*
51. *Ibid.*
52. *Ibid.*, 335–336.
53. David Wilkins, "An Inquiry into Indigenous Political Participation: Implications for Tribal Sovereignty," *Kansas Journal of Law and Public Policy* 9 (2000): 738.
54. *Ibid.*
55. RCAP, Volume 2.
56. Borrows, *Canada's Indigenous Constitution*, 157.

57. Wilkins, "An Inquiry into Indigenous Political Participation," 741.
58. Taiaiake Alfred, *Wasase: Indigenous Pathways of Action and Freedom* (Toronto: University of Toronto Press, 2009), 188.
59. *Ibid.*, 202, 205.
60. Borrows, "Landed' Citizenship," 329.
61. *Ibid.*
62. *Ibid.*
63. *Ibid.*
64. *Ibid.*, 326.
65. *Ibid.*, 332.
66. For more on this, see Jatinder Mann, *Redefining Citizenship in Australia, Canada, and Aotearoa New Zealand* (New York: Peter Lang Publishing, 2019).

Bibliography

Alfred, Taiaiake. *Wasase: Indigenous Pathways of Action and Freedom*. Toronto: University of Toronto Press, 2009.

Barsh, Russel Lawrence. "Indigenous Rights and the Lex Loci in British Imperial Law." In *Advancing Aboriginal Visions, Strategies, Directions*, edited by Kerry Wilkins: 91–126. Saskatoon: Purich Publishing, 2012.

Borrows, John. *Canada's Indigenous Constitution*. Toronto: University of Toronto Press, 2010.

Borrows, John. "Landed Citizenship: Narratives of Aboriginal Political Participation." In *Citizenship in Diverse Societies*, edited by Will Kymlicka and Wayne Norman: 326–344. Oxford: Oxford University Press, 2012.

Henderson, James Youngblood. "Empowering Treaty Federalism," *Saskatchewan Law Review*. 58, 1994: 241–300.

Kymlicka, William and Wayne Norman. "Citizenship in Culturally Diverse Societies: Issues, Contexts, Concepts." In *Citizenship in Diverse* Societies, edited by William Kymlicka and Wayne Norman: 1–44. New York: Oxford University Press, 1995.

Ladner, Kiera. "Treaty Federalism: An Indigenous Vision of Canadian Federalisms." In *New Trends in Canadian Federalism*, edited by Francois Rocher and Mariam Smith: 167–194. Peterborough: Broadview Press, 2003.

Ladner, Kiera and Michael McCrossan. "The Road not Taken." In *Contested Constitutionalism: Reflection on the Canadian Charter of Rights and Freedoms*, edited by James Kelly and Christopher Manfredi: 263–283. Vancouver: University of British Columbia Press, 2009.

Lenzerini, Federico. "Sovereignty Revisited: International Law and Parallel Sovereignty of Indigenous Peoples." *Texas International Law Journal*. 42, 2006–2007: 155–189.

Mann, Jatinder. *Redefining Citizenship in Australia, Canada, and Aotearoa New Zealand*. New York: Peter Lang Publishing, 2019.

Montour-Angus, Patricia. *Journeying Forward: Dreaming First Nations Independence*. Halifax: Fernwood Publishing, 1999.

Pitty, Roderic, and Shannara Smith. "The Indigenous Challenge to Westphalian Sovereignty." *Australian Journal of Political Science*. 46, 1, September 2011: 121–139.

Royal Commission on Aboriginal Peoples (RCAP), 1996. *Report of the Royal Commission on Aboriginal Peoples*, Volume 2. Ottawa: Canada Communications Group.

Wilkins, David. "An Inquiry into Indigenous Political Participation: Implications for Tribal Sovereignty." *Kansas Journal of Law and Public Policy*. 9, 2000: 732–751.

CHAPTER 10

"A Useful and Self-respecting Citizenship": Māori as Citizens in the Quest for Welfare in the Modern Aotearoa New Zealand State

Māmari Stephens

Introduction

The development of Māori-led welfare initiatives in Aotearoa New Zealand over the course of our social and political history offers some evidence to suggest a Māori-defined notion of citizenship that is arguably distinct from the broader national idea of citizenship in Aotearoa New Zealand.

Importantly, both welfare and citizenship are not merely, as might be supposed, distinct states to be achieved. Instead, the Māori imagined

I am extremely grateful to the editor of this collection, Jatinder Mann, for his detailed feedback and helpful suggestions on my chapter.

M. Stephens (✉)
Te Kauhanganui Tātai Ture - Faculty of Law, Te Herenga Waka Victoria University of Wellington,
Wellington, New Zealand
e-mail: mamari.stephens@vuw.ac.nz

J. Mann (ed.), *Citizenship in Transnational Perspective*, Politics of Citizenship and Migration,
https://doi.org/10.1007/978-3-031-34358-2_10

community, and the Māori concept of full citizenship, even in this urbanised age, is relational; it requires positive relations between Māori and the Crown as partners under the Treaty of Waitangi, as well as between Māori and other New Zealanders, and between Māori collectives. Further, Māori concepts of properly functional citizenship include different kinds of Māori collectives being able to exercise authority and autonomy in making effective decisions for Māori-specific welfare needs and aspirations.

Two seemingly unrelated current events help demonstrate this position. Both events illustrate specific Māori agency in seeking improved welfare outcomes for Māori individuals and collectives. Both events also illustrate relational ideas of citizenship.

Two Events

One event was the opening of an urban marae in Auckland, Aotearoa New Zealand's biggest city, to shelter homeless individuals and families in May 2016. As a noun, "marae" often denotes the courtyard of a traditional or contemporary Māori meeting house, where ritual welcomes take place that enable a collective of Māori people to extend appropriate hospitality to *manuhiri* (visitors). The word "marae" can also be used as an adjective or verb to express generous behaviour and being hospitable.[1]

Hundreds of marae serve specific tribal communities throughout the entire country, and since the 1950s, urban marae have also been established to serve Māori communities and individuals from all tribal areas and cultures. Te Puea Memorial Marae, an urban marae in Māngere, South Auckland, offered temporary residential support to needy *manuhiri* in response to a well-publicised increase in homelessness in Auckland. Manurewa Marae, another urban marae in South Auckland, also opened its doors in August 2016 to provide a similar service.[2] The sharp rise in numbers of people identifying as homeless in part has occurred due to a lack of government housing available to meet a growing accommodation shortage in urban areas.[3] Further, the problem may also reflect disengagement between individuals, families, and government welfare agencies. Almost half of the homeless people surveyed for a 2016 Salvation Army report stated they were not in direct contact with state agencies about their housing problems.[4]

By stepping into the space left vacant by government provision, even just for a temporary time, these marae use Māori traditional protocols of welcome, as well as other principles and processes relevant to hospitality in the provision of this short-term "indoor relief." *Manuhiri*, including individuals and families, are cared for on a collective basis, with *manaakitanga* (generosity) by the people who belong to that marae. Importantly, in accordance with most marae protocols, *manuhiri* themselves become incorporated within the *tangata whenua* (home people) for the duration of their stay. In addition, the marae staff and volunteers work alongside social services, including government social workers, in the provision of support. The marae have also received limited government funding and many public donations.[5]

Thus, located at the centre of a web of relationships, Te Puea Marae, Manurewa Marae, and other such centres have been able to offer better real welfare outcomes for families in need, as well as a sense of belonging that also provides the potential for ongoing relationships.

The second event involved the 2014 Treaty of Waitangi claim settlement between the Crown and Ngāi Tūhoe, the *iwi* (tribe) based in the Urewera area in the north of the Hawke's Bay region of the North Island of Aotearoa New Zealand. As a result of the settlement, several agencies of the Crown agreed to work alongside the people of Ngāi Tūhoe to bring to fruition a vision of a Tūhoe welfare system that would operate independently from (but collaboratively with) the national welfare system. Chief negotiator and Ngāi Tūhoe leader Tāmati Kruger sees the achievement of welfare independence for Ngāi Tūhoe as an important social goal: for "changing a mindset in Tūhoe around being beneficiaries of the state."[6]

A Crown-commissioned report made public in 2015 has briefly explored the possibility of the Crown devolving some of its liability for social security (including the benefit system) on to Ngāi Tūhoe in accordance with the 2014 settlement goals. According to this preliminary report, the Ministry of Social Development (the ministry unit responsible for the welfare system including benefits) is investigating the Crown's actuarial liability for Ngāi Tūhoe's long-term welfare costs. This inquiry is in keeping with the policy drive known as the "investment approach."[7]

One question posed by the Crown to the report writers (Sapere Group) was how the Crown would "sell" its welfare liability to Ngāi Tūhoe.[8] The report suggests one response could be "partial fiscal decentralisation" whereby beneficiaries could opt out of their rights to welfare, or their rights could be changed so that a calculated sum of money would be allocated to Ngāi Tūhoe to meet negotiated social and economic objectives.

Ngāi Tūhoe would have some freedom to achieve more effective spending of these funds.

The events described above call into direct question the nature of the relationship between Māori and the welfare state in Aotearoa New Zealand. While Māori individuals and *whānau* (families) have sought access to the social assistance available on the basis of need facilitated by the welfare state (as established fully under the *Social Security Act* 1938 in Aotearoa New Zealand), Māori have also claimed the space and freedom, often outside the existing legal welfare framework, to craft Māori solutions to providing for Māori welfare.

This chapter will consider the nature of what Benedict Anderson referred to as the "imagined community."[9] How Māori have viewed or understood themselves in connection to the welfare system, a system intended to provide support to all citizens in need (within certain limits), may reveal something of the nature of Māori citizenship and the Māori imagined community.

Welfare and Citizenship

Welfare is a matter of deep concern in the examination of citizenship, particularly in regard to obligations and social rights. The idea of the "social contract" is a very old one, centring on the idea that individual citizens gave up some of their rights to political autonomy (including the right to use force in resolving disputes), only in exchange for the sovereign's undertaking to extend to all citizens equally "justice, peace, and the possibility of a better life."[10] With the development of social security systems in the late-nineteenth and early to mid-twentieth centuries, for example, in the United Kingdom, Europe, the United States of America, Australia, and Aotearoa New Zealand, the idea of the social contract expanded to include the idea that citizenship was not only political, whereby citizens held a suite of enforceable political rights; the idea of "social citizenship" meant that citizens could also hold social rights that could be protected as part of the social contract. The status of citizenship could provide protection of both the political and social rights of individuals.

James Tully has identified the dominant liberal democratic view of citizenship as "civil citizenship" as a state: universalistic, constrained, and characterised by the institutions of the democratic representation and participation. Social and economic rights comprise one of the tiers of citizenship rights, serving mainly to assist the poor and unemployed to be able to access their other political citizenship rights.[11]

It is also possible to argue for a distinct view of social citizenship in the welfare paradigm that has become very narrow and constrained over the course of the past three or four decades. Increasing focus in this "tier" of citizenship is placed on the imposition of obligations alongside rights or entitlements to receive welfare. Thus, in order to qualify sufficiently to receive assistance from the State, benefit recipients must perform specific obligations. Increasingly many Western countries impose positive obligations upon social security recipients that require them to demonstrate certain kinds of approved, even morally just, behaviour in order to be eligible for support.[12]

Often ignored within social security nations are Indigenous notions of social citizenship. Indigenous notions of political citizenship cannot be restricted to liberal democratic citizenship ideals,[13] although they can certainly be influenced by them.

Recent scholarship confirms that other Indigenous or First Nations' experiences of social security reforms of the nineteenth and twentieth centuries reflect similar themes across developed Commonwealth countries. As pre-existing Indigenous legal and cultural systems were reformed and sometimes destroyed due to war, disease, and demographic upheaval, Indigenous peoples were usually thrust into some form of reliance on the new states for social assistance and on the new social security systems that were born in the late nineteenth century and in the early decades of the twentieth century. However, these systems were usually designed with the template of the house dwelling, nuclear family-focused, male, wage-earning worker in mind, often automatically or deliberately excluding Indigenous peoples who did not fit this social model.

Aboriginal Australians were routinely excluded from widows' benefits, child allowances, and maternity benefits and in some cases were required to meet competence thresholds in order to be able to obtain social security assistance.[14] Māori were effectively excluded from early Aotearoa New Zealand social security measures such as the 1898 *Old Age Pension Act* as Māori were often unable to prove their age and were deemed to have income if they held collectively owned shares in Māori land.[15] First Nations peoples were also often excluded from effective assistance within the Canadian federal and provincial social security systems. While the reservation and band registration system in Canada has thrown up different problems to those of the Māori, differing again to the experiences of Aboriginal Australians, the problem of early exclusion and marginalisation from social security systems has been common.[16]

Relational Citizenship and the Treaty of Waitangi

A distinguishing feature of the Aotearoa New Zealand situation is the existence of the Treaty of Waitangi. Māori citizenship discourse did not simply commence with the signing of the Treaty of Waitangi in 1840; Māori constitutional thinking within some tribal polities had already been developing for decades before that point. Nevertheless, the Treaty of Waitangi was a crucial stepping-stone in the evolution of modern Māori notions of social (and political) citizenship. The Treaty is not a starting point for defining modern Māori citizenship, but it preserved a space in which Māori concepts of civic life and decision-making could develop.

Over time the Treaty of Waitangi created the bedrock of the Crown/Māori relationship that has waxed and waned but never entirely broken over the past 176 years. Much comment has been made about Article 2 of the Treaty, whereby Māori received a guarantee that the Crown would protect Māori interests, including resources, that Māori would retain some degree of strong authority (*te tino rangatiratanga*) over those interests and other valued things, and that, in return, Māori would grant some form of authority or governorship (*kāwanatanga*) to the Crown to be exercised within Aotearoa New Zealand.

Of particular interest for the purpose of this chapter is Article 3 of the Treaty, which has been interpreted as an "assimilative weapon in the armoury of practices designed to incorporate indigenous peoples into the state."[17] The English text reads:[18]

> In consideration thereof Her Majesty the Queen of England extends to the Natives of New Zealand Her royal protection and **imparts to them** all the **Rights and Privileges** of British Subjects. [emphasis added]

The Māori text provides:

> Hei wakaritenga mai hoki tenei mo te wakaaetanga ki te Kawanatanga o te Kuini – Ka tiakina e te Kuini o Ingarani nga tangata māori katoa o Nu Tirani **ka tukua ki a ratou nga tikanga katoa** rite tahi ki ana mea ki nga tangata o Ingarani. [emphasis added]

In 1989 Sir Hugh Kāwharu published a simpler translation of the original Māori text:[19]

> For this agreed arrangement therefore concerning the Government of the Queen, the Queen of England will protect all the ordinary people of New Zealand and will give them the same rights and duties of citizenship as the people of England.

One important point to note as between the two versions of the Treaty of Waitangi is the use of the Māori term "tikanga" to denote "the rights and privileges of citizenship." Sir Kāwharu added by way of explanatory footnote his own doubts as to how Article 3 would have been understood by Māori at the time:[20]

> There is, however, a more profound problem about "tikanga". There is a real sense here of the Queen "protecting" (i.e. allowing the preservation of) the Māori people's tikanga (i.e. customs) since no Māori could have had any understanding whatever of British tikanga (i.e. rights and duties of British subjects.) This, then, reinforces the guarantees in article 2.

Former Prime Minister Sir Geoffrey Palmer identified in his explanation of the five legal principles derived from the Treaty that he viewed Article 3 as bequeathing a state of universal citizenship:[21]

> The Third Principle, the Principle of Equality, recognises the guarantee in the Third Article of the Treaty, of legal equality between Māori and other citizens of New Zealand. This means that all New Zealand citizens are equal before the law.

It is certainly possible to read the sentence "ka tukua ki a ratou nga tikanga katoa rite tahi ki ana mea ki nga tangata o Ingarani" as meaning something like "[Her Majesty] gives to them all the customs [rights and obligations][22] the same as those given to the people of England." In all likelihood, this will have been the meaning intended by the drafters.

On the other hand, support for Kāwharu's position can also be found in the use of the term "tuku" in Article 3. This term can bear the sense of "give" or "allow." Māori reading or hearing the text could well have understood the sentence above in a different way: "[Her Majesty] allows/

permits to them all their customs, the same as their customs are allowed to the English people."

However, Māori understood whatever they were guaranteed under Article 3; either that they were allowed to employ their own *tikanga* without obstruction or that they were given the right to share in the rights and obligations of the English, there is no doubt that most Māori, over the succeeding years and decades, came to understand both that a permanent relationship had been created between the Crown and Māori *iwi* and *hapū* (sub-tribe, or smaller tribal unit) by way of Article 2 and that Māori, simply by virtue of their status as signatories, were entitled to a suite of rights and subject to obligations (*tikanga*) flowing from that relationship or at the very least confirmed by it.[23]

Articles 2 and 3 of the Treaty appear to have affirmed a high degree of freedom to Māori to retain their modes of practice and possessions, as protected by the Crown. These articles also established and protected the relationship between the Crown and Māori. It is in this light that the Māori experiences of welfare ought to be considered, as Māori have continually sought to achieve welfare outcomes for Māori within the welfare system, but also outside all such systems employed by government since the middle of the nineteenth century.

Aotearoa New Zealand's Welfare State

The Aotearoa New Zealand welfare state, as constructed in 1938 with the passage of the *Social Security Act*, but also including (more broadly) other initiatives such as social housing, deliberately excluded and underpaid Māori for decades, on the administrative presumption that Māori were too communistic and simply not cut out for self-respecting universalistic understandings of citizenship. In 1937, when questioned about the Labour government's native housing policy, G. P. Shepherd, the Under-Secretary of Native Affairs, observed: "To put it in the broadest sense we must assimilate the Māori into useful and self-respecting citizenship."[24] An official standard was not applied to Māori who sought loans to build dwellings under that Act, but the standard of the "upstanding European" was applied to Māori so that by 1944 Judge Harvey could state: "The State housing programme has been sufficiently long in progress for it to be abundantly clear that Māoris—even the best of them—are not successful applicants for State houses."[25]

Notwithstanding this exclusion, Māori became, over the subsequent decades, the nonpareil subjects of the welfare state. Of course, as Māori lost land, *whānau* (family unit) connection, economic footing, and social standing, this process may well have been inevitable, but it has erased other powerful versions of the Māori welfare narrative.

Many Māori communities have long held a vision of Māori welfare that establishes Māori solutions to Māori poverty. However, the equally powerful vision in Māori society is that of sharing in the fruits of common citizenship with all New Zealanders of equal access to and equal participation in Aotearoa New Zealand society (or the "good life") that welfare at least makes possible. This is also part of a relational approach—that the benefits of citizenship flow not from the citizenship status itself, but from the functional relationships between Māori, between Māori and other New Zealanders, and between Māori and the Crown.

Māori communities have sought Māori solutions to welfare because the relationship between Māori and the Crown pursuant to the Treaty guarantees that freedom. The relationship with the Crown guarantees Māori the same status as everyone else, with concomitant access to the common good life.

This relational citizenship, as understood by many Māori, results from engaging in practices to maintain balance between seeking common benefit, or common good for all, and upholding *rangatiratanga* (autonomy, right to exercise authority) while retaining relationships with the Crown. This is more reflective of Tully's civic (as opposed to civil) citizenship, whereby individuals become citizens by democratising or cooperating their relationships of living and working together.[26]

Examples of Māori Autonomy and Relationships in Welfare

There are countless examples of structures, organisations, councils, and committees set up from the 1840s to the present day by Māori to provide welfare for poor Māori. For the purposes of this chapter, two examples will suffice to show how Māori constantly sought, often through legislation, to gain political as well as social control over Māori welfare outcomes. These examples can reflect this relational understanding of citizenship, as well as the drive for *rangatiratanga*. These two representative examples are entities established under the *Māori Councils Act* 1900 and the Māori War Effort Organisation (MWEO).

Māori Councils Act 1900

The Crown saw the potential of Māori group processes to create positive social and political outcomes very early on in Aotearoa New Zealand colonial history. There are some extraordinary accounts, in mid-nineteenth-century sources, of *rūnanga* (Māori traditional councils) being used by Māori as a way of making important political and social decisions over Māori lives.

The Crown attempted at certain points during this history to capitalise on, and co-opt, these processes, as in the enactment of the *Māori Councils Act* 1900. Under this legislation, thirty district councils were set up with more than 200 village councils. The Act originally granted a limited amount of self-government to Māori communities and gave councils limited power of self-regulation, often pertaining to Māori social well-being. Councils could:[27]

1. Regulate for the health and personal convenience of the inhabitants of Māori villages;
2. Enforce the cleansing of houses and other buildings 'in dirty and unwholesome state';
3. Suppress 'common nuisances'; and
4. Regulate to prevent 'drunkenness and sly grog selling.'

The councils also dealt with dog registration, the branding of cattle, registration of *tohunga* (local Māori cultural experts), the water supply, schools, sanitation, and general social matters. But even by 1911 Māori councils were largely ineffective due to underfunding and political difficulties. The councils had a degree of freedom to operate, but the relationship with the state markedly disintegrated within a few years, although some councils struggled on into the 1930s and even 1940s.

The MWEO

World War II prompted the growth of another critically important Māori entity concerned with welfare outcomes for Māori: the MWEO. Māori parliamentarians Paraire Paikea, Eruera Tirakatene, and H. T. Ratana drove the establishment of the MWEO, and it recruited Māori to be part of the war effort, leading to the establishment of the 28 (Māori) Battalion, comprising four companies established along tribal lines.[28] The MWEO proved a powerhouse, setting up 21 districts and more than 300 tribal committees. The MWEO also facilitated and carried out a good deal of welfare work at village level of considerable success and efficiency.[29] The MWEO's collective approach to recruitment and to welfare for families was extraordinarily successful in achieving high rates of Māori enlistment.[30] The general admiration for the MWEO and the service carried out by the 28 (Māori) Battalion ensured that at least something of the MWEO would survive the war.

By this stage the discourse of Māori citizenship in common with other New Zealanders was well and truly developing. The Māori contribution to Aotearoa New Zealand's role in World War II, as exemplified by the exploits of the Māori Battalion, led to high Māori expectations that they would be accepted as full citizens within mainstream society and attain a level of control over their own affairs.[31] This focus on the attainment or affirmation of citizenship in return for service proved extraordinarily powerful. Ngāti Porou leader and statesman Sir Apirana Ngata (who had first publicly articulated the idea of the Māori Battalion) famously urged Māori to enlist for military service in a 1943 pamphlet entitled "The Price of Citizenship." This was an important expression of an idea of common citizenship as demonstrated by Māori and Pākehā participation in the armed struggle for national defence. Ngata fully endorsed the Māori war effort on the basis of a shared, demonstrable, and highly relational citizenship. He asked:[32]

> ...whether the civilians of New Zealand, men, and women, fully realised the implications of the joint participation of Pakeha and Māori in this last demonstration of the highest citizenship.
>
> [...] We are participants in a great Commonwealth, to the defence of which we cannot hesitate to contribute our blood and our lives. We are the possessors of rights, which we must qualify to exercise, also of obligations, which the Māori must discharge always in the future as he has done in the past. We are of one house, and if our Pakeha brothers fall, we fall with them.

> How can we ever hold up our heads, when the struggle is over, to the question, 'Where were you when New Zealand was at war?

As the war ended, Māori MPs Eruera Tirikatene and Paraire Paikea formed a committee with the intention of capturing the MWEO's gains and maintaining momentum by way of legislation. They drafted early versions of what was to become the *Māori Social and Economic Advancement Act* 1945 which was supposed to herald a new dawn of Māori cooperation and involvement in decision-making with the State including the then Native Affairs Department. The Act that eventually passed bore a little true resemblance to that originally drafted and to some commentators seemed to be an opportunity missed for Māori to have some genuine control of Māori social outcomes.[33] The attempts to centralise, systemise, and decouple a grassroots movement from its own community and land base had stymied the movement's effectiveness.[34]

Other initiatives are easy to be found, over succeeding decades, including the *Māori Welfare Act* 1962 (later called the *Māori Community Development Act* 1962). This Act established fourteen district Māori councils with welfare objectives and the national body, the National Māori Council. The Māori Women's Welfare League established in 1951 was a highly effective welfare body. All such bodies sought to retain Māori structures and ways of doing things in urban contexts.[35]

Few such initiatives have proved to have lasting success. None of these initiatives has co-existed easily with the monolithic welfare state, but their success is not the concern of this chapter; instead the repeated efforts over nearly two centuries (as exemplified by the Māori councils of the early twentieth century, and the MWEO) show time and time again that Māori have sought to uphold a uniquely Māori vision of citizenship, including *rangatiratanga*, in being able to address Māori welfare needs, by working outside the legal system. Further, Māori have often been deeply invested in the notion of common benefit or common good shared with others as a further privilege of citizenship.

Conclusion

Welfare is a matter of deep concern in the examination of citizenship, particularly in regard to the enactment obligations and social rights. This chapter lightly touches upon the question of who, in the Aotearoa New Zealand context, truly has a claim upon the state for welfare, but also asks another question: who actually has the authority to provide welfare? It is in the flipping of the picture that we can get a clearer view of Māori and welfare; rather than understand Māori as subjects of welfare in order to understand the scope of their social citizenship, we ought to look at how Māori have sought to use authority and agency in providing welfare and in doing so in a way that need not threaten the notion of the shared imaginative Aotearoa New Zealand community. The social and legal history of Māori welfare-based initiatives in Aotearoa New Zealand thus offers a portal into the nature of Māori-defined citizenship.

Both welfare and citizenship are not merely, as might be supposed, distinct states to be achieved. Instead, to be effective, certain relationships must function properly in order that both welfare and citizenship be truly effective. The Māori imagined community, and the Māori concept of full citizenship, even in this urbanised age, is relational; it requires positive relations between Māori and the Treaty partner, as well as between Māori and other New Zealanders, and between Māori collectives. Further, Māori concepts of properly functional citizenship include different kinds of Māori collectives being able to exercise true *rangatiratanga* and make effective decisions for Māori-specific welfare needs and aspirations.

The examples of the Māori councils and the MWEO reveal, even in their ultimate failure to survive, that national legislation alone, in the absence of creating real space for Māori to be effective decision-makers, will usually be unsuccessful at providing for or engineering better Māori welfare outcomes.

The two matters that opened this discussion—the urban marae in Auckland opening their doors to the homeless and the Ngāi Tūhoe/Crown proposition to devolve welfare responsibility to Ngāi Tūhoe—are not isolated or unrelated matters. They are merely the most recent in a long series of moments where entities and organisations have attempted to take and articulate Māori collective responsibility for Māori welfare outcomes in a wide range of tribal and urban contexts.

The Ngāi Tūhoe Treaty settlement, as concluded in 2014, sets the scene for the creation of a "Tūhoe Welfare System," in negotiation and with the support of government agencies. Such a system will likely sit easily alongside other initiatives mentioned in this short chapter. Certainly, Ngāi Tūhoe expects that Tūhoe communities and families will seek to exercise agency in the provision of welfare outcomes. This as yet unformed system will also involve the creation of structures, but will also retain a certain degree of limited autonomy, largely free of legislative control, to allow

Māori collectives a degree of freedom within which to exercise *tikanga* in order to bring about better welfare outcomes for Māori. Whatever form the Ngāi Tūhoe solution to welfare takes, our social and political history suggests that good relationships between Māori and other Māori, and with other New Zealanders, and with the Treaty partner will be essential, as will the capacity for Ngāi Tūhoe to make their own substantive decisions, if this initiative is to uphold a truly relational and Māori vision of citizenship in the welfare context.

The more urbanised situation faced by Te Puea Memorial Marae (and Manurewa Marae) does not represent as obvious a challenge to the welfare system, as opening up to feed and house the homeless does not serve to create a separate system of welfare provision. Their actions do serve, however, as an important reminder of the web of relationships at the heart of Māori enterprise and the potential for relationship building that has been proving an effective tool in the provision of better, even if short term, welfare outcomes for families in need.

Both situations do raise an important question; how does Māori exercise of autonomy threaten or undermine the Crown role in the provision of welfare? What is the broader cost of the Crown retreating from its obligations in regard to certain groups in Aotearoa New Zealand society? Suggestions are now being canvassed about fiscal decentralisation—the notion that somehow the Crown might be able to sell welfare liability once the Ngāi Tūhoe welfare system is established. As a fiscal measure, this may make sense, but what are the longer-term implications for the relationship between the Crown and Ngāi Tūhoe or indeed any *iwi* or *hapū* that takes such a path? Caution might be warranted here, just as the Crown ought not restrict its considerations of Māori welfare to questions of beneficiary numbers and states of "welfare dependency," Māori too ought not see Māori welfare and citizenship, including autonomy, as only "states" to be achieved. In short, any connected party should not easily set the relational nature of Māori citizenship aside.

Glossary

Hapū:	tribal unit
Iwi:	larger tribal unit
Kāwanatanga:	governorship

Marae:	courtyard of a traditional or contemporary Māori meeting house used as an adjective or verb to express generous behaviour, and being hospitable
Manaakitanga:	generosity
Manuhiri:	visitors
Rangatiratanga:	authority, autonomy, self-determination
Rūnanga:	Māori traditional councils
Tangata whenua:	home people, people of the land
Tikanga:	rights and obligations, correct behaviour, customs
Tohunga:	local Māori cultural experts
Whānau:	family grouping

Notes

1. H. W. Williams, *A Dictionary of The Māori Language* (GP Publications, 1971), 180.
2. Rahia Timutimu, "Manurewa Marae Opens Doors to the Homeless for the Community's Sake," Māori Television Service. Available: http://www.maoritelevision.com/news/regional/manurewa-marae-opens-doors-homeless-communitys-sake [accessed 1 July 2016]. See also Chris Harrowell, "Paula Bennett Talks at Manurewa Marae about Homelessness," *Auckland Now*, 29 June 2016. Available: http://www.stuff.co.nz/auckland/81532562/paula-bennett-talks-at-manurewa-marae-about-homelessness [accessed 3 July 2016].
3. Shannon Haunui-Thompson and Tom Furley, "Marae opens its doors to those in need," Radio New Zealand. Available: http://www.radionz.co.nz/news/te-manu-korihi/304785/marae-opens-its-doors-to-those-in-need [accessed 30 June 2016].
4. R. T. Harris, *Invisible in the Supercity – Hidden Homelessness in Auckland* (Salvation Army Social Policy and Parliamentary Unit, 2016), 35.
5. Jo Moir, "Government set to Give Money to Te Puea Marae for Housing Homeless," *Stuff*, 9 June 2016. Available: http://www.stuff.co.nz/national/politics/80904066/Government-set-to-give-money-to-Te-Puea-Marae-for-housing-homeless [accessed 28 June 2016].
6. David Moore, Graham Scott, Rebecca Drew, Joanna Smith, and Claire Whelen, *Decentralising Welfare – Te Mana Motuhake O Tuhoe* (Wellington: Sapere Group 2014), 31. Available: http://www.srgexpert.com/wp-content/uploads/2015/11/Decentralising-welfare-te-mana-motuhake-o-tuhoe.pdf [accessed 29 June 2016].

7. This approach involves acknowledging the "fiscal, economic and social costs of long term dependency" and hence concluding that "[policy] initiatives must be seen as investments against the future costs." For further explanation of the investment approach and forward liability, see Simon Chapple, "Forward Liability and Welfare Reform," *Child Poverty Policy Quarterly* 9, 2 (May 2013): 56–62.
8. Moore et al., "Decentralising Welfare," 31.
9. Benedict Anderson, *Imagined Communities: Reflections on the Origin and Spread of Nationalism* (London: Verso, 1983). See also Paul Meredeth, "Urban Māori as New Citizens: The Quest for Recognition and Resources," Paper presented at Revisioning Citizenship in New Zealand Conference, University of Waikato, Hamilton, 2000.
10. Earl Johnson Jr., "Equality before the Law and the Social Contract: When will the United States Finally Guarantee its People the Equality before the Law the Social Contract Demands," *Fordham Urban Law Journal* 37 (2010): 159–160.
11. James Tully, "Citizenship for the Love of the World," Address given at Cornell University, 14 March 2013. See also Robert Nichols and Jakeet Singh, *Freedom and Democracy in an Imperial Context: Dialogues with James Tully* (New York: Routledge, 2014), 223.
12. See, for example, Peter Dwyer, "Creeping Conditionality in the UK: From Welfare Rights to Conditional Entitlements?," *Canadian Journal of Sociology* 29 (2004): 265–287; and Nicola Barker and Sarah Lamble, "From Social Security to Individual Responsibility: Sanctions, Conditionality and Punitiveness in the Welfare Reform Bill 2009 (Part One)," *Journal of Social Welfare and Family Law* 31 (2009): 321.
13. Nicole Roughan, "Te Tiriti and the Constitution: Rethinking Citizenship, Justice, Equality and Democracy," *New Zealand Journal of Public and International Law* 3 (2005): 290. See discussion in Iris Marion Young, "Polity and Group Difference: A Critique of the Ideal of Universal Citizenship," *Ethics* 99 (1989): 250, 252–254.
14. For a full discussion of such exclusions, see Thalia Anthony, "The Return to the Legal and Citizenship Void: Indigenous Welfare Quarantining in the Northern Territory and Cape York," *Balayi: Culture Law and Colonialism* 10 (2009): 30–31.
15. For a fuller account, see Margaret McClure, *A civilised community: A history of social security in New Zealand 1898–1998* (Auckland University Press in association with the Historical Branch, Department of Internal Affairs 1998), 10–48.
16. For example of ineligibility for social security assistance for Indigenous Canadians, see Hugh Shewell, *Enough to keep them alive: Indian welfare in Canada, 1873–1965* (Toronto: University of Toronto Press, 2004), 180, 197, 200, 268.

17. David Pearson, "The ties that unwind: Civic and ethnic imaginings in New Zealand," *Nations and Nationalism* 6, 1 (2000): 99.
18. See Ministry for Culture and Heritage, "Read the Treaty," 20 December 2012, New Zealand History. Available: www.nzhistory.net.nz [accessed 1 July 2016].
19. Footnotes omitted. See translation and footnotes at Waitangi Tribunal "The Kawharu Translation." Available: www.justice.govt.nz [accessed 2 July 2016].
20. "The Kawharu Translation".
21. Geoffrey Palmer, "The Treaty of Waitangi – principles for Crown action," *Victoria University Law Review* 19 (1989): 335 at 341–342.
22. After Kawharu.
23. For a nuanced account of the post-Treaty discourse among Māori, see Lachy Paterson, "The kohimarama conference of 1860: A contextual reading," *Journal of New Zealand Studies* 12 (2011): 29.
24. Interview with Shepard in David Williams, Crown Policy Affecting Māori Knowledge Systems, 55.
25. Judge Harvey, Native Housing, 10 January 1944, Archives New Zealand, MA 1 ACC W2459, BOX 249, 30/1 pt 2, cited in Bierre, Sarah, et al. "Institutional challenges in addressing healthy low-cost housing for all: learning from past policy," *Social Policy Journal of New Zealand* 30 (2007): 55.
26. Nichols and Singh, *Freedom and Democracy*, 224.
27. See s16 of the *Māori Councils Act* 1900.
28. Claudia Orange, "An Exercise in Māori Autonomy: The Rise and Demise of the Māori War Effort Organization," in *Aboriginal peoples and military participation: Canadian and International Perspectives*, eds. Whitney Lackenbauer, Craig Leslie Mantle, and R. Scott Sheffield (Winnipeg: Canadian Defence Academy Press, 2007), 237–266.
29. Te Ao Hou 1 (1952), 23.
30. M. Tennant, *The Fabric of Welfare: Voluntary Organisations, Government and Welfare in New Zealand, 1840–2005* (Wellington: Bridget Williams Books, 2007), 89.
31. This militaristic discourse can also be identified in other colonised nations, see Lackenbauer et al., and the account of unsuccessful attempts to establish Aboriginal fighting units for World War II, and the high enlistment numbers as discussed in Nicolas Peterson and Will Sanders, *Citizenship and indigenous Australians: Changing conceptions and possibilities* (Cambridge University Press, 1998), 9–14.
32. "Response to war – Māori and the Second World War," Ministry for Culture and Heritage. Available: http://www.nzhistory.net.nz/war/maori-in-second-world-war/response. See also P. Meredith, "Urban Māori as New Citizens: The Quest for Recognition and Resources."

33. See, for example, Richard Hill, *State Authority, Indigenous Autonomy: Crown-Māori Relations in New Zealand* (Wellington: Victoria University Press, 2004), 186.
34. Orange, "An Exercise in Māori Autonomy," 257.
35. Waitangi Tribunal, *Te Whanau o Waipareira Report*, Wai 414 (Wellington: GP Publications, 1998), 36–37.

Bibliography

Anderson, Benedict. *Imagined communities: Reflections on the Origin and Spread of Nationalism*. London: Verso, 1983.

Anthony, Thalia. "The Return to the Legal and Citizenship Void: Indigenous Welfare Quarantining in the Northern Territory and Cape York." *Balayi: Culture Law and Colonialism*. 10, 2009: 29–44.

Bierre, Sarah, Philippa Howden-Chapman, Louise Signal, and Chris Cunningham. "Institutional challenges in addressing healthy low-cost housing for all: learning from past policy." *Social Policy Journal of New Zealand*. 30, 2007: 42–64.

Chapple, Simon. "Forward Liability and Welfare Reform." *Child Poverty Policy Quarterly*. 9, 2, 2013: 56–62.

Hill, Richard. *State Authority, Indigenous Autonomy: Crown-Māori Relations in New Zealand*. Wellington: Victoria University Press, 2004.

Johnson, Earl Jr. "Equality before the Law and the Social Contract: When will the United States Finally Guarantee its People the Equality before the Law the Social Contract Demands." *Fordham Urban Law Journal*. 37, 2010: 157–254.

Nichols, Robert and Jakeet Singh. *Freedom and Democracy in an Imperial Context: Dialogues with James Tully*. New York: Routledge, 2014.

Orange, Claudia. "An Exercise in Māori Autonomy: The Rise and Demise of the Māori War Effort Organization." In *Aboriginal peoples and military participation: Canadian and international perspectives*, edited by Whitney Lackenbauer, Craig Leslie Mantle, and R. Scott Sheffield: 237–266. Winnipeg: Canadian Defence Academy Press, 2007.

Palmer, Geoffrey. "The Treaty of Waitangi – Principles for Crown Action." *Victoria University Law Review*. 19, 1989: 335–345.

Paterson, Lachy. "The Kohimarama Conference of 1860: A Contextual Reading." *Journal of New Zealand Studies*. 12, 2011: 29–46.

Pearson, David. "The ties that unwind: Civic and ethnic imaginings in New Zealand." *Nations and Nationalism*. 6, 1, 2000: 91–110.

Peterson, Nicholas and Will Sanders. *Citizenship and Indigenous Australians: Changing Conceptions and Possibilities*. Cambridge: Cambridge University Press, 1998.

Roughan, Nicole. "Te Tiriti and the Constitution: Rethinking Citizenship, Justice, Equality and Democracy." *New Zealand Journal of Public and International Law*. 3, 2005: 285–302.

Shewell, Hugh. *Enough to Keep Them Alive: Indian Welfare in Canada, 1873–1965*. Toronto: University of Toronto Press, 2004.

Tennant, Margaret. *The Fabric of Welfare: Voluntary Organisations, Government and Welfare in New Zealand, 1840–2005*. Wellington: Bridget Williams Books, 2007; Waitangi Tribunal. *Te Whanau o Waipareira Report*. Wai 414. Wellington: GP Publications, 1998.

Williams, H. W. *A Dictionary of The Māori Language*. Wellington: GP Publications, 1971.

Young, Iris Marion. "Polity and Group Difference: A Critique of the Ideal of Universal Citizenship." *Ethics*. 99, 1989: 250–274.

CHAPTER 11

Renegotiating Citizenship: Indigeneity and Superdiversity in Contemporary Aotearoa New Zealand

Paul Spoonley

Aotearoa New Zealand is a classic settler society that has experienced distinct phases of citizenship development in its modern history. In many respects, its colonial history—both as a colony and then as an independent country that retained extremely close political, economic, and cultural ties with its former coloniser—differs little from other settler societies such as Canada and Australia. Colonisation saw the erasure of the preceding sovereignty of the Indigenous Māori. However, by the 1970s, the country began to debate nationality and citizenship in ways that differed (in part) from other modern liberal (including settler) societies. It is this history

I am extremely thankful to the editor of this collection, Jatinder Mann, for his detailed feedback and helpful suggestions on my chapter.

P. Spoonley (✉)
Massey University, Palmerston North, New Zealand
e-mail: p.spoonley@massey.ac.nz

J. Mann (ed.), *Citizenship in Transnational Perspective*, Politics of Citizenship and Migration,
https://doi.org/10.1007/978-3-031-34358-2_11

and those departures which are the focus here. It has two key elements: a pre-eminent focus on a biculturalism which recognises the Indigeneity of the original settlers, Māori; and the shift in the ethnic diversity that resulted from changes to immigration policy in the 1980s so that a significantly enhanced diversity has altered debates about identity, nationalism, and citizenship. The result is new forms of pluralism and the recognition of rights in what David Pearson calls a "'post-settler's conception of multicultural nationhood in a globalised world."[1]

To Post-colonialism

Aotearoa New Zealand as a named entity was the result of European exploration and expansionism in the eighteenth century and the territory's colonisation by the British in the early 1800s. What happened next was influenced by domestic debates in the United Kingdom (UK) about the rights of those colonised. The British approach to expansionism and colonisation was influenced by those groups opposed to slavery and exploitation, notably the Church Missionary Society.[2] Aotearoa New Zealand was gathered into the British Empire by settlement—some would argue that it should be described as resettlement[3] to acknowledge the prior occupation by the Indigenous Māori—and confirmed by a treaty to conform with the new sensitivities of British expansionism. This included the protection of the British Sovereign over Māori property rights although this did not include the rights that would have been seen as central to twentieth-century citizenship rights.

The Treaty of Waitangi/Te Tiriti o Waitangi was signed during 1840 between the representatives of the British Crown and some representatives of Māori iwi (tribes). The semiotics of the treaty and its subsequent interpretation/reinterpretation is complicated by the fact that its three clauses were offered in both English and Māori, with some subtle and not so subtle differences in meaning between the two versions. (James Belich notes that there are five versions of the treaty,[4] see also Stephens' chapter in this collection.) Moreover, it is a product of its time and like other founding documents or statements of rights, it invites reinterpretation and renegotiation as the understandings of colonial agreements evolve. But for the purposes of this chapter, it remains the first statement of rights, including citizenship rights, with the affirmation of the rights, privileges, and duties of British citizenship alongside those that recognise—in a limited way—the rights of Māori to a sovereignty described as "te tino rangatiratanga," or the exercise of chiefly power that has been since defined as Māori sovereignty (see Jones and Linkhorn's chapter in this collection). The point of the treaty was to ensure Māori support for British sovereignty and an agreement by those about to be colonised for what was to follow. As Belich notes, the Māori version embodied a significant distinction between "kawanatanga" or governorship and "rangatiratanga" or the rights of chiefs to continue to exercise power.[5]

The treaty is important for two reasons (in the context of this chapter): the first is that it licensed the British to then begin full-scale colonisation which eventually resulted in the Land Wars in the late nineteenth century, a dispute between the settlers who wanted to usurp Māori control, particularly of land but also of other resources, and to marginalise Māori cultural identity and practices. These disputes occurred about 20 years after the signing as British settlers had reached population parity with Māori and they sought control of land for their own (individual and collective) purposes. Māori reacted and fought to retain land and control, largely unsuccessfully. The courts were also used to favour the more recent colonists, and in 1862, Judge James Prendergast ruled that the Treaty of Waitangi was a nullity, thereby denying the "citizenship" rights granted to Māori as part of the Māori version of the Treaty of Waitangi. The Crown continued to purchase land so that while settler ambitions were to alienate land, the Crown did act as a key broker—sometimes to moderate settler actions, at other times, on their behalf. Second, the treaty has been an important statement of intent and practice when it comes to the rights of Māori. But this was to take more than 130 years before there was the political and judicial renegotiation of what exactly these rights might entail.

Colonisation was in full stride by the 1860s, and the marginalisation of Māori, their demographic decline due to conflict and disease, and the establishment of British dominance and governance were rolled out through the late 1800s and continued through the twentieth century. There was outright conflict—the Land Wars—through this decade as an expression of both settler and Crown ambitions—and Māori resistance. There were some interesting permutations in this project to fully establish British sovereignty. Separate Māori representation in Parliament was established in 1866, essentially to overcome the power that would accrue to Māori due to their property rights and therefore voting rights. Separate Māori schooling was also established. These aside, Māori rights and "citizenship" were denied until politicisation of Māori identity and the rights associated with it occurred in the second half of the twentieth century.

Renegotiating Indigenous Rights

The marginalisation or denial of the rights associated with rangatiratanga (more recently defined as Māori sovereignty) were contested by the political renaissance of Māori from the 1970s.[6] There were three factors that contributed to this renaissance. The first was the involvement of Māori in the military campaigns (overseas) of the Second World War, with considerable losses as a result. The expectations of the state and the involvement of Māori in defence of that state spoke to one of the core responsibilities of citizenship and invited a new consideration of the rights of Māori. They were fulfilling their duties as citizens. The second was the post-war migration of Māori from rural areas to the developing cities of modern industrialism. This migration, which occurred over 30 years, saw a disconnect between the traditional centres of cultural identity and the decultured urbanism of post-migration Māori. Urban-born or raised generations felt aggrieved that they were denied this identity and access. And the third factor was the ongoing usurpation and denial of Māori rights. The Hunn Report (1960) did highlight the marginal location of Māori, and that assimilation, as a policy, had failed. Legislation in 1968 sought to further transfer land rights from Māori to local authorities and Pākehā (the majority group of European descent). The year 1970 was something of a turning point as new political groups emerged to contest this colonial history and the colonisation of Māori. The civil rights movement of the United States of America and a range of nationalist movements provided guidance in terms of both the message and the tactics that could be arrayed in a modern democratic state. Franz Fanon (and others) offered an intellectual guide to colonial racism and decolonisation. A period of confrontational politics emerged in the 1970s and continued into the 1980s (with some ongoing disputes and confrontations), a politics that confronted the state on its failure to protect rangatiratanga—and which also challenged Māori leaders who were seen as acquiescing to colonisation.

As Manjusha Nair notes, Indigeneity was a product of a group being self-defined as Indigenous who exercised precolonial sovereignty in ancestral territories and who embodied ethnic (cultural) practices.[7] The Māori political renaissance made the case for cultural integrity and offered arguments concerning the impacts of cultural and economic degradation/

marginalisation.[8] A new set of discursive claims for group rights associated with being Māori were articulated, and the case for recognition of the rangatiratanga rights specified in the Māori version of the Treaty of Waitangi was advanced.[9] In 1984, a book with the challenging title of "Māori Sovereignty" was published.[10] The notion that sovereignty (or some elements of it) could be detached from the liberal state and granted to Māori was indeed radical given the history of Aotearoa New Zealand as a nation-state. Aotearoa (one of the Māori names for New Zealand) was being reasserted.

A reforming Labour Government, elected in 1984, made significant changes to the constitutional landscape and began to include recognition of the Treaty of Waitangi in the opening clauses of legislation. The courts then took this up with some enthusiasm and a number of critical decisions were made that reinforced and expanded the rights of Māori, especially access to or the ownership of key resources such as land or minerals.[11] A review of a major government department, Puao-Te-Atatu, concluded that the department was institutionally racist in the way that it operated.[12] This provided a key moment for the development of biculturalism as a way of recognising Māori client interests within the operations of the state. Social services were de-universalised and customised to the interests of Māori communities and clients (not always successfully). The government began to recognise Māori language and cultural identity in policies and practices; Māori became an official language of the country. And the government began a process of recognising some of the damage done by colonisation through a reparation process.[13] While the amounts and recognition were seldom appropriate to the losses experienced, they were still often significant in terms of a transfer of funds, land or resource ownership—or as an acknowledgement of hurt. For example, half of all the inshore fisheries were granted to Māori in the late 1980s.

Interestingly, the conservative government that followed this reforming Labour Government in the 1990s continued to recognise Māori as right holders who deserved constitutional recognition and reparations, often with some enthusiasm. Some of the most significant settlements (now called Treaty settlements) were concluded in the 1990s by this government. Certainly, by the turn of the century, governments of whatever political persuasion operated with a new understanding of the rights of Māori in a modern state. The nation-state had been de-hyphenated so that there was no longer an assumption that the state in Aotearoa New Zealand was associated with a single nation, however defined. Māori had different rights and a different citizenship to other New Zealanders. This might mean the right to harvest seafood that was denied to others, or it might mean the right to use Te Reo Māori (Māori language) in a range of institutional settings. A Māori-controlled education system, delivered in Māori, rapidly evolved and involved everything from pre-schools to universities. A Māori television channel was established with the purpose of promoting and maintaining Māori language and culture and to reflect Māori interests. This has since expanded to include a Māori-language channel.

Not all New Zealanders were comfortable with these changes to rangatiratanga and the rights of Māori. There were political constituencies which strongly disagreed and organisations which campaigned against "Māori privilege." Don Brash, a former leader of the conservative National Party as well as the libertarian ACT Party, has campaigned for "one law for all" for many years and continues to be active in public campaigns and organisations opposing the recognition of Māori, describing it as separatist and anti-democratic. He helped form an organisation in 2016 called Hobson's Pledge. (William Hobson was one of those who was central in the early settlement of Aotearoa New Zealand as Lieutenant-General and Consul, appointed in 1839. He said at the time "He iwi tatou katoa," or "we are all one people.") Another politician, who is himself Māori, Winston Peters, has led the New Zealand First political party which is also critical of "Māori privilege." Despite this opposition, the debates concerning the rights of Māori and the centrality of the Treaty of Waitangi to the modern state have become largely accepted and there has been a general (although not complete) normalisation of such debates. A unitary sovereignty had been deconstructed and partially divided as the group rights of Māori were acknowledged. Māori are now, as Pearson describes them, "double citizens."[14] One of the interesting outcomes of these developments has been the naming of the majority group, Pākehā.

Ethnic Group Hegemony: Pākehā

As a new discursive landscape emerged in the 1980s, as the nation-state was being de-hyphenated and the rights of Indigeneity were renegotiated, the hegemonic position of the majority group came under scrutiny. Māori spokespeople and organisations challenged members of this majority group generally and those in positions of power directly, as contributing to Māori marginalisation and disadvantage. They were seen as complicit in the continuance of colonialism and institutional racism. Further, the state was not neutral because its key positions were filled by members of this ethnic group. They would, the argument went, act in their own interests even if this was not always as a result of a conscious or deliberate racism.

One of the interesting dimensions of these politics was the naming of the majority group as Pākehā. This is a Māori term that has uncertain linguistic origins but has now come to refer to members of the majority ethnic group who are the descendants of European/British settlers who have their own practices and values as a result of being the majority group in Aotearoa New Zealand. Through the 1970s and 1980s, both Māori and Pākehā themselves began to use this term more widely. In 1985, a prominent writer, Michael King, wrote a popular book on identity, *Being Pākehā*.[15] It explored the key elements of Pākehā identity, it made the case for Pākehā to be considered an ethnic group, and King argued that there were obligations associated with being Pākehā in relation to setting to right the wrongs of colonialism. Other prominent writers agreed with this stance and it became part of the naming of Pākehā: a willingness to see a degree of responsibility in rectifying past wrongs and to adopt a respectful and sympathetic approach to Māori claims.[16]

Pākehā has become widely and commonly used, although it can be used by both Pākehā and Māori in different ways. For some Pākehā, it is simply an ethnic label that does not imply any political responsibility towards Māori; it is depoliticised. For others, it is a statement about being a modern citizen with a particular approach towards inequality and rights. For another group, it is an offensive label ("we should all be New Zealanders") that has negative meanings and implications.

In debates about contemporary citizenship, the naming of this majority group has some interesting implications: a Māori term is used to name a group that is (at least implicitly) an ethnic group in a landscape that attributes both an identity and rights to such groups; for some, it describes the hegemony of the group as a contrast to the subjugated Māori—being Pākehā has historically derived implicit as well as explicit rights; and it implies a responsibility to engage in a discussion about the rights of Māori. Pearson refers to the "indigenization ... of settler majorities."[17] While Pearson's point is an important one—that Pākehā is a label and a set of politics that reflects an ethnic identification and positioning—the reference in this context to Indigenisation still feels awkward given the politics of Māori citizenship described above, and their prior and ongoing claim to an Indigenous status.

An Enhanced Diversity: Immigration and the Superdiversity of Aotearoa New Zealand

The colonial connections between the UK and Aotearoa New Zealand meant that immigration flows to the colony were completely dominated by immigrants from the UK and Ireland. For much the nineteenth and early twentieth centuries, about 98% of those arriving came from these two countries. This reflected the ambitions of the British Empire, reinforced by colonial administrators and governments in Aotearoa New Zealand. Nation building involved an explicit racial project that sought to continue the social and economic connections with the colonial power, and this was accompanied by exclusionary policies directed at Asian immigrants in particular.

The first Chinese immigrants arrived in Aotearoa New Zealand in the 1860s, and soon after this, anti-Asian groups were established and campaigns to restrict their arrival and citizenship rights ensued. From the 1880s, there were a series of acts (33 in total and based on legislation that had been enacted in California and Australia) that made it difficult for Asians to come to Aotearoa New Zealand, to settle in the country, or to be granted the same rights as other New Zealanders.[18] There were certain difficulties with these restrictions. They were applied to Indians until the British Colonial Office pointed out in the early 1900s that Indians were members of the British Empire and should not be subject to such crude restrictions. The Aotearoa New Zealand Government changed the legislation although the effect was still to discriminate against all Asians, including those arriving from India.[19]

The rights of settlement and citizenship were curtailed for Asians (and other non-Europeans), and this lasted until the mid-twentieth century. The 1935 Labour Government made some changes, and after the Second World War, further changes were made and rights progressively extended to non-Europeans. Family reunification was enabled (most Chinese immigrants were male sojourners who often left behind families in China), and in 1951, Chinese could become citizens for the first time. The normal welfare rights of New Zealanders were made available to Asians. But it was not until the 1980s that the racial preference elements of Aotearoa New Zealand's immigration policy were finally abandoned.

In 1986, a review of immigration policy was conducted and then new policies were introduced in 1987.[20] The preference countries' requirement was dispensed with and a system that sought to attract immigrants who could contribute, especially economically, was developed. Over time, the key elements of the points system that had been developed by Canada and Australia were adopted. After 2000, the Minister of Immigration, Lianne Dalziel, made some significant changes (more than 30) to immigration policy, and the structure and approach that now prevail were established. As with Canada and Australia, about 60% of those approved for permanent settlement came under the Skilled Migrant Category or one of the business and entrepreneur categories. Another 35% came under family reunification provisions while the remainder were refugees and asylum seekers.

The focus is on the recruitment of human capital with very explicit economic/market-driven criteria and approval. The key criteria are whether these immigrants will contribute to the national (economic) good and provide a modern economy with access to the labour skills required and have the international connections/experiences which contribute to twenty-first-century trading patterns (largely with Asia). The result is that traditional source countries, notably the UK and Ireland, have been displaced by Asian source countries, in order of significance, India, China, and the Philippines. In the 1990s, following the changes to immigration policy, the early Asian immigrants came from Hong Kong, Taiwan, and South Korea. After 2000, China and India quickly gained in importance. There was a period of lower-than-normal arrivals and of increased emigration during the Global Financial Crisis (GFC), but after 2012, the numbers of both permanent and temporary arrivals increased significantly.[21]

In mid-2020, as the borders were effectively closed as a result of public health measures in response to the Covid-19 pandemic, the net gain from permanent and long-term (PLT) migrants for the previous 12 months was 90,000 (1.6% of the total Aotearoa New Zealand population). The PLT figures are defined as those who indicate that they will stay for 12 months or more, so it includes some international students and returning New Zealanders. But these figures place Aotearoa New Zealand at the top of the OECD in terms of per capita arrivals. In addition, there are more than 80,000 international students and there were, in the same twelve-month period, 221,298 temporary workers (who arrive under a wide range of schemes from the Recognised Seasonal Employer scheme which sees temporary workers from the Pacific work in seasonal horticultural industries through to working holiday visa categories). These immigrant arrivals contribute significantly to Aotearoa New Zealand's annual population growth of 2.1%, especially in the major gateway city, Auckland.

Auckland was named the fourth most diverse city globally (behind Brussels, Dubai, and Toronto) by the 2016 World Migration Report. And 40% of the city's residents were born in another country and 56% are either immigrants or the children of immigrants. Māori comprise 12% of the city's population, while Pasifika (Samoan, Tongan, Cook Island Māori, Niuean, Tokelauan, and Fijian) make up another 7.4% of the population. Although the later still contain many immigrants who came in the 1960s and 1970s, the majority are now New Zealand-born. Of the remainder, 23% self-identify as members of one of the Asian communities, with those from China and India comprising the two largest by some way, and then followed by Filipinos and Koreans, and then a wide range of other Asian communities. The proportion of the Auckland population who self-identify as Asian is projected to increase to more than 30% of the resident Auckland population over the next decade or so and then to almost 40% by 2040.

The effect has been dramatic. From a country that was dominated by British immigrants with a Māori minority, the country has now become one that has seen the emergence of very significant ethnic minority communities (they are increasingly Asian, which is paradoxical given colonial policies that sought to exclude such immigrants), especially in Auckland. Moreover, in the period from 2013 to 2020, immigrant arrivals were at a level that contributed to a rapid and ongoing diversification as well as significant annual population growth. The arrivals, because of the recruitment and approval process, are skilled middle-class arrivals from Asian cities, who maintain connections with origin societies and communities. They operate across borders as relatively affluent and connected transnationals,[22] although they are also impacting on Aotearoa New Zealand's institutions and spaces. This is not to argue that the settlement and acceptance of these immigrants is unproblematic; there is evidence of gatekeeper discrimination and public anxiety,[23] as well as a degree of discursive homogenisation. Andrew Butcher points out that many New Zealanders associate the label Asian with being Chinese and that statistical convention refers to broad ethnic categories such as "Asian" or "Pasifika."[24]

Contemporary Citizenship Debates and Issues

Aotearoa New Zealand's current citizenship regime faces some interesting challenges, but it also has components which differ in certain ways from the citizenship regimes of comparator countries such as Canada and Australia. These include:

(a) A Soft Approach to Citizenship

In terms of official policy or community attitudes, there is no expectation that immigrant arrivals should become Aotearoa New Zealand citizens. This is not new and was originally apparent in official documents from the 1960s. The rights that are granted to those who are Permanent Residents are almost exactly the same as those that are attached to being a citizen. For example, it is possible to vote in local or national elections as a Permanent Resident (see McMillan's chapter in this collection). Moreover, Aotearoa New Zealand has some 56 visa waiver or dual citizenship agreements with other countries so that there is a recognition that dual loyalties are now commonplace that is not always apparent in the citizenship regimes of most similar countries.

The reasons for this are varied and a little unclear. One factor was that most arrivals to Aotearoa New Zealand up until the mid-twentieth century came from Britain and being a citizen of New Zealand and of the UK were similar; Aotearoa New Zealand passports reflected the dual heritage. The first time that this Britishness was seriously challenged was as a result of the political renaissance of Māori in the 1970s.[25] The conversation about national identity and sovereignty was tense and awkward, but the result was a degree of acceptance that the colonial ideas of racial unity (or purity) were no longer appropriate. By the time that immigration policies were changed in the late 1980s as part of the neo-liberal project to internationalise, there seemed little inclination to adopt a more rigorous set of expectations about citizenship and the need to become one for new arrivals. It was also reinforced by a relatively low-key approach to nationalism.

(b) Biculturalism and Multiculturalism

The debates around the group rights of Māori and rangatiratanga privileged biculturalism, the dual dominance of Māori and Pākehā, or the important relationship between Māori and the Crown. By the 1990s, there was an extensive set of understandings and arrangements that prioritised Māori relations with government, especially as client communities of the state. (This did not eradicate Māori disadvantage and the neo-liberal state, while recognising Māori as client communities with a set of constitutional rights, reinforced or created new forms of economic disadvantage in the wake of deindustrialisation and deregulation.) In terms of the recognition of group rights or rangatiratanga (including to post-migration, urban Māori as well as to tribes/iwi), the ongoing reparations for the disadvantages consequent to colonisation or the particular place Māori occupy a particular status in the exercise of citizenship reinforced the centrality of biculturalism.

The result is that the country is routinely defined as being bicultural. Unlike Canada and Australia, Aotearoa New Zealand has yet to adopt an official policy of multiculturalism. There are elements of multiculturalism in various policies and some government departments (e.g. Office of Ethnic Communities) that are charged with looking after the interests of minority ethnic and immigrant communities. But, for the moment, there is little political enthusiasm to create a policy platform that could be described as multicultural. It remains an omission (given the superdiversity of the country) and a point of tension (including Māori suspicion that it might be used to diminish the rights of Māori).

(c) Transnationalism and Diversity: Economic Drivers

Aotearoa New Zealand's soft approach to citizenship and the affirmation of dual citizenship has been increasingly seen as having a range of benefits, not the least in terms of encouraging affluent, highly mobile migrants from various parts of the world to maintain economic connections with their homeland. The post GFC high levels of inward migration have been justified by officials and recent governments as contributing to the country's economic vitality. Trans-border connections and divided loyalty are seen as having economic benefits, thereby overriding any inclination to tighten expectations about a singular loyalty or the uptake of Aotearoa New Zealand citizenship.

This is often in sharp contrast to other similar countries that have sought to tighten border control and security generally in the wake of events such as 9/11 or more recent trends involving populist and nationalistic political leadership. However, Aotearoa New Zealand operates a very economically focussed pick-and-choose system and has very little reason to anticipate on-shore conflict, including terrorism. (Of course, this expectation was significantly challenged when an Australian far-right activist shot dead 51 Muslim worshippers at two Christchurch mosques in 2019). The result is a degree of acceptance that churn, whether it is 3.5 million visitors per year or the almost 450,000 temporary or permanent arrivals (at least prior to the disruption in mobility and migration associated with Covid-19), is inevitable and that even those approved for permanent residence will continue to maintain residences or businesses in origin countries. This transnationalism is seen as having both individual and collective (national) benefits.

Conclusion

For much of Aotearoa New Zealand's colonial history post the 1840 Treaty of Waitangi, citizenship in the emerging state was defined by its British connections, ambitions to impose Britishness on the Indigenous Māori (including the move to establish Māori representation in Parliament), and to deny any citizenship rights to non-Europeans. There were many similarities with other British settler societies. But the post-colonial turn came with the direct challenges to colonial-influenced citizenship and the nation-state. A period of conflict and negotiation in the 1970s resulted in major changes to legislation and policy after 1984, which was reinforced by judicial decisions. A degree of rangatiratanga (iwi or tribal control) had been restored and the new relationship between the state and Māori (the latter as both a "partner" as well as a key client of the state) warranted the reference to biculturalism, with implications for a new group-defined Indigenous citizenship and sovereignty. But this was further complicated by changes to immigration policy that, by the last decade of the twenty-first century, had significantly altered the ethnic mix of Aotearoa New Zealand and especially Auckland. Although there is relatively little acknowledgement of the implications of this for official policy ("multiculturalism"), the country had adopted a "soft citizenship" regime that (unintentionally?) acknowledged the modern churn and trans-border activities of many migrants. The combination of this soft regime with a biculturalism which acknowledges a form of Indigenous citizenship provides a rather different mix to most other settler societies.

Notes

1. David Pearson, "Theorizing Citizenship in British Settler Societies," *Ethnic and Racial Studies* 25, 6 (2002): 989.
2. James Belich, *Making Peoples: A History of the New Zealanders from Polynesian Settlement to the End of the Nineteenth Century* (Auckland: Penguin, 1996).
3. Giselle Byrnes, "Introduction – Reframing New Zealand History" in *The New Oxford History of New Zealand*, ed. Giselle Byrnes (Melbourne: Oxford University Press, 2009); Katie Pickles. "Colonisation, Empire and Gender" in *The New Oxford History of New Zealand*, ed. Giselle Byrnes (Melbourne: Oxford University Press, 2009).
4. Belich, *Making Peoples.*
5. *Ibid.*
6. Roger Maaka and Augie Fleras, *The Politics of Indigeneity. Challenging the State in Canada and Aotearoa New Zealand* (Dunedin: University of Otago Press, 2005); Donna Awatere, *Māori Sovereignty* (Auckland: Broadsheet Publications, 1984).
7. Manjusha Nair, *Defining Indigeneity: Situating Transnational Knowledge* (Zurich: World Society Focus Paper, 2006).
8. Ranginui Walker, *Ka Whawhai Tonu Matou* (Auckland: Penguin Books, 2009).
9. Anne Salmond, *Tears of Rangi: Experiments Across Worlds* (Auckland: Auckland University Press, 2018).
10. Awatere, *Māori Sovereignty.*
11. Maaka and Fleras, *The Politics of Indigeneity.*
12. Ministerial Advisory Committee on a Māori Perspective for the Department of Social Welfare, *Puao-Te-Atatu* (Wellington: Department of Social Welfare, 1988).
13. Michael Belgrave, *Historical Frictions: Maori Claims and Reinvented Histories* (Auckland: Auckland University Press, 2005).
14. Pearson, "Theorizing Citizenship in British Settler Societies."
15. Michael King, *Being Pākehā* (Auckland: Penguin, 1985).
16. Michael King, *Pākehā: The Quest for Identity in New Zealand* (Auckland: Penguin, 1991).
17. Pearson, "Theorizing Citizenship in British Settler Societies," 989.
18. Paul Spoonley and Richard Bedford, *Welcome to Our World? Immigration and the Reshaping of New Zealand* (Auckland: Dunmore Press, 2012).
19. For more on this, see Jatinder Mann, "The Transnational Identities of the Global South Asian Diaspora in Australia, Canada, Aotearoa New Zealand, and South Africa, 1900s–1940s," *Journal of Australian, Canadian, and Aotearoa New Zealand Studies* 1, 1 (2021): 47–77.

20. *Ibid.*
21. Paul Spoonley, *The New New Zealand: Facing Demographic Disruption* (Auckland: Massey University Press, 2021), Chapter 5.
22. Hagyum Kim, Claire Hocking, Barbara McKenzie-Green, and Shoba Nayar, "Occupational Experiences of Korean Immigrants Settling in New Zealand," *Journal of Occupational Science* 23, 2 (2016).
23. *Ibid.*
24. Andrew Butcher, "An Irishman, a Samoan and a Korean walk into a church: Three encounters and New Zealand's struggle for its national identity," in *Migrant cross-cultural encounters in Asia and the Pacific*, eds. Jacqui Leckie, Angela Wanhalla, and Angela McCarthy (London: Routledge, 2017).
25. For more on this, see Jatinder Mann, "The end of the British World and the redefinition of citizenship in Aotearoa New Zealand, 1950s–1970s," *National Identities* 21, 1 (2019): 305–328; and Jatinder Mann, *Redefining Citizenship in Australia, Canada, and Aotearoa New Zealand* (New York: Peter Lang Publishing, 2019).

Bibliography

Awatere, Donna. *Māori Sovereignty*. Auckland, Broadsheet Publications, 1984.

Belich, James. *Making Peoples: A History of the New Zealanders from Polynesian Settlement to the End of the Nineteenth Century*. Auckland: Penguin, 1996.

Belgrave, Michael. *Historical Frictions: Maori Claims and Reinvented Histories*. Auckland: Auckland University Press, 2005.

Butcher, Andrew. "An Irishman, a Samoan and a Korean Walk into a Church. Three Encounters and New Zealand's Struggle for National Identity." In *Migrant Cross-Cultural Encounters in Asia and the Pacific*, edited by Jacqui Leckie, Angela Wanhalla, and Angela McCarthy, 79–97. London: Routledge, 2017.

Byrnes, Giselle. "Introduction – Reframing New Zealand History." In *The New Oxford History of New Zealand*, edited by Giselle Byrnes: 1–8. Melbourne: Oxford University Press, 2009.

Kim, Hagyum, Claire Hocking, Barbara McKenzie-Green, and Shoba Nayar. "Occupational Experiences of Korean Immigrants Settling in New Zealand." *Journal of Occupational Science*. 23, 2, 2016: 181–195.

King, Michael. *Being Pākehā*. Auckland: Penguin, 1985.

King, Michael. *Pākehā: The Quest for Identity in New Zealand*. Auckland: Penguin, 1991.

Maaka, Roger and Augie Fleras. *The Politics of Indigeneity: Challenging the State in Canada and Aotearoa New Zealand*. Dunedin: University of Otago Press, 2005.

Mann, Jatinder. "The end of the British World and the redefinition of citizenship in Aotearoa New Zealand, 1950s–1970s." *National Identities.* 21, 1, 2019a: 73–92. https://doi.org/10.1080/14608944.2017.1369019.

Mann, Jatinder. *Redefining Citizenship in Australia, Canada, and Aotearoa New Zealand.* New York: Peter Lang Publishing, 2019b.

Mann, Jatinder. "The Transnational Identities of the Global South Asian Diaspora in Australia, Canada, Aotearoa New Zealand, and South Africa, 1900s–1940s." *Journal of Australian, Canadian, and Aotearoa New Zealand Studies.* 1, 1, 2021: 47–77. https://doi.org/10.52230/VQGX5133.

Ministerial Advisory Committee on a Māori Perspective for the Department of Social Welfare. *Puao-Te-Atatu.* Wellington: Department of Social Welfare, 1988.

Nair, Manjusha. *Defining Indigeneity: Situating Transnational Knowledge.* Zurich: World Society Focus Paper, 2006.

Pearson, David. "Theorizing Citizenship in British Settler Societies." *Ethnic and Racial Studies.* 25, 6, 2002: 989–1012. https://doi.org/10.1080/01419870220000009403.

Pickles, Katie. "Colonisation, Empire and Gender." In *The New Oxford History of New Zealand*, edited by Giselle Byrnes, 219–241. Melbourne: Oxford University Press, 2009.

Salmond, Anne. *Tears of Rangi: Experiments Across Worlds.* Auckland: Auckland University Press, 2018.

Spoonley, Paul. *The New New Zealand: Facing Demographic Disruption.* Auckland: Massey University Press, 2021.

Spoonley, Paul and Richard Bedford. *Welcome to Our World? Immigration and the Reshaping of New Zealand.* Auckland: Dunmore Press, 2012.

Walker, Ranginui. *Ka Whawahi Tonu Matou. Struggle Without End.* Auckland: Penguin, 1990.

PART IV

Deep Diversity and Securitization

CHAPTER 12

Second-Generation Migrants in the Media and Politics: Enacting Cultural Citizenship, Claiming Belonging

Sukhmani Khorana

Introduction

Migrants have long been seen as striving for socio-economic mobility in the countries they migrate to. While these aspirations receive scholarly attention, less is known about how their subsequent generations experience belonging, what they mean by it, and how they enact it by trying to be part of the polity. This chapter begins with an overview of the concepts of "belonging" and "active citizenship" as they pertain to second-generation migrants before unpacking why this cohort of migrants merits

I am extremely grateful to the editor of this collection, Jatinder Mann, for his detailed feedback and helpful suggestions on my chapter.

S. Khorana (✉)
Faculty of Arts, Design, and Architecture, University of New South Wales, Sydney, NSW, Australia
e-mail: s.khorana@unsw.edu.au

J. Mann (ed.), *Citizenship in Transnational Perspective*, Politics of Citizenship and Migration,
https://doi.org/10.1007/978-3-031-34358-2_12

examination to understand how the enactment of citizenship is evolving in immigrant settler colonial nations like Australia. Two case studies pertaining to civic initiatives in the media and politics in Australia are then presented to exemplify the manifestation of belonging and citizenship. Media Diversity Australia (MDA) was founded by the children of migrants and has an explicit focus on advancing the media careers of this group. Pathways to Politics and Women for Election have a more generic emphasis on women in politics but have also been influential in facilitating the political careers of second-generation migrant women.

Claiming "Belonging"

This chapter departs from the emphasis on "identity" and migrant integration in settler colonial immigrant societies to frame questions of enacting citizenship through the lens of belonging. I contend that "belonging" is more useful than identity, not just as a concept to understand and unpack what takes place in migrants' everyday lives but also as a discursive tool that citizens with dual identities themselves employ to make sense of their present and future (see Jayawardena's chapter in this collection).

It is worth noting that trans-disciplinary academic research on belonging has been ongoing since the 1990s, and attempts to distinguish it from identity are also not new. For instance, in a 2019 edited volume, Anna Tsalapatanis argues that the two terms should not be conflated as belonging is an abstract relational concept, "compared to identity's more categorical individualistic bent."[1] Moreover, if belonging is to be re-conceptualised in settler immigrant societies as a pluralistic sense of being with diverse others, then it must be pushed beyond the "conceptual confines of identity."[2]

In re-conceptualising belonging, the key contribution of this chapter and its case studies on media and politics in Australia is in harnessing its progressive potential through civic initiatives in these realms by second-generation migrants (often in alliance with other socially disadvantaged communities). This progressive potential of belonging is premised on the notion that in the context of migration, belonging is the affective dimension of citizenship and thereby enables participation of migrants in a range of social, economic, cultural, and political activities. In enabling this participation and enactment of citizenship, migrant identity itself is unpacked so that ethnicity is not the sole determinant of how belonging is experienced and manifested in the host society.

According to conceptual work on belonging undertaken by sociologists, it has two dimensions: these include belonging in place and belonging as a discursive resource.[3] In the case studies examined in this chapter, the second one in particular is explored as second-generation migrants are seen as using their claim to belonging to the multicultural polity in their advocacy efforts for greater diversity. This means that the examples presented here will demonstrate how belonging is not just a matter of endowment through a passport but a feeling that is both experienced and insisted on through acts of civic participation.

There is also existing work on young people from immigrant backgrounds and their experiences of everyday life in diverse communities in Australia and comparable multicultural societies. For example, Anita Harris has studied diverse neighbourhoods across Australian capital cities and concludes that young people display affiliations with different communities.[4] In his research with young migrants and children of migrants in Leicester (UK), John Clayton has observed that they negotiate belonging in everyday life as a mix of local and transnational ties.[5] He adds that for this cohort, recognition of their liminal identities "does not merely entail the fracturing of bounded ethnic ties, implying a reduction of affiliation, but also the creation of new forms of solidarity."[6] Similarly, in the parts of western Sydney with a critical mass of multicultural populations, Noble has noted that migrants are actively engaged in code-switching. This kind of code-switching enables mobility across socio-cultural milieus, and it can be generative of belonging for them.[7]

At the same time, multiculturalism as government policy and everyday practice has been perceived to be under threat across the Global North, especially since the 9/11 attacks in the United States of America (USA). Moreover, this has impacted the belonging of visibly different minority groups in the countries of immigration, even when they have been born and raised there. Anita Harris and Melinda Herron looked at the socialisation of youth in the wake of the racially motivated Cronulla riots in Australia in 2005 and conclude that the capacity to relate to a place occurs along multiple axes of difference.[8] In other words, while the existence of casual as well as overt forms of racism in inter-cultural interactions cannot be overlooked, there is also mounting evidence of encounters that transcend these racialised power dynamics. To understand where and how this occurs, focusing on how these youth channel belonging to enact citizenship in a wide range of settings is vital. For instance, Maree Pardy and Julian Lee found that while multiculturalism as a policy of tokenism is critiqued in academic research, it has immense discursive value for migrants of varying backgrounds because it helps them lay claim and express belonging to the "multicultural nation."[9] This discursive value of a multicultural society to second-generation migrant youth in particular merits further attention.

Finally, the relational nature of belonging means that the dynamics of power and exclusion must also be noted, especially in terms of how they create barriers for those who should otherwise "feel" like citizens. As noted in the census of multicultural youth in Australia, high levels of migrant and refugee desire to belong to the nation-state of settlement are not matched with reciprocity from those who have been here longer. Boundaries of various kinds impact immigrants' belonging, and it also depends on the welcoming capacity of the majority community.[10] According to research by Mesa Mikola and Fethi Mansouri, un-belonging and racism are experienced by migrant youth in a spatial sense, as well as in everyday life.[11] In a similar vein, Zuleyka Zevallos notes that in the case of a sample of Australian women of Latin and Turkish backgrounds in Melbourne, "the women's experiences of racism and their awareness of a hierarchy of belonging have a strong impact on the ways in which they claim their identities."[12] Countering such forms of racism and exclusion has been found to be more successful when undertaken by youth collectives at the local level,[13] which in themselves are manifestations of cultural citizenship. In line with this, the chapter here attempts to unpack belonging and understand the enactment of citizenship from the perspective of grassroots initiatives in Australia, albeit with wider applicability.

Active Citizenship as the Affective Enactment of Belonging

In order to connect a feeling of belonging to participation in the polity, scholars have coined the term "active citizenship" and examined its practice amongst immigrant youth.[14] They reason that this framing of citizenship goes beyond the possession of legitimising documents and helps us focus on young migrants' agency, self-actualising practices, as well as self-reflexivity in their social networks. The case studies presented here are based on the premise that investigating and shaping such an affective and participatory dimension of citizenship is especially pertinent at a time when national debates about social cohesion and migrant/refugee integration are at cross purposes across the Global North. In other words, migrants are often demonised as causing problems for cohesiveness in urban areas, while also being considered crucial for a prosperous economy pivoted on real estate and skills. Such ambivalent messages about the value of migrants cause increasing emphasis on discourses of "integration" in the popular imaginary. While this is useful for the purposes of migrant settlement and attunement to the host nation, it takes away agency from migrants to shape their own surroundings, mediated stories, and policies that impact them directly.

Therefore, the framework of active citizenship enables migrants to contribute in a manner that fits in with the notion of integration and also (re)interprets representational politics as requiring input from old and new Australians alike.

An example of how belonging is affectively enacted through active citizenship is seen in Chloe Patton's research on youth from Muslim backgrounds in Australia. She notes that their citizenship practices can be usefully thought of as performative "by focusing on the acts through which marginalised subjects enact themselves as citizens."[15] Patton adds that this takes place through non-normative practices in sites of religious worship such as mosques, where youth combine the notion of being a good Muslim with that of being an engaged citizen who cares about social justice. These practices are considered non-normative because religious activity is not usually associated with being a good citizen in a secular state. Patton concludes that this particular combination of culture and citizenship is only possible when "in order to enact oneself as a citizen, particularly in the cultural sense, one has to develop the feeling that one rightfully belongs to the polis."[16] This feeling of rightful belonging, then, is what underpins any meaningful enactment of citizenship.

What Is New About "Second-Generation Migrants" and Their Belonging and Citizenship Practices

Inclusion in workplaces and broader society is considered key by scholars and independent bodies like the Australian Human Rights Commission for the integration of culturally and linguistically diverse (CALD) communities in contemporary multicultural Australia. However, despite recent momentum in terms of representing cultural diversity in sectors such as the media due to the efforts of industry advocates and institutional initiatives, progress has been slow and/or staggered.[17] Research indicates that those with ethnic names and the same qualifications as white candidates are less likely to be called for an interview.[18] Also of significance is the fact that the cultural diversity of the population is not reflected at the leadership levels of sectors of society with high visibility.[19] Moreover, many second and further-generation migrant Australians have grown up with globally accessible digital media and are looking for diverse representation since representation in Australia's mainstream media is still lacking. They are finding new ways to mobilise and self-represent using digital platforms and social media. The impact of global and digital media influences, and the modes in which immigrant young people's belonging is being expressed, have thus far not been sufficiently addressed in scholarly assessments of what constitutes migrant "aspirations." Yet, examining both these channels of belonging and enactments of citizenships is vital to fully understand how their aspirations are being shaped and articulated, and to centre their perspectives in achieving inclusion.

The group of second- and further-generation migrants co-emergent with digital media is already of growing interest in a comparable immigrant society such as the USA, where it is referred to as "the new second generation."[20] In the Australian setting, this chapter builds on the theory of the distinctiveness of "the new second generation" which is deployed here to characterise young people aged 18–40 years from CALD backgrounds who are second- and further-generation migrants. CALD youth is arguably a heterogenous group with a range of class and ethnic backgrounds as well as career aspirations. It must also be acknowledged that the "CALD" label is insufficient as it does not account for racial disadvantage, yet is considered a functional term in policy settings, and more strengths-based than the term that was previously employed in its place, "Non-English Speaking Background."[21] While research on first-generation CALD migrants is primarily concerned with issues of settlement and mobility,[22] literature on the second generation also deals with acculturation concerns, hybrid identities, and negotiations of home and host culture media consumption.[23] At the same time, participation in the increasingly digitised and global nature of youth cultures (beyond the home and host nations) now offers possibilities and challenges for the kinds of aspirations CALD migrant youth now have in their immediate contexts—for education, work, travel, relationships, environmental change, politics, and the hope for a better life in a collective sense. However, those attempting to pursue careers in "white-bread" institutions like traditional media or formal politics are faced with a lack of cultural diversity.[24] The largely online civic initiatives spawned to address such systemic exclusion have thus far not been examined as enactments of active citizenship.

Digital media has become an important site to understand what impacts the individual aspirations of second- and further-generation CALD young people, and how their collective aspirations are shaped and expressed.[25] At the same time, Australian youth are growing up in times of the normalisation of cultural diversity.[26] This means that youth experience higher levels of cultural diversity in their everyday lives as well as in the media they consume. However, there is little empirical work on how the normalisation of cultural diversity is directly shaped by their engagement with global digital media and how the media in turn funnels their aspirations and everyday practices. While youth studies as a field acknowledges that young people around the world are subject to some fundamental megatrends such as economic insecurity, greater mobility, and the ubiquity of the digital,[27] there are increasingly calls for youth research to deepen understanding of how these trends play out in local contexts.[28] The chapter aims to begin to address this gap with regard to CALD second- and further-generation migrant youth, referred to here as "the new second generation."

CALD migrant communities' under-representation in highly visible sectors such as media, formal politics, and activist social movements has remained entrenched in Australia despite some efforts to address it. Children of migrants from CALD backgrounds who are born in Australia attain higher levels of social and economic integration than their parents.[29] However, the realisation of their aspirations continues to be marred by racial and ethnic discrimination and consequent feelings of not belonging that impact their contribution to Australian society.[30] For instance, according to the 2016 census, Australians claiming Asian ancestries constitute about 13% of the population and are growing every year. Chinese and Indian Australians (amongst others) also tend to be highly educated, and working in white-collar jobs, but are under or mis-represented in the media.[31] Accounting for the socio-economic mobility of migrants by measuring their education and income levels over time is an important dimension of migration research in immigrant settler societies.[32] However, their growing expectations for representation in sectors of society with high visibility and decision-making potential need to be integrated into the narrative about migrant aspirations. Moreover, the needs, experiences, and aspirations of the "new second generation" are distinct from both (a) newly arrived young migrants (including international students and asylum seekers) who are usually the focus in policy and scholarly studies of settlement and citizenship and (b) previous cohorts of second-generation migrants who grew up before the advent of digital media and its influence on local cultures.

Case Study 1: Media Diversity Australia

According to the official website of the initiative, MDA was founded in 2017 by Isabel Lo and Antoinette Lattouf and is a "national not-for-profit organisation, working towards creating a media landscape that looks and sounds like Australia." The homepage also mentions that they have expertise in delivering evidence-based research, "bespoke programs, strategic memberships and partnerships that disrupt the status quo and pave pathways for diverse representation across Australian media."[33] Their activities are focused on "setting the agenda," "creating pathways," and "partnering for change." MDA constitutes a valuable case study for examining the phenomenon of second-generation migrant belonging and enactment of citizenship through the media as it is the first initiative of its kind in Australia that combines advocacy for people of colour aspiring to work in the media with high-profile publicity, evidence-based research, and dedicated training or mentoring programmes. This relative success shows the growing momentum of representational politics and how they are seen as connected with belonging and citizenship in the popular imaginary in immigrant settler colonial nations.

The current CEO of MDA is Mirian Veiszadeh who is a human rights lawyer, author, and media commentator (as well as a second-generation migrant like the founders). Her bio on the official website of MDA also states that she was born in Afghanistan and came to Australia in 1990 with her family as a refugee. Also of note is Waleed Aly, a prominent member of the organisation's advisory board who is Egyptian-Australian and well-known for his media career and advocacy across platforms. The New South Wales state chapter of MDA includes many second-generation migrant Australians with emerging media careers such as Wenlei Ma (film critic), Farid Farid (news reporter), Kishor Napier-Raman (columnist), and Kamin Gock (journalist). Those across the Victorian, Queensland, and newly launched Australian Capital Territory chapters have similar profiles, with children of migrants with a wide range of media experience dominating.

The website serves as not just a hub for information about the initiative, its executive team, and highly publicised research reports (often in partnership with universities) but also crucially has a focus on capacity-building opportunities and resources. These include the summer fellowships, political fellowships, women of colour mentorships, and a Chinese-Australian secondment opportunity. The "political fellowships," for instance, are worth $15,000 each and "take place during the federal election and will be Canberra-based for Australians under the age of 30, who are passionate about media, politics and diversity."[34] They are also targeted at 12 current journalism students and give them a taste of working for a mainstream media organisation. Of note in the selection criteria is that the fellowships are designed to address what is perceived as an obvious gap: "*culturally diverse perspectives* in the coverage of Australian federal politics."

The "women of colour mentorships," on the other hand, are designed for "mid-career women journalists of First Nations and culturally and linguistically diverse backgrounds to undertake a 12-month program to help pave a pathway into leadership roles."[35] Therefore, these particular mentorships are in recognition of the fact that leadership positions in the media are even less likely to be occupied by those hailing from this cohort, although this is not explicitly stated.

Also of significance is the "research and resources" section of the website which can be used for finding an expert in a particular area or topic and has links for guidebooks on Indigenous reporting and disability reporting. It is also possible to download the two MDA research reports, titled "Who Gets to Tell Australian Stories?" (2020) and "Who Gets to Tell Australian Stories? 2.0" (2022), from this section. As the titles of the reports themselves suggest, the organisation is deeply invested in what gets counted as "Australian" in terms of representation and who decides. Through their partnerships and paid pathways for early and more established professionals from diverse backgrounds working in the media (or aspiring to do so), they are attempting to change the landscape of not just the Australian media but also the very sense of belonging and symbolic citizenship that CALD Australians experience. In her book on Latina migrants in search of belonging in the USA, Jillian Baez concludes that their place within the nation is often thought to be "not only imagined by media, but also secured by media."[36]

Finally, it is worth noting that while MDA partners with several major media outlets, including digital media (such as Google Australia), the focus of their capacity-building efforts and reports is largely on achieving parity of representation in the media workforce (and relatedly what gets reported/represented). It is likely that the reports in particular have been critiqued by the likes of the Australian public broadcaster, the ABC on the grounds that understanding of representation needs to go beyond the ethnicity of news presenters, particularly when most media consumption takes place across a range of platforms these days.[37] While the MDA initiative is a substantive starting point in enacting citizenship by second-generation migrant Australians, it could go further and deeper in exploring the radical potential of representation as well as online self-representation by these communities.

Case Study 2: "Pathways to Politics" and "Women for Election" Programmes

On the global stage, the election of Kamala Harris as Vice-President of the USA, an American woman of South Asian and Black descent has led to a renewed focus on the representation of women of colour in formal politics. Research from the USA shows that her election slogan, "that she is the first but not the last—self-consciously opens the door for women and girls from all racial/ethnic backgrounds to follow in her footsteps."[38] Also worth noting is that in the campaign coverage, Harris was often characterised as a "woman of colour," or "WOC," and self-identifies with the label as well. While it is important to reflect on what this positioning means for WOC candidates more broadly and for the voters who identify with the term, it is important to point out slow progress on this front. For example, "no Black woman or Native American woman has ever won the office of governor, and just three WOC have ever been elected governor."[39] In terms of barriers to standing for election and enacting one's citizenship using that route, online attacks are a significant hurdle as "gender-based, race-based, and intersectional attacks on 'the Squad' and other prominent WOC officials under President Donald Trump" have constituted a backlash to small wins.[40]

In the Australian context, similar challenges are faced by the handful of WOC who are in elected office. For instance, Greens Senator Mehreen Faruqi, who became Australia's first Muslim woman to be a member of an Australian parliament in 2013, said in an interview that "our political system is steeped in patriarchy and racism that go hand-in-hand to oppress women of colour."[41] The same article also cites the story of Charishma

Kaliyanda who was "born in India and migrated to Australia with her family in the early 90s, and said the 'biggest challenge people of colour face in politics is lack of institutional knowledge and access.'"[42]

In the 2022 federal parliament, "The biggest gains have been made in the proportion of women representatives, now making up 38% of the House of Representatives and 57% of the Senate—a record for both chambers."[43] However, the parliament is still not adequately reflective of the nation's cultural and linguistic diversity. Even though "23% of Australians claim a non-European ancestry, just 6.6%—or 15 out of the 227 MPs—have overseas non-European backgrounds."[44] Furthermore, "4.4% of MPs in the parliament have Asian heritage, compared with 18% of the Australian population at large."[45]

It is worth adding that one successful Asian-Australian candidate, Sally Sitou, who happens to be a second-generation migrant did successfully win the marginal seat of Reid in inner west Sydney in the most recent federal election. Amongst other factors, the "Pathways to Politics" programme is noted as contributing to her electoral success. According to its official website, "the program is focused on women and is a national, proudly non-partisan initiative that aims to change the face of politics by equipping women with the skills, knowledge, confidence and networks they need to run for elected office and thrive as political leaders."[46] In her testimonial for the programme on its website, Sitou says:

> I've always felt compelled to serve. The value of this program was it made me think about the contribution I wanted to make to my community. It made me be brave and bold and see a bigger role for what that contribution might look like. It was a wonderfully supportive environment and gave me a unique opportunity to meet a cohort of women across the political spectrum who are all guided by the desire to serve their community.[47]

Another noteworthy alumna of the programme is second-generation Asian Australian Wesa Chau who stood as the Labor candidate for the seat of Prahran in the state election in Victoria in 2022. On the "Knowledge Hub" section of Pathways to Politics website, Chau mentions that she has been an advocate for inclusion for a long time and even established "Poliversity"—a platform to increase cultural diversity and participation in the membership base in the Australian Labor Party. Moreover, Chau sees programmes such as Pathways as facilitating ways for people of colour to be at the centre of decision-making when this has been historically denied to them. In other ways, candidates like Sitou and Chau are making use of programmes available for all women to make space for WOC and enhance their belonging and symbolic citizenship.

The "Women for Election" programme has similarly trained second-generation migrant women who are emerging as influential or aspiring politicians. Examples include Charishma Kaliyanda, a councillor in the Western Sydney Local Government Area of Liverpool and who ran as a Labor candidate for the seat of Liverpool in the recent New South Wales state election and won; and Greens candidate for the seat of Summer Hill in the same election, Izabella Antoniou identifies as young, queer, and from a migrant background. Both claim to have benefited from the training courses for aspiring woman-identifying candidates.[48] The website for the programme contains more information about what it entails and the topics covered. Within the "Equip" programme that is a series of online workshops, aspiring women candidates or campaign managers are trained in campaign planning, budgeting and fundraising, engaging with the community, public speaking, legal duties, and resilience. There does not appear to be a specific targeting of barriers faced by WOC, though the "in conversation" series includes interviews with a few and the masterclass option has tailored material focused on particular skills/issues.

Conclusion

To summarise, this chapter has explored how second-generation migrants in a settler colonial immigrant nation like Australia are claiming belonging and enacting active citizenship. To do so, it frames their belonging as an affective dimension of citizenship they are insisting on rather than waiting on it to be endowed by the polity. The case studies used to illustrate this kind of enactment of active citizenship include civic initiatives in media such as Media Diversity Australia and in the field of politics like Pathways to Politics and Women for Election. Both feature a high representation of people/women of colour in their founders and/or alumni, and therefore manifest the belonging and enactment of citizenship that extends beyond possessing legal documents.

Notes

1. Anna Tsalapatanis, "Naming belonging: When national vocabularies fail," in *Social Beings, Future Belongings: Reimagining the Social*, eds. Anna Tsalapatanis, Miranda Bruce, David Bissell, and Helen Keane (London and New York: Routledge, 2019), 13.
2. David Bissell, Miranda Bruce, Helen Keane, and Anna Tsalapatanis, "Introduction: Belonging unbound," in *Social Beings, Future Belongings: Reimagining the Social*, eds. Anna Tsalapatanis, Miranda Bruce, David Bissell, and Helen Keane (London and New York: Routledge, 2019), 4.
3. Marco Antonsich, "Searching for belonging – an analytical framework," *Geography Compass* 4, 6 (2010): 644–659.
   Rebecca Williamson, "Everyday space, mobile subjects and place-based belonging in suburban Sydney," *Journal of Ethnic and Migration Studies* 42, 14 (2016): 2328–2344.
4. Anita Harris, "Belonging and the uses of difference: young people in Australian urban multiculture," *Social Identities* 22, 4 (2016): 359–375.
5. John Clayton, "Living the multicultural city: acceptance, belonging and young identities in the city of Leicester, England," *Ethnic and Racial Studies* 35, 9 (2012): 1673–1693.
6. *Ibid.*, 1688.
7. Greg Noble, "'It is home but it is not home': habitus, field and the migrant," *Journal of Sociology* 49, 2–3 (2013): 341–356.
8. Anita Harris and Melinda Herron, "Young People and Intercultural Sociality after Cronulla," *Journal of Intercultural Studies* 38, 3 (2017): 284–300.
9. Maree Pardy and Julian C. H. Lee, "Using buzzwords of belonging: everyday multiculturalism and social capital in Australia," *Journal of Australian Studies* 35, 3 (2011): 297–316.
10. Kristina B. Simonsen, "How the host nation's boundary drawing affects immigrants' belonging," *Journal of Ethnic and Migration Studies* 42, 7 (2016): 1153–1176.
11. Masa Mikola and Fethi Mansouri, "Race lines and spaces of political action among migrant youth," *Journal of Youth Studies* 18, 4 (2015): 500–514.
12. Zuleyka Zevallos, "You Have to be Anglo and Not Look Like Me': identity and belonging among young women of Turkish and Latin American backgrounds in Melbourne, Australia," *Australian Geographer* 39, 1 (2008): 21–43.
13. Mikola and Mansouri, "Race lines and spaces of political action among migrant youth," 210.

14. Fethi Mansouri and Liudmila Kirpitchenko, "Practices of active citizenship among migrant youth: beyond conventionalities," *Social Identities* 22, 3 (2016): 307–323.
15. Chloe Patton, "Multicultural Citizenship and Religiosity: Young Australian Muslims Forging a Sense of Belonging after 9/11," *Journal of Intercultural Studies* 35, 1 (2014): 109.
16. *Ibid.*, 110.
17. James Arvanitakis, Carolyn Cage, Dimitria Groutsis, Annika Kaabel, Christine Han, Ann Hine, Nic Hopkins, Antoinette Lattouf, Irene Jay Liu, Isabel Lo, Catharine Lumby, Usha Rodrigues, Tim Soutphommasane, and Subodhanie Umesha Weerakkody, "Who gets to tell Australian stories?," (Media Diversity Australia, 2020), https://apo.org.au/node/307889.
18. Alison L. Booth, Andrew Leigh, and Elena Varganova, "Does ethnic discrimination vary across minority groups? Evidence from a field experiment," *Oxford Bulletin of Economics and Statistics* 74, 4 (2012): 547–573.
19. Australia Council for the Arts, "Towards Equity: A research overview of diversity in Australia's arts and cultural sector" (2020).
    Juliet Pietsch, "Australian ethnic change and political inclusion: finding strength in diversity in responding to global crises," in *Re-imagining Australia: Migration, culture, diversity: Practical suggestions on the challenges and opportunities ahead*, eds. Shamit Saggar and Anna Zenz (Perth: UWA Public Policy Institute, 2020).
20. Min Zhou and Carl L. Bankston, *The Rise of the New Second Generation* (Cambridge: Polity, 2016).
21. Pooja Sawrikar and Ilan Katz, "How useful is the term 'Culturally and linguistically diverse (CALD)' in Australian research and policy discourse?," Social Policy Research Centre, UNSW, 2009.
22. Farida Fozdar and Susan Banki, "Settling refugees in Australia: achievements and challenges," *International Journal of Migration and Border Studies* 3, 1 (2017): 43–66.
    Shanthi Robertson, "Suspending, settling, sponsoring: the intimate chronomobilities of young Asian migrants in Australia," *Global Networks* 20, 4 (2020): 677–696.
    Christina Ho, *Aspiration and Anxiety: Asian Migrants and Australian Schooling* (Melbourne: Melbourne University Press, 2020).
23. Melissa Butcher, "FOB Boys, VCs and Habibs: Using Language to Navigate Difference and Belonging in Culturally Diverse Sydney," *Journal of Ethnic and Migration Studies* 34, 3 (2008): 371–387.
    Patton, "Multicultural Citizenship and Religiosity."
24. Andrew Jakubowicz, "Diversity and news in Australia," in *Cosmopolitan Civil Societies Research Centre University of Technology Sydney, & Institute*

for Cultural Diversity Presentation to Symposium on News and Inclusion: Journalism and the Politics of Diversity, Stanford University, 2010, vol. 4.

25. Centre for Multicultural Youth, "Culturally and Linguistically Diverse Young People and Digital Citizenship: A Pilot Study," 2018, 1–34.
    Amelia Johns, "Muslim Young People Online: 'Acts of Citizenship' in Socially Networked Spaces," *Social Inclusion* 2, 2 (2014): 71–82.
26. Anita Harris and Sherene Idriss, "Lifeworlds and Cultures of Australian Youth in a Globalised World," in *Youth Cultures in a Globalized World*, eds. G. Knapp and H. Krall (Cham: Springer, 2021).
27. Peter Kelly and Annelies Kamp, *A critical youth studies for the 21st century* (Leiden and Boston: Brill, 2014).
    Mark Cieslik and Donals Simpson, *Key concepts in youth studies* (London and Los Angeles: Sage, 2013).
28. Harris and Idriss, "Lifeworlds and Cultures of Australian Youth in a Globalised World," 91.
29. Glenda Ballantyne and Aneta Podkalicka, "Dreaming Diversity: Second Generation Australians and the Reimagining of Multicultural Australia," *M/C Journal* 23, 1 (2020).
30. Jock Collins, Carol Reid, and Charlotte Fabiansson, "Identities, aspirations and belonging of cosmopolitan youth in Australia," *Cosmopolitan civil societies: an interdisciplinary journal* 3, 3 (2011): 92–107.
    Andrew Jakubowicz, Jock Collins, Carol Reid, and Wafa Chafic, "Minority Youth and Social Transformation in Australia: Identities, Belonging and Cultural Capital," *Social Inclusion* 2, 2 (2014): 5–16.
31. Sukhmani Khorana, "The problem with Apu: why we need better portrayals of people of colour on television," *The Conversation*, 2018, https://theconversation.com/the-problem-with-apu-why-we-need-better-portrayals-of-people-of-colour-on-television-106707 [Accessed 10 November 2021].
32. Jenny Chesters, "Does migrant status affect educational achievement, aspirations, and attainment?," *Multicultural Education Review* 7, 4 (2015): 197–212.
33. Media Diversity Australia official website, https://www.mediadiversityaustralia.org.
34. *Ibid.*
35. *Ibid.*
36. Jillian M. Báez, *In search of belonging: Latinas, media, and citizenship* (Champaign: University of Illinois Press, 2018), 8.
37. Gavin Fang, "ABC response: 'Who Gets to Tell Australian Stories? 2.0'", *ABC News*, 2022, https://about.abc.net.au/statements/abc-response-who-gets-to-tell-australian-stories-2-0/ [Accessed 25 February 2023].

38. Stacey Greene, Yalidy Matos, and Kira Sanbonmatsu, "Women Voters and the Utility of Campaigning as 'Women of Color,'" *Journal of Women, Politics & Policy* 43, 1 (2022): 25.
39. *Ibid.*
40. *Ibid.*, 26.
41. Alicia Vrajlal, "'It's A White Boys' Club': How WOC Are Sidelined In Aussie Politics," *Refinery29.com*, 2021, https://www.refinery29.com/en-au/2021/09/10678622/australia-politics-racism-sexism [Accessed 20 February 2023].
42. *Ibid.*
43. Amy Remeikis, "The 47th parliament is the most diverse ever – but still doesn't reflect Australia," *The Guardian*, 25 July 2022, https://www.theguardian.com/australia-news/2022/jul/25/the-47th-parliament-is-the-most-diverse-ever-but-still-doesnt-reflect-australia [Accessed 20 February 2023].
44. *Ibid.*
45. *Ibid.*
46. Pathways to Politics for Women official website, https://pathwaystopolitics.org.au/.
47. *Ibid.*
48. Ashleigh Raper, "The women hoping to be voted into lower house at NSW election," *ABC News*, 26 February 2023, https://www.abc.net.au/news/2023-02-26/women-candidates-for-nsw-state-election/102022994 [Accessed 27 February 2023].

Bibliography

Antonsich, Marco. "Searching for belonging–an analytical framework." *Geography Compass*. 4, 6, 2010: 644–659.

Australia Council for the Arts. "Towards Equity: A research overview of diversity in Australia's arts and cultural sector." 2020.

Báez, Jillian M. *In search of belonging: Latinas, media, and citizenship*. Champaign: University of Illinois Press 2018.

Ballantyne, Glenda and Aneta Podkalicka. "Dreaming Diversity: Second Generation Australians and the Reimagining of Multicultural Australia." *M/C Journal*. 23, 1, 2020. https://doi.org/10.5204/mcj.1648.

Bissell, David, Miranda Bruce, Helen Keane, and Anna Tsalapatanis. "Introduction: Belonging unbound." In *Social Beings, Future Belongings: Reimagining the*

Social, edited by Anna Tsalapatanis, Miranda Bruce, David Bissell, and Helen Keane: 1–10. London and New York: Routledge, 2019.

Booth, Alison L., Andrew Leigh, and Elena Varganova. "Does ethnic discrimination vary across minority groups? Evidence from a field experiment." *Oxford Bulletin of Economics and Statistics*. 74, 4, 2012: 547–573.

Butcher, Melissa. "FOB Boys, VCs and Habibs: Using Language to Navigate Difference and Belonging in Culturally Diverse Sydney." *Journal of Ethnic and Migration Studies*. 34, 3, 2008: 371–387. https://doi.org/10.1080/13691830701880202.

Centre for Multicultural Youth. "Culturally and Linguistically Diverse Young People and Digital Citizenship: A Pilot Study." 2018: 1–34.

Chesters, Jenny. "Does migrant status affect educational achievement, aspirations, and attainment?." *Multicultural Education Review*. 7, 4, 2015: 197–212. https://doi.org/10.1080/2005615X.2015.1112561.

Cieslik, Mark and Donals Simpson. *Key concepts in youth studies*. London and Los Angeles: Sage, 2013.

Clayton, John. "Living the multicultural city: acceptance, belonging and young identities in the city of Leicester, England." *Ethnic and Racial Studies*. 35, 9, 2012: 1673–1693.

Collins, Jock, Carol Reid, and Charlotte Fabiansson. "Identities, aspirations and belonging of cosmopolitan youth in Australia." *Cosmopolitan civil societies: an interdisciplinary journal*. 3, 3, 2011: 92–107.

Collins, Patricia H. *Black feminist thought: Knowledge, consciousness and the politics of empowerment*. Boston: Unwin Hyman, 1990.

Fozdar, Farida and Susan Banki. "Settling refugees in Australia: achievements and challenges." *International Journal of Migration and Border Studies*. 3, 1, 2017: 43–66. https://doi.org/10.1504/IJMBS.2017.081197.

Greene, Stacey, Yaledi Matos, and Kira Sanbonmatsu. "Women Voters and the Utility of Campaigning as 'Women of Color'." *Journal of Women, Politics & Policy*. 43, 1, 2022: 25–41. https://doi.org/10.1080/1554477X.2022.2007467.

Harris, Anita. "Belonging and the uses of difference: young people in Australian urban multiculture." *Social Identities*. 22, 4, 2016: 359–375.

Harris, Anita and Melinda Herron. "Young People and Intercultural Sociality after Cronulla." *Journal of Intercultural Studies*. 38, 3, 2017: 284–300.

Harris, Anita and Sherene Idriss. "Lifeworlds and Cultures of Australian Youth in a Globalised World." In *Youth Cultures in a Globalized World*, edited by G. Knapp and H. Krall: 77–95. Springer, Cham., 2021. https://doi.org/10.1007/978-3-030-65177-0_6.

Ho, Chris. *Aspiration and Anxiety: Asian Migrants and Australian Schooling.* Melbourne: Melbourne University Press, 2020.

Jakubowicz, Andrew, Jock Collins, Carol Reid, and Wafa Chafic. "Minority Youth and Social Transformation in Australia: Identities, Belonging and Cultural Capital." *Social Inclusion.* 2, 2, 2014: 5–16.

Johns, Amelia. "Muslim Young People Online: 'Acts of Citizenship' in Socially Networked Spaces." *Social Inclusion.* 2, 2, 2014: 71–82.

Kelly, Peter and Annelies Kamp. *A critical youth studies for the 21st century.* Leiden and Boston: Brill, 2014.

Mansouri, Fethi and Liudmila Kirpitchenko. "Practices of active citizenship among migrant youth: beyond conventionalities." *Social Identities.* 22, 3, 2016: 307–323.

Media Diversity Australia official website: https://www.mediadiversityaustralia.org.

Mikola, Masa and Fethi Mansouri. "Race lines and spaces of political action among migrant youth." *Journal of Youth Studies.* 18 4, 2015: 500–514.

Noble, Greg. "'It is home but it is not home': habitus, field and the migrant." *Journal of Sociology.* 49, 2–3, 2013: 341–356. https://doi.org/10.1177/1440783313481532.

Pardy, Maree and Julian C. H. Lee. "Using buzzwords of belonging: everyday multiculturalism and social capital in Australia." *Journal of Australian Studies.* 35, 3, 2011: 297–316.

Pathways to Politics for Women official website: https://pathwaystopolitics.org.au.

Patton, Chloe. "Multicultural Citizenship and Religiosity: Young Australian Muslims Forging a Sense of Belonging after 9/11." *Journal of Intercultural Studies.* 35, 1, 2014: 107–122.

Pietsch, Juliet. "Australian ethnic change and political inclusion: finding strength in diversity in responding to global crises." In *Re-imagining Australia: Migration, culture, diversity: Practical suggestions on the challenges and opportunities ahead*, edited by Shamit Saggar and Anna Zenz: 57–64. Perth: UWA Public Policy Institute, 2020.

Robertson, Shanthi. "Suspending, settling, sponsoring: the intimate chronomobilities of young Asian migrants in Australia." *Global Networks.* 20, 4, 2020: 677–696.

Simonsen, K. B. "How the host nation's boundary drawing affects immigrants' belonging." *Journal of Ethnic and Migration Studies.* 42, 7, 2016: 1153–1176.

Sawrikar, Pooja and Ilan Katz. "How useful is the term 'Culturally and linguistically diverse (CALD)' in Australian research and policy discourse?." Social Policy Research Centre, UNSW, 2009.

Tsalapatanis, Anna. "Naming belonging: When national vocabularies fail." In *Social Beings, Future Belongings: Reimagining the Social*, edited by Anna Tsalapatanis, Miranda Bruce, David Bissell, and Helen Keane: 13–25. London and New York: Routledge, 2019.

Williamson, Rebecca. "Everyday space, mobile subjects and place-based belonging in suburban Sydney." *Journal of Ethnic and Migration Studies.* 42, 14, 2016: 2328–2344.

Zevallos, Zuleyka. "'You Have to be Anglo and Not Look Like Me': identity and belonging among young women of Turkish and Latin American backgrounds in Melbourne, Australia." *Australian Geographer.* 39, 1, 2008: 21–43.

Zhou, Min and Carl L. Bankston. *The Rise of the New Second Generation.* Cambridge: Polity, 2016.

CHAPTER 13

The Vulnerability of Dual Citizenship: From Supranational Subject to Citizen to Subject?

Kim Rubenstein

Introduction

This chapter provides an overview of the trajectory of the place of citizenship in Australian law today. It argues that the journey has involved travelling from an acceptance and foundation of a form of cosmopolitan or supranational citizenship to one of vulnerability for dual citizens. The 2015 amendments to the *Australian Citizenship Act* 2007 extended the context for stripping dual citizen Australians of their citizenship, and not sole citizens, due to Australia's "commitment" to the Convention on the

I am extremely thankful to the editor of this collection, Jatinder Mann, for his detailed feedback and helpful suggestions on my chapter.

K. Rubenstein (✉)
Faculty of Business, Government and Law, University of Canberra, Bruce, ACT, Australia
e-mail: kim.rubenstein@canberra.edu.au

J. Mann (ed.), *Citizenship in Transnational Perspective*, Politics of Citizenship and Migration,
https://doi.org/10.1007/978-3-031-34358-2_13

Reduction of Statelessness.[1] However, in doing so, it changed the relationship between the individual and the state, reverting Australian citizens back to their "subject" like status in principle, even if not in title.

Beginnings as a Supranational Status[2]

The place of citizenship law in Australia today is grounded in an interesting journey charting Australia's development as a nation. At Federation, the status of people in Australia centred around their being British subjects or subjects of the Queen. Those who were not British subjects were aliens. Even so, Australian citizenship was discussed during the drafting of the Constitution. John Quick, a member of the Convention who, with Robert Garran, later published the first commentary on the Constitution,[3] had sought the insertion in the Constitution of a power over Commonwealth citizenship. When this was not successful, he suggested that a new clause be inserted to confer citizenship on all people resident within the Commonwealth, being natural-born or naturalised subjects of the Queen, and not under any disability by the Parliament. Quick wanted to create a national citizenship above State citizenship, and he was also concerned with the treatment of residents of one State in relation to another State and the wording of s 17 of the Constitution.[4] The proposed conferral of citizenship was similarly rejected. The omission of citizenship was based on many contentious grounds, including race.[5]

Thus, citizenship in Australia is not a constitutional concept. Furthermore, in failing to create or discuss Australian citizenship, the Commonwealth's power to legislate and define citizenship is uncertain. It is generally accepted that the Commonwealth has the power to naturalise aliens under s 51(xix). The High Court has held that:

> Within the limits of the concept of "alien" in s 51(xix), it is for Parliament to decide who will be treated as having the status of alienage, who will be treated as citizens, and what the status of alienage, or non-citizenship, will entail.[6]

However, the limits of the concept, within which this power must be exercised, are not clear. The High Court has considered the definition of aliens in s 51(xix) in several cases concerning non-citizens who were about to be deported under the *Migration Act* 1958. However, these cases have been brought in a number of different contexts, and the Court's interpretation of the concept has been inconsistent.[7]

From 1901 through until 26 January 1949, the major distinction of membership in Australian law was between British subjects and aliens. At common law, a person's formal legal status was determined by their allegiance to the monarch, whether by birth or through naturalisation.[8] Even so, David Dutton has explained that:

> [a] *de facto* administrative Australian citizenship operated during the period which arose from the necessity of distinguishing between those British subjects who were permanent residents and belonged to the Commonwealth (in the sense that they could not be deported), and those British subjects who were merely visitors or who were yet to reside in Australia long enough to be regarded as belonging.[9]

Thus, there were three forms of membership—those who were British subjects permanently residing in Australia, those who were British subjects and temporarily in Australia, and those who were not British subjects and were aliens. This broader distinction between aliens and British subjects, which framed Australian citizenship in the first 48 years of the nation's existence, has continued to this day with the current distinction between citizen and non-citizen. The preference for British subjects has disappeared relatively recently (see Mann's first substantial chapter in this collection).[10] The confusion about membership in Australia has been further complicated by British subject status—a factor that continued until the 1980s.

Despite the constitutional lack of certainty over the power regarding citizenship and the extent to which the Commonwealth could legislate given there was no direct head of power, in 1948 Australian citizenship as a legislative status "initially crept into our lives quietly, almost unnoticed,"[11] with the introduction of the *British Nationality and Australian Citizenship Act* 1948 in 1949. As the then Minister for Immigration Arthur Calwell put it, the time had come for Australia to recognise its maturity legally and officially as a member of the British Commonwealth.[12] For the next twenty years, Australians remained British subjects but were also citizens of Australia. In Calwell's words:

> The [Act was] not designed to make an Australian any less a British subject, but to help him express his pride in citizenship of this great country. To say

> that one is an Australian is, of course, to indicate beyond all doubt that one is British; but to claim to be of the British race does not make it clear that one is an Australian.[13]

The Act was renamed the *Australian Citizenship Act* 1948 in 1973, but everyone also remained a British subject. Finally, in 1984, the definition of the status of British subject was repealed to accord with the government's aim that the Act reflects the national identity of all Australians.[14]

It was this straddling of two forms of membership—British subject and Australian citizen that give rise to my argument that the foundations of citizenship law in Australia recognised a form of cosmopolitan or supranational citizenship. From Federation until 1949, Australians' legal status was linked to membership of the British Commonwealth—a supranational and cosmopolitan membership that went beyond the boundaries of a single state. And from 1949 until 1987 Australia felt comfortable as a nation maintaining this dual status alongside its own citizenship. Indeed, it is only since 1987 when the 1984 *Amendment Act* came into force that Australians have been solely citizens of Australia and no longer dual British subjects and Australian citizens.[15]

However, that did not preclude some Australians from holding citizenship of another nation state at the same time as being Australian citizens. It is to the evolution of policy about holding two or more nation states' citizenship that I shall now turn.

Dual Citizenship in Australian Law[16]

Dual citizenship involves two aspects. First, there are questions of dual citizenship for those persons seeking Australian citizenship by grant. What are the consequences for those persons for their existing citizenship? This is not necessarily a question of Australian law but rather a question of law for the country of origin. There is nothing in the provisions of the Act for the grant of Australian citizenship requiring a person to renounce their former citizenship. Second, there is the issue of dual citizenship for existing Australian citizens who took up citizenship of another country in addition to their Australian citizenship. Up until 4 April 2002, Australian citizens lost their Australian citizenship when taking up a new citizenship.

In the first case, where citizens of another country become Australian citizens, the approach in practice, not law, has varied. The pledge taken upon becoming an Australian citizen has changed over the years. Between

1966 and 1986 the words included "renouncing all other allegiance."[17] However, this wording had no legal consequence for their status as citizens of the other country. The High Court of Australia confirmed this in *Sykes v Cleary (No 2)*[18] where two of the persons who ran for Parliament, and whose positions were challenged, were citizens of other countries.[19] It was alleged that they were ineligible for election due to s 44(i) of the *Constitution* disqualifying people who owe an allegiance to another country. [20] While both persons had taken an oath of allegiance to Australia with words indicating they were renouncing their former citizenship,[21] it was not sufficient in law to shed them of their former citizenship. The court held that the foreign citizen must comply with the laws of the foreign country regarding renunciation of citizenship in order to be divested of that citizenship. Many countries allow their citizens to take up a new citizenship without losing their original or existing citizenship.[22] This is an example of where principles of international law and the sovereignty of nation states are affirmed—that is Australia must respect the law of another country regarding its own determination of who is a citizen of that country.

In the second case, since the inception of the *Australian Citizenship Act* 1948 until 4 April 2002, there had been a provision mandating loss of Australian citizenship for a person who acquired a new citizenship.[23] Although the provision has been repealed, it has enduring relevance, due not only to the implications of dual citizenship for Parliamentary membership under s 44(i) of the *Constitution* but because some individuals who lost their Australian citizenship under this provision prior to 4 April 2002 may not yet be aware that this has occurred.

The journey to the repeal of s 17 mandating loss of Australian citizenship when becoming a citizen of another country reflects upon the changing nature of citizenship in a globalised world, and an earlier comfort with the reality and concept of multiple or cosmopolitan citizenship.

S 17 operated in law so that as soon as people satisfied that section, they were no longer Australian citizens. S 17 was repealed by the *Australian Citizenship Legislation Amendment Act* 2002, which commenced on 4 April 2002. When the amendment legislation was debated in the Senate on 14 March 2002, Senator Nick Bolkus tabled a memorandum of advice, dated 27 June 1995, prepared by the late A. R. Castan QC,[24] regarding the constitutional validity of s 17. In that advice it was argued that s 17 fell beyond the limit of constitutional power because it sought to exclude from "the people of the Commonwealth," in its constitutional sense, persons who in truth have not ceased to be such people but who nevertheless wish to take out dual citizenship. Some of Castan QC's reasoning relied upon the constitutional concept of "equality" under the law. While this concept has not been well-developed by the High Court since the date of that advice, the decision of the High Court in *Patterson* lends support to some of the concepts raised by Castan QC in his memorandum. Castan's memorandum may also be relevant to the recent Amendments to the Act regarding deprivation of citizenship to which I will return.

S 17 and the deterrence of dual citizenship was one of the most contested and contentious areas of the *Australian Citizenship Act* 1948. Dual citizenship was the subject of a 1976 review by the Joint Committee on Foreign Affairs and Defence[25] and it was also considered in the context of the national consultations on multiculturalism and citizenship conducted in 1982.[26] Then two further reviews in the 1990s considered the worthiness of s 17,[27] and a related Parliamentary review of s 44(i) disqualifying dual citizens from becoming members of Parliament also considered related policy matters.[28]

At one level there was a basic inequality in the former system. Persons who are born with another citizenship and who also have, or later acquire, Australian citizenship were entitled to dual citizenship.[29] However, once a person was an Australian citizen, he or she could not take up a new citizenship. Thus, some people were able to be dual citizens and others were not entitled to this privilege; it depended upon the order of obtaining the citizenship.

Questions of Allegiance

More pertinent, perhaps, was the question of how appropriate it was to divest an Australian of citizenship if he or she became a citizen of another country. The arguments against repealing the section and maintaining the status quo revolved around issues of allegiance and loyalty. It was argued that one was necessarily disloyal to Australia in taking up another citizenship. However, both the Joint Standing Committee on Migration and the Australian Citizenship Council were swayed by arguments to the contrary, that s 17 should be repealed. The Joint Standing Committee on Migration stated:

> The overwhelming view in submissions was that Australia's insistence on single citizenship for those born in Australia is outmoded and discriminatory. In a world of increasing mobility, it was considered anachronistic that one section of the Australian population should be disadvantaged by a prohibition on accessing more than one citizenship.[30]

Considering matters such as globalisation, the Australian Citizenship Council stated:

> As we move into the twenty-first century, the prevalence of dual citizenship internationally will rapidly increase. The law and practice of most countries with which Australia likes to compare itself permits citizens of those countries to obtain another citizenship without losing their original citizenship … These countries simply recognize that they have an internationally mobile population and that they can retain connection with this population even if another citizenship is acquired.[31]

The issue of allegiance and commitment is at the heart of the dispute. The pledge of commitment is now set out in Sch 1 of the 2007 Act:

> From this time forward (under God)
> I pledge my loyalty to Australia and its people,
> whose democratic beliefs I share,
> whose rights and liberties I respect, and
> whose laws I will uphold and obey.

The use of the term "loyalty" is interesting. The Preamble uses the term "loyalty to Australia" and this is used within the content of the Preamble. Yet the title of the pledge in Schedule 1 to the Act is "Pledge of Commitment as a Citizen of the Commonwealth of Australia." Is there a difference between the terms "loyalty" and "commitment"? "Loyalty" is defined in the *Shorter Oxford English Dictionary* as, inter alia:

> Faithful adherence to one's promise, oath, word etc; conjugal fidelity
> Faithful adherence to the sovereign or lawful government. Also *now* enthusiastic devotion to the sovereign's person and family
> Legality (of marriage).

The notion of being faithful to one's country has connotations, particularly with its link to fidelity, of being loyal to one country only. In contrast, "commitment" is defined in the *Shorter Oxford English Dictionary* as:

> The action of entrusting, giving in charge, or commending.

To invest with trust is to create a relationship of responsibility. Committing oneself to Australia is putting oneself in a special relationship of acting in the best interests of the country. It has less of a sense of sole allegiance—one can be responsible to, or committed to, more than one country.

The analogy that I like to use is that of marriage and parenthood.[32] If you see citizenship like marriage, then there is a clear and understandable rejection of multiple partners. But if you view citizenship as being more akin to parenthood, then we all accept and affirm that you can have more than one child without that undermining your commitment and connection to all your children. It is only when there is a direct conflict between those connections that a singular notion of connection or an overriding connection needs to be identified.

Australian law accepted the concept of multiple connections with the repeal of the former s 17 of the 1948 Act. The government issued another discussion paper on dual citizenship in June 2001[33] and called for further public comment. The discussion paper provided a comprehensive overview of the topic of dual citizenship and included topics such as "How Current Citizenship Law Works," "What Other Countries Do," "Proposed Repeal of Section 17," "Arguments for the Change," and "Arguments Against the Change." Having received further submissions from the public,[34] the government then announced its decision to repeal s 17.[35] With the repeal of s 17, adult Australian citizens acquiring the nationality or citizenship of another country have not lost their Australian citizenship from 4 April 2002.

This change in 2002 saw Australia as a nation return to a comfort with cosmopolitan citizenship—and in my view fully affirmed Australia as a multicultural society. That had existed in law earlier given those individuals who migrated to Australia and later became citizens, as a matter of international law could retain their former citizenship, if that country allowed them to. By moving to allowing dual citizenship for all Australians, no matter which order the other citizenship was derived or bestowed, Australia moved towards a more unifying and inclusive notion of citizenship, affirming of a multicultural nation.

Finally, on this point, it is well to remember also that one does not have to hold a formal citizenship of another country to have a sense of connection to it. So, for instance, those individuals whose countries did not allow them to keep their former citizenship when they took up Australian citizenship did not necessarily wipe their slate clean on their emotional, psychological, or practical link to that sense of connection. Or closer to home, those Australians who did take up a new citizenship before 2002 and lost their Australian citizenship may still have felt similarly connected to Australia. Questions of allegiance and identity are not solely legally bound. We only need to think about the numbers of Australian citizens who have a connection to another nation state, either through family, or religion, or a personal experience, to appreciate that questions of law do not always fit well with questions of practice. This is an appropriate segue into the more recent changes to the *Australian Citizenship Act* 2007.

Changes in the International Environment and International Law

Questions about dual citizenship are relevant to the changes to the *Australian Citizenship Act* 2007 that were prominent in public policy discussions in 2015 and led to the passing of the *Australian Citizenship Amendment (Allegiance to Australia) Act* 2015 which received Royal Assent on Friday, 11 December 2016 and came into operation the following day.

Until that time, the simplified outline of the 2007 Act explained that there were five ways in which a person could cease to be an Australian citizen. From the perspective of the citizen, he or she could renounce their Australian citizenship, although this is still in the Minister's discretion and the Minister is precluded from accepting the application if it means a person will be stateless. For those who became citizens by "application" as opposed to automatically (in certain circumstances including birth in Australia) their citizenship can be revoked due to the commission of certain offences and/or fraud and failure to comply with special residence requirements. In addition, s 35 set out a particular provision, never used or relied upon, that a person, who is a national or citizen of another country (i.e. a dual citizen), who serves in the armed forces of another country at war with Australia, "ceases to be an Australian citizen at the time the person commences to so serve." This provision has been at the centre of other new ways in which a dual citizen Australian can now lose their Australian citizenship.

The three new ways of losing Australian citizenship as a matter of policy were explained by the government as revolving around the change in the international environment regarding terrorism. In the supplementary material tabled before Parliament, the government explained:

> On 23 February 2015, the Prime Minister delivered his National Security Statement outlining the Government's response to the Review of Australia's Counter-Terrorism Machinery for a Safer Australia ('the Review'). The Review found that the terrorist threat in Australia is rising, specifically:
>
> - the number of foreign fighters is increasing;
> - the number of known sympathisers and supporters of extremists is increasing; and
> - the number of potential terrorists is rising.
>
> The Government is taking a multi-faceted approach to countering these threats to national security. This includes implementing the Review's recommendations to strengthen the coordination of agencies, introduce initiatives to counter violent extremism and manage the return of foreign fighters, and implement measures to improve the community understanding of the threat level.
>
> As part of the response, the Government is also amending the Australian Citizenship Act 2007 (the Citizenship Act) to broaden the powers relating to the cessation of Australian citizenship for those persons engaging in terrorism and who are a serious threat to Australia and Australia's interests.
>
> As the basic requisite for participation in and adherence to the values and institutions of Australia's secular democracy, citizenship does not simply bestow privileges or rights, but entails fundamental responsibilities. As set out in the preamble to the Citizenship Act, Australian citizenship gives full and formal membership of the Australian community and is a common bond, involving reciprocal rights and obligations, uniting all Australians while respecting their diversity. *Those who are citizens owe their loyalty to Australia and its people.* This applies to those who acquire citizenship automatically through birth in Australia and to those who acquire it through application. *Where a person is no longer loyal to Australia and its people, and engages in acts that harm Australians or Australian interests, or engages in acts that are intending to harm Australians or Australia's interest, they have severed that bond and repudiated their allegiance to Australia.*

Those highlighted areas centre on questions of loyalty, but that breach of loyalty can only lead to loss of citizenship if the person is a dual citizen. If you are a single citizen who seeks to sever that bond, the government chose not to offend the International Convention on the Reduction of Statelessness.

What the Act now does is expand the earlier framework for revoking citizenship. The previous s 35 has been expanded to include people aged fourteen or older who are dual citizens and in addition to serving in the armed forces of a country at war with Australia, now includes "fights for, or is in the service of, a declared terrorist organization," as defined under s 35AA, and that fighting occurs outside Australia. In addition, there is a new provision 33AA of *Renunciation of Conduct* for people fourteen years or older and a new provision s 35A for *Conviction for terrorism offences and certain other offences.* These provisions mark a dramatic step in the life of citizenship as a legal status in Australia.

Conclusion: Having More now Means Having Less

In 1901 Australians were solely British subjects. When Australia was encouraged by Canada to follow it in holding a separate Australian status, as well as maintaining the status of British subject, there was strong resistance in Parliament.[36] But the introduction of the new status of Australian citizen that came into effect on Australia Day in 1949 was an important step in recognising Australians could remain part of the Commonwealth by retaining the British subject status, as well as becoming independent Australian citizens. As I have argued, it also displayed a comfort in maintaining a dual sense of connection to Britain and Australia.

But the addition of the term citizen was important because being a citizen is different to being a subject. To be a subject is to be subjected to the power of the Crown. To be a citizen reflects a more even footing. Citizens elect their Parliaments and Parliaments are bound by the rule of law. There is an equality of membership, an equality of power. The citizen is not subject to the whim of the state but rather equal to the state and can challenge the state's exercise of power in the Courts.

So, when the state is able to take away that person's citizenship and their claim to equality within the state, it represents a dramatic change in the balance of power. With these new provisions, dual citizens become subject to the heavy hand of the state in determining whether they remain citizens. If the government can legislate, in this instance for the stripping of citizenship for terrorist activity, what is to stop dual citizens being vulnerable to losing their Australian citizenship for other reasons? Society abhors paedophilia—why not then determine dual citizens found guilty of paedophilia should be stripped of their Australian citizenship and deported to another country or not allowed to return on leaving Australia?

Dual citizenship has been part of the Australian landscape since 1949 beyond the concept of being both a British subject and an Australian citizen. For those who took up Australian citizenship after 1949, if their country of first citizenship allowed them to keep that former citizenship they were dual citizens. Since 2002 in addition to foreign-born citizens being able to have dual citizenship, Australia has recognised that Australian citizens can take up another citizenship without losing their own. Lawmakers recognised that dual citizenship has been increasingly accepted in a world of international mobility and that it is possible to maintain strong and meaningful connections with Australia even when they acquire another citizenship. By allowing dual citizenship Australia moved towards a more unifying and inclusive notion of citizenship, affirming of a multicultural nation.

While the problem of Australian citizens being involved in violent conflicts on foreign soil certainly must be addressed, it is a regressive step to deprive dual citizens of their citizenship. Once a person is an Australian citizen, the consequences of committing a criminal offence should be a matter for the criminal law. Australia has a suite of laws that criminalise acts committed on foreign soil, including the existing offence of treachery. Criminalising these acts and prosecuting citizens is the best way to act as a good international citizen. How responsible is Australia to the world fight against terrorism if the punishment is to exclude dual citizens from Australian territory?

The Preamble to the *Australian Citizenship Act* 2007 states that Australian citizenship unites "all Australians, while respecting their diversity." To politicise citizenship, and to use it as a tool of exclusion and as the basis of a threat, undermines its purpose and ignores the contribution that dual citizens make to Australia. Ironically, those who now have more than one citizenship have less protection of their Australian citizenship—this becomes a case of having more, meaning having less.[37]

Notes

1. (1961) 989 UNTS 175.
2. See also Kim Rubenstein, "From Supranational to Dual to Alien Citizen: Australia's Ambivalent Journey," in *Citizenship in a Post-National World Australia and Europe Compared*, eds. Simon Bronitt and Kim Rubenstein (Sydney: Federation Press, 2008), 1.
3. John Quick and Robert Garran, *Annotated Constitution of the Australian Commonwealth* (Sydney: Angus and Robertson, 1901).
4. See *Official Record of the Debates of the Australasian Federal Convention* (Sydney: 1891), Vol. I, 93, 546–547; *Ibid* (Sydney: 1897), Vol. II, 101; *Ibid* (Melbourne: 1898), Vol. IV, 664–691; *Ibid.* (Melbourne: 1898), Vol. V, 1750–1768, 1780–1782, 2397–2398; Cheryl Saunders, "Citizenship under the Commonwealth Constitution," *Constitutional Centenary Foundation Newsletter* 3, 3 (1994): 6.
5. See Kim Rubenstein, "Citizenship and the Constitutional Convention Debates: A Mere Legal Inference?," *Federal Law Review* 25 (1997): 295, and some further work I did on the place of race in the 1890s, parts of which also appear in Kim Rubenstein, "Citizenship and the Centenary: Inclusion and Exclusion in 20th Century Australia," *Melbourne University Law Review* 24 (2000): 576.
6. *Koroitamana v The Commonwealth (Koroitamana)* [2006] 227 CLR 31 at 38, citing *Singh v Commonwealth* (2004) 222 CLR 322, 329.
7. I discuss this in greater detail in Chap. 4 of my book Kim Rubenstein, *Australian Citizenship law*, 2nd edition (Sydney: Thomson Reuters, 2017). Since the second edition of this collection, further citizenship law cases have been heard before the High Court of Australia—including *Love v Commonwealth of Australia; Thoms v Commonwealth of Australia* [2020] HCA 3 regarding Indigenous membership of Australia https://www.hcourt.gov.au/cases/case_b43-2018 (see Pillai and Hobbs' chapter in this collection) and *Alexander v Minister for Home Affairs* [2022] HCA 19 https://www.austlii.edu.au/cgi-bin/viewdoc/au/cases/cth/HCA/2022/19.html regarding s 36B of the *Australian Citizenship Act* 2007.
8. See Michael Pryles, *Australian Citizenship Law* (Sydney: Lawbook Company, 1981), 14–16. In particular, Australia was influenced by the common code of the *British Nationality and Status of Aliens Act* 1914 (UK) 4 & 5 Geo 5, c 17, which was intended to form the basis of a common, uniform law of nationality throughout the Empire. This period is discussed in greater detail in Chap. 3.
9. David Dutton, *Citizenship in Australia: A Guide to Commonwealth Government Records* (Canberra: National Archives Australia, 1999), 13.

See also David Dutton, *Strangers and Citizens: The Boundaries of Australian Citizenship* (Ph.D. Thesis, University of Melbourne, 1998) and David Dutton, *One of Us? A Century of Australian Citizenship* (Sydney: UNSW Press, 2002).

10. See also Jatinder Mann, *Redefining Citizenship in Australia, Canada, and Aotearoa New Zealand* (New York: Peter Lang Publishing, 2019).
11. Sir Ninian Stephen, "Australian Citizenship: Past, Present and Future," *Monash University Law Review* 26 (2000): 333.
12. Commonwealth, *Parliamentary Debates,* House of Representatives, 30 September 1948, 1060 (Arthur Calwell).
13. *Ibid.*
14. *Australian Citizenship Amendment Act* 1984. For detail regarding the evolution of Australian citizenship law, see Michael Klapdor, Moira Coombs, and Catherine Bohm, "Australian citizenship: a chronology of major developments in policy and law" (Background Note, 11 September 2009, Parliamentary Library, Commonwealth, 2009). See also Kim Rubenstein (ed), *Individual, Community, Nation: 50 Years of Australian Citizenship* (Melbourne: Australian Scholarly Press, 2000) and Kim Rubenstein, *Australian Citizenship Law in Context*, 2nd edition (Sydney: LawBook Co, 2016).
15. The term was removed by the Australian Citizenship Amendment Act 1984 which commenced on 1 May 1987.
16. The term "dual citizenship" also could be "multiple citizenship" as there may be instances where a person holds more than two citizenships.
17. Introduced by Act No 11 of 1966, s 11 (commenced 6 May 1966) and repealed by Act No 70 of 1986, s 11 (commenced 28 August 1986).
18. *Sykes v Cleary (No 2)* (1992) 176 CLR 77.
19. As a matter of international law, it is for the country of citizenship to determine when a citizen loses his or her citizenship. In this case, neither Greece nor Switzerland mandated the loss of citizenship upon the adoption of a new citizenship.
20. S 44(i) states: "Any person who is under any acknowledgment of allegiance, obedience, or adherence to a foreign power, or is a subject or a citizen or entitled to the rights or privileges of a subject or a citizen of a foreign power; shall be incapable of being chosen or of sitting as a senator or a member of the House of Representatives."
21. The second respondent, Mr. Delacretaz, was born in Switzerland and in 1960 was naturalised as an Australian citizen pursuant to the *British* Nationality and Australian Citizenship Act 1948. The oath or affirmation of allegiance required by the 1948 Act, as it stood in 1960, did not involve the renunciation of prior allegiance. Despite this, Mr. Delacretaz, in fact, formally renounced all other allegiance as a preliminary to taking the oath.

It appears from the Second Reading speech for the Nationality and Citizenship Act 1967 (which introduced the form of oath and affirmation involving renunciation of all other allegiance) that, for some time past, there had been a "practice of requiring applicants ... to renounce allegiance to their former countries" in "a prominent and separate part of the naturalisation ceremony." It was clear from Mr Delacretaz' naturalisation certificate that that is what happened in his case: see Sykes v Cleary (No 2) (1992) 176 CLR 77 (Gaudron J) at 138–139. The third respondent, Mr Kardamitsis, was born in Greece and became an Australian citizen in 1975 pursuant to the Australian Citizenship Act 1948 and, in so doing, renounced all other allegiance and swore the oath of allegiance in a form similar to, but not identical with, that sworn by the second respondent. The form of oath and affirmation required by the Citizenship Act, as it stood in 1975, was introduced in 1966 when s 11 of the Nationality and Citizenship Act 1966 amended the Sch 2 to the 1948 Act "by inserting after the letters 'AB' ... the words 'renouncing all allegiance.'" At the same time, s 12 of the 1966 Act introduced Sch 3, which contained the form of oath and affirmation required in the case of women wishing to be registered as British subjects without citizenship. This also involved the renunciation of all other allegiance: see Sykes v Cleary (No 2) (1992) 176 CLR 77 at 133 per Gaudron J.

22. See Parliament of the Commonwealth of Australia, Joint Standing Committee on Migration, *Australians All: Enhancing Australian Citizenship* (1994). Table 6.1 lists countries that allowed dual citizenship at the time of taking evidence. See also 181–188, paras [6.16]-[6.36], which explain overseas practice at the time of the report. See also Kim Rubenstein "From Supranational to Dual to Alien Citizen: Australia's Ambivalent Journey," in *Citizenship in a Post-National World Australia and Europe Compared*, eds. Simon Bronitt and Kim Rubenstein (Sydney: Federation Press, 2008).
23. In fact, the prevention of dual nationality began before the legal concept of Australian citizenship existed. S 21 of the *Nationality Act* 1920 provided that a person would lose their British nationality when, through a "voluntary and formal" Act, they became naturalised in a foreign state.
24. See Australia, Senate, *Parliamentary Debates* (14 March 2002), 552–557.
25. Joint Committee on Foreign Affairs and Defence, *Dual Nationality*, Report (1976), 8. The Committee supported the policy that every person should have one nationality only but recognised that the holding of dual nationality by some Australian nationals was inevitable given the differences in domestic nationality laws.

26. Department of Immigration and Ethnic Affairs, *National Consultation on Multiculturalism and Citizenship*, Report (1982). See in particular the discussion on dual citizenship, 28.
27. See Parliament of the Commonwealth of Australia, Joint Standing Committee on Migration, *Australians All*, Chap. 6, where it is stated that the issue of dual citizenship attracted most attention throughout the inquiry. See also Australian Citizenship Council, above n 97, 60–66, where it is stated that nearly three-quarters of the submissions to the Council addressed the issue of loss of Australian citizenship upon the acquisition of another. The Council sets out in detail many personal comments received regarding the consequences of s 17, 62–63.
28. Parliament of Australia, Standing Committee on Legal and Constitutional Affairs, *Aspects of Section 44 of the Australian Constitution* (July 1997).
29. This is because, according to international law, it is up to each state to determine under its own law who are its nationals.
30. Parliament of the Commonwealth of Australia, Joint Standing Committee on Migration, *Australians All*, paragraph [6.90], 206.
31. Australian Citizenship Council, above n 97, 65.
32. Kim Rubenstein, "Why We Are Not All Born Equal," *The Age*, 1 July 1999; Kim Rubenstein, "Let's Face It. Today We're Citizens of the World," *The Australian*, 22 May 2001; Kim Rubenstein, "Loyalty and Membership: Globalization And its Impact on Citizenship, Multiculturalism, and the Australian Community," in *Political Theory and Australian Multiculturalism*, ed. Geoffrey Braham Levey (New York: Berghahn Books, 2008), 171.
33. Department of Immigration and Multicultural Affairs, *Loss of Australian Citizenship on the Acquisition of Another Citizenship*, Discussion Paper on Section 17 of the *Australian Citizenship Act* 1948 (June 2001).
34. The Discussion Paper led to a detailed response from the Southern Cross Group. The Group submitted to the Department a comprehensive document entitled "Section 17 of the Australian Citizenship Act 1948; Grounds for Appeal and Associated Issues" (6 July 2001). This is available on their website http://www.southern-cross-group.org. See also Chap. 7 at [7.5.1].
35. The *Australian Citizenship Legislation Amendment Act* 2002 repealed s 17 through Schedule 1, item 1.
36. See Jatinder Mann, "The evolution of Commonwealth citizenship, 1945–48 in Canada, Britain and Australia," *Commonwealth and Comparative Politics* 50, 3 (2012): 293–313.
37. *Postscript:* Since the first edition of this book, amendments were made in 2020 to the stripping of citizenship provisions following the 2019 Independent National Security Legislation Monitor (INSLM) review of

the 2016 amendments. See https://www.timebase.com.au/news/2020/AT05118-article.html for a summary of this. The case of *Alexander v Minister for Home Affairs* [2022] HCA 19 https://www.austlii.edu.au/cgi-bin/viewdoc/au/cases/cth/HCA/2022/19.html regarding s 36B of the *Australian Citizenship Act* 2007 involved *one* of the citizenship stripping provisions which the High Court of Australia determined was unconstitutional. As Rayner Thwaites identified, the decision leaves open the fate of other deprivation mechanisms under the *Australian Citizenship Act*. Confining attention to mechanisms directed at "disallegiant" conduct, s 36D provides for a ministerial power of deprivation conditioned on prior conviction and sentence by a court with respect to a nominated set of terrorism offences. The application of Alexander's case to this provision will turn on whether, in authorising citizenship deprivation, s 36D "authorises the imposition of a new or additional punishment for a person committing an offence," for instance. See further https://globalcit.eu/citizenship-deprivation-as-banishment-the-high-court-of-australia-in-alexanders-case/. This further case affirms the final sentence of this chapter—"those who now have more than one citizenship have less protection of their Australian citizenship—this becomes a case of having more, meaning having less."

References

Bronitt, Simon and Kim Rubenstein, eds. *Citizenship in a Post-National World Australia and Europe Compared*. Sydney, Federation Press, 2008.

Dutton, David. *Strangers and Citizens: The Boundaries of Australian Citizenship*. Ph.D. Thesis, University of Melbourne, 1998.

Dutton, David. *One of Us? A Century of Australian Citizenship*. Sydney, UNSW Press, 2002.

Levey, Geoffrey Braham, ed. *Political Theory and Australian Multiculturalism*. New York: Berghahn Books, 2008.

Mann, Jatinder. "The evolution of Commonwealth citizenship, 1945–48 in Canada, Britain and Australia." *Commonwealth and Comparative Politics*. 50, 3, 2012: 293–313. https://doi.org/10.1080/14662043.2012.692923.

Mann, Jatinder. *Redefining Citizenship in Australia, Canada, and Aotearoa New Zealand*. New York: Peter Lang Publishing, 2019.

Pryles, Michael. *Australian Citizenship Law*. Sydney: Lawbook Company, 1981.

Quick, John and Robert Garran. *Annotated Constitution of the Australia Commonwealth*. Sydney, Angus and Robertson, 1901.

Rubenstein, Kim. "Citizenship and the Constitutional Convention Debates: A Mere Legal Inference?." *Federal Law Review*. 25, 1997: 295–316.

Rubenstein, Kim, ed. *Individual, Community, Nation: 50 Years of Australian Citizenship*. Melbourne, Australian Scholarly Press, 2000a.

Rubenstein, Kim. "Citizenship and the Centenary: Inclusion and Exclusion in 20th Century Australia," *Melbourne University Law Review*. 24, 2000b: 576–608.

Rubenstein, Kim. "From Supranational to Dual to Alien Citizen: Australia's Ambivalent Journey." In *Citizenship in a Post-National World Australia and Europe Compared*, edited by Simon Bronitt and Kim Rubenstein: 1–15. Sydney, Federation Press, 2008a.

Rubenstein, Kim. "Loyalty and Membership: Globalization and its Impact on Citizenship, Multiculturalism, and the Australian Community." In *Political Theory and Australian Multiculturalism*, edited by Geoffrey Braham Levey: 171–187. New York: Berghahn Books, 2008b.

Rubenstein, Kim. *Australian Citizenship Law*. 2nd Edition. Sydney: Thompson Reuters, 2016.

Saunders, Cheryl. "Citizenship under the Commonwealth Constitution." *Constitutional Centenary Foundation Newsletter*. 3, 3, 1994: 6.

Stephen, Sir Ninian. "Australian Citizenship: Past, Present and Future." *Monash University Law Review*. 26, 2000: 333–338.

CHAPTER 14

Building a New Citizenship Regime? Immigration and Multiculturalism in Canada

Yasmeen Abu-Laban

Since the end of World War Two, Canada has stood out internationally for developing an inclusive model of citizenship when it comes to immigration, cultural pluralism, and civil rights. As a "white settler colony" modelled after Britain in ethnic, linguistic, and cultural terms—like Australia and Aotearoa New Zealand—it is notable that Canada was the first Commonwealth country to advance its own citizenship as a distinct legal status from that of "British subject" in 1947.[1] Reflecting on the occasion of the seventy fifth anniversary of Canadian citizenship, on 1 January 2022, Liberal Prime Minister Justin Trudeau observed:

I am extremely grateful to the editor of this collection, Jatinder Mann, for his detailed feedback and helpful suggestions on my chapter.

Y. Abu-Laban (✉)
Department of Political Science, University of Alberta, Edmonton, AB, Canada
e-mail: yasmeen@ualberta.ca

J. Mann (ed.), *Citizenship in Transnational Perspective*, Politics of Citizenship and Migration,
https://doi.org/10.1007/978-3-031-34358-2_14

> Today, Canadian citizens across the country and around the world proudly share freedoms and rights, while embracing the responsibilities given to them by their status. In the past decade, more than two million people have taken the oath of citizenship to become Canadian citizens. The Government of Canada recognizes that investing in immigration helps strengthen and grow our economy, but we also know that the pandemic has caused delays for those looking to build a future in Canada…We also know that there is still work to do to make Canada a fairer, more inclusive, and more equitable place for everyone, including new Canadians. No matter their background, a Canadian is a Canadian. Unfortunately, many have faced additional barriers to social and economic participation due to the pandemic. Prejudice, discrimination, and systemic racism also continue to be a lived reality for many immigrants across the country.[2]

Justin Trudeau's 2022 statement is noteworthy for its emphasis on citizenship rights and responsibilities, the economic benefits of immigration to the country, as well as in stating that since a "Canadian is a Canadian" lingering discrimination and systemic racism demand attention. It is a statement that pairs well with another anniversary statement given by the prime minister in 2021, this time on the occasion of the fiftieth anniversary of Canadian multiculturalism. Multiculturalism as a term as well as an official policy owes its origins to Canada.[3] In 1971 Justin Trudeau's own father, Prime Minister Pierre Elliott Trudeau, announced an official policy of multiculturalism within a framework of English and French bilingualism. Exactly fifty years later his son observed the policy brings prosperity and other benefits:

> The diversity of Canadians is a fundamental characteristic of our heritage and identity. For generations, newcomers from all over the world, of all backgrounds, ethnicities, faiths, cultures, and languages, have been coming to Canada with the hopes of making it their home. Today, in addition to First Nations, Métis, and Inuit peoples, people from more than 250 ethnic groups call Canada home and celebrate their cultural heritage with pride—they are at the heart of our success as a vibrant, prosperous, and progressive country.[4]

In many ways these anniversary statements on citizenship and multiculturalism capture the path Justin Trudeau has forged since first becoming prime minister in 2015 with a majority Liberal government (and being re-elected with minority governments in 2019 and 2022).

As this chapter will trace further, the anniversary statements also capture key elements of Canada's citizenship regime. Jane Jensen uses the idea of a citizenship regime to refer to "the institutional arrangements, rules and understandings that guide and shape concurrent policy decisions and expenditures of states, problem definitions by states and citizens, and claims-making by citizens."[5] This chapter analyses Canada's contemporary citizenship regime when it comes to the regulation of citizenship, not only through the *Citizenship Act* but through immigration and multiculturalism policies. While the majority of Canadians—close to 80%—have received their citizenship as a result of birth, the extension of formal citizenship is also implicated by immigration policy. Immigration effectively serves to determine who is let in to Canada and the possibility of being considered for citizenship. Multiculturalism provides a possibility for a pluralistic form of substantive citizenship when it comes to national belonging in a settler colonial context. However, certain elements of the post-war iteration of immigration and multiculturalism relating to inclusion, cultural pluralism, and civil rights have also faced challenges in the twenty-first century. Such challenges stem from cuts to social spending, the turn towards greater control over immigration and borders, as well as securitization evident across Western polities since 9/11.[6]

In what follows attention is paid to the similarities and/or differences between the governments of Prime Minister Stephen Harper (2006–2015) and Prime Minister Justin Trudeau since late 2015, as well as other Liberal governments in power from 2000. What I argue is that under Justin Trudeau there has been a decisive discursive shift back to the *status quo ante* of the pre-Harper period when it comes to focusing on the value of diversity for Canada. As a consequence, both immigrants and refugees tend to be presented in a positive light for their contributions. Under Justin Trudeau there has also been more explicit recognition given to the idea that racism, discrimination, and social exclusion are ongoing challenges—a feature that deepened as a result of the racialized inequities exacerbated by the COVID-19 pandemic.[7] However, these discursive shifts have taken place in a context where neoliberal principals and concerns relating to security remain central material practices and also part of partisan and popular discourse. In this sense, it is more appropriate to speak of an evolving citizenship regime, as opposed to an entirely different regime. The period since 2015 has witnessed some shifting back to the more inclusive side of the citizenship regime advanced when the Liberals were in power under Prime Ministers Jean Chrétien and Paul Martin in the early 2000s, but not a break with either neoliberalism or securitization. In making this argument this chapter takes a three-fold approach, focusing firstly on the politics and policies relating to citizenship, followed by immigration, and finally multiculturalism.

A "Canadian is a Canadian"?: The Politics of Citizenship Revocation and Acquisition

Justin Trudeau and his government's emphasis on the idea that a "Canadian is a Canadian" stems from language first employed to distinguish himself and the Liberal Party from the Conservative Party of Prime Minister Harper, in power from 2006 to 2015. The Harper Conservatives' approach to citizenship ultimately sharpened the differences between the Canadian-born and naturalized citizens. More specifically, through new legislation that went into effect just in advance of the 2015 election, greater security was accorded to those holding citizenship acquired at birth (as well as mono citizenship) as opposed to those holding citizenship acquired by naturalization (and dual or multiple citizenships).[8] Amongst other things, this legislation, known as Bill C-24—*Strengthening Canadian Citizenship Act*, allowed for the revocation of citizenship from dual/multiple nationals on grounds of security, and introduced new financial and linguistic barriers to getting citizenship. Changes were justified by then Immigration Minister Chris Alexander as necessary to "protect and strengthen the great value of Canadian citizenship and to remind individuals that citizenship is not a right, it's a privilege."[9] The kind of language associated with the bill, and eventually law, implicated all immigrants, new citizens, and dual/multiple citizens, and also drew heavily on themes relating to fraud and security. As such federal officials could revoke citizenship if it was decided that a naturalized citizen did not intend to live in Canada, committed a crime or fraud, or acted "contrary to the national interest of Canada." Moreover, if citizenship was revoked there were no grounds of appeal in Federal Court.[10] Such broad categories for revoking citizenship raised concerns for many NGOs for their potential negative impact. This included the Canadian Arab Institute, which in a policy brief noted that the changes could disproportionately and unfairly effect Canadians of Arab origin, who were often stereotyped to be security threats.[11]

In the months following the 2015 election, the Trudeau Liberals introduced new legislation (Bill C-6) designed to neutralize the controversial new grounds for citizenship revocation. In the words of the then newly appointed Liberal Minister for Immigration, Refugees, and Citizenship, John McCullan, "we would make it impossible for the government to take away someone's citizenship, and we would reduce the barriers currently in place that people have to overcome."[12] When this legislation was eventually passed in June 2017, the Trudeau Liberals repealed the provisions enabling the revocation of citizenship from dual citizens convicted of spying, treason, and terrorism offences; removed mention of the "intention" to reside in Canada if granted citizenship; and also allowed for the possibility that minors could apply for citizenship without a parent.[13]

While these represented important changes, considering all details of Bill C-6 as passed in 2017 I would suggest that the Liberal changes were more about "tweaks" to the system rather than jettisoning it.[14] The new legislation shifted to requiring a physical presence for three out of five years before the date of an application for citizenship (from four out of six with a minimum of 183 days, though before 2015 residency was not defined as physical presence); it reduced the requirements for language testing and the citizenship test from 14–64 back to 18–54 (but did not get rid of testing); and it required tax filing to be done for three out of five years (as opposed to four out of six years).[15]

The idea of tweaks to the *Citizenship Act* and the Harper changes, rather than a complete replacement, might be said to characterize other aspects of Bill C-6. For one, revocation was still possible on grounds of fraud, and the Liberal government of Justin Trudeau actually made use of this provision more than the Harper Conservatives had.[16] As well, there were many things left untouched from the Harper period, as the Canadian Council for Refugees noted at the time.[17] These included the fees for citizenship (which in 2023 amounted to C$630), waiting times for processing applications, denying citizenship and removing refugee status from some applicants through cessation (i.e. claiming they are no longer refugees), restoring Canadian citizenship to the second generation born abroad which was rescinded in 2009,[18] and improving procedural rights for those who lose citizenship on the basis of fraud or misrepresentation. Given all this, it would be more accurate to consider the citizenship regime evolving rather than being replaced. This theme carries into issues relating to immigration where Canada's responses are not unique.

Immigration and Refugee Policy in a World of Inequity: Security, Economic Prosperity, and Welcoming Newcomers

In general, certain patterns relating to immigration can be traced in relation to responses from Northern states that can be summed as the "3 S" words "skills, securitization, and sovereignty." First on skills, it is clear that while migration impacts all world regions, the flows have been disproportionately from countries of the South to countries of the North, reflecting on an unequal division of wealth globally. This unequal division of wealth helps propel what economists like to call the "push factors" of immigration. Moreover, countries of the North have tended to try and attract those they deem desirable, and in recent years this has involved competition for the highly skilled. This might be seen as one of the "pull" factors of migration.

Of course, with the global COVID-19 pandemic, migration was impacted by border closures, and stay at home/quarantine measures also led to greater awareness and government support in Canada for "essential workers" in the care and service sectors, but it is unclear that the emphasis on attracting those deemed highly skilled will dissipate.[19] In light of these trends, it is notable that many recent reports from the Organization for Economic Cooperation and Development (OECD) are highlighting new ways in which the longstanding concern over a North/South brain drain is combining with a new concern and that is that immigrants do not always get work commensurate with their high skills in the wealthy Northern countries.[20] Globally in 2019 there were approximately 272 million international migrants with some two-thirds (62%) being migrant workers and the bulk (67%) residing in high-income countries.[21]

In more recent decades, migrants, and refugees in particular, have come under suspicion giving rise to securitization so that even people fleeing the worst of state persecution can be cast as threats rather than victims. The end of the Cold War really serves to demarcate two very different approaches to refugees. Generally speaking, the era of the Cold War (roughly 1946–1991) drew a very different response from Western states because the offering of asylum served other goals. The core of the international refugee regime, as represented by the 1951 United Nations (UN) Convention, emerged from the context of the forty million Europeans displaced after World War Two, as well as the Cold War. Offering asylum to those fleeing Communist persecution enhanced the propaganda arsenal of the Liberal-democratic West over the Soviet bloc.[22] However, as refugees from countries of the global South increased, and especially once the Cold War ended, the response of Western states altered. As observed by the late migration specialist Stephen Castles, after 1991 the refugee policies of the global North shifted from welcoming Cold War refugees to "a 'non-entreé regime' designed to exclude and control asylum seekers from the South."[23]

The non-entry regime has also been justified through a discursive shift. Refugees came to be "securitized" over the course of the 1980s and 1990s. As legal scholar Sharryn Aiken suggests, "the refugee has been reconceived as the 'bogus asylum seeker' illegal migrant, and even worse, criminal or terrorist."[24] It should be noted that the discourse around "international terrorism" began to come to the fore in American policies as far back as the 1980s and at the same time associated some countries and groups in the Middle East with both the Soviet bloc and terrorism.[25] After 9/11 this discourse was further reinforced in Northern countries, as was surveillance directed at both citizens and non-citizens perceived to be Middle Eastern and/or Muslim.

Finally, when it comes to sovereignty, it is clear that Northern states are finding ways to exert sovereignty and control in relation to migrants. From visa controls to innumerable barriers in far-flung airports worldwide, Northern states have increased the ways in which they control movement. They also have all manner of ways to control who gets citizenship. In fact, the exclusion of long-term residents, mostly from the developing world from nationality in many European Union (EU) countries, is a case in point, and these people are also not eligible for EU citizenship since they do not have the national citizenship of an EU member state. Barriers to citizenship in the form of the use of temporary migrant labour or greater and more punitive testing for citizenship are also in evidence in Northern states in the past couple of decades. What is perhaps most striking is how controls have been directed at refugees. It is striking because the one seeming single exception to the lack of a human right to movement, and specifically a right to enter and stay in a different state than of one's nationality, might be seen to pertain to refugees.

Writing of the period between World War One and World War Two, Hannah Arendt poignantly highlighted the connection between statelessness and rightlessness. As Arendt put it, a person's "right to have rights" was contingent on membership in a state.[26] Because the observations of Arendt reflected a world system where there was no international framework governing people who were stateless, it was distinct that in the decades following World War Two, there was the growth of a strong discourse around human rights and the emergence of international agreements including ones dealing with refugees.

In particular, the United Nations (UN) has played a critical role in defining who is entitled to asylum and the responsibility of states. Two important agreements, signed by Canada, are the 1951 UN Convention Relating to the Status of Refugees and the 1967 Protocol which define a refugee as someone who is outside his or her country and cannot return because of a "well-founded fear of being persecuted for reasons of race, religion, nationality, membership of a particular social group or political opinion." Canada has incorporated this definition of refugee into domestic laws and by extension has agreed to the principle of non-refoulement, namely that a refugee will not be returned to a country where his or her life or freedom is in danger.[27]

Yet, the fact remains that international agreements are only binding on signatory states and moreover, can even be potentially ignored by signatories, and Western states have proved adept at finding ways to get around the refugee convention and protocol by making it difficult to even reach Western states to make claims.[28] Moreover, policies have been designed to control access to countries to make claims but also to limit the number of countries where claims could be directed. For example, in the EU, the 1990 Schengen Convention aimed to create a border free Europe internally, but external borders were fortified. And the 1990 Dublin Convention (which came into force in 1997) created criteria for determining the sole European country in which a refugee had to make their claim, generally the country where s/he first arrived. Scholars quickly demonstrated how these agreements have allowed EU countries to circumvent the UN Convention and Protocol.[29]

Although Canada and the United States of America (USA) are not party to an arrangement quite like what has developed in the continent of Europe, the two countries are close in relation to trade. And of special note is the Canada-USA so-called Safe Third Country Agreement, which Canada under the Liberal governments of Chrétien and Martin really pushed for. This came in force at the end of 2004 covering the official land ports of entry, and numerous studies and press releases by groups like the Canadian Council for Refugees showed the Safe Third Country Agreement worked to reduce claims made in Canada by preventing refugees arriving from the USA on official land ports from even making claims.[30] This only changed following the election of Donald Trump in the USA in 2017, when numerous refugee claimants started to make often dangerous journey from the USA and cross at irregular (non-official) points of the Canadian border not covered by the agreement to make claims.

For the period in which Harper was in power, the Safe Third Country Agreement worked as anticipated in reducing claims. Nonetheless, when the Harper Conservatives came to power, yet more restrictive legislation was passed (in particular the 2012 *Protecting Canada's Immigration System Act*—Bill C-31 and the *Balanced Refugee Reform Act*—Bill C-11). This 2012 legislation was widely deemed to be problematic by many analysts because of the ministerial discretion left to determining whether a country produces refugees and the fact that "irregular" arrivals can face automatic detention (in what is akin to a medium security prison).[31] Overall, since the end of the Cold War, and especially since 9/11, this kind of restrictive legislation was justified by saying some kind of combination of things: that refugees are not really refugees (they are bogus refugees and really economic migrants out there shopping for asylum) or they may be refugees but they are criminal or security or terrorist threats.

Since coming to power, the Justin Trudeau government has vacillated between wanting to be open to refugees in a way not done by his predecessor Harper (including by welcoming Syrians and more recently Ukrainians), increasing immigration intake, but also wanting to stem the backlash from irregular crossings not covered by the USA-Canada Safe Third Country Agreement and invoking discourses and policies of closure.

To understand these different dimensions, it can be noted that the new and dramatic flow of Syrian refugees eventually led to public challenge of the march to greater restriction under the Harper government. As is well known, the numbers of refugees globally began to swell to levels unseen since the end of World War Two and by 2014 the then United Nations High Commissioner for Refugees (UNHCR) said the world was not facing a crisis but rather a "mega crisis."[32] In 2015 there were over sixty-five million refugees and internally displaced persons (IDPs) globally; that was equivalent to 1 in every 113 people worldwide and therefore more than the populations of Canada, Australia, and Aotearoa New Zealand combined.[33] It has only increased since then, standing at 80.3 million refugees and internally displaced persons.[34] Today many refugees come from the Middle East, with Syria accounting for 6.8 million in 2021.[35] Since these refugees were uprooted from the civil war, Syria's crisis underscores how the production of refugees is tied to conflict as well as global inequality. It is important to note as well that refugees worldwide are primarily concentrated in countries of the developing world, often ending up in camps in neighbouring developing countries.

For Canadians, the 2015 national election campaign served to raise profound questions about the specific lack of response by the Harper Conservative government to Syrian refugees. A real turning point in the campaign for Canadians (as well as the global community) was seeing the photographic image of a lifeless Aylan Kurdi, a three-year-old Syrian boy who drowned trying to reach the shores of the Greek island of Kos with his family in September 2015. The photographer who captured the chilling image of young Aylan called it a "silent scream,"[36] but it was his Canadian aunt, Tima Kurdi, who gave that image sound by doing media interviews. Recounting her own bureaucratic difficulties in getting family members who fled Syria to safety in Canada, she beseeched the world to "step in and help the refugees."[37] As legal scholar Audrey Macklin averred in an op-ed in *The New York Times*, "the moral distance between Syrian refugees and Canada evaporated with the revelation that Aylan Kurdi's Canadian aunt made an urgent and futile application to sponsor family members to Canada."[38]

The more open Trudeau Liberal response to Syrian refugees contrasted with the Conservatives and resonated with a more open Canadian tradition. Many Canadians see Canada as having a long and proud tradition of welcoming refugees. Indeed, the United Empire Loyalists are frequently upheld as Canada's first major wave of refugees.[39] Moreover, the xenophobic and antisemitic responses that conditioned a "none is too many" response to Jewish refugees fleeing Nazi persecution[40] are now widely condemned by Canadians. There is a monument at Halifax's Pier 21 (home to the Canadian Museum of Immigration) reflecting on the tragic historic response to the M.S. St. Louis, when Jewish refugees were denied entry to Canada and turned back to their deaths. The resettlement of some 37,000 Hungarians in 1956, 11,000 Czechs in 1968, 7000 fleeing Uganda in 1972, 7000 from Chile in 1973, 60,000 Vietnamese between 1978 and 1980, and 5000 Kosovars in 1999 are readily pointed to as exemplifying a tradition that made Canada the first country to be awarded the UN Nansen Medal.[41]

Under current rules refugees may find initial support through sponsorship by the government or privately (by organizations like churches or groups of five or more Canadians). Justin Trudeau pledged that he would bring in 25,000 Syrian refugees with a combination of government and private sponsorship and re-settle them in Canada, and made good on this pledge once he was elected. Still, historically in Canada in the nineteenth century, Syrians were stereotyped to be habitual liars and carriers of disease, and today's version of this would be that they are carriers of terrorism. Of course, the reality is that anybody admitted to Canada has to go through intensive screening. Nonetheless, there are many elected politicians at all levels, as well as journalists and members of the Canadian public, who focus on security and control, making it seemingly unavoidable in relation to discourse.

More recently, themes of security, sovereignty, and control have manifested in relation to the irregular crossing from the USA into Quebec known as Roxham Road. Following the election of Republican Donald Trump and more draconian policies with respect to protected persons and refugees, the numbers crossing from the USA to Canada to claim asylum began to increase. With the border closures during the height of the COVID-19 pandemic, Justin Trudeau announced in 2020 that those crossing at irregular points of the border would be detained and returned to the USA, but with the border re-opening we can see the trend has continued under Democratic President Joe Biden. Indeed, between January and March 2023 alone, there was a record of 44,000 crossings at Roxham Road,[42] which drew criticism both from the Premier of Quebec, François Legault, and the Conservative Party (now led by Pierre Poilievre). In March 2023 Prime Minister Justin Trudeau and President Biden announced a new agreement whereby the Safe Third Country agreement would be extended along the entire border between the USA and Canada, raising considerable concerns about Canada living up to international obligations under the UN refugee convention (like non-refoulement) since the Safe Third Country was already facing a Supreme Court Challenge.[43]

On other dimensions of immigration, namely the non-refugee immigration intake, it is notable that the government moved on 5 July 2016 to have a formal "national conversation about immigration," explicitly stating the interest in "how we can continue to grow our nation through immigration" and stressing that "Canada's strength lies in its diversity. Our diversity is closely tied to immigration and is a valued part of Canada's story."[44] Since coming to power, the trend has been towards an increase in overall numbers. However, with the emphasis being on skilled immigrants who effectively pay for their own integration and greater use of expendable temporary labour, the details of immigration rest heavily on neoliberal logics.[45] In short, the immigration trend has been towards greater discursive emphasis on diversity, within a context in which both the security and economic imperatives, which create other forms of exclusion, have not disappeared. This discourse on the value of diversity is also being reflected in multiculturalism.

Multiculturalism: (Re)embracing Diversity as National Identity

Turning to consider multiculturalism it is notable that unlike the context of Europe where both publics and many former European politicians like Germany's former Chancellor Angela Merkel or former United Kingdom Prime Minister David Cameron have questioned multiculturalism, this has not happened in Canada. Indeed, the Conservative government of Prime Minister Harper supported multiculturalism, as has the Canadian public. For example, a 2010 poll found that just the word "multiculturalism" generated very positive or positive responses from 73% of respondents across Canada, including 71% of those from Quebec (even if successive Quebec governments have stressed interculturalism as opposed to multiculturalism).[46] As well, a 2012 poll found overall 58% of Canadians had a very positive or somewhat positive attitude towards the federal multiculturalism policy.[47] More recently, a 2018 poll found without any prompting that 43% of Canadians defined Canada by multiculturalism.[48]

However, when Harper came to power, there were clear efforts made to make multiculturalism more connected to immigration policy as opposed to Canadian identity, by moving the multiculturalism directorate from the Department of Canadian Heritage into the Department of Citizenship and Immigration Canada. This move can be read as symbolically linking multiculturalism with incoming immigrants and also marginalizing multiculturalism from the relative status and resources accorded to official languages, still housed in the Department of Canadian Heritage. As well, there were clear efforts to give a different, more explicit, and more traditional content to Canadian identity and history. This was achieved by stressing themes relating to military history and Canada's historic ties to Britain, as evidenced in a 2009 guide to citizenship acquisition put out by the Harper Conservatives.[49] This guide also made use of globally widespread racialized and gendered tropes relating to "apparent Muslim excess"[50] and was followed by the Harper Conservatives banning the extension of citizenship to anyone covering their face at a citizenship ceremony (a move widely understood to be directed at the tiny minority of Muslim women in Canada who wear the niqab).[51]

During the 2015 election campaign, intense focus concerned the legal case of Zunera Ishaq, an immigrant from Pakistan seeking Canadian citizenship, who refused to remove her niqab during the citizenship ceremony. In February 2015, a Federal Court judge ruled that requiring her to do so violated the *Citizenship Act* and religious freedom.[52] The Federal Court of Appeal unanimously upheld this interpretation in September 2015.[53] One of the first things that the new Liberal government did on assuming power was to withdraw the legal efforts that the Harper government had begun to pursue in relation to the Supreme Court after lower courts ruled that women should be able to wear a face covering, and more specifically the niqab, when receiving citizenship at an official ceremony. In the words of the former Liberal Justice Minister Jody Wilson-Raybould in making the announcement: "in all of our policy as a government, we will ensure that we respect the values that make us Canadians: those of diversity, inclusion and respect for those fundamental values."[54]

However, when it comes to anti-terrorism measures, even if they infringe or are seen to infringe on civil rights, Justin Trudeau has been largely in step with the Harper Conservatives. This was seen very clearly in the support given to Bill C-51 by Justin Trudeau when he was in opposition, even though this legislation was roundly criticized by many Canadian NGOs for its negative implications for civil liberties and also questioned by the UN Human Rights Committee in 2015.[55] Specifically, the Human Rights Committee was concerned about the implications of expanding powers to the Canadian Security Intelligence Service (CSIS) and changes to information sharing and the no-fly programme.[56]

The manner in which securitization targets some minorities join with other dimensions of racialized inequality in contemporary Canada. These other dimensions include statistically evident and growing forms of racialized and gendered socioeconomic inequality, as well as the rise in the number of temporary migrant workers who are denied citizenship.[57] As such, issues of anti-racism are critical for minorities in Canada. Under the federal Conservatives of Stephen Harper, anti-racism was far less on display in relation to funded projects or ongoing discourse on multiculturalism. Rather, under the Harper Conservatives the discourse was more on "bridge building" aimed at providing mentorship and employment training for second-generation youth as exemplified by a programme linking

Somali-Canadian youth with Jewish-owned businesses and professions. Notably, while the "Somali-Jewish Canadian Mentorship Project" was billed as a model for other "cross-cultural projects,"[58] it was really about fostering conditions for individual success, rather than acknowledging or attempting to eliminate structural barriers that might produce inequalities.

Efforts to bypass discussions relating to racism in Canada were also seen in statements made by the former Conservative Minister of Multiculturalism, Citizenship, and Immigration Jason Kenney, including in March 2013 on the United Nations-sponsored International Day for the Elimination of Racial Discrimination when he basically said racism was only a problem outside Canada, since Canada was a model of "successful pluralism."[59] Paradoxically, and unlike any other previous federal government since multiculturalism was introduced in 1971, the Harper Conservatives did show a high degree of willingness to entertain redress for select examples of historic discrimination relating to measures taken during war (in particular World Wars One and Two) as well as immigration restrictions.[60] While entertaining apologies or statements of regret and funding commemorative and educational activities about important historical events that have shaped the experience of groups, and Canada's history, is arguably positive, critical attention to the limitations of this approach is also needed. For one, collective injustices may happen outside of a war or immigration context.

More broadly, Matt James argues the overall approach can be critiqued as one of "neoliberal heritage redress."[61] Neoliberal heritage redress twins with neoliberal multiculturalism by placing limitations on the possibility and use of state funding, allowing the government to pick select groups to reward, as well as working to make contemporary claims for social justice, equity, and anti-racism disappear.[62]

Thus, under the Conservatives while there were growing forms of racialized inequality experienced by both incoming immigrants and minorities in Canada, multicultural discourse and funding retreated from a focus on racism and anti-racism. This contrasts heavily with the discourse of the Liberals. For example, on 21 March 2016—the UN International Day for the Elimination of Racial Discrimination—Justin Trudeau himself made an announcement in which racism was acknowledged and where the focus was on challenging acts of discrimination "whenever and wherever they occur."[63] By 2019 a new federal secretariat of anti-racism was announced that takes a "whole of government" approach across federal agencies to address the impacts of policies, services, and programmes.[64]

Focusing on the idea of the value and strength of diversity, Trudeau also delivered a statement on Multiculturalism Day (27 June 2016), arguing, "Canada has shown time and time again that a country can be stronger not in spite of its differences, but because of them."[65] What is equally noteworthy is that in 2016 Multiculturalism Day was merged into a new "Celebrate Canada" four-day celebration, which culminates in the national holiday of Canada Day and simultaneously bridges multiculturalism, Indigenous peoples, and Quebec. As indicated by the then Canadian Heritage Minister Mélanie Joly:

> This special day is part of Celebrate Canada, a four-day celebration that highlights cultural diversity in our country, beginning with National Aboriginal Day on June 21 and Saint-Jean-Baptiste Day on June 24. Celebrations continue today with Canadian Multiculturalism Day and finish on Canada Day on July 1.[66]

This emphasis on valuing cultural diversity is also in keeping with the discursive tenor of the Liberal government in multiculturalism, as is the emphasis that there is remaining discrimination and racism.[67]

Given all this, unlike the emphasis on the military and Canada's British heritage characterizing the Harper plans, the Liberal government's approach to the 150th anniversary of Confederation (i.e. the founding of the modern Canadian state) occurring in 2017 focused on promoting and celebrating Canadian identity and "ethnic, linguistic, cultural and regional diversity."[68] And, by the fiftieth anniversary of multiculturalism in 2021, Trudeau's statement also implored Canadians to "confront painful truths about our history and society, learn from them, and take meaningful action together to address systemic discrimination and ensure everyone is treated with respect and able to participate equitably in economic, social, cultural, and political life in Canada."[69]

Conclusion

To conclude, what has been happening under the Justin Trudeau Liberals is a reminder that discourse and symbolism can matter in the articulation of ideas of inclusion. In many ways the track they are following is in keeping with earlier Liberal governments, including those of Chrétien and Martin, as well as with the prime minister who first articulated multiculturalism, Pierre Elliott Trudeau.[70] This makes it hard to speak of a new citizenship regime. However, this also serves as a reminder that economistic rationales stemming from neoliberalism and securitization, stemming from post 9/11 policy responses, still remain central in the articulation of Canadian citizenship in the twenty-first century. This is the case even if Justin Trudeau is a unique and popular prime minister who seems to go against the grain by having a tattoo and calling himself a feminist. As such, immigration and multiculturalism remain deeply connected to a world, and a country, of unequal relations.

Notes

1. Yasmeen Abu-Laban, "Multiculturalism: Past, Present and Future," *Canadian Diversity*, Special Issue on "Multiculturalism at 50: Promoting Inclusion and Eliminating Racism," Guest Edited by Will Kymlicka, 18, 1 (2021): 9–12; and Jatinder Mann, *Redefining Citizenship in Australia, Canada, and Aotearoa New Zealand* (New York: Peter Lang, 2019).
2. Prime Minister of Canada Justin Trudeau, "Statement by the Prime Minister on the 75th Anniversary of Canadian Citizenship," Ottawa, 1 January 2022. Available: https://pm.gc.ca/en/news/statements/2022/01/01/statement-prime-minister-75th-anniversary-canadian-citizenship [Accessed 8 March 2023].
3. Yasmeen Abu-Laban, Alain-G. Gagnon, and Arjun Tremblay, "Reflecting on Multiculturalism at its Semicentennial: Over the Hill or Just Getting Started?," in *Assessing Multiculturalism in Global Comparative Perspective: A New Politics of Diversity for the 21st Century?*, eds. Yasmeen Abu-Laban, Alain-G. Gagnon, and Arjun Tremblay (London and New York: Routledge, 2023), 5–7; and Jatinder Mann, *The Search for a New National Identity: The Rise of Multiculturalism in Canada and Australia, 1890s–1970s* (New York: Peter Lang Publishing, 2016).
4. Prime Minister of Canada Justin Trudeau, "Statement by the Prime Minister on the 50th Anniversary of Canada's Multiculturalism Policy," Ottawa, 8 October 2021. Available: https://pm.gc.ca/en/news/statements/2021/10/08/statement-prime-minister-50th-anniversary-canadas-multiculturalism [Accessed 8 March 2023].
5. Jane Jensen, "Social Citizenship in 21st Century Canada: Challenges and Options," 2001 Timlin Lecture, University of Saskatchewan, 7. Available: http://www.cprn.org/documents/26232_en.pdf [Accessed 4 June 2016].
6. Yasmeen Abu-Laban, "The Political Economy of International Migration and the Canadian Example," in *International Political Economy*, eds. Greg Anderson and Christopher J. Kukucha (Don Mills: Oxford University Press, 2016), 476–491.

7. Abu-Laban, "Multiculturalism: Past, Present and Future."
8. Laura van Wass and Sangita Jaghai, "All Citizens are Created Equal but Some are More Equal Than Others," *Netherlands International Law Review* 65 (2018): 413–480.
9. Cited in Debra Black, "Immigration Experts Say Bill C-24 Discriminatory and Weakens Citizenship," *TheStar.com*, 27 June 2014. Available: https://www.thestar.com/news/immigration/2014/06/27/immigration_experts_say_bill_c24_discriminatory_and_weakens_citizenship.html [Accessed 8 March 2023].
10. Abu-Laban, "The Political Economy of International Migration and the Canadian Example."
11. Andrew S. Thompson, "The Need to Protect Rule of Law: A Response to Bill C-24," *Canadian Arab Institute* Policy Brief, May 2014.
12. Quoted in Katherine Starr, "Changes Coming Soon to Citizenship Act, John McCallum Says," *CBC News*, 18 February 2016. Available: https://www.cbc.ca/news/politics/mccallum-immigrants-citizenship-act-language-requirement-1.3453658 [Accessed 14 March 2023]. In January 2017, Prime Minister Trudeau appointed Ahmed Hussen to this post. Hussen, a lawyer by training, arrived in Canada as a sixteen-year-old refugee from Somalia in 1993. Since 2021 the post has been filled by Sean Fraser.
13. Yasmeen Abu-Laban, Ethel Tungohan, and Christina Gabriel, *Containing Diversity: Canada and the Politics of Immigration in the 21st Century* (Toronto: University of Toronto Press, 2023), 229.
14. Quoted in Starr, "Changes Coming Soon to Citizenship Act."
15. Canada, Government of Canada, "Backgrounder: An Act to Amend the Citizenship Act: A Comparative View of Proposed Amendments," 2016. Available: http://news.gc.ca/web/article-en.do?nid=1036049 [Accessed 3 July 2016].
16. Abu-Laban, Tungohan, and Gabriel, *Containing Diversity*, 230.
17. Canadian Council for Refugees, "Reforming the Citizenship Act: Bill C-6," (2016). Available: http://ccrweb.ca/en/bill-c-6-citizenship-concerns [Accessed 14 March 2023].
18. Lois Harder and Lyubov Zhyznomirska, "Claims of Belonging: Recent Tales of Trouble in Canadian Citizenship," *Ethnicities* 12, 3 (June 2012): 293–316.
19. Abu-Laban, Tungohan, and Gabriel, *Containing Diversity*, 308–309.
20. Yasmeen Abu-Laban, "North American and European Immigration Policies: Divergence or Convergence?," *European View*, European People's Party, EU Parliament 5, (Spring 2007): 10.
21. Marie McAuliffe and Anna Triandafyllidou (eds.), *World Migration Report 2022* (Geneva: International Organization for Migration, 2021), 36.

22. Stephen Castles, "The International Politics of Forced Migration," in *Fighting Identities: Race, Religion and Ethno-nationalism*, eds. Leo Panitch and Colin Leys (London: Merlin Press, 2002), 178.
23. *Ibid.*, 181.
24. Sharryn Aiken, "Of Gods and Monsters: National Security and Canadian Refugee Policy," *Revue québécoise du droit international* 14, 1 (2001): 9.
25. See Yasmeen Abu-Laban and Abigail B. Bakan, "The 'Israelization' of Social Sorting and the 'Palestinianization' of the Racial Contract: Reframing Israel/Palestine and the War on Terror," in *Surveillance and Control in Israel/Palestine: Population, Territory and Power*, eds. Elia Zureik, David Lyon, and Yasmeen Abu-Laban (London and New York: Routledge, 2011), 276–294.
26. Hannah Arendt, *The Origins of Totalitarianism* (New York: Schocken Books, [1951] 2004).
27. Audrey Macklin, "The Value(s) of the Canada-US Safe Third Country Agreement," Paper Prepared for the Caledon Institute of Social Policy, December 2003, 1.
28. Abu-Laban, "The Political Economy of International Migration and the Canadian Example."
29. G. Gudrun Hentges, "Refugee and Asylum Policy Influenced by Europeanisation," in *Europe's New Racism? Causes, Manifestations and Solutions*, ed. The Evans Foundation (New York and Oxford: Berghahn Books, 2002), 118.
30. Abu-Laban, "The Political Economy of International Migration and the Canadian Example."
31. See Naomi Alboim and Karen Cohl, *Shaping the Future: Canada's Rapidly Changing Immigration Policies* (Toronto: Maytree Foundation, 2012), 30–40.
32. Abu-Laban, "The Political Economy of International Migration and the Canadian Example."
33. Adrian Edwards, "Global Forced Displacement Hits Record High," *United Nations High Commissioner for Refugees*, 20 June 2016. Available: http://www.unhcr.org/news/latest/2016/6/5763b65a4/global-forced-displacement-hits- record-high.html [Accessed 14 March 2023].
34. United Nations High Commissioner for Refugees, *Global Trends: Forced Displacement in 2021* (Copenhagen: 2022), 2.
35. *Ibid.*, 3.
36. Rob Virtue, "Photographer Behind Image of Dead Syrian Boy: 'I wanted to Express his Silent Scream," *Express*, 5 September 2015. Available: http://www.express.co.uk/news/world/603140/Aylan-Kurdi-photographerspeaks-out-about-syrian-dead-child-photo [Accessed 14 March 2023].

37. Quoted in Peter Edwards and Robin Levinson King, "'I want to tell the rest of the world at this point, to step in and help the refugees,' says aunt of drowned Syrian boys," TheStar.Com, 3 September 2015. Available: https://www.thestar.com/news/canada/2015/09/03/father-of-aylan-kurdi-describes-how-his-family-drowned.html [Accessed 14 March 2023].
38. Audrey Macklin, "Canadians Have a Decision to Make that Will Affect Syrian Refugees," *The New York Times*, 15 September 2015. Available: http://www.nytimes.com/roomfordebate/2015/09/15/what-can-countries-do-to-help-refugees-fleeing-to-europe/canadians-have-a-decision-tomake-that-will-affect-syrian-refugees [Accessed 14 March 2023].
39. See Gerald Dirks, *Canada and Refugees: Indifference or Opportunism?* (Montreal and Kingston: McGill-Queen's University Press, 1977).
40. Irving Abella and Harold Troper, *None is Too Many: Canada and the Jews of Europe 1933–1948* (Toronto: Lester and Orpen Dennys, 1982).
41. Macklin, "Canadians Have a Decision to Make that Will Affect Syrian Refugees."
42. Verity Stevenson and Kwabena Oduro, "Migrants Still Attempting to Cross at Roxham Road, with News of Canada-US Deal Slow to Spread." *CBC News*, 27 March 2023. Available: https://www.cbc.ca/news/canada/montreal/migrants-attempt-roxham-after-deadline-1.6791810 [Accessed 27 March 2023].
43. Abu-Laban, Tungohan, and Gabriel, *Containing Diversity*, 89.
44. Canada, Government of Canada, "National Conversation on Immigration Launched," 5 July 2016. Available: http://news.gc.ca/web/article-en.do?nid=1094449 [Accessed 5 July 2016].
45. Abu-Laban, Tungohan, and Gabriel, *Containing Diversity*.
46. Association for Canadian Studies, "Canadian Words," 18 June 2010.
47. Association for Canadian Studies, "Younger Canadians Believe Multiculturalism Works; Older Canadians, Not so Sure," 24 April 2012. Available: http://www.acs-aec.ca/en/social-research/multiculturalism diversity/ [Accessed 13 September 2012].
48. Abu-Laban, Tungohan, and Gabriel, *Containing Diversity*, 236.
49. Yasmeen Abu-Laban, "Reform by Stealth: The Harper Conservatives and Canadian Multiculturalism," in *The Multiculturalism Question: Debating Identity in 21st Century Canada*, ed. Jack Jedwab (Montreal and Kingston: School of Policy Studies, Queen's University and McGill Queen's University Press, 2014), 149–172.
50. Alana Lentin and Gavan Titley, *The Crises of Multiculturalism: Racism in a Neoliberal Age* (London: Zed Books, 2011), 30.
51. Abu-Laban, "Reform by Stealth."

52. Mark Kennedy, "Liberals Drop Legal Bid to Ban Niqab at Citizenship Ceremonies," *The Ottawa Citizen,* 16 November 2015. Available: http://ottawacitizen.com/news/politics/liberal-government-drops-legal-bid-to ban-niqab-at-citizenship-ceremonies [Accessed 3 July 2016].
53. *Ibid.*
54. Quoted in Kennedy, "Liberals Drop Legal Bid to Ban Niqab at Citizenship Ceremonies."
55. Stephanie Levitz, "Bill C-51 Not in Keeping with Canada's International Obligations: UN," *The Globe and Mail,* 23 July 2015. Available: http://www.theglobeandmail.com/news/politics/bill-c-51-not-in-keeping-with-canadas-international-obligations-un/article25642360/ [Accessed 8 March 2023].
56. *Ibid.*
57. Abu-Laban, "The Political Economy of International Migration and the Canadian Example"; and Abu-Laban, "Reform by Stealth."
58. Jason Kenney, "Foreword by the Minister," in Canada, Citizenship and Immigration Canada, *Annual Report on the Operation of the Canadian Multiculturalism Act* 2008–2009 (Ottawa: Minister of Public Works and Government Services Canada, 2010), iii.
59. Jason Kenney, "Minister Kenney Issues Statement on the International Day for the Elimination of Racial Discrimination," 21 March 2013. Available: http://www.cic.gc.ca/english/department/media/statements/2013/2013-03-21.asp [Accessed 16 June 2013].
60. Abu-Laban, "Reform by Stealth."
61. Matt James, "Neoliberal Heritage Redress," in *Reconciling Canada: Critical Perspectives on the Culture of Redress*, eds. Jennifer Henderson and Pauline Wakeham (Toronto: University of Toronto Press, 2013), 31–46.
62. *Ibid.*
63. Prime Minister of Canada Justin Trudeau, "Statement by the Prime Minister of Canada on the International Day for the Elimination of Racial Discrimination," Ottawa, 21 March 2016. Available: http://pm.gc.ca/eng/news/2016/03/21/statement-prime-minister-canada-international-day-elimination-racial-discrimination [Accessed 3 July 2016].
64. Canada, Department of Canadian Heritage, *Annual Report on the Operation of the Canadian Multiculturalism Act 2019–2020: Building a Better Canada through Diversity* (Her Majesty the Queen in Right of Canada, 2021).
65. Prime Minister of Canada Justin Trudeau, "Statement by the Prime Minister of Canada on Multiculturalism Day,“ Ottawa, 27 June 2016. Available: http://pm.gc.ca/eng/news/2016/06/27/statement-prime-minister-canada-multiculturalism-day [Accessed 14 March 2023].

66. Canada, Department of Canadian Heritage, ***Annual Report on the Operation of the Canadian Multiculturalism Act: Building a Diverse and Inclusive Society*** (Her Majesty the Queen in Right of Canada, represented by the Minister of Immigration, Refugees and Citizenship, 2016), 5. Available: http://www.cic.gc.ca/english/pdf/pub/multi-ar-en-2015.pdf [Accessed 3 July 2016].
67. *Ibid*., 36.
68. Canada, Government of Canada, "Backgrounder: The 150th Anniversary of Confederation in 2017," 25 May 2016. Available: http://news.gc.ca/web/article-en.do?mthd=index&crtr.page=2&nid=1072209 [Accessed 3 July 2016].
69. Prime Minister of Canada Justin Trudeau, "Statement by the Prime Minister on the 50th Anniversary of Canada's Multiculturalism Policy," Ottawa, 8 October 2021. Available: https://pm.gc.ca/en/news/statements/2021/10/08/statement-prime-minister-50th-anniversary-canadas-multiculturalism [Accessed 8 March 2023].
70. See Yasmeen Abu-Laban and Christina Gabriel, ***Selling Diversity: Immigration, Multiculturalism, Employment Equity and Globalization*** (Peterborough: Broadview Press, 2002).

References

Abella, Irving and Harold Troper. *None is Too Many: Canada and the Jews of Europe* 1933–1948. Toronto: Lester and Orpen Dennys, 1982.

Abu-Laban, Yasmeen. "Multiculturalism: Past, Present and Future," *Canadian Diversity*. Special Issue on "Multiculturalism at 50: Promoting Inclusion and Eliminating Racism." Guest Edited by Will Kymlicka. 18, 1, 2021: 9–12.

Abu-Laban, Yasmeen. "The Political Economy of International Migration and the Canadian Example." In *International Political Economy*, edited by Greg Anderson and Christopher J. Kukucha: 476–491. Don Mills: Oxford University Press, 2016.

Abu-Laban, Yasmeen. "Reform by Stealth: The Harper Conservatives and Canadian Multiculturalism." In *The Multiculturalism Question: Debating Identity* in 21st Century Canada, edited by Jack Jedwab: 149–172. Montreal and Kingston: School of Policy Studies, Queen's University and McGill-Queen's University Press, 2014.

Abu-Laban, Yasmeen. "North American and European Immigration Policies: Divergence or Convergence?." *European View*. European People's Party, EU Parliament. 5, Spring 2007: 9–16.

Abu-Laban, Yasmeen and Abigail B. Bakan. "The 'Israelization' of Social Sorting and the 'Palestinianization' of the Racial Contract: Reframing Israel/Palestine and the War on Terror." In *Surveillance and Control in Israel/Palestine: Population, Territory and Power*, edited by Elia Zureik, David Lyon, and Yasmeen Abu-Laban: 276–294. London and New York: Routledge, 2011.

Abu-Laban, Yasmeen and Christina Gabriel. *Selling Diversity: Immigration, Multiculturalism, Employment Equity and Globalization.* Peterborough: Broadview Press, 2002.

Abu-Laban, Yasmeen, Ethel Tungohan, and Christina Gabriel. *Containing Diversity: Canada and the Politics of Immigration in the 21st Century.* Toronto: University of Toronto Press, 2023a.

Abu-Laban, Yasmeen, Alain-G. Gagnon, and Arjun Tremblay. "Reflecting on Multiculturalism at its Semicentennial: Over the Hill or Just Getting Started?." In *Assessing Multiculturalism in Global Comparative Perspective: A New Politics of Diversity for the 21st Century?*, edited by Yasmeen Abu-Laban, Alain-G. Gagnon, and Arjun Tremblay: 3–17. London and New York: Routledge, 2023b.

Aiken, Sharryn. "Of Gods and Monsters: National Security and Canadian Refugee Policy." *Revue québécoise du droit international.* 14, 1, 2001: 7–36.

Alboim, Naomi and Karen Cohl. *Shaping the Future: Canada's Rapidly Changing Immigration Policies.* Toronto: Maytree Foundation, 2012.

Arendt, Hannah. *The Origins of Totalitarianism.* New York: Schocken Books, [1951] 2004.

Castles, Stephen. "The International Politics of Forced Migration." In *Fighting Identities: Race, Religion and Ethno-nationalism,* edited by Leo Panitch and Colin Leys: 172–92. London: Merlin Press, 2002.

Dirks, Gerald. *Canada and Refugees: Indifference or Opportunism?.* Montreal and Kingston: McGill-Queen's University Press, 1977.

Harder, Lois and Lyubov Zhyznomirska. "Claims of Belonging: Recent Tales of Trouble in Canadian Citizenship." *Ethnicities.* 12, 3, June 2012: 293–316.

Hentges, Gudrun. "Refugee and Asylum Policy Influenced by Europeanisation." In *Europe's New Racism? Causes, Manifestations and Solutions* edited by The Evans Foundation: 105–29. New York and Oxford: Berghahn Books, 2002.

James, Matt. "Neoliberal Heritage Redress." In *Reconciling Canada: Critical Perspectives on the Culture of Redress,* edited by Jennifer Henderson and Pauline Wakeham, 31–46. Toronto: University of Toronto Press, 2013.

Lentin, Alana and Gavan Titley. *The Crises of Multiculturalism: Racism in a Neoliberal Age.* London: Zed Books, 2011.

McAuliffe, Marie and Anna Triandafyllidou. Eds. *World Migration Report 2022.* Geneva: International Organization for Migration, 2021.

Mann, Jatinder. *The Search for a New National Identity: The Rise of Multiculturalism in Canada and Australia, 1890s–1970s.* New York: Peter Lang Publishing, 2016.

Mann, Jatinder. *Redefining Citizenship in Australia, Canada and Aotearoa New Zealand.* New York: Peter Lang Publishing, 2019.

United Nations High Commissioner for Refugees. *Global Trends: Forced Displacement in 2021.* Copenhagen: 2022.

van Wass, Laura and Sangita Jaghai. "All Citizens are Created Equal but Some are More Equal Than Others." *Netherlands International Law Review* 65, 2018: 413–480.

CHAPTER 15

(Re)reading Citizenship in Relational Contexts: Race, Security, and Dissidence

Nisha Nath

Introduction

On 1 January 2022, Canada celebrated the 75th anniversary of the *Canadian Citizenship Act*. In his statement to Canadians, Prime Minister Justin Trudeau drew links between citizenship as an expression of Canada's national identity and reinforced the role of immigration in strengthening and growing the Canadian economy.[1] Critically, the prime minister wrote the life of the nation by asserting that generations of immigrants and new Canadians embody "the values of openness, compassion, and respect that

My thanks are extended to Rita Dhamoon and Yasmeen Abu-Laban who have seen the earliest iterations of my work on race, security and citizenship, and whose scholarship and ongoing mentorship prompt me to look for intersections amidst so many siloes.

N. Nath (✉)
Centre for Interdisciplinary Studies, Athabasca University, Athabasca, AB, Canada
e-mail: nnath@athabascau.ca

J. Mann (ed.), *Citizenship in Transnational Perspective*, Politics of Citizenship and Migration,
https://doi.org/10.1007/978-3-031-34358-2_15

define and unite us." While stressing that work remains to be done to ensure Canada is "a fairer, more inclusive, and more equitable place for everyone," he goes on to assert that "No matter their background, a Canadian is a Canadian."

I open this chapter with this seemingly innocuous address because it is precisely that it reads as innocuous that it is analytically interesting when thinking about citizenship. What is being rehearsed in narratives of repetition around citizenship? What does it mean to celebrate citizenship? What is being asked of us when we are invited or expected to invest our hopes in this status?

In this chapter, I offer a (re)reading of citizenship that is meant to query the erasures and presumptions built into the prime minister's address. To be clear, these are not his erasures and presumptions alone, and as implied above, they are rehearsed with striking regularity, across myriad historical and contemporary Canadian institutional contexts. I am snagged by the erasure of "security" in celebratory appeals to the promises of liberal multicultural citizenship and want to pause on the framing of "[p]rejudice, discrimination, and systemic racism" as being "unfortunate," but somehow separate from citizenship in the first place. Thus, in this chapter, I add to a body of critical citizenship scholarship that positions citizenship as a regulatory strategy. As opposed to focusing on citizenship as a legal status, a set of rights, an act of participation, or an identity or form of solidarity,[2] this chapter works to disrupt the contention that citizenship is solely or primarily an expression or practice of belonging to a national community.[3] Instead, I consider the white settler colonial state's interest in citizenship as a governmental strategy. Contextualized within the imperatives of *this* state, I make two key contentions about citizenship. First, citizenship *regulates* the boundaries of political normativity, or what I am terming dissidence, through the processes of racialization and securitization. Second, contrary to siloed understandings of political community that are often present in renderings of "ethnocultural diversity" in "Canada the liberal multicultural state," I contend that this regulation of citizenship is *relational*. Put differently, citizenship regulates political normativity through relational securitization, wherein the positioning of white, racialized, non-Indigenous people and Indigenous people is specifically relational *as a strategy of the state*.[4]

To consider this, I home in on a set of political encounters in and around Canada's *Anti-Terrorism Act (ATA)*, specifically amendments in the form of Bill C-51 in 2015 *(ATA)*. The intention here is to offer a (re) reading of citizenship as regulatory strategy, through the framework of relational securitization. In doing so, I am wanting to (re)read citizenship by considering the white settler colonial state's interest in particular dissident subjects, how they are cultivated as threats in relational ways, and how this functions to secure the state's authority and jurisdiction as somehow legitimate and natural. To explore this, this chapter engages in three (re)readings of citizenship: first, I extend my analysis of citizenship as a regulatory strategy; second, I position Canadian anti-terrorism legislation within relational contexts by exploring the tight co-implication of race, security, and dissent in the white settler colonial state; and, third I trace out specific ways in which a critical engagement with the *ATA* illuminates how citizenship regulates access to political subjectivity through the legal exception, hyperpoliticization, and (in)visibility. Throughout this chapter, the intention is to examine the internal and external forms of regulation made visible by and enacted through the *ATA*; this site is revelatory of how racialized people and Indigenous people are securitized through citizenship (and non-citizenship) in dialectical and overlapping ways. With a more complicated rendering of citizenship, I end by returning to the question, "What is being asked of us when we are invited or expected to invest our hopes in this status?"

(Re)reading Citizenship as Regulatory Strategy

The prime minister's statement at the opening of this chapter is not exceptional in that it finds resonance with much of the mainstream Canadian scholarship on citizenship. Here, context matters. The purpose of citizenship, and indeed the relationship of citizenship to the state (i.e. what does citizenship do *for* the state), is fully bound up in how we understand the state in the first place. The state this chapter theorizes is in tension with the imaginary of "Canada, the liberal multicultural state." That state is one that is often characterized as benevolent or perhaps somewhat "neutral" in that it is under pluralistic contestation; it holds centrally the normative values of inclusion and belonging, and in doing so, a primary locus of attention or fixation is "the actuality of a plurality of social identities and the singular identity implied by citizenship."[5] Here, the question that is posed time and again has been some version of: "how does, or can, a concept which has at its core the principles of universality and equality of status accommodate the politics of particularity and difference?"[6] In fact, one might argue that in the Canadian context this tension between universality and particularity has been canonical within scholarship on citizenship.[7] This has shaped notions of crisis and risk, with advocates of liberal multiculturalism offering "sophisticated" rationales for legitimated exclusion and regulated inclusion as it pertains to particular ethno-cultural and religious practices and groups.[8]

Critically, this fixation on this as "The Problem" that should be asked and answered about citizenship relies on a conceptualization that does not necessarily resonate with those who experience fundamental and structured precarity and inequity as the problem needing to be addressed. Rather, this diagnosis of unity-difference as "The Problem" is from the perspective of a state that sees difference as diversity on a horizontal plane and imagines that the appropriate role of the state is to manage this difference.

Instead, as others have done, I want to (re)orient and locate citizenship within the ordering logics of Canada as a white settler colonial state. Rather than focusing on the state's role as "manager of difference," I turn to the state's interest in consolidating itself (e.g. its power, authority, and jurisdiction to act). This is germane to the purpose of citizenship, which is after all an institution of the state. As opposed to conceptualizing citizenship as a status of promise, I propose instead that we think about citizenship in three key ways. First, citizenship is a form of regulation that is meant to secure and consolidate the state. Second, citizenship regulates subjects and secures itself through interacting notions of race, security, and dissidence. Third, the way in which citizenship regulates through race, security, and dissidence is *relational*. Hence, in this section, I want to trace out how relational racialized securitization is integral to how citizenship is deployed as a form of regulation that is meant to cultivate and/or contain the "right" and "wrong" kinds of political subjectivity.

First, in thinking about the role of citizenship and asserting that race, security, and dissidence are modalities through which citizenship regulates, I draw from Mitchell Dean's[9] analytics of government to lay out an articulation of citizenship as regulation. For scholars of citizenship, this shift in orientation is important because it also prompts different questions to be asked about citizenship. Here, citizenship as a regulatory strategy of government visualizes who and what is to be governed, how relations of authority and obedience are constituted, what problems are to be solved, and what objectives are sought.[10] With this (re)orientation, instead of being focused on the promises of inclusive citizenship as a kind of end goal that formalizes rights and entitlements, we might query through what "means, mechanisms, procedures, instruments, tactics, techniques and vocabularies" are authority and rule secured and accomplished through citizenship?[11] Moreover, what forms of "knowledge, expertise, strategies, means of calculation, or rationality" are being deployed in and through citizenship, and how do these presuppose particular identities or processes of identification?[12] Critically, this requires a relational understanding in that these "statuses, capacities, attributes and orientation" are affixed to those who are governed *and* those who govern.[13]

Second, the context in which citizenship is deployed as regulatory strategy is far from neutral; where strategy may shift, and regulation gets enacted in local, located, and at times situational ways, the organizing logics of the state are structural and systemic. The context of citizenship is one in which the modern state has always conceived of itself as racially configured.[14] This racial state is not simply a condition of being but rather a description of a state of *governance*.[15] Where querying the politics of racial dominance tells us something about what racist exclusion looks like, why the racial composition of state personnel matters, or what the racialized implications of state politics and policies are,[16] to contextualize citizenship within the racial state is to position it within a state where race is integral to the state's conceptual and institutional emergence, development, and transformation.[17] For subjects of the state—citizens, non-citizens, potential citizens—racial states constitute their subjects not simply by "knowing" them but by attempting to create and assert their "truth conditions."[18] This cultivation of a racialized non/citizen subject happens through bold assertions of state authority and jurisdiction but also through implicit modes of discipline and surveillance, as well as the diffuse production of consent.[19]

In these ways, the link between the state, citizenship, race, and security starts to become clearer. Consider Rita Dhamoon's[20] rich intervention on multicultural securitization, in which she challenges the notion that multiculturalism and security have an oppositional relationship. Instead, she argues that liberal multiculturalism is intrinsically constitutive of security mechanisms.[21] As a mechanism of security, liberal multiculturalism "performs to *secure* hegemonic nation-building endeavors in ways that re-entrench unequal relations of power,"[22] doing so through the consolidation of colonized territory; the consolidation of a national identity that is "tolerant"; the consolidation and securing of the dominance of whiteness;[23] and the consolidation of a capitalist economy committed to the business value of multiculturalism.[24]

In conceptualizing liberal multiculturalism as constitutive of security mechanisms, Dhamoon is interrupting a pointed silence or absenting of the word security in much of the scholarship on multicultural citizenship, even as this body of work engages in the language of crisis in its anxiety over diversity.[25] This absenting of security is all the more curious given that within liberal social contract theory, security itself is understood as a right or first freedom wherein individuals surrender to the state the power to protect their lives and property.[26] As an "interlocking system of knowledge, representations, practices and institutional forms that imagine, direct, and act upon bodies, spaces, and flows in certain ways,"[27] an orientation to citizenship as securitization challenges the liberal presumption that security is an *essential* value, and invites an interrogation of how citizenship regulates relationally.

Yet, the specific strategy of securitizing inclusion and diversity is grounded in the imperatives of a white settler colonial state. *This* is the state that is being articulated and consolidated through Canadian citizenship as regulatory strategy. The positioning of precarious, racialized, non-Indigenous citizens and non-citizens can either uphold or disrupt the state's legitimacy, authority, and jurisdiction to act on lands it has no entitlement to. In the Canadian settler colonial context, that the state is seemingly founded on the promise to secure its members *against each other*, belies the fact that what is also being secured is access to Indigenous land, through the "*transfer of* property" and the "*transformation into* property."[28] "Belonging" then is not simply an affective response or an iteration of substantive citizenship; rather, belonging is an assertion of state sovereign power, jurisdiction, and ownership in the context of ongoing settler colonial processes that target Indigenous people through occupation, dispossession, usurpation, and appropriation—of land, systems of law and governance, identity, and culture. These processes are territorial and material but also enduring and eliminatory: "[settler] colonialism destroys to replace."[29] This enduring temporality of settler colonialism fully undermines the mythologies associated with liberal temporalities of linear progress, given that settler colonialism, through its continual reassertion, rearticulation, and reinvigoration, is "both an historical *and* contemporary matrix of relations and conditions."[30]

Third, and considering the above, we can see how within the context of the white settler colonial state, citizenship as a mechanism of racialized securitization is a site of consolidation but also of *emplacement*. Settler colonial dispossession, usurpation, and appropriation constitute a kind of erasure that necessitates emplacement, meaning that how citizenship regulates is necessarily relational. Citizenship is both regulatory ***and*** pedagogical; it requires that we are positioned upon and against each other, and for the state's authority and jurisdiction to be consolidated, citizenship works to ensure that we participate in the state's desired (read: safe) relational logics. Teasing this out, capitalist, Orientalist, colonial, and imperialist projects shape how racialized citizens and non-citizens become subject(ed) to the institution of white supremacy and white settler citizenship.[31] The rewriting of the Canadian white settler colonial state as the liberal multicultural state scripts us as a nation of immigrants, where citizenship is a promise not a peril. Yet, Sunera Thobani describes the relational complexity here: "The category citizen, born from the genocidal violence of colonization, exists in a dialectical relation with its Other, the Indian, for whom *the emergence of this citizenship was deadly, not emancipatory*."[32] Inseparable from "the forced internal migrations of Aboriginal peoples onto reserves and the destruction of their communities as sovereign entities," the institution of Canadian citizenship bundles together settler colonialism, nation-building, economic development, settlement, white supremacy, and security.[33]

In the remainder of this chapter, I turn towards Canada's *ATA* 2015 and its amendment in 2015 through Bill-51. The intention here is to think through and expand on my framework of relational securitization to explore how, in the context of citizenship, the "state's focus on securing the border, on 'managing diversity', and on securing its governance over Indigenous People and their territories represent not simply ***different*** regulatory strategies for ***differently*** marginalized people; rather these relationships of governance are intrinsic to each other and to the regulatory apparatus of the white supremacist settler colonial state."[34] Here, in turning to the *ATA*, the intention is not to engage in an in-depth critical policy analysis but rather to hold the *ATA* as a provisional locus of analysis at a given moment in time and to think through this legislation as one site through which we can trace how "policies that infringe on Indigenous peoples' self-determination, the securitization of Canadian state borders, and imperialism abroad" are working together[35] as citizenship regulates through race, security, and dissent. This relational orientation that I am adopting is focused on the structured relationships between Indigenous and non-Indigenous racialized peoples, but also between citizens and non-citizens. Moreover, the relational orientation to my analysis focuses on the consolidation, constitution, and reconstitution of the state's legitimacy and authority as part of those scripts. In this, I want to both illustrate how the state is invested in "particular kinds of connections *and* disconnections" amongst and within citizens and non-citizens, and that through the mechanism of citizenship, this kind of regulation and securitization is happening in "profoundly reliant and relational ways."[36]

(Re)reading Anti-terrorism Legislation in Relational Contexts

The dominant understanding of national security or anti-terrorism legislation is that this legislation meant to support the policing and containment of those deemed outside the borders of a given political community. These persons or groups constitute a fundamental risk to "our" security, with "us" and "them" invoking moves towards bordering and the protection of those borders. The presumptions accompanying this conceptualizing of security often cast outwards in a focus on external threats; these threats may reside outside of domestic borders, or they may be brought into a domestic context by those whose claims to belonging are not authorized or legitimized through citizenship. But bordering and political normativity do not always neatly coincide with the actual borders of the state. The complexity here, of course, is that there is also a scripting of domestic terrorists as well. Whether focused internally or externally, the process of designating a subject or subjects as a "threat" to the state is not neutral and has been well documented as being profoundly racialized.

Harsha Walia's conception of "territorial diffusion" is particularly helpful in drawing our attention to a more complex rendering of the supposed binary of inside(r) citizen and outside(r) non-citizen.[37] Territorial diffusion is a border governance strategy that works through the "internalization and externalization of border enforcement."[38] The border is not just selectively porous but is mobile in that it can be enforced anywhere within the state. In this way, internal bordering differentiates between those who are deemed part of the political community and those who are not. This bordering happens discursively, but also materially, through actual government infrastructure, shared databases and enforcement mechanisms, agency collaboration, etc.[39] Moreover, bordering is enacted both vertically and horizontally. For example, the internalization of bordering has impacts within domestic communities, shaping how both formal and substantive citizenship are exercised.[40] On this, we have witnessed the distinct chilling impact of national security and anti-terrorism legislation within Muslim, Arab, and South Asian communities (citizens or not) after 9/11, in which communities experienced visceral day-to-day fear and regulation considering this dialectic of internal and external racialized surveillance. Or, as Robyn Maynard has so clearly demonstrated, the policing of Black lives occurs not only across child welfare systems, schools, border security, and systems of incarceration, rather these systems work together in deeply interrelated and reliant ways.[41] Territorial diffusion is also analytically helpful to think of horizontal ways in which regulation, policing, and surveillance through citizenship occur across groups, with these forms of regulation often working together. Here, we can see how differently racialized groups might be called into the work of co-surveillance and nation-consolidation in the white settler state.

Krista Johnston, for example, details how, historically, amendments to immigration and citizenship legislation have often occurred in close proximity to proposed changes to the *Indian Act*.[42] In the more contemporary post-2001 period, the *Immigration and Refugee Protection Act* (*IRPA*) 2001, the proposed *First Nations Governance Act* 2002, the omnibus Bill C-45, the *Jobs and Growth Act* 2012, the *Strengthening Canadian Citizenship Act* 2014, the *Zero Tolerance for Barbaric Cultural Practices Act* 2015, and Bill C-51, the *ATA* 2015 all coalesced to reinforce a preoccupation with fraud, terrorism, and criminality, but also more broadly with citizenship, surveillance, the curtailment of dissent, and the securitizing of the settler state.[43] Working together, these proposed and passed legislation attempted to "eliminate Indigenous sovereignty, maintain white settler dominance, and increasingly limit access to secure citizenship status, particularly for racialized migrants."[44]

Narrowing in on the 2015 amendments to the *Anti-Terrorism Act*, Bill C-51 made several radical amendments to existing legislation (e.g. *Criminal Code of Canada*, the *Canadian Security Intelligence Service Act*, the *Secure Air Travel Act*, and the *Security of Canada Information Sharing Act*) that are revelatory of the links between citizenship, race, security, and dissent. Amongst other changes, the legislation constituted a profound departure in authorizing that government institutions share information broadly and internally about activities "that undermine the security of Canada."[45] While exclusions were made for "advocacy, protest, dissent and artistic expression," nine activities including "terrorism" and "interference with critical infrastructure" were listed as those undermining the "sovereignty, security or territorial integrity of Canada or the lives or the security of the people of Canada."[46] Bill C-51 also amended the *Criminal Code* to enact a new terrorism offence of propagation crimes. This criminalized knowingly "[advocating] or [promoting] the commission of terrorism offences in general ... while knowing that any of those offences will be committed or being reckless as to whether any of those offences *may* be committed."[47] As opposed to the previous legislation, the speaker's intent in communicating did not matter, and communications made in private would also be subject to the Code. Related to this, Bill C-51 allowed for the preventative arrest and detention of a person by a peace officer who has "reasonable grounds" to believe that a "terrorist activity *may* be carried out"[48] or where the arrest is "*likely* to prevent the carrying out of the terrorist activity."[49] This lowered the *Criminal Code*'s threshold for preventative detention, as well as the evidentiary thresholds to obtain a terrorism peace bond.[50] In addition to radically authorizing a kinetic or active role for the Canadian Security Intelligence Service (CSIS), the legislation sanctioned CSIS to seek special authorization, in *secret* warrant proceedings, to engage in *secret* disruption tactics even if these tactics violate the *Canadian Charter of Rights and Freedoms* or other Canadian laws. Finally, the legislation amended the *IRPA*, reversing the onus of the Minister to provide all evidence to a special advocate, and instead authorized the government to withhold information in cases where individuals are detained on security certificates.[51] This was in direct contravention to the spirit of Supreme Court rulings that had mandated the implementation of a special advocate role.[52]

Security operates in at least two dominant and interrelated ways: as a political strategy and as a technology of subjectivity. As strategy, governing through security necessitates the active production of and insistence on insecurity or the existential threat.[53] Related to this, in a white settler colonial context, state security does not refer to an objective reality; rather, it is an ongoing strategy that actively represents particular categories of people, engagement, and political assertions as threats.[54] From the outset, the *ATA* was premised on the following definition:

> 'Activity that undermines the security of Canada' means any activity, including any of the following activities, if it *undermines the sovereignty, security or territorial integrity* of Canada or the lives or the security of the people of Canada: (a) interference with the capability of the Government of Canada in relation to intelligence, defence, border operations, public safety,

the administration of justice, diplomatic or consular relations, or the economic or financial stability of Canada.[55]

While the amendments in Bill C-51 were framed as "targeting Islamic militants,"[56] the breadth of this framing invites a pause given that "Indigenous sovereignty remains an Achilles heel" for the white settler colonial state.[57] Guided by a logic of elimination, Indigenous presence alone constitutes a threat to the mythology of the liberal multicultural state whose "sovereignty, security or territorial integrity" are taken as a given. Moreover, operating in multiscalar ways, security is also inseparable from the notion of protection and the white possessive logic of private property—here, protection from Indigenous people "rises as a historical spectre of white citizens protecting their white kin from Indigenous threat."[58]

The threat of presence is different than the threat posed by non-Indigenous people of colour, hence invites a different kind of regulation through citizenship. The liberal multicultural state *needs* those settlers in service of its assertion of sovereignty and ongoing capitalist economic exploitation. Moreover, racialized immigrant communities can be differentially pulled into desiring the promise of citizenship in the settler colonial state, even as they are excluded from shaping (or claiming) the national imaginary. For example, writing on the tar sands industry in Alberta, Canada, Nishant Upadhyay describes how dominant caste Indian migrants working in this industry get pulled into and participate in white settler colonial logics as "model minorities," wherein non-Indigenous labour "serves to reproduce the settler state while simultaneously rendering Indigenous labor as nonlabor."[59] The desire for a citizenship that is bound up in the terms of the white settler colonial state can transform "potential allies to Indigenous struggles into accomplices of the settler state."[60] This gets enacted through both a kind of "regulated inclusion" and a "relational othering."[61] To be clear, however, beyond complicity and implication, border regulation as a site of securitization, even if territorially diffuse in its internal working through citizenship, also involves explicit forms of violent *exclusion*, containment, and incarceration. This is, however, different than the kind of securitization directed towards Indigenous peoples in its focus on *erasure/elimination*, containment, and incarceration. These overlapping yet distinct strategies are intrinsic to the regulatory apparatus of the white settler colonial state, given its continuing preoccupation with Indigenous mobility and sovereignty.[62] In this sense, the positioning of racialized, non-Indigenous people vis-à-vis Indigenous people is specifically relational *as a strategy of the state*.[63]

This manifests in material ways. While the "public" face of terrorism has been scripted onto the bodies of Brown and Black people, the infrastructure of the national security state has been (and has arguably always been) turned inwards as well. For example, the Integrated Terrorism Assessment Centre (ITAC) is described as the "independent, expert federal body responsible for assessing terrorism threats to Canada."[64] Beyond "[examining] the terrorism threat environment, relying on information and intelligence from Canadian and international security partners," the ITAC "provides *objective*, expert recommendations about the threat level."[65] Notably, while the ITAC falls within the provisions and authorities of the *CSIS Act*, the ITAC has been structured in such a way "to facilitate the exchange of knowledge, experience, and contacts within the Canadian national security sector."[66] In that sense, the ITAC was intentionally meant to be staffed almost exclusively by staff seconded from other partner agencies, for example the Royal Canadian Mounted Police (RCMP), Canada Border Services Agency, National Defence, and Transport Canada.[67] In 2007, Indian and Northern Affairs Canada (INAC) established a series of weekly reports or a Hot Spot Reporting System, meant to identify "the First Nations leaders, participants and outside supporters of First Nations occupations and protests and to closely monitor their actions."[68] Russel Diabo and Shiri Pasternak describe these INAC briefings and the close relationship between INAC and the RCMP as "almost indistinguishable from a presentation one would expect to see from security forces, rather than from a government ministry."[69]

The overlapping mechanisms of surveillance that are all linked through ITAC are dizzying, with the RCMP's Suspicious Incident Report Platform mandated to protect Canada's critical infrastructure, their Integrated Security Unit mandated to gather and distribute intelligence involving Indigenous peoples, and the creation of Integrated National Security Enforcement Teams to protect natural resource extraction infrastructure.[70] Focusing on "multi-issue extremism" threats, the internalization and externalization of security and surveillance mechanisms turns towards external security threats, Indigenous peoples, activists groups, environmentalists, and those refusing and protesting government policy.[71] Consider that during the 2007 National Day of Action for the Idle No More movement, staff from INAC were seconded to ITAC "to facilitate the exchange of information and to 'enhance [its] analytic capacity' in producing threat assessments on 'aboriginal protests'."[72] This continued a well-established historical and ongoing practice wherein intelligence information has been shared between INAC, law enforcement, and security intelligence agencies.[73]

Shiri Pasternak and Tia Dafnos write about the securitization of critical infrastructure, in which the threat that Indigenous people pose by asserting jurisdiction and sovereignty is a threat to commodity flows.[74] Here, capital specifically relies on the elimination of Indigenous people, a dynamic we see time and again in moments emblazoned in our public consciousness: the Kanehsatà:ke Resistance, the raid at Elsipogtog, the slow warfare against the Algonquins of Barriere Lake, the Lubicon Cree struggle against tar sands development in Alberta, the murder of Dudley George in Ipperwash, the Gustafsen Lake Standoff, the resistance of the Mi'kmaq at Burnt Church, Six Nations land defenders in Caledonia, and the Unist'ot'en Camp, to offer just an abbreviated list. Moreover, capital simultaneously relies on the maintenance of selective flows of precarious short-term racialized labour, which again is wrapped into transnational projects of political and capitalist imperialism which are themselves framed as implicating security.[75] If then, liberalism, settler colonialism, security, and capitalism are so fundamentally connected, at the same time that race, security, and dissidence are fundamental to how citizenship regulates, these relationships become even more tightly "knotted." The risk becomes what happens to the knot if the wrong thread is pulled.

(Re)reading Citizen Subjects: From Political Subject to Threat

Within these broader contexts, a (re)reading of citizenship through the framework of relational securitization illuminates how the classification of political subjects occurs according to a racial continuum of white normativity, "where conduct associated with the white liberal norm is rewarded, and conduct associated with indigeneity is viewed as a mark of abnormality, uncertainty, and dangerousness."[76] Part of the work being done through racialization is to delineate relationships of power, to signify difference, and to enable the sorting of non/citizen subjects into categories of worthiness ("good") and unworthiness ("bad").[77] Consider, for example, Orientalist and gendered discourses of secularism that are often bound up in notions of security: they are uncivilized, "we" are civilized;

they are irrational, "we" are rational; they must be saved, "we" can save them. The key here is that these qualities, which rely on their opposition, are constructed as inherent. When this kind of race thinking is taken up by the bureaucracy, "it is systematized and attached to a project of accumulation, it loses its standing as a prejudice and becomes instead an organizing principle."[78] This organizing principle doubles as an intense justificatory strategy, such that "[suspensions] of rights [appear] not as a violence but as the law itself."[79]

Worthiness/unworthiness, and other associated binaries, are also read into the classification accompanying the surveillance of Indigenous people. Keith Smith writes that the surveillance of Indigenous people in the Canadian west did not produce "simple innocent reflections of Indigenous reality."[80] What emerged instead were a series of contradictory images that were consistently inferior to white Anglo-Canadians, functioning to bolster the image of the colonizer as "benevolently superior."[81] Rita Dhamoon and Yasmeen Abu-Laban further remark upon this process, explaining how Indigenous people have been marked "as barbarians who posed a militant threat to national identity (territorially and colonially defined), economic development (defined as property), and civilization (culturally and racially defined)."[82]

The production of these dissident subjectivities are consequential in their service to advancing the material interests of the white settler state.[83] For example, in the decades following confederation, the monitoring, tracking, and information gathering done by the Department of Indian Affairs were meant to "provide a portrait of the progress of colonial rule."[84] In a more contemporary context, Andrew Crosby and Jeffrey Monaghan trace how historical forms of racialized surveillance continued at full pace via the Aboriginal Affairs and Northern Development Canada, Public Safety's Government Operations Centre, the RCMP, and the Department of National Defence, and CSIS in their policing of the Idle No More movement.[85] During just the two-year period (2014–2015) surrounding the passing of Bill C-51, the RCMP monitored and tracked 313 Indigenous activists.[86] Consider, for example, the following deeply racialized characterization of Idle No More in correspondence between RCMP Corporal Wayne Russett, the Aboriginal liaison for the national capital region to Inspector Mike LeSage, the acting director general for National Aboriginal Policing:

> This Idle No More Movement is like bacteria, it has grown a life of its own all across this nation. It may be advisable for all to have contingency plans in place, as this is one issue that is not going to go away...There is a high probability that we could see flash mobs, round dances and blockades become much less complaint to laws in an attempt to get their point across. The escalation of violence is ever near.[87]

As noted before, there is longevity here as we consider the increasing militarization of state responses to the policing of Indigenous nations and communities, a longevity of the racialized and racist deployment of state power that goes some way towards explaining why some subjects can be treated with dehumanizing impunity by the state. In addition, we can see how in a settler colonial racial state, some forms of conduct are deemed not just incompatible with the values and imperatives of white settler society but are so fundamentally challenging that they become cast (out) as essential and ongoing threats.

In this final section, I want to explore how these binaries reconfigure the political subjectivity made available to particular non/citizens. A key strategy in that reconfiguration is the way in which non-normative political subjects are moved out of the realm of the "political" and into the realm of "security." This securitization is meaningful because when security is "deployed," it deactivates political issues into security ones, thereby removing them from the realm of political contestation.[88] National security forecloses political debate and contestation, it justifies increasing investment in a surveillance infrastructure, it exempts the state from having to explain or legitimize itself to the public, and it provides a vocabulary that shuts down further examination. This depoliticizing gesture matters especially when the targets of security practices are regularly people of colour and Indigenous people.[89] In this section, I describe three interrelated and relational ways in which this happens: rightlessness, the exception and law; hyperpoliticization; and visibility.

Rightlessness, the Exception and Law

As mentioned previously, with the *ATA*, new powers were granted to CSIS to allow for the withholding of evidence in cases where suspects are held on security certificates. In brief, security certificates are exceptional removal orders that can be issued to clear the way for non-citizens to be deported from Canada if they are deemed to threaten the state's national security.[90] Through these certificates, non-citizens, who have overwhelmingly been racialized men originally from countries in Southwest Asia or North Africa, can be detained, held without charges, and are denied the capacity to make full answer and defence.[91] This makes the security certificate process function as a normalized exception,[92] in which those named in a certificate ultimately exist in a state of rightlessness.[93] While many of the men subject to these detention orders have practised extraordinary refusal and resistance under untenable circumstances, to the state, they are effectively treated as without legal or political subjectivity. Put differently, they have been securitized out of the political realm. The security certificate regime reinforced and legislated through the *ATA* is not simply a story about non-citizens, detention, and deportation, but it inextricably linked to the governance of citizens and non-citizens through security and race, borders, and arguably belonging.

Law functions centrally in this process. Historically, the state's position has been to deny non-citizens involved in immigration proceedings the legal protections afforded to defendants in the criminal justice system. This has been done either by adopting a stance where immigration is framed as a privilege and not a right, or by characterizing deportation and removal as qualitatively different from criminal punishment.[94] This strategy of rendering exceptional is not unfamiliar in a white settler colonial state that regularly characterizes nation-to-nation agreements as "special treatment" or "entitlements" in which the assertion of any negotiated treaty *always* borders on the risk of being too threatening or too risky to state sovereignty. Moreover, the legal questions surrounding land, land claims, accountabilities to treaty, and Indigenous land-based direct action that occurs outside the legal system are regularly securitized; as opposed to being understood as political questions, they are moved to the realm of security given that they so profoundly challenge the basis of settler state jurisdiction and sovereignty.[95] The space of legal exception evident in legislation like the *Indian Act* has and continues to authorize a range of dehumanizing treatment that consolidates and secures the state, as it works to undermine the political status of Indigenous peoples.

Returning to the *ATA* and its bolstering of the security certificate regime, through the law, deportation is somehow *not* seen as an intrinsic deprivation of liberty that is about the security of the person.[96] For non-citizens who are faced with deportation or indefinite detention, this premise is clearly flawed and reflects how those named in certificates are positioned in the first order as threats, *not* as rights bearers; the subject position available to them cannot sustain both dimensions.[97] Commenting on rightlessness in this context, Temitope Oriola writes that “the right to know the case against you, to have a fair hearing in order to defend yourself, the right of the dignity of the human person” are inalienable human rights and are not tethered to state-based citizenship.[98] Yet, in these cases, there is also an absolute loss of protection by any government or any state; this lack of legal subjectivity can lead to an inability to claim or inhabit the legality of international treaties and agreements which are ultimately a function of sovereign states. The loss of home, the loss of state protection, the loss of legal subjectivity, or the loss of belonging to any community—they are not simply “not equal before the law, but no law exists for them.”[99] This means that those named in security certificates become very real exceptions in this zone of ambiguity between human rights and citizenship rights.

One *could* say that this violence and rightlessness becomes possible because security certificate detainees are non-citizens. But, if centred within the context of the white settler colonial state, this becomes tenuous given that we know that the state has and continues to authorize itself to carry out a range of oppressive actions against Indigenous people and people of colour precisely through citizenship and the law. Dafnos describes how law is a central means by which the settler colonial state engages in pacification.[100] Legal strategies “[fabricate] settler colonial order,” which includes “the expropriation of land and resources, the displacement and confinement of Indigenous peoples, the criminalization of means of subsistence outside of waged labour, and assimilationist mechanisms such as residential schools and outlawing of cultural practices.”[101] A range of policing techniques are deployed against Indigenous people, in order to protect private property, to protect the class structure, to protect conceptions of settler morality, to protect the settler oversight of mobility, and to protect the capitalist labour market.[102] Here, then, the bordering of citizenship and specifically the policing of Indigenous peoples are also diffuse as we see the ways in which non-Indigenous people are pulled into policing and criminalizing Indigenous peoples, particularly when they are on white property. The recent murder of Colten Boushie by Gerald Stanley demonstrates this vividly but also raises a fundamental question about why white settler terror is rarely if ever the target of the state.[103] In this way, Dafnos’ adoption of the term lawfare overlaps with counter-law, illustrating the “simultaneously destructive and constitutive power of law in settler-colonialism" when it comes to regimes of citizenship and security.[104]

Pulling together these threads is not meant to collapse our conceptualizations of the state's regulation of Indigenous people and racialized non/citizens, even though the state itself has reframed Indigenous political protesters or land defenders as "insurgents on par with Islamic terrorists or as economic and environmental criminals standing in the way of progress."[105] Rather, the intention here is to illuminate a linkage wherein we can see and consider an overlapping strategy of regulation and containment within the white settler colonial state. It is not simply "security" that functions to depoliticize and delegitimize, but law itself. These spaces of exception in which citizenship is turned in on itself are not absent of law, but rather replete with the law; this is because law legitimizes sovereign and executive prerogative. The state is making and remaking its own sovereignty not just through the bodies of non-citizens who are detained as threats but by asserting their authority and jurisdiction to define subjects as threats. *This* is an exercise of state sovereignty that is intimately and relationally bound up in the state's refusal of Indigenous sovereignty. This constitutes "an ongoing settler colonial terror structure."[106]

Hyperpoliticization

Despite being denied political subjectivity, the "birthing" of a subject as a "terrorist" or "extremist" is a deeply political exercise that also serves to hyperpoliticize. Take for example the status of refugees. One of the critiques of the *ATA* was regarding its overbroad and unconstitutionally vague definition of national security. Amongst academics, there is widespread consensus that terrorism is in fact an elastic concept that is variable depending on socio-political context. Despite the stripping of political status from security certificate detainees, definitions of terrorism, particularly amongst refugee communities, are a live political issue given that many refugees are persecuted precisely for political reasons, and many refugees are engaged in support for oppositional politics or movements in their home countries.[107] In this labelling as threat, refugees get (re)coded through Canadian law, which changes "its conception of refugees from victims and survivors, to terrorists, a recoding where political activism that is in theory lawful for citizens, becomes the basis for expelling non-citizens."[108] In this sense, security certificate detainees, particularly those who are racialized, Arab and/or Muslim, and with a background as convention refugees, can be said to be exceptionally at risk in that their political context and past political affiliations and lives position them as potentially inadmissible to Canada given their potentiality as threat.[109]

With that said, while public narratives of national security tend to focus on the racialized figure of the "Muslim terrorist" and the potential ***inherent*** risk they pose, historically the white settler colonial state has ***always*** turned inwards to identify Indigenous people as threats. For example, surveillance was key to eliminating Indigenous opposition to settler colonial expansion in the North-West, with surveillance being necessary "for identifying indigenous peoples and sorting them based on their adoption of, or resistance to, practices of European liberalism imposed by the Canadian settler state."[110] Or, while the government publicly rationalized the *ATA* in terms of a "relatively new manifestation of an existing terrorism security threat; namely domestic radicalization and the growing reality of terrorist action taken within Western societies."[111] The actual context of the legislation was one in which the government had already released an anti-terrorism strategy focused on foreign threats and "domestic extremism" that was "based on grievances—real or perceived—revolving around the promotion of various causes such as animal rights, white supremacy, environmentalism and anti-capitalism."[112] The "irony" is not lost that in the context of the white settler colonial state, Indigenous challenges to capitalist exploitation and to the settler state's continual assertions of its sovereignty are equated with white supremacy. In an open letter in 2012, then Minister of Natural Resources, Joe Oliver, would describe "environmental and other radical groups" as threatening to "hijack our regulatory system to achieve their radical ideological agenda."[113] And, as we would come to find out after the passage of the *ATA*, the context of the *ATA* was one of extreme and extensive surveillance and policing of the Idle No More movement in light of its commitments to "honour Indigenous sovereignty, and to protect the land and water."[114]

This surveillance extended far beyond Idle No More, intensifying after the election of Stephen Harper in 2006 when INAC received a directive to spy on Indigenous communities.[115] With this, the surveillance apparatus monitoring Indigenous people would continue to grow, with INAC establishing a "Hotspot Reporting System" noted earlier in this chapter and a "Standard Information Sharing Forum," chaired by the RCMP and involving several government departments (e.g. INAC, CSIS, Fisheries and Oceans, Natural Resources, Transport Canada).[116] The RCMP formed the "Aboriginal Joint Intelligence Group" (JIB) to investigate lawful protest engaged in by Indigenous groups, and despite an Access to Information request showing otherwise, CSIS denied spying on Idle No More, given that under pre-*ATA* legislation, it would be illegal to spy on civilians without specific justification.[117]

While Sherene Razack describes the dynamics informing post-9/11 racialized surveillance as a "casting out" or an expulsion from political community, this does not fully capture the state's pacification process and its "ongoing war" against resistance by Indigenous people.[118] While in the context of settler colonial governmentality the decolonial politics of asserting Indigenous sovereignty are treated as "criminal" and "abnormal,"[119] pacification "has a historical-materialist basis in imperialism and colonialism whereby imperial powers attempts to transform societies in ways that facilitate the territorial expansion necessary to the accumulation of capital."[120] As Dafnos notes, settler colonial state "colludes with capital in a multitude of ways; land-centered, it requires private companies and public agencies to work together to secure access to land and resource which strategically managing the 'Indian problem'."[121] In this sense, the "vigilant gaze" of colonial surveillance is quite narrowly fixed on its target.[122] Indigenous people who insist on treaty provisions and defend Indigenous lands are "deviant" and threats to "prosperity through liberalism."[123] This suggests *perhaps* that for people of colour, the "vigilant gaze" of the white settler colonial state is watchful for what these subjects can do for the state's settler and imperialist imperatives. For Indigenous people, the gaze is activated merely by presence.

(In)visibility

This raises important considerations with respect to visibility and surveillance through citizenship in a white settler colonial context. Certainly, when thinking about the *ATA* broadly, especially with respect to the breadth of its amendments, we know that anti-terrorism or counter-terrorism policies do not have a uniform effect on individuals or groups. As political subjects we are not positioned equally before the law. Non-citizens, persons with dual citizenships from certain states, Muslims, Arabs, those perceived to be Muslim and/or Arab, Brown and Black people of colour, caste-oppressed persons, and racialized men are all individuals and group who are disproportionately impacted by increased surveillance, preventative detention, indefinite detention, and things like extraordinary rendition.[124] As Razack has described with specific reference to security certificate detainees in the post 9/11 period, these men are not simply the victims of racial profiling, "their Arab origins, and the life history that mostly Arab Muslim men have had, operate to mark them as individuals likely to commit terrorist acts, people whose propensity for violence is indicated by their origins."[125] They are characterized as "Islamic terrorists" that are governed by religion not rationality.[126] The inference is clear—these men are marked by an *inherent* capacity for violence. [127] Race becomes crucial to this pre-emptive punishment and the possibility for indefinite detention.[128]

Mike Larsen explains how the "Labeled Individual" and the "Potential Threat" "experience the effects of 'security threat' claimsmaking in different but related ways."[129] Where some individuals may be not be aware they are the focus of long-term surveillance, others experience the consequences of being designated as a security threat immediately, with the intensity varying depending on whether individuals are aware of their status, whether members of their community are aware, whether the public and the media are aware, and so forth.[130] Individuals may be subject to increased surveillance, increased scrutiny, electronic surveillance, and wiretapping, all of which curtails their capacity to be employed or make and maintain connections with family, friends, colleagues, community organizations, and businesses.[131]

Yet, again signalling this dialectical relationship, the infrastructure developed to monitor and track external security threats has historically been turned inwards but arguably also outwards. Monaghan explains how the securitization in the white settler colonial state is premise on the need to "know" Indigenous peoples and their territories.[132] This has meant that surveillance has a long history when it comes to Indigenous peoples, manifest through status cards, the pass system to leave the reserve, and numbered identification for Inuit people.[133] This need to "know" is accompanied by identification, categorization, and enumeration, with reserves having been a primary tool of surveillance allowing for a broad network of state agents to keep track of, systemically report in, and create a body of knowledge "about Indigenous peoples, their use of land and resources, the way they provided for themselves and their families, their way of life, and a myriad of less significant details."[134] Craig Proulx continues that between 1877 and 1927, a well-developed machinery of surveillance targeting Indigenous people meant that Indigenous people were distinctive in terms of the level surveillance and the length of time that they were surveilled.[135] As Matthew Banninga notes with respect to the attempted pacification of Idle No More, the national security apparatus of the white settler state is dynamic, engaging "nation-wide surveillance program and providing integrated security intelligence to law enforcement management, and national security agencies, other government departments and agencies not usually associated with policing, as well as private sector 'stakeholders'."[136] The "interference with critical infrastructure" provisions of the *ATA* ultimately authorized even broader parameters of surveillance, monitoring and data gathering on Indigenous peoples both on and off reserves.

While not fully resolvable within the context of this chapter, the point here is to at least note that this raises different implications of surveillance and visibility for people of colour than for Indigenous people. Leanne Simpson, for example, speaks about colonialism's logic of elimination and the "fear of disappearance—a basic, terrifying, omnipresent reality of being Indigenous and particularly of being an Indigenous woman or queer person and occupied by Canada."[137] Dafnos adds to this complexity, by noting that within liberal democratic society, the repertoire of political engagement includes the electoral process, the enforcement of the rule of law and rights through judicial procedures, but also "participating in acts of political dissent in public spaces."[138] As Dafnos notes, this is because public dissent brings Indigenous people into contact with institutions of law enforcement and policing.[139] In this way, to be counted and tracked by the colonial state, in fact to be "recognized" by the colonial state, carries distinctive and substantive risks for Indigenous people.

Conclusion

In 2016, I defended a dissertation about citizenship as a regulatory strategy of the Canadian racial state. In my final case study, I wrote about security certificates, a chapter in which the word "Indigenous" appears once and "settler colonial" appears twice. As I reflect on this, I "cringe" because of what this signals to me in terms of my erasures, complicities, and avoidances. Echoing Ghaida Moussa's words, this chapter emerges from *my* positionality, in which I am actively rethinking "dynamics beyond me/whiteness, Indigenous peoples/whiteness, all the while still being aware of the settler-colonial white-supremacist context in which I live."[140] Like Moussa, I am also still "very much wrapped in the complexity of this shift."[141]

In some ways, the goal of this chapter has been purposefully constrained. I have focused on illustrating that the positioning of racialized settlers vis-à-vis Indigenous is specifically relational as a strategy of the state and that the securitization of dissidence and resistance is key to this. Here, as opposed to doing a critical policy analysis, I wanted to reflect on a set of issues that emerge from this iteration of the *ATA*, a piece of legislation that is often seen as outside of the bounds of multicultural citizenship theory. In doing so, I wanted to purposefully blur the lines of how we think about citizenship, race, and security. Our analyses can shift profoundly depending on the kind of state we contextualize citizenship within. As a political strategy and technology of racialized subjectivity, white supremacist settler governmentality *needs* immigrants of colour and racialized labourers in service of the liberal multicultural state's assertion of sovereignty and in service of ongoing capitalist economic exploitation. Through the securitization of resistance, rightlessness, hyperpoliticization, and (in)visibility all adhere to racialized settlers and Indigenous people in distinct but profoundly reliant ways.

At the outset of this chapter, I posed a question about what is being asked of us when we are invited or expected to invest our hopes in the status accompanying citizenship? To this, I want to pose another series of questions to demonstrate where the framework of relational securitization might take us as we think of the complexities of citizenship in a contemporary political moment. Whose struggles speak through citizenship and whose do not? How do we sustain an analysis of how racialized persons are regulated through borders and citizenship, while still holding at the forefront of our minds that the state that is being bordered is the white supremacist settler colonial state? What do we do with citizens and non-citizens (and those who cast-off this label entirely) who reject not just the terms of inclusion but inclusion itself? What happens to our analyses and our sense of repertoires of resistance when we frame a range of political contestation as dissidence? Most critically, what holds emancipatory promise for both racialized settlers and Indigenous people, and what functions as a tool of legitimation that reinscribes the oppression of the white settler colonial state?

Notes

1. Statement by the Prime Minister on the 75th anniversary of Canadian citizenship, 1 January 2022, Ottawa, Ontario. Available: https://pm.gc.ca/en/news/statements/2022/01/01/statement-prime-minister-75th-anniversary-canadian-citizenship.
2. Janine Brodie, "Citizenship and Solidarity: Reflections on the Canadian Way," *Citizenship Studies* 6, 4 (2002): 379.
3. Giovanna Procacci, "Governmentality and Citizenship," in *The Blackwell Companion to Political Sociology*, eds. Kate Nash Alan Scott (Blackwell Publishing, 2004), Blackwell Reference Online.
4. Given that these identity-based categories are limiting in that they mask power differentials within and across these groups, the language I am using here is provisional, while the frameworks I am deploying make space for more intentional and nuanced thinking through these intersecting relationalities.
5. Trevor Purvis and Alan Hunt, "Identity versus Citizenship: Transformations in the Discourses and Practices of Citizenship," *Social and Legal Studies* 8, 4 (1999): 458.
6. *Ibid.*
7. Nisha Nath, "Far from belonging: Race, Security, Dissent and the Canadian Citizenship Story after 9/11," Ph.D. Thesis, University of Alberta, 2016, 37.
8. Rita Dhamoon, "Exclusion and Regulated Inclusion: The Case of the Sikh Kirpan in Canada," *Sikh Formations* 9, 1 (2013): 11.
9. Mitchell Dean, *Governmentality: Power and Rule in Modern Society* (London: Sage Publications, 1999).
10. *Ibid.*, 30.
11. *Ibid.*, 31.
12. *Ibid.*, 31–32.
13. *Ibid.*, 32.
14. David Theo Goldberg, *The Racial State* (Oxford: Blackwell Publishing), 2.
15. *Ibid.*, 98.
16. *Ibid.*, 2.
17. *Ibid.*, 4.
18. *Ibid.*, 34.
19. *Ibid.*, 106.
20. Rita Dhamoon, "Security Warning: Multiculturalism Alert!," in *Ashgate Research Companion to Multiculturalism*, ed. Duncan Ivison (Surrey, UK: Ashgate, 2010).
21. *Ibid.*, 256–257.
22. *Ibid.*, 256.

23. *Ibid.*, 265.
24. *Ibid.*, 273.
25. Nath, *Far from Belonging*, 42.
26. Rita Dhamoon and Yasmeen Abu-Laban, "Dangerous (Internal) Foreigners and Nation-Building: The Case of Canada," *International Political Science Review* 30, 2 (2009): 168.
27. B. J. Muller, "(Dis)qualified Bodies: Securitization, citizenship and 'identity management'," *Citizenship Studies* 8, 3 (2004): 281.
28. Robert Nichols, *Theft is Property!: Dispossession and critical theory* (Durham, NC: Duke University Press, 2018), 14—emphasis in original.
29. Patrick Wolfe, "Settler Colonialism and the Elimination of the Native," *Journal of genocide research* 8, 4 (2006): 387.
30. Eve Tuck and Rubén Gaztambide-Fernández, "Curriculum, replacement, and settler futurity," *Journal of curriculum theorizing* 29, 1 (2013): 74.
31. Sunera Thobani, *Exalted Subjects: Studies in the Making of Race and Nation in Canada* (Toronto: University of Toronto Press, 2007), 71–74.
32. *Ibid.*, 74—emphasis added.
33. *Ibid.*, 74.
34. Nisha Nath, "Curated hostilities and the story of Abdoul Abdi: relational securitization in the settler colonial racial state," *Citizenship Studies* 25, 2 (2021): 293.
35. Shaista Patel, Ghaida Moussa, and Nishant Upadhyay, "Complicities, Connections, and Struggles: Critical Transnational Feminist Analysis of Settler Colonialism," *Feral Feminisms* 4 (2015): 15.
36. Nath, "Curated hostilities," 294.
37. Harsha Walia, *Border and rule: Global migration, capitalism, and the rise of racist nationalism* (Chicago: Haymarket Books, 2022).
38. *Ibid.*, 102.
39. *Ibid.*, 102; Nath, "Curated Hostilities," 299.
40. Nath, *Far from Belonging*, 29–30.
41. Robyn Maynard, *Policing Black lives: state violence in Canada from slavery to present* (Halifax; Winnipeg: Fernwood Publishing, 2017).
42. Krista Johnston, "Unsettling Citizenship: Movements for Indigenous Sovereignty and Migrant Justice in a Settler City," Ph.D. Thesis, York University, 2015, 150; Nath, "Curated hostilities."
43. Johnston, "*Unsettling Citizenship*," 140–141.
44. *Ibid.*, 141.
45. *Anti-Terrorism Act (ATA)*, s. 2.
46. *Ibid.*
47. *ATA*, s. 83.221(1)—emphasis added.
48. *ATA*, s. 17(1)a—emphasis added.

49. *ATA*, s. 17(1)b—emphasis added.
50. Voices-voix, "Bill C-51: Anti-Terrorism Act, 2015." Available: http://voices-voix.ca/en/facts/profile/bill-c-51-anti-terrorism-act-2015 [Accessed 3 May 2018].
51. Canadian Bar Association, "Bill C-51, *Anti-terrorism Act*, 2015," 5 October 2016. Available: https://www.cba.org/CMSPages/GetFile.aspx?guid=94bd7a6e-87c2-4143-a288-e780504d2f51 [Accessed 5 April 2023].
52. Nath, "*Far from Belonging*," 457.
53. Daiva Stasiulis and Darryl Ross, "Security, Flexible Sovereignty, and the Perils of Multiple Citizenship," *Citizenship Studies* 10, 3 (2006): 337.
54. Muller, "(Dis)qualified bodies," 281; Stasiulis and Ross, "Security," 336.
55. *ATA*, s. 2.
56. Andrew Crosby and Jeffrey Monaghan, *Policing Indigenous Movements: Dissent and the Security State* (Halifax: Fernwood Publishing, 2018), 290.
57. *Ibid.*, 193.
58. Erin Morton, "White settler death drives: settler statecraft, white possession, and multiple colonialisms under Treaty 6," *Cultural Studies* 33, 3 (2019): 444.
59. Nishant Upadhyay, "Making of 'Model' South Asians on the Tar Sands: Intersections of Race, Caste, and Indigeneity," *Critical Ethnic Studies* 5, 1–2 (2019): 155.
60. *Ibid.*, 155.
61. Dhamoon, "Exclusion"; Rita Dhamoon, "Relational Othering: Critiquing dominance, critiquing the margins," *Politics, Groups, and Identities* 9, 5 (2021).
62. Nath, "Curated hostilities," 297; A. Smith, "Foreword," in *Undoing Border Imperialism* by Harsha Walia (Oakland: AK Press/Institute for Anarchist Studies, 2014), x–xi.
63. Nath, "Curated hostilities," 297–298.
64. Public Safety Canada, "2016 Public Report on the Terrorist Threat to Canada: Building a Safe and Resilient Canada," (Her Majesty the Queen in Right of Canada, 2016), 9.
65. *Ibid.*, 9—emphasis added.
66. Stephanie Carvin, "The Integrated Terrorism Assessment Centre (ITAC)," in *Top Secret Canada*, eds. Stephanie Carvin, Thomas Juneau, and Craig Forcese (Toronto: University of Toronto Press, 2021), 96.
67. *Ibid.*; Tia Dafnos, "Pacification and Indigenous Struggles in Canada," *Socialist Studies* 9, 2 (2013): 67.
68. Russel Diabo and Shiri Pasternak, "First Nations Under Surveillance: Harper Government Prepares for Unrest," *Media Co-op*, 7 June 2011. Available: https://mediacoop.ca/story/first-nations-under-

surveillance/7434 [Accessed 5 April 2023].; Craig Proulx, "Colonizing surveillance: Canada constructs and Indigenous terror threat," *Anthropologica* 56, 1 (2014): 89.
69. Diabo and Pasternak, "First Nations."
70. Proulx, "Colonizing surveillance," 89; Jen Preston, "Neoliberal settler colonialism, Canada and the tar sands," *Race & Class* 55, 2 (2017): 44.
71. Proulx, "Colonizing surveillance," 89.
72. Dafnos, "Pacification," 67.
73. *Ibid.*, 67.
74. Shiri Pasternak and Tia Dafnos, "How does a settler state secure the circuitry of capital?" *Environment and Planning D: Society and Space* 36, 4 (2017): 739.
75. Jen Preston, "Racial extractivism and white settler colonialism: An examination of the Canadian Tar Sands mega-projects," *Cultural Studies* 31, 2–3 (2017): 353–75.
76. Jeffrey Monaghan, "Settler Governmentality and Racializing Surveillance in Canada's North-West," *Canadian Journal of Sociology* 38, 4 (2013): 489.
77. *Ibid.*, 488.
78. Sherene Razack, *Casting Out: The Eviction of Muslims from Western Law and Politics* (Toronto: University of Toronto Press, 2008), 9.
79. *Ibid.*, 9.
80. Keith D. Smith, *Liberalism, Surveillance and Resistance: Indigenous Communities in Western Canada, 1877–1927* (Edmonton, AU Press, 2009), 20.
81. *Ibid.*, 20.
82. Dhamoon and Abu-Laban, "Dangerous," 177.
83. Smith, *Liberalism*, 20.
84. *Ibid.*, 16–17.
85. Andrew Crosby and Jeffrey Monaghan, "Settler colonialism and the Policing of Idle No More," *Social Justice* 43, 2 (2016).
86. Voices-voix, "Criminalization of Indigenous Communities," 1 August 2017. Available: http://voices-voix.ca/en/facts/profile/criminalization-indigenous-communities [Accessed 3 May 2018].
87. As cited in Crosby and Monaghan, "Settler colonialism," 49.
88. Stasiulis and Ross, "Security," 335.
89. *Ibid.*
90. Nath, "*Far from belonging*," 398.
91. *Ibid.*, 405.
92. Mike Larsen and Justin Piché, "Exceptional State, Pragmatic Bureaucracy, and Indefinite Detention: The Case of the Kingston Immigration Holding Centre," *Canadian Journal of Law and Society* 24, 2 (2009):

208; Colleen Bell, "Surveillance Strategies and Populations at Risk: Biopolitical Governance in Canada's National Security Policy," *Security Dialogue* 37, 2 (2006): 147–65; Rob Aitken, "Notes on the Canadian exception: security certificates in critical context," *Citizenship Studies* 12, 4 (2008): 381–96.

93. Christiane Wilke and Paula Willis, "The Exploitation of vulnerability: Dimensions of Citizenship and Rightlessness in Canada's Security Certificate Legislation," *Windsor Yearbook of Access to Justice* 26, 1 (2008): 25–51.
94. Nath, "*Far from belonging*," 428.
95. Proulx, "Colonizing surveillance," 87.
96. Nath, "*Far from Belonging*," 428.
97. *Ibid.*, 25.
98. Temitope Oriola, "Counter-terrorism and alien justice: the case of security certificates in Canada," *Critical Studies on Terrorism* 2, 2 (2009): 266.
99. *Ibid.*; Nath, "Curated hostilities," 429.
100. Dafnos, "Pacification," 59.
101. *Ibid.*
102. *Ibid.*
103. Morton, "White settler death," 441.
104. Dafnos, "Pacification," 60.
105. Proulx, "Colonizing surveillance," 87.
106. Morton, "White settler death," 442.
107. Peter J. Carver, "Shelter from the Storm: A Comment on Suresh v. Canada (Minister of Citizenship and Immigration)," *Alberta Law Review* 40, 2 (2002): 471.
108. Sharryn Aiken, "Manufacturing 'Terrorists': Refugees, National Security, and Canadian Law," *Refuge* 19, 3 (2000): 55.
109. Carver, "Shelter," 471.
110. Monaghan, "Settler governmentality," 488.
111. Scott Newark, "C-51: An Analysis Without the Hype or Hysteria," *A Macdonald-Laurier Institute Publication—Commentary*, March 2015. Available: https://www.macdonaldlaurier.ca/files/pdf/MLICommentaryNewark03-15WebReadyV4.pdf [Accessed 3 May 2018].
112. "Ottawa's new anti-terrorism strategy lists eco-extremists as threats," *Globe and Mail*, 10 February 2012. Available: https://www.theglobeandmail.com/news/politics/ottawas-new-anti-terrorism-strategy-lists-eco-extremists-as-threats/article533522/.
113. "An open letter from Natural Resources Minister Joe Oliver," *Globe and Mail*, 9 January 2012. Available: https://www.theglobeandmail.com/

news/politics/an-open-letter-from-natural-resources-minister-joe-oliver/article4085663/.

114. Crosby and Monaghan, "Settler governmentality," 42.
115. Voices-voix, "Criminalization of Indigenous Communities."
116. *Ibid.*
117. *Ibid.*
118. Razack, *Casting Out*; Dafnos, "Pacification," 60.
119. Crosby and Monaghan, "Settler governmentality," 42.
120. Dafnos, "Pacification," 59.
121. *Ibid.*, 49.
122. Monaghan, "Settler governmentality," 491.
123. *Ibid.*, 493–494.
124. Wilke and Willis, "Exploitation," 33.
125. Razack, *Casting out*, 6.
126. *Ibid.*
127. *Ibid.*
128. *Ibid.*; Maureen T. Duffy and Rene Provost, "Constitutional Canaries and the Elusive Quest to Legitimize Security Detentions in Canada," *Case Western Reserve Journal of International Law* 40 (2009): 549.
129. Mike Larsen, "Talking About Terrorism: An Analysis of Official Canadian Insecurity Narratives in the Post-September 11 Context," Master's Thesis, University of Ottawa, 2006, 62.
130. *Ibid.*
131. *Ibid.* 67.
132. Monaghan, "Settler governmentality," 488.
133. Proulx, "Colonizing Surveillance," 83.
134. Smith, *Liberalism*, 18; Monaghan, "Settler governmentality," 488.
135. Proulx, "Colonizing Surveillance," 83.
136. Matthew Banninga, "The Pacification of Indigenous Resistance: An *Anti*-Security Analysis of Idle No More Protest Policing and Surveillance Operations," Master's Thesis, Carleton University, 2015, 9.
137. Leanne Betasamosake Simpson, *As we have always done: Indigenous freedom through radical resistance* (Minneapolis: University of Minnesota Press, 2017), 176.
138. Dafnos, "Pacification," 60.
139. *Ibid.*
140. Patel, Moussa and Upadhyay, "Complicities," 7.
141. *Ibid.*

References

Aiken, Sharryn. "Manufacturing 'Terrorists': Refugees, National Security, and Canadian Law." *Refuge*. 19, 3, 2000: 54–73.

Aitken, Rob. "Notes on the Canadian exception: security certificates in critical context." *Citizenship Studies*. 12, 4, 2008: 381–96.

Bell, Colleen. "Surveillance Strategies and Populations at Risk: Biopolitical Governance in Canada's National Security Policy." *Security Dialogue*. 37, 2, 2006: 147–65.

Brodie, Janine. "Citizenship and Solidarity: Reflections on the Canadian Way." *Citizenship Studies*. 6, 4, 2002: 377–94.

Carver, Peter J. "Shelter from the Storm: A Comment on Suresh v. Canada (Minister of Citizenship and Immigration)." *Alberta Law Review*. 40, 2, (2002): 465–92.

Carvin, Stephanie. "The Integrated Terrorism Assessment Centre (ITAC)." In *Top Secret Canada*, edited by Stephanie Carvin, Thomas Juneau, and Craig Forcese: 90–105. Toronto: University of Toronto Press, 2021.

Crosby, Andrew and Jeffrey Monaghan. "Settler colonialism and the Policing of Idle No More." *Social Justice*. 43, 2, 2016: 37–57.

Crosby, Andrew and Jeffrey Monaghan. *Policing Indigenous Movements: Dissent and the Security State*. Halifax: Fernwood Publishing, 2018.

Dean, Mitchell. *Governmentality: Power and Rule in Modern Society*. London: Sage Publications, 1999.

Dhamoon, Rita. "Exclusion and Regulated Inclusion: The Case of the Sikh Kirpan in Canada." *Sikh Formations*. 9, 1, 2013: 7–28.

Dhamoon, Rita. "Security Warning: Multiculturalism Alert!." In *Ashgate Research Companion to Multiculturalism*, edited by Duncan Ivison: 255–76. Surrey, UK: Ashgate, 2010.

Dhamoon, Rita and Yasmeen Abu-Laban. "Dangerous (Internal) Foreigners and Nation-Building: The Case of Canada." *International Political Science Review*. 30, 2, 2009: 163–83.

Duffy, Maureen T. and Rene Provost. "Constitutional Canaries and the Elusive Quest to Legitimize Security Detentions in Canada." *Case Western Reserve Journal of International Law*. 40, 2009: 531–60.

Goldberg, David Theo. *The Racial State*. Oxford: Blackwell Publishing, 2001.

Larsen, Mike and Justin Piché. "Exceptional State, Pragmatic Bureaucracy, and Indefinite Detention: The Case of the Kingston Immigration Holding Centre." *Canadian Journal of Law and Society*. 24, 2, 2009: 203–29.

Maynard, Robyn. *Policing Black lives: state violence in Canada from slavery to present*. Halifax: Fernwood Publishing, 2017.

Monaghan, Jeffrey. "Settler Governmentality and Racializing Surveillance in Canada's North-West." *Canadian Journal of Sociology*. 38, 4, 2013: 487–508.

Morton, Erin. "White settler death drives: settler statecraft, white possession, and multiple colonialisms under Treaty 6." *Cultural Studies.* 33, 3, 2019: 437–59.
Muller, B. J. "(Dis)qualified Bodies: Securitization, citizenship and 'identity management'," *Citizenship Studies.* 8, 3, 2004: 279–94.
Nath, Nisha. "Curated hostilities and the story of Abdoul Abdi: relational securitization in the settler colonial racial state." *Citizenship Studies.* 25, 2, 2021: 292–315.
Nichols, Robert. *Theft is Property!: Dispossession and critical theory.* Durham, NC: Duke University Press, 2018.
Oriola, Temitope. "Counter-terrorism and alien justice: the case of security certificates in Canada." *Critical Studies on Terrorism.* 2, 2, 2009: 257–74.
Pasternak, Shiri and Tia Dafnos. "How does a settler state secure the circuitry of capital?" *Environment and Planning D: Society and Space.* 36, 4, 2017: 739–57.
Patel, Shaista, Ghaida Moussa, and Nishant Upadhyay. "Complicities, Connections, and Struggles: Critical Transnational Feminist Analysis of Settler Colonialism." *Feral Feminisms.* 4, 2015: 5–19.
Preston, Jen. "Racial extractivism and white settler colonialism: An examination of the Canadian Tar Sands mega-projects." *Cultural Studies.* 31, 2–3, 2017: 353–75.
Procacci, Giovanna. "Governmentality and Citizenship." In *The Blackwell Companion to Political Sociology*, edited by Kate Nash Alan Scott: Blackwell Reference Online. Blackwell Publishing, 2004.
Proulx, Craig. "Colonizing surveillance: Canada constructs and Indigenous terror threat." *Anthropologica.* 56, 1, 2014: 83–100.
Purvis, Trevor and Alan Hunt. "Identity versus Citizenship: Transformations in the Discourses and Practices of Citizenship." *Social and Legal Studies.* 8, 4, 1999: 457–82.
Razack, Sherene. *Casting Out: The Eviction of Muslims from Western Law and Politics.* Toronto: University of Toronto Press, 2008.
Smith, A. "Foreword." In *Undoing Border Imperialism* by Harsha Walia. Oakland: AK Press/Institute for Anarchist Studies, 2014.
Smith, Keith D. *Liberalism, Surveillance and Resistance: Indigenous Communities in Western Canada, 1877–1927.* Edmonton: AU Press, 2009.
Stasiulis, Daiva and Darryl Ross. "Security, Flexible Sovereignty, and the Perils of Multiple Citizenship." *Citizenship Studies.* 10, 3, 2006: 329–48.
Thobani, Sunera. *Exalted Subjects: Studies in the Making of Race and Nation in Canada.* Toronto: University of Toronto Press, 2007.
Tuck, Eve and Rubén Gaztambide-Fernández. "Curriculum, replacement, and settler futurity." *Journal of Curriculum Theorizing.* 29, 1, 2013: 72–89.
Upadhyay, Nishant. "Making of 'Model' South Asians on the Tar Sands: Intersections of Race, Caste, and Indigeneity." *Critical Ethnic Studies.* 5, 1–2, 2019: 152–73.

Walia, Harsha. *Border and rule: Global migration, capitalism, and the rise of racist nationalism*. Chicago: Haymarket Books, 2022.
Wilke, Christiane and Paula Willis. "The Exploitation of vulnerability: Dimensions of Citizenship and Rightlessness in Canada's Security Certificate Legislation." *Windsor Yearbook of Access to Justice*. 26, 1, 2008: 25–51.
Wolfe, Patrick. "Settler Colonialism and the Elimination of the Native." *Journal of Genocide Research*. 8, 4, 2006: 387–409.

Index[1]

[1] Note: Page numbers followed by 'n' refer to notes.

J. Mann (ed.), *Citizenship in Transnational Perspective*, Politics of Citizenship and Migration,
https://doi.org/10.1007/978-3-031-34358-2